Yale Germanic Studies, 5

Poetry in East Germany

Adjustments, Visions, and Provocations,
1945–1970

by John Flores

New Haven and London, Yale University Press, 1971

Published with assistance from the Louis Stern
Memorial Fund.
Copyright © 1971 by Yale University.

Library of Congress catalog card number: 77-115368
International standard book number: 0-300-01339-6

Designed by Marvin Howard Simmons
and set in Janson type.
Printed in the United States of America by
Vail-Ballou Press, Binghamton, N.Y.

Distributed in Great Britain, Europe, and Africa by
Yale University Press, Ltd., London; in Canada by
McGill-Queen's University Press, Montreal; in Mexico
by Centro Interamericano de Libros Académicos,
Mexico City; in Central and South America by Kaiman
& Polon, Inc., New York City; in Australasia by
Australia and New Zealand Book Co., Pty., Ltd.,
Artarmon, New South Wales; in India by UBS Publishers'
Distributors Pvt., Ltd., Delhi; in Japan by John
Weatherhill, Inc., Tokyo.

To My German Friends
Wolf Biermann and Rudi Dutschke

Contents

Preface

In 1958 Ad den Besten, a Dutch poet from Amsterdam, became the first Westerner to cross over to the "other side" of Germany in search of lyric poetry worth mentioning to all German readers. After his return he published a long article and an excellent anthology[1] in which he documented his discovery, at the time startling to many West Germans, that Bertolt Brecht and Johannes R. Becher were not the only poets to have written in the DDR. He found that the official dogma demanding a narrowly conceived "socialist realism" in verse had failed to take hold among a good number of poets, and he recognized that many of the writings of Erich Arendt, Stephan Hermlin, Georg Maurer, Hanns Cibulka, Christa Reinig, Günter Kunert, Peter Jokostra, Johannes Bobrowski, and Peter Huchel deserve their place in the history of modern German poetry.

Since Ad den Besten's pioneering expedition much has happened that would tend to counteract the impact of his findings. In 1961 the Berlin Wall was built, and another act of separation was the law passed in the DDR in February 1966, forbidding East German writers from publishing their works "abroad" (that is, in West Germany) before they had been checked by the Party's "copyright office." Further, two of the most promising poets, Peter Jokostra and Christa Reinig, now live in the West, Peter Huchel has gone into complete isolation as a result of repressive measures taken against him, and Johannes Bobrowski is dead.

1. "Deutsche Lyrik auf der anderen Seite," *Eckart, 28* (1959), 224–63; *Deutsche Lyrik auf der anderen Seite* (Munich, 1960).

However, the importance of Ad den Besten's conclusions has steadily increased. The works of Stephen Hermlin and Franz Fühmann have been published, and studied, in the West; Peter Huchel and Johannes Bobrowski are fully recognized as two of the finest poets in modern German literature; and the poems of Günter Kunert and many younger writers compare favorably with those of their contemporaries in the Federal Republic. The two most exciting anthologies to have appeared in West Germany in recent years—Hildegard Brenner's *Nachrichten aus Deutschland* (1967) and Peter Hamm's *Aussichten* (1966)—as well as the best anthology published in the DDR, Adolf Endler and Karl Mickel's *In diesem besseren Land* (1965), provide striking evidence of the excellence of poetry in the DDR; each of the collections contains a thoughtful, penetrating introduction.

The literature of the DDR has become a standard topic in all books on contemporary German writing, including the *Handbuch der deutschen Gegenwartsliteratur* (1965) edited by Hermann Kunisch, Marcel Reich-Ranicki's *Deutsche Literatur in West und Ost* (1963), and in English the collection of *Essays on Contemporary German Literature* (1966) edited by Brian Keith-Smith. In addition, some of the most eminent critics in the West— Franz Schonauer, Karl-Otto Conrady, and Hans Mayer—have written substantial essays on the situation of literature in the DDR. Major Western periodicals, such as *Der Spiegel, Die Zeit,* and *The Times Literary Supplement,* include regular columns on East German writers, and several prominent West German publishers (Hanser, Rowohlt, Wagenbach, and Luchterhand) have printed many works from the DDR. Among East German critics, Dieter Schiller, Günter Hartung, and especially Dieter Schlenstedt are often excellent on postwar poetry. Gerhard Wolf, however, in *Deutsche Lyrik nach 1945* (East Berlin, 1965) does not get beyond the familiar Cold War clichés; similarly, the book *Dichter im Dienst* (1963) by the West German critic Lothar von Balluseck is informative, but too polemical to be of great value. Most depressing of all is Hermann Pongs' volume *Dichtung im gespaltenen Deutschland* (Stuttgart, 1966), which attempts to trace the division evident in contemporary German literature to a kind of primordial dichotomy in the German soul. It is clear that Pongs, who is at ease with such jargon as "urpolarities of creation" and the "pre-logical realm" ("Ursprungszone aus prä-logischem Bereich"), has still not changed his vocabulary since his days as a leading literary ally of National Socialism.

Generally speaking, however, the attention devoted to literature of the DDR is becoming increasingly subtle, intensive, and free of political ax-grinding. Ad den Besten had good reasons for describing the literary situation "on the other side" as something qualitatively different from that in the German-speaking countries of the West; he was also justified in presenting lyric poetry as the genre most worthy of detailed analysis. Now, a decade after his visit to East Berlin, it may be possible to study the outstanding poets in the DDR, and the conditions under which they write, with somewhat greater precision.

Acknowledgments

I received much guidance in the preparation of this book. My gratitude is due first of all to the poets, all of whom (except for Johannes Bobrowski and Karl Mickel) I had the opportunity to meet personally during a Fulbright Research Grant to Berlin in 1966–67. The warm hospitality and active interest in my work shown by Stephan Hermlin, Franz Fühmann, Peter Huchel, Günter Kunert, Volker Braun, Wolf Biermann, and their families, proved indispensable to me in my attempts to gain familiarity with the contemporary cultural situation in the DDR, and with the particular concerns of each poet. I am also grateful to Mrs. Anna Bobrowski and her family, Fritz and Sigrid Decho of the Volksbühne, Professor Siegfried Streller of the Humboldt Universität, Gerhard Rostin of Union Verlag, and all of my other friends in the DDR for introducing me to life in their country. Further acquaintance with the position of intellectuals in Eastern Europe came to me in meaningful conversations with Robert Havemann, Eduard Goldstücker, and Georg Lukács, whom I thank for their time and useful advice.

In West Berlin and the Federal Republic, I had the opportunity to discuss my project with many critics and interested observers of literature and politics of the DDR. Hans Mayer, Klaus Wagenbach, Hildegard Brenner, Marcel Reich-Ranicki, Hans Magnus Enzensberger, Walter Jens, Peter Szondi, Gregor Laschen, Eberhard Lämmert, Peter Ludz, Wolfgang Schiwelbusch, and Arwed Gorella all contributed their rich experiences and generous suggestions to my work. I want to thank them, as well as Hans and Helga Rinne and their beautiful family, Jim Timner, Ekkehart and Eve

Krippendorff, Rudi and Gretchen Dutschke, and my other friends in West Berlin who kept me in close touch with the political pulse of that exciting city during a time of important changes and challenges. Although my study concentrates on the DDR, I recognized early in my stay that it is impossible to assess the situation there without contact with simultaneous developments in the West. Special gratitude is due to Frau Emma Biermann, a human link between the two Germanies never sufficiently acknowledged.

I received further crucial assistance from friends, colleagues, and teachers in the United States. I am deeply indebted, above all, to Professor Peter Demetz, whose initial inspiration, sustained interest, meticulous criticism, and generous encouragement were invaluable to me at all stages of my work. My sincere gratitude is also due to Professors Jeffrey L. Sammons, Konstantin Reichardt, and A. Peter Foulkes for their careful reading of the entire manuscript, valuable suggestions for its improvement, and enthusiastic recommendation to submit it for publication. I am further indebted to my friends Dave and Feelie McCann, Mark Goldberg, Heinz Osterle, Peter Frank, Sigfrid Hoefert, Peter Beiken and Henry Polin, and to my typist Mrs. Angela Wanninger, for their support and assistance. I also wish to thank Ruth Hein, Wayland Schmitt, and Barbara Folsom, of Yale University Press for their friendly encouragement and expert editorial and technical guidance in preparing the manuscript for publication.

My deepest thanks go to my wife Sue, my daughters Diana and Andrea, and my whole family. Without their love and unflinching support I might never have written this book, and certainly would never have accomplished anything worthwhile.

To all of them, to Professor Herbert Marcuse, and to my comrades in Cuba and the Third World: ¡Venceremos!

Introduction

The Literary Order: Policies and Poets

Preliminary Thoughts

The question of the unity, or division, of postwar German literature has troubled many observers. Literature in the West—represented by such authors as Günter Grass, Max Frisch, Ingeborg Bachmann, and Hans Magnus Enzensberger—has so much overshadowed developments in the German Democratic Republic (DDR) in interest and international acclaim that it would be difficult to speak of two equal rivals on the scene. Yet writers in East and West share a common historical past (National Socialism, World War II, and subsequent occupation) as well as a common literary heritage, from Goethe and Heine to Thomas Mann and Brecht; and it is a mistake when dealing with writers in the DDR to place too much emphasis on the influence of Johannes R. Becher and to disregard that of Franz Kafka, Gottfried Benn, and others. Brecht has served as a literary bridge linking the ideologically torn country, as in different ways have Uwe Johnson and Peter Weiss. There are some authors, notably Heinrich Böll and Johannes Bobrowski, whose work is appreciated equally in East and West Germany. Perhaps the most satisfactory answer was given by the Soviet critic Lew Kopelew, who argues that there are really three German Literatures: one characteristic of the DDR, one typical of the Federal Republic, and a third which, by generality of interest and sheer artistic quality, transcends the fact of political division.[1] Above all else, writers in East and West Germany share a common language.

1. Lew Kopelew, "Gibt es zwei deutsche Literaturen?" *Neue Zeit* (Moscow), December 22, 1965, pp. 22–24. See also Hans Mayer's essay "Über die Einheit der

But there can be no doubt that the border running through
Germany is of far more pronounced significance than that separat-
ing the Federal Republic from Austria and German-speaking
Switzerland; the DDR is not to be considered a mere "literary
province" in the usual sense of the term. The binding past and
literary tradition are absorbed differently by authors on either
side, and with the years attention has increasingly shifted to steadily
diverging social conditions. Contemporary German literature in the
West is ordinarily assumed to have begun at the "zero point"
(Nullpunkt) of 1945 with "rubble poetry" (Trümmerlyrik) and
"homecomer literature" (Heimkehrerliteratur), in which language and historical dilemma were exposed to a "clearing"
(Kahlschlag) of all ideological attachments except a kind of vague
existentialism. In the DDR such origins are emphatically denied,
at least in official statements. In an article entitled "We did not
begin in the Year Zero" (1965), for example, Wolfgang Joho
of the (East) German Writers' Union stated: "Our new German
literature neither began with a *Kahlschlag* nor did it emerge out
of nothing. Rather, it took up the tradition of humanist bourgeois
literature, represented by such names as Arnold Zweig, Lion
Feuchtwanger, Heinrich and Thomas Mann, and Leonhard Frank,
and it is linked to such writers of German proletarian-revolution-
ary literature as Johannes R. Becher, Erich Weinert, Willi Bredel,
Hans Marchwitza, Karl Grünberg, and Hans Lorbeer." [2] This
description (by an old-guard Communist novelist) may contain
more wishful thinking than historical accuracy, but it does indicate how differently postwar literary developments are conceived
of in East and West.

Still more disturbing is the fact that even the German language
has shown evidence of a rapid differentiation as a result of the
political division. Eminent linguists and critics in both parts of

deutschen Literatur," *Zur deutschen Literatur der Zeit* (Reinbek, 1967), pp. 344–
57.

2. Wolfgang Joho, "Wir begannen nicht im Jahr Null," *Neue Deutsche Literatur*, *13* (May 1965), 8: "Die neue deutsche Literatur bei uns begann weder mit
einem Kahlschlag noch entstand sie aus dem Nichts. Sie übernahm das Erbe der
humanistischen bürgerlichen Literatur, repräsentiert durch Namen wie Arnold
Zweig, Lion Feuchtwanger, Heinrich und Thomas Mann, Leonhard Frank und
sie knüpfte an die Leistungen solcher Vertreter der proletarisch-revolutionären
Literatur Deutschlands an wie Johannes R. Becher, Erich Weinert, Willi Bredel,
Hans Marchwitza, Karl Grünberg, Hans Lorbeer."

Germany—Victor Klemperer and F. C. Weiskopf in the East, Werner Betz and Hugo Moser in the West—have written convincing detailed studies of this phenomenon.[3] By the mid-1960s some of the recent East German works were leaving even the most attentive Western readers totally perplexed because of diverging linguistic usage.[4]

The most serious factor of literary division (related to an estrangement within the language) was described by Uwe Johnson, an author who knows perhaps more intimately than anyone else the differences between East German and West German writing. A simple sentence, according to Johnson, is read differently in the two states of Germany. Speaking as a West German writer, Johnson maintains: "We say (and I admit that we are justified by nothing but our own personal opinions) that this or that sentence (let's say in *Der geteilte Himmel* by Christa Wolf) is 'bad' ['schlecht']. . . . East German criticism, however, says that this book or this sentence by a West German author, is 'harmful' ['schädlich']." [5] In the DDR and in the German-speaking countries of the West there are two different realms of aesthetic discourse, two separate languages for the critical evaluation of literature. In the West the quality of a text is determined by the reader's taste, his past experience of literature, and certain artistic norms; a work is either "good" or "bad." In the East literature is judged by its "function," its success or failure in fulfilling an assigned "task"; since it has a responsibility within what is considered the "objective" historical development, it is therefore regarded as either

3. Klemperer, "Verantwortung für die Sprache," *Neue Deutsche Literatur, 3* (March 1955), 122–26; F. C. Weiskopf, " 'Ostdeutsch' und 'Westdeutsch' oder Über die Gefahr der Sprachentfremdung," *Über Literatur und Sprache* (East Berlin, 1960), pp. 416–33; Werner Betz, "Der zweigeteilte Duden," *Der Deutschunterricht, 12* (1960), 82–98; Hugo Moser, "Die Sprache im geteilten Deutschland," *Wirkendes Wort, 11* (1961), 1–21 (extended as *Sprachliche Folgen der politischen Teilung Deutschlands, Wirkendes Wort,* supplement 3, 1962).

4. See Jürgen Sturtz, "Innerdeutsche Sprachentfremdung," *alternative, 7* (1964), 135–41. Also Hildegard Brenner's introduction to her anthology *Nachrichten aus Deutschland* (Reinbek, 1967,) pp. 6–14.

5. " 'Sie sprechen verschiedene Sprachen'?" *alternative, 7* (1964), 97–100; Uwe Johnson, p. 100: "Wir sagen—und ich gebe zu: durch nichts gerechtfertigt als durch die persönliche Meinung—dieser Satz und jener Satz, sagen wir im 'Geteilten Himmel' von Christa Wolf, ist 'schlecht.' . . . [D]ie ostdeutsche Kritik sagt, dieses Buch, oder sagen wir, dieser Satz eines westdeutschen Autors ist 'schädlich.'"

"helpful" or "harmful." The real danger lies not so much in the categories themselves but, as Johnson maintains, in the tendency on both sides to treat them as mutually exclusive.

Literature in the DDR, in a way very different from that in the West, must be studied in relationship to what I would term a "literary order"—by which I mean the policies stating the "task" of literature—and the writers who follow those policies most faithfully. The "order" by no means embraces all literature written in East Germany; on the contrary, I hope to show that the writers who come into conflict with the prescribed policies, or seem to ignore them altogether, are generally the ones most worthy of discussion. But even in these cases the tension between literary creativity and official social demands is an integral component of the works themselves and is not to be omitted from any interpretation. Even those standing outside the order do so by deliberate choice, and the reasons for this choice are embodied in the formal and thematic characteristics of their writings.

Policies

In the years immediately following the war many German intellectuals returning from exile decided to settle in the part of Germany then known as the Soviet Occupied Zone (Sowjetische Besatzungzone—SBZ). Many came from Moscow, others from Mexico or the United States. A majority of them had been Communists since before Hitler's ascent to power, and in the period 1928–33 many had belonged to the League of Revolutionary Proletarian Writers, the German equivalent of the RAPP group in the Soviet Union. To some extent literature and cultural politics in the DDR represent a continuation of this workers'-movement tradition—though, as Franz Schonauer has shown, the agitational function which characterized it earlier has been largely replaced by a kind of apologetic dilettantism.[6]

Despite this relative uniformity in political persuasion, however, the period 1945–49, from the end of the war to the founding of the DDR, is with some validity called by East German historians

6. See Franz Schonauer, "DDR auf dem Bitterfelder Weg," *Neue Deutsche Hefte, 13* (1966), 91–117.

the "antifascist, democratic reconstruction of German culture." [7]
The major thematic concern in art and literature in those years
was "coming to terms with the past" (Bewältigung der Vergangenheit); virtually all formal techniques were permitted. Intellectual
activity centered around the Cultural Union for the Democratic
Renewal of Germany (Kulturbund zur demokratischen Erneuerung Deutschlands), which was established in July 1945 for the
purpose of integrating and furthering all constructive, democratic
efforts in the field of culture, regardless of specific ideological
leanings. In the Cultural Union and its periodical, *Aufbau*, the
first signs of a diversified cultural life appeared. Germany's greatest
living playwright, Bertolt Brecht, returned to East Berlin in
October 1948 and directed the classic performance of his *Mutter
Courage* at the Deutsches Theater on January 11, 1949.

But in the meantime greater and greater emphasis was placed
on art of the Soviet Union, and several important social changes
in the Soviet Occupied Zone had the effect of sealing the division
of Germany at all levels. Many of these steps, it must be noted,
were undertaken as strategic responses to the ill-calculated politics
of the Allied powers occupying the western part of Germany.
Beginning in September 1945, steps were taken for thoroughgoing land reform, followed shortly thereafter by similar measures
in the field of industry. In April 1946 the Communist and Social
Democratic parties were merged to form the Socialist Unity Party
of Germany (Sozialistische Einheitspartei Deutschlands—SED);
the coalition entailed the exclusion of many "bourgeois" and
liberal Social Democrats. Later in 1946 extensive restructuring
of the educational system was undertaken, and in June 1948 the
Central Committee announced the currency reform and defined
the Two-Year Plan for 1949–50. Finally, with the establishment
of the DDR on October 7, 1949, the second stage of East German

7. See *Kultur in unserer Zeit*, ed. Institut für Gesellschaftswissenschaften beim
ZK der SED (Berlin, 1965), especially Chapter 2, "Die Hauptetappen der kul-
turellen Entwicklung in der Deutschen Demokratischen Republik," pp. 68–143.
For a sketch of the general development, see also Peter Demetz, "Literature in
Ulbricht's Germany," *Problems of Communism*, 11 (1962), 15–21; Jan Peddersen,
"Die literarische Situation in der DDR," *Handbuch der deutschen Gegenwarts-
literatur*, ed. Hermann Kunisch (Munich, 1965), pp. 746–58; and Helmut Wagner,
"The Cultural Sovietization of East Germany," *Social Research*, 24 (1957), 395–
426.

art politics was initiated: the transition to a socialist cultural revolution.

The main points of emphasis for this period of transition (and they reappear in all policy statements to the present) were formulated at the first SED Party Conference in January 1949. The resolution proclaimed that all work of the party in the field of culture was to be based on the foundations of Marxism-Leninism, and that the "contribution of artists and writers to the Two-Year Plan consists in the development of a 'realistic' art." [8] The famous words of Andrey Zhdanov at the First Congress of Soviet Writers in 1934, defining the principles of socialist realism, were often quoted in the DDR in its founding years.[9] These principles were directly adopted by the new East German government, in total disregard for the historical circumstances under which they were introduced in the Soviet Union and without even a mention of the dialogue of the late 1930s between Anna Seghers, Bertolt Brecht, and Georg Lukács about the implications of socialist realism.[10] In the early 1950s all East German literary journals and daily newspapers were filled with demands for an art with realistic, "popular" expression and socialist, "partisan" content. Literature was called a weapon against decadence and formalistic perversions and a tool with which to elevate the popular consciousness in the spirit of socialism. In March 1951 the party's Central Committee concluded its fifth session with a resolution, "Against Formalism in Art and Literature, for a Progressive German Culture," which contains the codified directives for socialist realism in the postwar German

8. Quoted in Peddersen, p. 747: "Nunmehr müsse 'die gesamte Arbeit der Partei auf dem Gebiet der Kultur auf der Grundlage des Marxismus-Leninismus beruhen' . . ."

9. Zhdanov's words in his "Speech at the First All-Union Congress of Soviet Writers, 1934" were: "The truthfulness and historical exactitude of the artistic image must be linked with the task of ideological transformation, of the education of the working people in the spirit of socialism. This method in fiction and literary criticism is what we call the method of socialist realism." A. A. Zhdanov, *On Literature, Music and Philosophy* (London, 1950), p. 15. The pronouncement was quoted in the DDR, for example in *Einheit*, 6 (1951), 586.

10. It is one of history's ironies that Lukács, who took the more orthodox position and whose thoughts during the war years exerted a formative influence on many of the men who became East Germany's cultural authorities, has been condemned as a "revisionist" in the DDR since 1956; whereas Brecht and Seghers, who vehemently defended a less rigid conception of realism, are now considered the two greatest writers of the DDR.

context.[11] In an attempt to centralize all aspects of cultural activity, a State Commission for Affairs of Art, under the dogmatic supervision of Alexander Abusch and Wilhelm Girnus, was formed to replace the Cultural Union.

The ideas of socialist realism have peculiar theoretical ramifications when applied to the literary situation of postwar Germany, particularly because the term "nation" was inextricably bound up with the concept in its Soviet origins. The demand for a theme "partisan" to socialism presented little difficulty: the transformation to socialism meant freeing the German "nation" from capitalism and fascism and a continuing struggle against their revival in the other half of Germany. In the minds of nearly all writers concerned, the road to socialism was the road to a peaceful and just society; and even nonsocialist writers agreed that a "literature of national self-criticism" (Abusch) was the goal of their work.

The matter of a "national" form, however, was far more problematic. For national in the Soviet sense invariably meant "popular" (volkstümlich) and therefore implied the previous work of only a small number of authors writing in the DDR in the early 1950s. The others were forced to adjust their means of expression to the nationwide campaign for a "popular" culture, most often to the absolute detriment of their writing. There was also a serious terminological difficulty in adopting the category "national" in the divided Germany: literature in the DDR was claimed to be national but also (because of its relation to Soviet culture) international; conversely, West German literature had to be attacked both as nationalistic and (because of its ties with trends in Western Europe and the United States) as cosmopolitan. Policy statements in these years, therefore, were characterized by this two-pronged polemic, which rarely amounted to more than rhetorical double-talk. The demand for literature "socialist in content and national in form" was more suggestive than was clear to most of the officials: socialist realism, a policy appealing to the "genuine" culture of the German people, often sounds frighteningly similar to National Socialism.

The period 1949–53, from the founding of the DDR until

11. The full text of the resolution "Der Kampf gegen den Formalismus in Kunst und Literatur, für eine fortschrittliche deutsche Kultur" was printed in *Einheit*, 6 (1951), 579–92.

Stalin's death, was the "winter" in East German cultural life. Policies were set and rigidly enforced, dogmatic functionaries were given free rein to detect "deviations" in all corners, and artistic productivity of any significance was at a complete standstill. The works of even the most committed progressive writers—such as Arnold Zweig, Heinrich Mann and Brecht—came under bitter attack for their "formalism" and lack of revolutionary "perspective." One fact not sufficiently emphasized in Western accounts, however, is that the great majority of intellectuals living in the DDR at this time were genuinely sympathetic toward the changes, especially at the economic level; there was, indeed, a mild but heartfelt "revolutionary spirit," even among those who were later to demand change most adamantly. But with regard to actual works, the only continuity with the earlier, "antifascist, democratic" phase was maintained by three institutions: Brecht's Berliner Ensemble, the newly formed Academy of Arts presided over by Johannes R. Becher, and the literary journal *Sinn und Form* under the editorship of Peter Huchel. Otherwise there was such obvious stagnation in East German literature and the arts that even the authorities began to grow anxious.

The first stirrings of discontent, in June 1953, came from below. Unappeased by the promises of a "new course," adopted on June 9, workers and farmers in many parts of the DDR demonstrated a week later, in the famous uprising of June 17, against a sudden raise in work norms amid acute shortages of food and consumer goods.[12] This "attempted fascist putsch," as it is referred to in the DDR, was quickly brought under control by the Soviet military, but it did usher in some degree of liberalization by the shaken government. The discredited State Commission controlling the arts was temporarily dissolved, or rather replaced by the Ministry of Culture (Kulturministerium), which was founded in 1954 under the direction of Johannes R. Becher. Some of the leading intellectuals, who had played little or no part in the popular revolt and had even in some instances been the target of the workers' attacks, began to speak out publicly for economic reforms and an easing of administrative supervision of art and literature. Theaters began offering plays other than the usual Soviet propaganda, and in literary discussions the concepts of formalism and

12. See Arnulf Baring, *Der 17. Juni 1953* (Cologne, 1965).

partisanship became subject to slightly more subtle scrutiny than before.

The most important impetus of all came in philosophy. In 1955 the ideas of Ernst Bloch (b. 1885) began to receive explicit support from many East German students and young intellectuals. Bloch, who moved from the West in 1948 to accept a chair of philosophy at the University of Leipzig, is an unorthodox Marxist with an explicitly prophetic orientation, his major work being entitled "The Principle of Hope" (*Das Prinzip Hoffnung*). His particular contribution to the growing resistance against dogmatic orthodoxy occurred with his widely attended lecture series, "Differentiation in the Concept of Progress," which he held in East Berlin in 1955. Bloch, the "philosopher of hope," provided the broad groundwork for a critical reexamination of the optimism and "socialist perspective" demanded of all artists and all scholars engaged in the humanities and social sciences. Bloch's Marxism is inclusive enough to take account of the "differentiations" and contradictions of social reality and even of the possible frustration of human progress. The impact of his thought was clear in the contributions during 1955–56 to the Leipzig philosophy journal, *Deutsche Zeitschrift für Philosophie;* it has remained alive among intellectuals in the DDR ever since, even after Bloch moved back to West Germany in 1961.[13]

The "thaw" came in the year 1956, which in many respects represents the turning point in East German cultural developments because it began a trend of critical dissent which has proven irreversible. Of decisive importance was the impact throughout Eastern Europe of the Twentieth Congress of the Soviet Communist Party, which convened in February 1956. Yet even a month before that, at the Fourth Writers' Congress in East Berlin, voices of discontent were raised by old and young German Communists alike. Willi Bredel (b. 1901)—who had been active in the workers' movement since the days of the Spartacists (1917)—Anna Seghers, and Georg Lukács, all spoke out for a refinement and broadening of theoretical concepts and an atmosphere more conducive to significant literary productivity. Seghers in particular complained

---

13. See the chapter on Bloch in Jürgen Rühle, *Literatur und Revolution: Die Schriftsteller und der Kommunismus,* 2nd ed. (Munich and Zurich, 1963), pp. 253–65.

openly about the empty schematism and colorlessness of East
German literature, while Lukács in his speech argued for a recon-
sideration of "the problem of perspective." [14] Younger writers
joined them, and throughout the year pressure mounted for a
thoroughgoing reform of cultural affairs. In October, Gomulka's
victory in Poland and Soviet intervention in Hungary brought the
unrest to a peak, when students demonstrated at Humboldt University in East Berlin. But the movement was crushed, and Wolfgang Harich, the editor of *Deutsche Zeitschrift für Philosophie*,
was arrested.

One of the most revealing critical documents of this period was
Hans Mayer's radio speech, "Concerning the Current State of Our
Literature," scheduled to be broadcast in November 1956. Mayer
not only condemned the naïve category of "optimism" applied to
all literature in the DDR but spoke frankly of the meager and
even sickly condition of East German writing. He contrasted it
with the wealth of German literature of the 1920s and called for
a familiarity with some of the great writers of the twentieth
century (Trakl, Kafka, Joyce, and the "real" Brecht). Mayer
stated that "modern literature is not possible without a knowledge
of modern literature." "Furthermore," he noted, "many administrative and bureaucratic restrictions will have to be removed before
matters in our literary life can take a turn for the better." He even
mentioned Alfred Kurella by name when speaking of the sectarian-
ism dominating East German cultural affairs. But Mayer's speech
was never broadcast. [15]

Reaction and countermeasures by the authorities were not long
in coming, and the new restrictions were harsher than ever before.
The initial signs, at the Third Party Conference in March 1956,
were promising, apparently indicating that the writers' demands
of their congress two months earlier would be respected. But the
party soon came to recognize the seriousness of the present danger;

14. Seghers, *Die grosse Veränderung und unsere Literatur* (East Berlin, 1956);
Georg Lukács, "Das Problem der Perspektive" in *Schriften zur Literatursoziologie*,
ed. Peter Ludz (Neuwied, 1961), pp. 254–60.

15. Hans Mayer, "Zur Gegenwartslage unserer Literatur" was first published in
the East Berlin weekly *Sonntag*, December 2, 1956. Mayer reprinted it in his book
Zur deutschen Literatur der Zeit, pp. 365–73. "Übrigens wird man viele administrative und bürokratische Hemmnisse beseitigen müssen, sollen sich die Dinge in
unserem literarischen Leben zum Besseren wenden" p. 372.

for unlike the uprising of 1953—a public protest by the labor force for better working conditions and more material goods—the resistance in 1956 was conducted largely within the Communist ideological leadership itself and was waged over the critical question of alternatives in political strategy.[16] The ruling circle, therefore, had to immediately consolidate its forces and begin a full-fledged campaign against all traces of "deviationism" (Zurückweichen) or, as they were called at the thirtieth meeting of the Central Committee in January 1957, defenders of "ideological coexistence" and "the third way."[17] (Unquestionably the deaths of Brecht in August 1956 and of Becher in 1958 had far-reaching political consequences in these and subsequent years.)

Alfred Kurella (b. 1895), long-time party functionary and one of the country's most uncompromising dogmatists, was chosen to direct the newly formed Cultural Commission (1957) which took over control of all matters of art from Becher's Ministry of Culture. One after another the spokesmen of the short-lived "thaw" were called to task: Harich and his friends received long prison sentences, Ernst Bloch was forced into retirement and the movement he initiated was condemned, Lukács' books were withdrawn from the market, and he and Hans Mayer were labeled "bourgeois revisionists." It was in these years, between 1958 and 1961, that some of the leading intellectuals in the DDR left for West Germany. In addition to Bloch and Mayer, Uwe Johnson (b. 1934), Alfred Kantorowicz (b. 1899), and Gerhard Zwerenz (b. 1925)—all Marxists of international renown—chose to join the flow of emigrants from East Germany. This irreparable rift between institutionalized culture and the most respected intellectuals, together with the impossible demands of the first Seven-Year Plan (1958–65), made the East German government more unpopular than ever. These two factors together help explain the final, most momentous measure of national consolidation: the erection of the Berlin Wall on August 13, 1961.

Another phase of official literary politics in the DDR was begun at a conference in the industrial town of Bitterfeld on April 24, 1959; this period extends through 1961, when the imminent failure

16. Compare Ernst Richert, *Das zweite Deutschland* (Frankfurt and Hamburg, 1966), pp. 133–34.
17. See Martin Jänicke, *Der dritte Weg* (Cologne, 1964).

of the Seven-Year Plan became obvious. The thrust of the famous
Bitterfeld Movement (Bitterfelder Weg), announced in speeches
by Walter Ulbricht and Alfred Kurella, was indicated by two
main directives: writers were requested henceforth "to contribute
actively to the enormous economic and social developments," and
the working masses were encouraged "to take by storm the higher
reaches of culture" ("die Höhen der Kultur erstürmen").[18] Practically speaking, all writers and artists were asked to take jobs in
factories, industrial plants, and agricultural collectives, while the
workers were bidden to try their hand at the fine arts (the slogan
most frequently associated with the Bitterfeld program is: "Greif
zur Feder, Kumpel!"—"Grasp the pen, chum!"). The motivating
purpose of these measures, which have their obvious precedent in
the Soviet Proletkult movement of the 1920s, was primarily economic, as Franz Schonauer has shown in an excellent essay on the
Bitterfelder Weg.[19] Official attempts to eliminate the dangers of
cultural "revisionism" were very conveniently identified with the
call for artists' direct participation in the productive process.
Cultural "progress" was made to compete, as it were, with the
pace of economic advance.

The result of this wholly reactionary move was the "harvest"
of Bitterfeld: a slew of sentimental, trashy stories and prose anecdotes by the "talented" workers and superficial, totally unreadable
"industry novels" (Betriebsromane) by some of the recognized
writers. The "new reality" was not presented in its full wealth and

18. See the protocol of the Bittersfeld meeting, *"Greif zur Feder, Kumpel!"*
(Halle, 1959). The speeches by Ulbricht and Kurella also appear in Marianne
Lange, ed., *Zur sozialistischen Kulturrevolution 1957-1959* (East Berlin, 1960), *2*,
pp. 455-91.

19. Schonauer, "DDR auf dem Bitterfelder Weg." See also Hans-Peter Gente,
"Versuch über 'Bitterfeld'," *alternative*, 7 (1964), 126-31, and Hans Koch, "Bitterfeld und die Folgen," *Unsere Literaturgesellschaft* (East Berlin, 1965), pp. 173-
205. It is interesting to note that in both major speeches held at Bitterfeld even
the ideological implications of the new policy were expressed in terms of economic efficiency. Ulbricht defined what for him was the main problem: "Die
Aktivisten, die Mitglieder der Brigaden der sozialistischen Arbeit haben ein
schnelleres Tempo als ein Teil unserer Schriftsteller und unserer Künstler"; in
Alfred Kurella's introductory words, "Wir werden also auf unserer Konferenz
einige Fragen unserer Literatur und unseres literarischen Lebens auf eine ähnliche
Weise behandeln müssen, wie es unsere Wirtschaftsplaner in ihrem Aufgabenge-
biet tun: sowohl in ihrer Bindung an die Tagesaufgaben, als auch in der Perspektive einer zeitlich sehr weit gesteckten Planung." In Lange, ed., *Zur Kulturrevolution, 2*, 463 and 478.

complexity, as had been hoped for, but appeared as a trivial, unreal pastoral, peopled by simple-minded nonentities operating old-fashioned industrial equipment. Walter Ulbricht took as a joke the concern of many authors over the feasibility of writing about the "new life" and its "conflicts," as they had been directed, without coming into difficulties with the party.[20] Another aspect of the Bitterfeld program was the newly prescribed "path of development of a writer in socialist society." After completing their secondary schooling, and before going on to the university and embarking on a literary career, prospective writers would be required to spend time at "practical labor" and simultaneously attend "literary workshops," for which the Johannes R. Becher Institute (founded in Leipzig in 1955) was the model. This breeding process was meant to assure an active participation in social developments on the part of all future authors and artists during their formative years. The insurmountable problem of such a method is that the decision concerning anyone's "qualifications" to pursue literary endeavors at a higher level is largely left to the authorities. Yet with regard to the goals proclaimed at Bitterfeld this process is far more constructive than the idea of herding middle-aged and elderly writers, many from bourgeois backgrounds, into factories and collectives and forcing them to develop themes that had never concerned them previously. The policy of planning literary careers from the outset, despite all its sinister connotations, has shown undeniable signs of success and is in part responsible for the emergence in recent years of a significant East German literature qualitatively different from that in the Federal Republic.

The "new" indigenous literature of the DDR, the long-suppressed product of the "thaw" period, first came to light in 1961. Particularly after the construction of the Wall there was a pronounced easing of cultural restrictions. At a meeting of the Central Committee in November 1961 Ulbricht for the first time emphasized the need to build a socialist society independently of developments in West Germany.[21] Literary directives since late 1961 have laid stress on the concepts of the specifically "socialist image of man" ("das sozialistische Menschenbild") and the "new style of

20. Lange, ed., *Zur Kulturrevolution*, 2, 466–67.
21. See *Kultur in unserer Zeit*, p. 134.

life" ("der neue Lebensstil"). This period is characterized by the irregular alternation of promising stretches, during which controls are relatively loose and impressive new works appear, and sudden sharp crackdowns against individual writers and groups of writers.

In the years 1961–62, for example, Johannes Bobrowski (1917–1965), Franz Fühmann (b. 1922), Peter Hacks (b. 1928), Günter Kunert (b. 1929), and several others first emerged as important writers, and not at all in the sense implied by official policies. But, beginning in December 1962, stringent reaction set in, to a large extent sparked by simultaneous similar measures in the Soviet Union (Khrushchev's criticism of Ehrenburg, Yevtushenko, and others). Stephen Hermlin was publicly denounced for having organized a reading by many of the young poets at which attitudes boldly critical of conditions in the DDR were voiced. Peter Huchel was removed from his post as editor in chief of *Sinn und Form*, to be replaced by more reliable party men, such as Bodo Uhse and Wilhelm Girnus; he eventually withdrew from cultural activity altogether. Even Alfred Kurella was considered too "soft," and his Cultural Commission was superseded in the Central Committee by a Commission for Ideology (Ideologiekommission), with the ruthless Kurt Hager as its head.[22]

Although at the Second Bitterfeld Conference in April 1964 officials tried futilely to revitalize the plans proposed five years earlier, circumstances were generally more lax from early 1964 through 1965. Wolf Biermann captivated youthful audiences throughout the DDR and was permitted a highly successful tour of West Germany. A large group of new talents appeared, many of whom had first spent time working in factories and attending "literary institutes"; they include Hermann Kant (b. 1926), Heiner Müller (b. 1929), Christa Wolf (b. 1929), Rolf Schneider (b. 1932), Manfred Bieler (b. 1934), Sarah and Rainer Kirsch

22. Other prominent writers who were called to task as a result of the Sixth Party Congress (January 1963) were Peter Hacks, for his play *Die Sorgen und die Macht*, and Günter Kunert. On the occasion of the Kafka conference, held in Prague in December 1963, various official spokesmen for the DDR sharply denounced the attempts by such liberal western Marxists as Roger Garaudy and Ernst Fischer to reconsider the relevance of Kafka's work in Communist countries. For an informative description of the cultural situation in the DDR in the year 1963, see Lothar von Balluseck, *Literatur und Ideologie 1963: Zu den literatur politischen Auseinandersetzungen seit dem VI. Parteitag der SED* (Bad Godesberg, 1963).

(b. 1935 and 1934), Karl Mickel (b. 1935), Volker Braun (b. 1939), and Bernd Jentzsch (b. 1940). It was in these years, too, that many serious critics and writers in the West began to turn their attention to the phenomenon of literature in the DDR.

The most recent countermeasure occurred at the Eleventh Plenum of the Central Committee in December 1965, and its impact on East German cultural life has extended through the end of the decade. Here again, as in the case of the Bitterfeld Movement, the interplay of ideological and economic factors is of great importance. The chief target in the "superstructure"—aside from the clear influence of "demoralizing, Western" habits and attitudes among the younger generation—was the dangerous and growing popularity of Wolf Biermann and Professor Robert Havemann.[23] After a nearly miraculous economic boom the authorities felt in a position to minimize resistance to their acts of cultural repression by buying the confidence of the populace with timely offers of material benefits. By the end of a month-long smear campaign, accompanied by the announcement of conciliatory "surprises" for the working population, Biermann and Havemann were totally eliminated from the public scene. One final measure against dissident intellectuals was taken in February 1966, when an official copyright office (Büro für Urheberrechte) was established, where all literary works intended for publication "abroad" were to be submitted. Thus West Germany could no longer be used as an outlet for writers in the DDR, as it had been so often before, notably by Johannes Bobrowski, Peter Huchel, Günter Kunert, and above all, Wolf Biermann. To the absolute dread of East German officials, Biermann's book of songs, *Die Drahtharfe*, was published in West Berlin in October 1965 and became an immediate best-seller throughout Germany (including the East). The copyright law has since become known as the lex Biermann.

One of the direct consequences of East Germany's spectacular economic advance, which established it as one of the ten leading industrial powers in the world, was a harsh and virtually unchallenged harnessing of cultural diversification. The fact of material

23. Havemann is a world-respected professor of chemistry, formerly at Humboldt University, whose lectures on socialism and freedom were attended by huge audiences in 1964–1965; they appear collected in *Dialektik ohne Dogma?* published in Reinbek, West Germany, in 1964.

prosperity has not brought with it a general liberalizing trend, as might have been expected. Rather, it has been used as a tactical guarantee that ideological divergence could be forced into submission without giving rise to any substantial opposition at the popular level. The German Democratic Republic—which towers economically over its faltering neighbors, Poland and Czechoslovakia—remains a grotesque dwarf, clinging to policies which are isolating it more and more even from the socialist countries around it. But in Peter Huchel, Robert Havemann, Wolf Biermann, and many more of its citizens than it is willing to admit, the DDR has gathered some painful thorns, which may some day become more than its calloused flesh can bear.

Literature and the Genres

The development of East German cultural politics has passed through six main phases: the "antifascist, democratic reconstruction" ending with the foundation of the DDR (1945–49); the "transition to a socialist cultural revolution," at which time Soviet categories of socialist realism were introduced (1949–53); a gradual movement toward the 1956 "thaw," from Stalin's death to the signs of de-Stalinization in the Soviet Union, Poland, and Hungary (1953–56); the period of official reaction to "ideological coexistence" and the "third way" (1957–59); the initiation of the Bitterfeld Movement in accordance with the proposed Seven-Year Plan (1959–61); and finally, the period of sporadic loosening and tightening since the construction of the Berlin Wall. It is too early to state with certainty whether a new stage began as a result of the Eleventh Plenum in December 1965.[24]

24. In general, the development as I have described it corresponds roughly to the four-stage periodization of the history of the DDR according to the East German version, as in Stefan Doernberg's *Kurze Geschichte der DDR* (Berlin, 1964). Doernberg's chapters are entitled: "Die antifaschistisch-demokratische Umwälzung im Osten Deutschlands" (1945–1949), "Die Schaffung der Grundlagen des Sozialismus" (1949–1956), "Die Erhaltung des Friedens und der Sieg der sozialistischen Produktionsverhältnisse" (1956–1961), "Der Beginn des umfassenden Umbaus des Sozialismus" (1961–1964). The periodization suggested by Helmut Wagner in his essay "The Cultural Sovietization of East Germany" (loc. cit., note 7 above) fails, I believe, to delineate clearly the major changes both in the direction of official cultural policies and in the situation of art and literature.

Whatever the authorities prescribed, it is perhaps not too misleading to view the literature of East Germany since 1945 as falling into two broad periods. The first period is characterized by the attempt on the part of older writers (many belonging to the generation of the Weimar Republic) to adjust their literary methods to the norms of socialist realism. The main difficulty in adjustment, as I mentioned above, was stylistic: to meet the demand for a "popular" language meant for most of these authors a more radical break with their earlier writing than they were able to assimilate. But there was also a very fundamental thematic obstacle to the required transformation: the reality which they were now to "reflect" in their art, unlike that in their books about Hitler's Germany or the Spanish Civil War, was no longer antagonistic to their basic ideological convictions. The result is the meager, colorless, schematic literature deplored by Anna Seghers and Hans Mayer in their speeches of 1956. (Anna Seghers' own career, of course, provides a classic example of that unsuccessful adjustment from oppositional to apologetic writing.) The authors of the second period in East German literature (usually referred to as "recent literature of the DDR"—"die neuere DDR-Literatur") all began writing after the war and as citizens of the newly founded society. Their main problem, clearly, is not in developing a "popular" style or in adjusting to the new conditions; rather, they are concerned with the meaning of the demand for socialist realism when applied to a society already engaged in the construction of socialism.

But there can be no precise chronological separation of these two phases in the development of East German literature. In fact, it is possible to discern a "middle generation" (writers born around the year 1920) which in many ways forms a link between old and new. Yet generally speaking, the earlier phase, in which older writers were adapting themselves to the new conditions, began to wane around the mid-1950s; and the new situation, characterized by young talents grappling for an honest literary representation of their own reality, emerged in the early 1960s. Only with regard to the more recent stage can one really begin to speak of a literature with a clearly defined identity of its own. In the future the late works of Communist exile writers may come to be recorded as no more than a preparatory transition from the immediate postwar situation to the development of conditions required for a new literary society.

In addition to this distinction between the periodization of the socialist cultural revolution and actual literary history, a difference can be seen in the effect of official policies on the genres. No elaborate genre theory is needed to ascertain that prose fiction and the drama are more susceptible to administrative supervision than is lyric poetry; Käte Hamburger's convincing systematic differentiation between the "mimetic" fictional genres and the "existential" lyric provides a convenient framework for discussion.[25] The greater a genre's public potency—that is, the more directly it addresses and involves the external world—the more meticulous will be the surveillance and direction of works in that genre.

The doctrine of socialist realism has as its primary model the nineteenth-century realistic novel, and works of narrative prose have therefore remained the most conventional and least noteworthy literature of the DDR. Prose writers who had enjoyed productive and successful years in exile were uniformly hampered by demands for "typical" situations and for the "positive hero" when these terms became current in their new homeland. Anna Seghers, Arnold Zweig, and Stefan Heym, to cite the three most prominent examples, have never duplicated their fine prewar and wartime novels; their work of the 1950s has been depressingly retrospective, schematic, and generally unconvincing. Even the careers of the major proletarian writers from the 1920s, such as Willi Bredel and Hans Marchwitza, illustrate this same sharp decline after 1950. The most popular East German novel of the 1950s, Bruno Apitz' *Nackt unter Wölfen* (1958) is thrilling, but it treats the concentration-camp setting in terms of the most naïve clichés. Prose works about the "new life," notably Eduard Claudius' *Menschen an unserer Seite* (1951) and Hans Marchwitza's *Roheisen* (1955), are entirely colorless and strictly functional propaganda; the conventions they introduced found their continuation in the scores of *"Betriebsromane"* (industrial novels) written in line with the Bitterfeld program. In the early 1960s

25. *Die Logik der Dichtung* (Stuttgart, 1957, 1968).

Dieter Noll and Max Walter Schulz wrote long novels—*Die Abenteuer des Werner Holt* (1960) and *Wir sind nicht Staub im Wind* (1962)—in which they attempted to combine the methods of socialist realism with the German tradition of the novel of development (*Entwicklungsroman*) but never reached a level beyond popular entertainment. Perhaps the most readable fictional works are Johannes Bobrowski's stories and his novel *Levins Mühle* (1964), stories by Franz Fühmann in the collection *König Ödipus* (1966), and the sketches and anecdotes of Günter Kunert in *Tagträume* (Munich, 1964) and *Die Beerdigung findet in aller Stille statt* (Munich, 1968). However, Bobrowski's and Fühmann's narratives deal almost exclusively with the German past, and none of these works, particularly Kunert's has much in common with the main body of East German prose.

Along official lines Erwin Strittmatter's *Ole Bienkopp* (1963) and Erik Neutsch's *Spur der Steine* (1964) are interesting because they introduced a critical dimension into the usual settings of the rural collective and the state-owned factory and thus awakened some serious disaffection among the authorities. More recently attention in East and West has been attracted by three novels: *Bonifaz oder Der Matrose in der Flasche* (1963) by Manfred Bieler, *Der geteilte Himmel* (1962) by Christa Wolf, and *Die Aula* (1965) by Hermann Kant. These works do suggest a new and not insignificant trend in East German prose writing, all of them touching on some of the tenderest nerves of life in the DDR. But in none of them—nor in the novels by Strittmatter and Neutsch, nor even in the important new novel by Christa Wolf, *Nachdenken über Christa T.* (1969)—are the problems probed deeply and in all their implications, nor do the linguistic and formal techniques offer any original contribution to the mainstream of contemporary European prose literature. These writers are still too plagued by conservative regulations and are too isolated from the great works of the twentieth century. It will obviously be a long time before they attain the controlled subtlety and technical sophistication of Uwe Johnson.

If the situation of dramatic writing in the DDR appears to be more favorable than that of prose fiction, it is only because of the influential presence of Bertolt Brecht from 1948 until his death in

1956 and the activity of his Ensemble at the Deutsches Theater
and the Theater am Schiffbauerdamm.[26] Despite all Brecht's difficulties with the demands of orthodoxy, his theory of the epic
theater and first-rate performances of some of the most important
plays in modern German literature have succeeded in maintaining
an atmosphere conducive to serious theatrical writing. Brecht's
impact has also helped counteract recurrent calls for a less experimental "realism," by which is meant the conventions of the nineteenth-century "well-made play" combined with those of socialist
realism: naïve, mechanical empathy with the "positive hero."
Younger playwrights, therefore, have been able to evade these
dangers as well as the straightforward techniques of the Soviet
agitprop plays which flooded East German theaters in the early
1950s. They have developed more subtle treatments of dialectical
situations than would have been possible had Brecht not been on
the scene.

But Brecht's presence has proven a mixed blessing, to say the
least. In Heiner Müller (b. 1929), Helmut Baierl (b. 1926), Hart-
mut Lange (b. 1937), and above all Peter Hacks (b. 1928), who
moved to East Berlin from Munich in 1955, Brecht has some outstanding young disciples. None of them, however, has succeeded
in going beyond their master in any respect, and even their best
works are haunted by the unmistakeable style and techniques of
the genius from whom they learned. In addition to this unintended
domination, Brecht's famous method of the alienation effect and
some of his true masterpieces have never really been accepted by
East German policy makers. In the early 1950s, and even later,
cultural authorities extolled the traditional old-timer, Friedrich
Wolf (1888–1953), over Brecht, whose activity they encouraged
only with severe reservations.

The real restrictions to which significant dramatic writing and
public performance are subject became clear after Brecht's death,
most notably in the case of Peter Hacks and his play *Die Sorgen
und die Macht* (1962, first version 1958). Brecht's concept of
dramatic alienation is interpreted in the terms of official doctrine as

26. On the drama, see Peter Demetz, "*Galileo* in East Berlin: Notes on the
Drama in the DDR," *The German Quarterly*, 37 (1964), 239–45. See also Henning
Rischbieter and Ernst Wendt, *Deutsche Dramatik in West und Ost* (Velber,
1965), and Hermann Kähler, *Gegenwart auf der Bühne von 1956–1963/4* (East
Berlin, 1966).

running directly counter to the insistence on *Parteilichkeit*—political commitment. The theory of socialist realism when applied to the theater calls for expressively culinary techniques, including dramatic illusion and emotional empathy. A rational, calculating audience may have been Brecht's goal, but the official notion of didacticism remains of a cruder sort. For this reason the prospect of a strong East German drama moving out from Brecht seems extremely dim, and so far no promising alternatives have suggested themselves. Dramatic writing, in fact, is in an even less developed condition in the DDR than is prose fiction, the most significant achievement thus far being, in my opinion, Peter Hacks' adaptations and his remarkable play *Moritz Tassow* (1965).

Lyric poetry, the private, "existential" genre, has been least susceptible to administrative limitations and has therefore remained more open to a variety of expressive and thematic possibilities. This fact is not at all obvious if an assessment of poetry in the DDR is limited to the abysmal verse propaganda written in the early 1950s. Whatever innovations lingered into the immediate postwar period were brought to an abrupt halt in 1949, and for years virtually nothing was written but the most perishable of verse platitudes. Like writers of the worst religious poetry, poets at this time were warmly sincere in their devotion, but their confessions were sterile, trivial, uninspiring. The most common forms were, in fact, those of sacred poetry: the cantata, the oratorio, the chorale, and the hymn. Demands for a "popular" language were followed so faithfully that these texts by Johannes R. Becher, Louis Fürnberg, Kuba, and Max Zimmering (to name a few) are virtually interchangeable; as familiar as their authors' names were made, the poems might as well be regarded as anonymous. The most common shorter forms were the totally artificial "folksong," the "tractor poem," and brief hymns of allegiance to the Party.

This depressing situation, continuing through the 1960s, was the main basis for Western impressions of poetry in the DDR until only a few years ago. But it no longer constituted the dominant trend as soon as the first traces of a general thaw became apparent. Between 1954 and 1957 there were definite, though still isolated, signs of a differentiation and deepening of poetic styles and themes.

Another low was reached in the period 1958–60, with official reaction to the thaw and the cultivation of trivial "Sputnik" poetry. In 1961, though, East German poetry came into its own as a phenomenon of far-reaching significance; despite occasional, harsh crackdowns, as in 1963 and 1965, it will never be the same as it was in its days of provincial socialist realism.

It is of crucial importance to note that this new phase in poetry, far more than the promising recent developments in prose and the drama, was foreshadowed and anticipated by a substantial group of "middle generation" writers. The ground had already been broken as early as the mid-1950s, in the work of such different poets as Erich Arendt (b. 1903), Peter Huchel, Georg Maurer (b. 1907), Johannes Bobrowski, Hanns Cibulka (b. 1920), Franz Fühmann, Günther Deicke (b. 1922), Paul Wiens (b. 1922), and Heinz Kahlau (b. 1931). All of these poets, except for Huchel and Bobrowski, are mediocre by international standards; little of their verse is directly political or critical of social conditions; and none of them exerted as immediate an influence on the younger poets as did Brecht. But without them the emergence of a critical social poetry in the manner and spirit of Brecht would not have been nearly as noteworthy as it is. They are important because they created the climate necessary for the dissolution of enforced literary uniformity. They began introducing a diversity in the means of poetic expression and raising poetic language above the level of common speech. Quickly they rediscovered the dimension of myth and vision in poetry and restored the indirectness and ambiguity essential to good literature. In their best works the clichés, the mindless avowals, and the vacuous optimism which were typical of East German verse in the early 1950s had all but disappeared.

These historical developments form the background for my critical study of eight individual poets in the DDR. The reason for my selection, aside from my personal attraction to these particular writers, is my feeling that of all East German poets Stephan Hermlin, Franz Fühmann, Peter Huchel, Johannes Bobrowski, Günter Kunert, Volker Braun, Karl Mickel and Wolf Biermann are of greatest interest to an international reading audience; the quality of their work and their dilemmas as talented artists in East

German society warrant the attention of all observers of contemporary European poetry. I plan to discuss them individually, each time undertaking to determine the specific artistic and social problems peculiar to each of them, and I hope that the justification for such a method will clearly emerge from each essay.

My different sections are to be considered in relationship to my description of the literary order and the general direction of literary history in the DDR. Part One, "Adjustments," corresponds to the first phase of the development—that is, the period when DDR cultural policies characteristically compelled authors who had written during and immediately after the war to adapt their stylistic means and thematic concerns to meet official demands for socialist realism; and Stephan Hermlin and Franz Fühmann impress me as the outstanding examples of poetic reeducation. In Part Two, "Visions," I am chiefly concerned with that middle group of poets who prepared the way for the emergence of a new, specifically East German poetry in the 1960s. Peter Huchel and Johannes Bobrowski are far and away the most important poets to have written in the DDR—excepting, of course, Bertolt Brecht. Their entire work (Huchel's extending back to the 1920s, Bobrowski's for the most part having little to do directly with conditions in the DDR) is worthy of detailed, exhaustive analysis. A real opposition poetry did not appear, however, until the 1960s. In Part Three, "Revisions," I discuss the major trends of recent East German poetry, characterized by an application of Brechtian techniques to a criticism of social conditions, and the most prominent young poets to have emerged in these years. Günter Kunert (b. 1929), Volker Braun (b. 1939), Karl Mickel (b. 1935) and Wolf Biermann (b. 1936) are all disciples of Brecht, and all are "social" poets; that is, their verse stands in an active relationship with society, sensing its contradictions, criticizing its blatant shortcomings, and challenging it to realize its promises. In my discussion I hope to determine the personal dilemma peculiar to each of them, and to indicate the type of poetry at which each seems to excel. Most important, I would like to give a sense of the striking diversity and vitality evident in recent poetry of the DDR.

My study, then, is organized in such a way that its three parts correspond to three phases in the development of East German poetry: Part One to the literary "adjustments" characteristic of the early 1950s, Part Two to the growing diversification of literary techniques and the deepening of poetic vision in the later 1950s, and Part Three to the emergence of a critical, specifically East German poetry in the 1960s. In each chapter I concentrate on the individuality of the poet discussed and attempt to present a unified interpretation of his particular concerns. Yet I also intend to introduce each poet as a kind of model illustrating certain characteristic tendencies and literary phenomena. For this reason each of the writers may be seen to have parallels and revealing contrasts in the work of other East German poets whose names are often mentioned but whom I do not discuss in detail.

The overall reason for this three-part organization is to suggest that there is a discernible evolution in the situation and quality of poetry in the DDR. At first no more than the depressing record of obedience to Soviet literary categories, East German verse gradually begins to challenge the enforced shallowness and uniformity to which it was confined. In the powerful visions of Peter Huchel's late poetry and the work of Johannes Bobrowski there is no trace of respect for the codified order of the cultural functionaries; and in the younger poets this resistance becomes an active defiance, an explicit refusal to give in to the provincial restrictions which threaten their art. These changes in the relationship between poetry and imposed literary order will be of crucial importance in all parts of my essay.

Part One: Adjustments

I

Stephan Hermlin: "Volkstümlichkeit" and the Banality of Language

> Volkstümlich und funktionärstümlich.
> Ausserdem wünscht das Volk nicht tümlich zu sein.
> Bertolt Brecht

Expressionism and Résistance *(1940–45)*

The career of Stephen Hermlin (b. 1915), one of the most intriguing political poets in modern German literature, extends back to the early 1940s. The core of his poetry is contained in his first volume—and the one for which he is best known still today—*Zwölf Balladen von den Grossen Städten* (1944). These high-pitched, erratic "ballads" clearly do not belong to the tradition of German narrative poetry; rather, they read like the hymnic outbursts and personal litanies of a man caught in the sweep of historical events and enraptured by the great lyric poets of the past.[1] In Hermlin's first book the striking eclecticism of all his writing is already evident. Nearly all of his verses—some compellingly powerful, many hopelessly crippled by awkward stylizations and far-fetched metaphoric concoctions—are pervaded by the familiar voices of more original poets and previous traditions. His lines resound with echoes from the lyrical past: from Luther to Georg Heym, from Gryphius, Michael Drayton, Goethe and Hölderlin to Shelley, Eichendorff, Mörike, Rimbaud and Apollinaire, from Whitman, George and Rilke, Trakl and Gottfried Benn to the

---

1. For a fine discussion of Hermlin's early poetry, see Hans Mayer, "Stephan Hermlins 'Zwölf Balladen von den Grossen Städten'," *Deutsche Literatur und Weltliteratur* (East Berlin, 1957), pp. 649–54.

early Brecht and the early Johannes R. Becher, German baroque poetry, expressionism, and surrealism. Hermlin is at his best a versatile eclectic and a skillful adapter (see especially his adaptations from Eluard's poetry in the volume *Nachdichtungen*, 1957); at his worst he is a slave to the outworn tones and techniques of earlier poets.

West German critics have sufficiently emphasized Hermlin's derivativeness, and particularly the "bourgeois," even aristocratic, origins and extremely decorative nature of his vocabulary: the castles and marble statues, words like "Gestad," "Sirene," "Asphodelenhain," "Katarakt," phrases such as "Wälder aus Marmor und Licht," "Flöten und marmorne Bilder," "Schloss im mondenen Haine," and "Vor des Wahnsinns süssem mohnfarbnen Saft"—all taken from romantic and neoromantic tradition.[2] Surprisingly, though, one name that has never been mentioned in this regard is that of Swinburne, long one of Hermlin's favorite poets.

Even more generally acknowledged, in both East and West, is Hermlin's relationship to the late stages of French surrealism, the poetry of the French resistance; in fact, in nearly every brief discussion of his poetry his historical importance is declared to have been the importing of surrealism into the German lyric.[3] Hermlin was personally acquainted with Paul Eluard and Louis Aragon during the years of the French resistance, and many of his better verses show a spontaneity and melodic fluidity characteristic of Eluard's poetry. Hermlin's technique in *Zwölf Balladen* (but not in later volumes containing the "ballads") of omitting all commas and punctuation which would interrupt the flow of the lines was clearly borrowed from Eluard and Aragon. As Peter Huchel has stated, perhaps a bit too generously, "Hermlin's profound knowledge of modern French literature may have set the tone of much of his poetry and lent it an intellectual clarity, a depth and gracefulness not often present in German poetry." Nevertheless, as Huchel also points out, and I think rightly, "Hermlin is neither a pupil of Paul Eluard nor did he write his poems in the shadow of Aragon. What he does share with those poets, however, is the

2. See especially Marcel Reich-Ranicki, "Stephan Hermlin, der Poet," *Deutsche Literatur in West und Ost* (Munich, 1963), pp. 386–410, and the review by Jürgen P. Wallmann in *Neue Deutsche Hefte, 13* (1966), 140–46.

3. See, for example, Hermann Kunisch, ed., *Handbuch der deutschen Gegenwartsliteratur*, (Munich, 1965), p. 268.

conception of his literary pursuit as a 'social task,' to use a word of
Mayakovsky." [4] The influence of Eluard and Aragon on Stephen
Hermlin was actually more biographical than literary; poetically,
their impact was more thematic than stylistic. It is for the idea of
secret community in a period of deep isolation, the sense of hope
in a time of desperation, that Hermlin is most indepted to his activity in the French resistance movement. This factor of political
commitment and affirmation made the thematic transition to his
later poetry, written in the DDR, a relatively unproblematical one.

The real, immediate influence on Hermlin's poetic language
came not from the French surrealists, but from the first, prewar
stage of German expressionist poetry, specifically the early Johannes R. Becher and, above all, Georg Heym. All of Hermlin's
pathos and visionary fervor, the bold metaphors and startling
syntactical constructions, even much of the markedly "romantic"
or "aristocratic" vocabulary, the exoticisms and archaisms, derive
directly from Heym. Moreover, many of the weaknesses that tend
to mar early expressionist verse, particularly the excessive use of
genitive metaphors and awkward constructions of all varieties,
occur again, often with annoying frequency, in Hermlin's poetry.

One need only juxtapose typical Heym stanzas with lines characteristic of the early Hermlin to see the obvious similarities:

Heym, "Die Dämonen der Städte":

Um ihre Füsse kreist das Ritornell
Des Städtemeers mit trauriger Musik,
Ein grosses Sterbelied. Bald dumpf, bald grell
Wechselt der Ton, der in das Dunkel stieg.

Sie wandern an dem Strom, der schwarz und breit
Wie ein Reptil, den Rücken gelb gefleckt
Von den Laternen, in die Dunkelheit
Sich traurig wälzt, die schwarz den Himmel deckt.[5]

4. *Sonntag,* April 27, 1958, p. 8: "Hermlins profunde Kenntnis der modernen
französischen Literatur mag das Klima mancher Verse mitbestimmt und ihnen eine
intellektuelle *clarté,* eine Tiefe, mit Grazie verbunden, gegeben haben, die man
in der deutschen Lyrik nur allzu selten findet." "Hermlin ist weder ein Schüler
Paul Eluards, noch hat er im Schatten Aragons seine Verse geschrieben. Gemeinsam mit den beiden Dichtern hat er allerdings, dass er seine literarische Arbeit,
um ein Wort Majakowskis zu gebrauchen, als 'sozialen Auftrag' empfindet."
5. *Dichtungen und Schriften,* ed. Karl Ludwig Schneider (Hamburg and
Munich, 1964), *1,* 186.

Hermlin, "Die Ebene":

Tieren gleich brüllten aus Kneipen verflucht Grammophone.
In den Kasernenhöfen schlugen den Takt
Schüsse. Es warfen von Brückenbögen Spione
Sich ihrem Wild nach in der Stadt Katarakt.

Liessen wir uns nicht auch in die Wälder versetzen,
Wo unter Schlingpflanzen und dem zaubrischen Flug
Giftfarbner Kolibris Wahnsinn und Entsetzen
Uns aus verdrehten Pupillen entgegenschlug? (7) [6]

Both of these samples illustrate the same flair for bold, shocking
imagery, characterized by striking genitive constructions ("das
Ritornell des Städtemeers," "der zaubrische Flug giftfarbner Kolibris") and the same apocalyptic vision, dominated by metaphors
of primitive jungle habitation. The big-city setting is the same,
Hermlin being deeply indepted to Heym (as well as to Ernst
Stadler, Gottfried Benn, and the early Becher) for that demonic,
mythic urban atmosphere. The vocabulary is also similar, common
usages alternating with elaborate, sometimes technical words such
as "Ritornell," "Katarakt," and "Kolibri." Word order is generally
inverted, the syntax complicated and intricately hypotactic, as in
the second stanza of each passage. The rhythmic cadence is highly
erratic, with sharp, abrupt periods giving way to long units
extending over several lines. Furthermore, despite these startling
specific qualities, the overall effect in both cases is not one of
irregularity, much less of dissolution. Heym and Hermlin exhibit
here, and in all their poetry, the same stubborn attachment to the
complete grammatical sentence, regular rhyme schemes, and symmetrical stanza patterns. These conventions are espoused as indispensable building blocks; they function as harnesses to the visionary pathos and as sturdy columns supporting the clashing details. As
ominous and jarring (and very often haphazard) as the statements

6. Page references are to the collection *Dichtungen* (East Berlin, 1956). In the
case of the early poems I generally cite the original versions as they appear in
the volumes *Zwölf Balladen von den Grossen Städten* (Zürich, 1944), *Wir verstummen nicht* (Zürich, 1944), and *Strassen der Furcht* (Singen, 1944). Most of
the poems referred to also appear in the selection *Gedichte* (Leipzig, 1963) and in
the two West German editions of Hermlin's poetry, *Gedichte und Prosa*, ed.
Klaus Wagenbach (Berlin, 1965) and *Die Städte*, ed. Alfred Karnein (Munich and
Esslingen, 1966).

and images are, the poem as a whole leaves the impression of controlled solidity. All of these common stylistic features, and others, are extolled by Hermlin in the introduction to his recent edition of Heym's poetry, which has appeared in both East and West Germany.[7]

Hermlin's formal reliance on this immediate source is extremely heavy, but there is a fundamental thematic difference which must not be overlooked. Because of his virtually lifelong commitment to the Communist cause, which became crucial during the period of resistance against fascism, Hermlin invariably added an element of ideological direction lacking in Heym's poetry. All Heym's visions of horror, isolation, and destruction are almost without exception answered in Hermlin's poems by a closing sense of community and faith in political courage and activity. Even the very early work "Die Ebene," for instance, the first three-fourths of which represent entirely scenes of death and shattered illusions, ends in tones worthy of the most unflinching political revolutionary:

> An jeder Ecke erschossen wir Hunger und Sterben,
> Wahnsinn, Pest und Verrat. Wir reichten der zögernden Hand
> Waffen und Bücher. Und gegen das Grosse Verderben
> Schmiedeten wir wie beflügelt den Grossen Verband.
>
> . . . .
>
> Auf den dröhnenden Feldern der Sang der Traktoren.
> Ebenen warteten riesig auf uns überall.
> Und der mächtige Tag, im Osten geboren,
> Flog aus unserer Hand wie ein feuriger Ball. (9)

Another example is the "Ballade von unserer Zeit mit einem Aufruf an die Städte der Welt," which is also an accumulation of visions of desperation. Here again there is the final "Aufruf," a pledge of confidence in the future:

> Darum erwarten wir euch: die Schatten vom Städtege-
>   schlechte.
> So sind verschworen wir euerer Zukunft oder dem Fall
> In die staubigen Gräber der Nacht. Doch unsere Rechte

7. Georg Heym, *Gedichte*, ed. Stephan Hermlin (Leipzig, 1967, and Frankfurt, 1967).

Krönt euch mit Zuversicht. Und unsrer Stimme ersterbender
   Hall
Sagt euch von der Erwartung der Schatten vom Städtege-
   schlechte. (12)

In fact, as Hans Mayer pointed out in an early review, the volume
Zwölf Balladen is actually one long "ballad" in twelve movements, each section and the composition as a whole proceeding
in the same direction from horror to confidence, from visions of
destruction and isolation to an appeal for collective reconstruction.
By the end, Mayer notes, the cycle's direction is "prepared thematically for the 'overcoming of isolation,' so that the strange,
gigantic voice of the 'cities' judges' can echo forth. For it is not
destruction that is the final word of this twelve-part ballad, but
reconstruction and confidence." [8]

Hermlin's historical importance, then, lies not in the fact that
he introduced French surrealist poetry into the modern German
lyric; this was more the achievement of Karl Krolow, Paul Celan,
and others. Rather, his accomplishment was that he adapted the
tone and poetic means of his most immediate predecessor, Georg
Heym, to the firmly hopeful, committed spirit of the French
resistance movement. At his best he achieved this combination
without reverting to a kind of vague "O Mensch" poetry in the
fashion of Werfel and Hasenclever.

Another reason for emphasizing Hermlin's reliance on the tradition of lyric poetry—aside from merely pointing to the derivativeness of his verse—is its thematic role. Hermlin's cities, unlike
Heym's, are not only demonic settings for visions of cosmic
destruction; they are also seats of culture and civilization, threatened, wounded, yet always the basis of hope for retaliation and
eventual conquest. In "Litanei für die Grossen Städte der Welt,"
the opening poem in the volume *Zwölf Balladen*, the last vision
before the summoning of courage is the sight of book burnings:
"Aus allen Kellern drang der Sterbenden Gebrüll / Und Werk
der toten Dichter brannt auf Plätzen still / Wir beugten uns.
Es war des Grossen Moloch Will" (15). In the closing poem,

---

8. Mayer, "Hermlins 'Zwölf Balladen'," p. 653: "bis thematisch alles für die
'Überwindung der Einsamkeit', für das Echo der seltsam-grossen Stimme dieser
'Richter vom Städtegeschlechte' vorbereitet ist. Nicht Vernichtung nämlich ist das
letzte Wort dieser zwölfgeteilten Weltballade, sondern Aufbau und Zuversicht."

"Ballade von einem Städtebewohner in tiefer Not," the speaker
again bemoans his "poets buried in the morning wind" ("Dichter
verscharrt im Morgenwind") and in the stanza following specifies
his regret:

> Wie mich in meinen Sinnen friert!
> Die Brüder die ich fern gekannt
> Die Toten die mein Herz regiert
> Zu jeder Zeit sind längst verbannt
> Und Percy Friedrich Wolfgang sind
> Verschlagen in das grosse Wehn
> Von Bannern die im weissen Wind
> Der Ewigkeiten weit vergehn. (49)

Between the prologue and the finale of the volume there are
numerous other references to the cultural past—buildings, statues,
historical figures, music, poets. Of greatest relevance in this respect
is the "Ballade von der Königin Bitterkeit," in which the speaker's
relation to the "dead poets" is the central theme of the poem. In
the first two stanzas an idyllic setting is presented, housed by
"voices" of tranquillity: "Stimmen der Bienen im Wald / Stimmen
der Heide im Sonnenglast." This idyll becomes more and more
treacherous, until the first elegiac note is sounded: "Warum blieb
es nicht so." We then learn the nature of the voices and what has
become of them:

> Ihr toten Dichter die ihr für mich spracht
> Ihr verliesst mich doch ich euch nie
> Ich versank in der Bitterkeiten Meer
> Und ihr hörtet nicht als ich schrie. (33)

The long middle section of the poem is an evocation of the
present-day "land of misery," ruled over by "Queen Bitterness"
and from which the sweet voices are excluded ("Und die toten
Dichter sind nicht zu Gast / In Babel und Ninive"). Though the
speaker first identifies with this brotherhood of outcast poets, he
ends by realizing that the only alternative left him is the power
to steel himself against the times with the power of conviction:

> Wenn dir nichts mehr blieb als die Bitterkeit
> Mag die abschiedsmüde Hand

Jäh sich ballen zur Faust Das verschleierte Aug
In stählernem Hass gespannt

Und erbarmungslos in die Laden gelegt
Siehst Sonaten du und das Wort
Toter Dichter Und aus des Abends Meer
Und Erinnerung gehst du fort
Ohne Tränen und ohne Gedächtnis hin
In die Horizonte der Zeit
Durch die Lande des Jammers die mächtig regiert
Die Königin Bitterkeit (25)

The comforting voices of dead poets have betrayed him in the
time of need, leaving moral determination as his only answer
to the uncomforting, unpoetic present. In the "Ballade vom Land
der ungesprochenen Worte"—another poem dealing with the
cultural heritage and political engagement—the speaker's preoccupation with the past resembles an intoxication, leading to
indifference toward his contemporaries and in part responsible
for the curse which seems to hover over the present day.[9]

The tension, then, between the aesthete and the revolutionary,
on which Marcel Reich-Ranicki bases his perceptive essay about
Hermlin,[10] is apparent not only in the discrepancy between his

---

9. *Die Strassen der Furcht*, p. 22:

Ja berauscht sind wir von vergangenem Tag
Und verdammt zur Einsamkeit
Miteinander Das Auge rückwärts gewandt
Sieht Lippen vergangener Zeit
(Wie aus Marmor) in unerhörtem Kuss
Vereint—jenes Meer jenen Baum
Und auf der Zunge verdorrt uns das Wort
Und die Gegenwart welkt vor dem Traum

10. "Hermlin, der Poet." It is interesting to note that Marcel Reich-Ranicki,
who as a West German critic has written the most exhaustive analysis of Hermlin's development in his book *Deutsche Literatur in West und Ost*, once had different thoughts about literature and about the poet Hermlin. In an earlier book
on modern German literature, published in Warsaw in 1955, Marceli Ranicki (his
name then) had praised Hermlin for his discovery of a clear, "popular" language.
(See *Z dziejów literatury niemieckiej*, pp. 345–51.) He did not then consider
Hermlin's "Stalinist" poetry—*Mansfelder Oratorium* (1949) and the volume *Der
Flug der Taube* (1952)—"books of compromise," nor did he doubt Hermlin's
ability "to be a Communist and a poet at the same time." In the early 1950s
Marceli Ranicki also wrote for publication in the DDR and employed all of the
categories current among East German "critics" at the time. For an excellent

esoteric lyrical means borrowed from an "unrevolutionary" tradition and his will to political activism; it is also of thematic importance within the work itself. The praise of political courage,
with which so many of Hermlin's poems end, grows in large part
out of the poet's disappointment with the "sweet voices" of the
past and his feeling of their inadequacy to face the challenges of
the day. The real futility of his position derives not from his un-
awareness of this tension, but from his singular inability to develop
a means of expression appropriate to his revolutionary message.
Even the "Ballade von den Unsichtbar-Sichtbaren in den Grossen
Städten"—a powerful poem in praise of the steadfast and selfless
commitment of the resistance fighters—for instance, does not end
with a straightforward, agitational rallying of forces. Rather, the
three final stanzas are a mystical, magical incantation, much in the
style of Gottfried Benn:

> Ihrer Gesichter sind viele doch immer das eine
> Wie die Erde sind sie uns der wandernde Strom
> Ihre Stummheit ihr Reden fallen wie Steine
> Schwer in den Schacht unseres Seins seit Memphis und Rom
>
> Liebe sind sie und Hass Der Schatten von Schilden
> Völker Verzückung Trunkene Schleier der Nacht
> Worte die sich versuchen im Wind von Gefilden
> Wenn der Falter des Morgen zu Fluge erwacht
>
> Zahl die beweist und Formel Zeichen Tabelle
> Unerhörtes Raunen geheimster Musik
> Magisches Bild ganz schleierlos an unsrer Schwelle
> Mund o blutender du der sich gab und verschwieg! (34)

Perhaps past critics are unaware that Hermlin submitted a batch
of early poems to Benn and received a very encouraging reaction.
Later, of course, in a speech before the East German Writers'

---

example of his use of the term "Volkstümlichkeit" in reference to poetic language,
see his essay "Erich Weinert: Ein Dichter des deutschen Volkes," *Sinn und Form*,
5 (1953), 139. Reich-Ranicki, then, has clearly undergone adjustments and made
made compromises of his own. Between his "Stalinist" period and his polemical
criticism of the 1960s he wrote another essay on Hermlin: "Der Weg des Stephan
Hermlin," *Die Welt*, April 18, 1959. It is here, in my opinion, that he most satisfactorily combined the admiration and disappointment which are appropriate to a
study of Stephan Hermlin as a lyric poet.

Union, Hermlin was to refer to Benn as an "esoteric Fascist."[11]
Political conviction, this time specifically commitment to the
Party, finds similar incantatory expression in the final stanzas of
the "Ballade von einem Städtebewohner in tiefer Not," and thus
at the very end of the *Zwölf Balladen:* "Du warst der Blick der
mich nicht liess / Sage von Tyrus und Korinth / Du warst das
Wort das nicht verwies / Vers bist du grösser als der Wind" (48).
Hermlin's sincere political persuasions are unmistakably present
as a theme of his poetry, and he clearly hoped that his writings
would have an impact on historical events. But these rallying cries
are proof that he had no place on a tribunal, since his expressive
means are totally lacking in the directness and concreteness of
reference required of functional political verse.

That Hermlin was consciously struggling for a new vocabulary
more appropriate to his conception of poetry as a social instrument
is clear in the "Ballade von den alten und den neuen Worten"
(1945). Here the conflict between idyllic, personal voices and a
poetic language of direct political consequence becomes the exclusive theme of the poem; this text, in fact, is generally (especially
in the East) interpreted as programmatic of a transition to a new,
more "actual" poetry. The poem begins with a condemnation of
the "old words" as inadequate and even at odds with the present
day: "Weil die alten Worte lügen, / Weil der Unschuld die
Stunde schlägt, / Ich weiss, dass sie nicht mehr genügen" (53).
The speaker goes on to specify that the "old words" are those
born of a kind of mystical inspiration, "die Worte, / Die mir eine
Nacht verrät, / Die beflügelten Magierkohorte, / Wie vom Rauch
der Dämonen umdreht" (53). He then speaks of his suffering
because of words which were beautiful but not clear enough in
their affirmations or negations.[12] The remainder of the poem

---

11. For Hermlin's comment on Benn, see his speech *Der Kampf um eine
deutsche Nationalliteratur* (Berlin, 1952), p. 15. Hermlin told me of his early contact with Benn in private conversation.

12. "Ballade von den alten und den neuen Worten" was first published, in a
longer version, in the volume *Strassen der Furcht* (1944). There it is precisely
the "sweetness" of the old language which is now, in the reign of "Königin Bitterkeit," rejected:

Denn die Süsse war nicht die Süsse
Die ins Bittere sich nicht kehrt
Und auf steinigem Weg unsre Füsse
Blieben beinahe unversehrt
Ungenügend war diese Süsse.

presents the various characteristics of the "new words" as the speaker conceives of them. They are not to be "betrayed" to him by the night during an irrational trance, but to be "given" to him, presumably by society. He is to control his language rationally and make it serve specific functions: "Drum gebt mir eine neue Sprache! . . . / Wie ein Fluss, ein Pflug, ein Gewehr . . . / Über die Sprache will ich verfügen / Wie über mein Hemd, meine Hand, . . . / Ich will eine neue Sprache, wie einer, der sein Werkzeug wählt" (53–54). It is to be a language which he can use for his cause and which will have an immediate effect ("Eine Sprache für meine Sache, / Die euch tröstet und euch quält"), sharply defined purposes, and clearly distinguishable meaning. The "new words" are to serve as guides in the future, for example by naming the victims of the immediate past, a suggestion which leads thematically to Hermlin's poetry of the immediate postwar years: "Worte, Wegbereiter, / Sie können wie Namen sein: / Andre oder Lechleiter" (56).

What is in the end most striking about this poetical manifesto is that it demonstrates, above all else, the unfeasibility of its own insistent program. The need for a rationally controlled, socially effective poetic language is unquestionably present, and it is sincerely and eloquently expressed. Unfortunately, however, the means of expression remain far too eloquent; the plea for a rational, functional language it itself a document resulting from a highly irrational, inspirational relation to language. Programmatic declarations are continually sidetracked by such conjuring outbursts of images as the following:

> Enorm wie die Morgenröten,
> Wie Blicke verheissend, fatal,
> Wie Verzückungen, die uns töten,
> Wie die Schiffe auf dem Kanal . . .

> Worte wie Astern, Syringen,
> Wie in den Staub ein Kuss,
> Worte, die wie Städte klingen. (54–55)

These lines illustrate perfectly Hermlin's slavish reliance on modes and devices typical of German poetry thirty years earlier, from the initial adjective "Enorm" to the torrent of plural noun usages and words straight from the vocabulary of Gottfried Benn, such as "Astern" and "Syringen."

The last stanza of "Ballade von den alten und den neuen Worten" does not at all present a clear, unambiguous conclusion; instead, it renders a rather vague symbolic setting, more in the "old" language than in the "new":

> Unser Brot gewürzt mit Qualen,
> Unser Wein berauschend wie Hass.
> Wer soll unsern Wein bezahlen . . .
> Am Boden liegt das Glas
> Und das Brot gewürzt mit Qualen. (56)

The poem is, contrary to its own intentions, a prophetic announcement of a new poetic style lacking in credibility because it is made with precisely those poetic means which it condemns as no longer adequate to the contemporary situation. The same observation applies to another programmatic poem written in the same year (1945), "Forderung des Tages," which begins,

> Sage, Sprache des Dichters, herber du als Holunder,
> Tagstimme, Nachtflöte, unendlicher Flug
> Unenträtselter Vögel, verwundendes Wunder,
> Sag den Schrei und die Stille, den Durst und den Krug. (73)

Here again, what would be a call for a socially more "effective" poetry ("Dass ihr Stachel in eurem Fleische mich nennt") is made in the same derivative and often esoteric language characteristic of Hermlin's early verse, although in this case he has succeeded in composing a concise and poignant poem. Neither poem, however, should be viewed as signaling a transition from one phase of Hermlin's development to another, since it was not until the volume *Der Flug der Taube* (East Berlin, 1952), poetry written in response to the official appeal for greater "Volkstümlichkeit," that he wrote truly functional, rationally conceived poems.

Postwar Reminiscences (1945–50)

In the years after the war, following his return to Germany in 1945, Hermlin pursued his literary interests, so harassed until then, in two ways. Beginning in December 1945, he collaborated with Hans Mayer in a series of broadcasts for American-sponsored Radio Frankfurt entitled "New Books" ("Neue Bücher"), the purpose of which was to familiarize the German public with the major literary and intellectual events of the time. His other contributions were his poems expressing reaction to the war's end; they are contained in the cycle "Die Erinnerung," which is devoted to the remembrance of the fallen victims of the war and the brutality of National Socialism.

The radio speeches were later compiled in book form under the title *Ansichten über einige Bücher und Schriftsteller* (1947), which was dedicated to Golo Mann and prefaced by a brief statement of intention. According to this, Hermlin and Mayer wished to influence German literary criticism by introducing, on the French model, a new form of the essay which steers cautiously between the tradition of pondersome scholarship, in all its thoroughness and unreadability, and impressionism. More important, they hoped to cultivate and direct public taste both by viewing literary events on an international scale and by distinguishing between "genuine" German literature and works distorted and destroyed by remnants of fascist ideology.

Stephan Hermlin's contributions to the program—including discussions of Heinrich Mann and Karl Kraus, Mayakovsky and John Steinbeck, Kafka and Anna Seghers, contemporary English literature and contemporary German poetry—demonstrate at once the sincerity of his didactic intention and his distinguished literary judgment. He was a receptive critic, with a wide range of appreciation, capable of discussing with equal understanding and insight *The Grapes of Wrath* and *Das Schloss, Henri IV* and *Ulysses*, the poetry of Eliot, Eluard, and Mayakovsky. Yet his essays are not merely random expressions of praise meant to exhibit a formidable reading knowledge; they are also united by a general viewpoint and delimiting criteria, clear even from the selection of topics. In addition to the emphasis on realistic, social literature, Hermlin expressed intolerance of absolute cultural pessimism or, as regards style, formal conventionality. The first of these "limits" may be seen in his rejection of Friedrich Georg Jünger's essay on the consequences of modern technology, *Perfektion der Technik* (1946), and his assertion of the "actuality" in Kafka. The questions posed by Kafka's works, according to Hermlin, although unanswered and perhaps ultimately unanswerable, nevertheless remain questions, to be continually raised anew. Jünger's thesis is unacceptable not because it describes the correspondence between technological advance and military destruction, but because it is without direction, it fails to point to or even to suggest a way beyond the evils of modern-day reality.[13]

Still more revealing for a study of Hermlin's poetry is the second basis of judgment, his opposition to pseudoclassical conventionality. In his discussion of Mayakovsky on the occasion of the appearance of Hugo Huppert's German translation (Berlin, 1946), Hermlin ends with the hope that the Russian poet will exert a positive influence on contemporary German writers by preventing their complete submergence "in the sticky flow of Rilkean lyricisms and classicistic sonnets." Hermlin reveres not only the revolutionary inspiration of Mayakovsky's poetry, but also the originality and cosmic power of his language.[14] The same condemnation of slavish adherence to Hölderlin and Rilke and false classicism occurs in the essay on contemporary poetry. In the course of that discussion one particularly tragic example is singled out: the former expressionist and long-time Communist poet Johannes R. Becher. Although he is in basic sympathy with Becher's political intentions, Hermlin can only denounce the false direction his aesthetic endeavors took. "This case is very complex," Hermlin noted, "and calls for thorough consideration. But it has been proven beyond doubt that concern for a new realism has in this instance destroyed the substance and autonomy of poetry: Becher has arrived at neoclassical smoothness and conventional verse concoctions." [15] Becher's poetic talent and artistic production are, according to Hermlin at this time, totally incompatible with the far-reaching political goals he had set himself. Becher, the poet of national reconstruction, is considered to be still another illustra-

13. Stephan Hermlin and Hans Mayer, *Ansichten über einige Bücher und Schriftsteller* (Wiesbaden, 1947). The essay on Kafka appears on pp. 158–63; the discussion of *Perfektion der Technik* on pp. 126–30.

14. P. 146: "im zähen Fluss rilkescher Lyrismen und klassizistischer Sonette. . . . die jäh zupackende, von phantastischen Bildern erfüllte, stabreimhämmernde Sprache."

15. P. 191: "Dieser Fall ist sehr kompliziert und erfordert eine gründliche Auseinandersetzung. Es liegt aber unleugbar der Beweis vor, dass die Bemühung um einen neuen Realismus hier die Substanz und Eigengesetzlichkeit des Lyrischen zerstört hat: Becher ist in neo-klassizistischer Glätte und konventioneller Verseschmiederei gelandet."

tion, perhaps the most unfortunate of them all, of the mediocrity
of German poetry at the war's end.

Hermlin's ideological position, his rejection of complete cultural
pessimism, remained the same throughout his writings, from the
"ballads" he composed as a resistance fighter in France through
his poems, stories, and literary essays of the 1950s. Significantly,
however, his attitude toward stylistic conventionality can be seen
to have changed severely between the immediate postwar period
and the founding years of the German Democratic Republic. Less
than ten years after his Frankfurt radio speeches Hermlin was to
retract his criticism of Johannes R. Becher; he came to regard
Becher's unsuccessful poems as exceptions to the rule of high
aesthetic quality, the neoclassicism as a "complexity veiled in
simple forms," and his own earlier judgment as an error committed
in a moment of impatience.[16] This reappraisal, made in a tone
typical of political self-criticism, has more to do with tactical
reverence for the "poet of the nation," as Walter Ulbricht calls
Becher, than with any "thorough consideration" of Becher's work.
Nevertheless, Hermlin's revised judgment is extremely indicative
for a study of his own development as a poet. The demand made
on him by the society in which he came to live after 1947 was for
a "new realism" precisely in line with the program of Becher; his
political commitment was to be linked with a "popular" style,
a poetic language directly accessible to the broad masses of the
people. Indeed, by the early 1950s Hermlin was writing verse
which is virtually interchangeable with Becher's volumes of the
same period. His language, and his relation to the means of expression available to him, had undergone a complete alteration.
Before this decisive adjustment, however, in the years just after the
war, Hermlin wrote some of his most successful poems.

The "Erinnerung" cycle consists of poems written predomi-
nantly in the latter half of the 1940s in Western Germany and
the Soviet Occupied Zone; they are bound together by the theme
of remembrance of the fallen war victims. Hermlin did not abandon the decorative, often unwieldy language of his wartime poems

16. See Hermlin's essay on Becher in *Begegnungen 1954–1959* (East Berlin,
1960), pp. 260–61.

(as might have been expected from the proclamations in "Ballade von den alten und den neuen Worten") but merely tempered it and handled it with greater precision. The lines still occasionally suffer from that glossy, clumsy stylization which characterized his early writing. But the poetic medium is unquestionably more appropriate to the slow pace and contemplative tone than to the erratic outbursts of the "ballads." The newer verses are haunted by traces left by the dead and demonstrate their inescapable presence: lurking shadows, footsteps beneath the window, voices behind the curtain, flowers and ashes, faces and hands. Yet the victims return not only as terrifying, nightmarish apparitions, as uninvited reminders of what would be forgotten, but also as inspiration to turn to the brightening future. These two aspects of remembrance are expressed most clearly at the end of the programmatic poem "Forderung des Tages": "Die Oboen der Toten bezaubern mein Blut. / Weisse Städte! Ihr Schwäne der Zukunft! Du Reigen / Gemordeter, nimm mich in deine Hut!" (73) The "demand of the day" is, by mentioning the victims of the past, to torture the present into an intoxication with the future.

In gentler tones, more typical of the postwar cycle, the remarkably constructed "Blühe, blühe mir näher" [17] presents these relationships in a sequential way, as a progression from an exclusive concern for the dead (the conversation with the moon) to an awakened interest in what is to come (the sign of new light on the horizon as the moon sets). The intriguing aspect of the poem lies in its two overlapping structures, one strictly symmetrical (abccba) according to the recurrence of images and syntactical constructions, the other progressive (aabbcc) according to the passage of time from evening to night to the first trace of dawn. Thus what

17. Blühe, blühe mir näher,   Ach, ich irre sehr
   Holdes Abendgesicht.   Im Labyrinth des Erträumten.
   Grüsse im scheidenden Licht   Aus dem Versäumten
   Den erblindenden Späher.   Rettet uns niemand mehr.

   Weisses Antlitz. Wie weiss   Lege die zu weisse Hand
   Unter dem kalten Mond,   Tödlich mir aufs Haar.
   Der die Nacht bewohnt,   Nacht schwillt wunderbar
   Hinzieht auf Sternengleis.   Ins versinkende Land.

   Horch, jemand singt im Traum . . .   Weiter, o weiter
   Weint mir dein banger Mund   Klagendes Gesicht.
   Zu in später Stund   Verlass im dämmernden Licht
   Unterm Mitternachtsbaum?   Deinen Begleiter.

would seem at first to be a circular experience, returning at the
end to the form of direct address with which the poem had begun,
is in fact one which has undergone a full development. It proceeds
from a beckoning to the rising moon for companionship in the
night through the traumatic confrontation with the forces of night
to a farewell to the setting moon as the light of morning rises.
The final stanza implies that only when the moon is setting can
the light of dawn shine in full brightness—only when the remembrance of the dead is of less immediate impact can inspiration for
the future be complete; and contrarily, only when the morning is
breaking, when the future begins to show itself, does the moon
become truly a companion, is our remembrance of the dead complete.

Two poems, "Die Zeit der Wunder" and "Ballade nach zwei
vergeblichen Sommern," perhaps the finest Hermlin has written,
may best exemplify the linguistic mastery he reached in the few
years between the war's end and the foundation of the German
Democratic Republic. Both were written in 1947, and both take
as their theme the speaker's reaction to that year in German history. They are poems of disappointment and disillusion, mourning
the loss of the "miraculous" period immediately after the surrender
and the wasted, frustrated ambitions of reorienting the German
nation. In this respect they stand out in Hermlin's work as
virtually the only poems not directed toward and not concluding
with a glorification of political courage and hope in the future;
both poems begin and end on a negative note of resignation and
skepticism. The "Ballade nach zwei vergeblichen Sommern" opens
with a setting of freezing, dismal winter and ends with complete
stagnation:

> Doch der Reigen der Möglichkeiten
> Hebt nächtens an sich zu drehen,
> Weil die Zeiten nicht weiterschreiten,
> Weil die Zeiger im Frost stillstehn. (60)

Even the gloomy signs of a cyclical course of events are suggested,
and the conclusive halt is emphasized in the three successive
stresses with which the poem closes. "Die Zeit der Wunder" is
filled with the same sense of dashed illusions and halted progress,
ending with the lines, "Der Worte Wunden bluten heute nur

nach innen. / Die Zeit der Wunder schwand. Die Jahre sind vertan." (83)

The real uniqueness of these poems, though, is the mastery of language and formal technique. They have lost none of their diversity and emotional verve to the program of poetic functionality announced in the "Ballade von den alten und den neuen Worten" and realized in Hermlin's later verse. Yet they are handled with a caution and discrimination not evident in the early work: the vocabulary and rhythmic cadence are more perfectly suited to the context and changing moods within the poem. In "Ballade nach zwei vergeblichen Sommern," for instance, the words are plain and unelaborate, and the line is deliberately tense in sections reporting the wintery stagnation of the present day:

> Man friert in den grossen Städten.
> An Pfosten klettert der Reif,
> Wenn die Kinder in den Schatten sich retten,
> In den Schatten, in der Ratten Gekeif . . .
>
> Die Krähen hängen im Winde.
> An den Herzen wächst der Schorf. (57)

The language is more evocative and metaphorical in the long middle portion of the poem, where the speaker thinks of the hope-filled year or two after the war, and here too the rhythm is interrupted less abruptly from line to line:

> Grüne Blitze aus Oleander
> Haben unsern Mittag entzückt.
> Wenn des Blutes schwarzer Mäander
> Das Pflaster der Städte bestickt,
> Gekreuzigt von brüllenden Sonnen
> Flogen Arme und Münder im Föhn
> Der Revolten, von Glorie umronnen,
> Lasst sie, lasst sie wieder geschehn! (58)

The poem is weakest at the end, when the speaker returns his glance to the present. The diction is again direct and straightforward, but the images are really no more than the usual commonplaces attached to tendencies of a restorative society: "Die Magier singen die neuen Lieder / Auf die alte Melodie, . . . / Gaukler und Kartenschläger / Vertauschen auf den Märkten den /

Gejagten mit dem Jäger, / Und wir lassen es wieder geschehn"
(60). The careful poetic modulation breaks down in this final
stanza, where recourse is taken to tiring political clichés.

It is in "Die Zeit der Wunder" that Hermlin puts his poetic
means to most perfect use. The images and usages remain striking
but are freed of the excesses and clumsiness which so often mar
his earlier verse. Particularly successful is the second stanza, where
the speaker recalls that "miraculous" time which has now passed:

> Es war die gute Zeit der Schwüre und der Küsse.
> Verborgen waren die Waffen, offen lag der Tod.
> Die Schwalben schrien in einem Abend voller Süsse.
> Man nährte sich von Hoffnung und vergass das Brot.
> Die halben Worte, die im Dunkel sich verfingen,
> Waren so unverständlich wie Orakelspruch.
> Hörst du es noch: Wenn wir die Zeit der Kirschen singen . . .
> Ich weiss noch heut der blauen Nebel bittren Ruch. (82)

Here, by skillfully blending straightforward declarations and suggestive metaphors, Hermlin manages to truly evoke a historical
situation by associating it with the personally felt mood of innocence and unsuspecting youth. Statement gives way to an image
filled with sensual associations ("Verborgen waren die Waffen,
offen lag der Tod. / Die Schwalben schrien in einem Abend voller
Süsse"), and description of that earlier state, when hope supplied
whatever nourishment was required, is followed by a direct reminder: "Hörst du es noch: Wenn wir die Zeit der Kirschen
singen."

With this evocation of the famous nineteenth-century French
folksong by the follower of Béranger, Jean-Baptiste Clement, the
time of unfaltering political courage is fully integrated with the
ahistorical period of youthful love, "die Zeit der Wunder" with
"les temps des cerises." The allusion is especially fortunate because
it refers to a song of melancholy remembrance which was popular
among the active resistance fighters in France. "Les temps des
cerises" is also a singing of days which could only be understood in
their full bitter-sweetness after they have passed. The prophetic
warnings which had surrounded those earlier days, so incomprehensible then ("Die halben Worte . . . waren so unverständlich
wie Orakelspruch"), are perceived only now, in a state of reflec-

tion; similarly the French folksong, which had been sung in the
"Zeit der Wunder" of the French resistance, is understood only
now, after the movement's dissolution, to be not an idyllic love-
song but one of painful remembrance:

> C'est de ce temps-là que je garde au coeur
>   Une plaie ouverte!
> Et dame Fortune, en m'étant offerte,
> Ne pourra jamais fermer ma douleur . . .
> J'aimerais toujours le temps des cerises
> Et le souvenir que je garde au coeur! [18]

With this perfectly placed allusion, Hermlin suggests his answer
to the calamity described in the first two stanzas, where the un-
promising, empty present was posed in shocking contrast to that
dreamlike past, "die gute Zeit der Schwüre und der Küsse." The
force of memory, the open wound of "le souvenir," is meant to
stand up against the disappointment of the day, and this despite the
finality of the closing lines, "Der Worte Wunden bluten heute
nur nach innen. / Die Zeit der Wunder schwand. Die Jahre sind
vertan." Resignation and skepticism are unquestionably present and
determine the tone of the poem, but they are significantly modified
by their continual interplay with lines demonstrating the capacity
to remember and almost bring back to life a time of unshaking
optimism ("Ich weiss noch," "Ich hör noch"; the word "noch"
occurs eight times in the final eighteen lines).

   This thematic complex, with its steady shifting of mood from
inspired remembrance to melancholy awareness of the present,
finds convincing expression in the slow-moving, superbly modulated language, the alternation of direct statement and metaphoric,
allusive suggestion. At the end of the poem, for a further example,
the two last lines are significantly modified, their conclusiveness
at once emphasized and tempered by the line which immediately
precedes them: "Ich hör im Nachtwind brausen noch den wilden
Schwan." The complete halt to which the poem is brought by
the two irreversible statements of the final line becomes even more

18. The text of "Les temps des cerises" appears in *La chanson française du XVe
au XXe siècle* (Paris, n. d.), p. 288. The fact that this song was frequently sung
in France during the time of his activity there was emphasized by Hermlin in
conversation.

pronounced in contrast to the tumultuous movement recalled here.
Yet, because of the complex syntactical structure of the line, with
the ambiguous reference of "im Nachtwind" (does it modify "ich"
or the "Brausen" of the swan?) and the intentionally misleading
position of "noch" (it almost seems as though the swan is "still" in
wild motion), there is a suggestion that a remnant of movement
lingers on even in the present standstill and that the activity of
yesterday still bears influence on today's inactivity. The same
suggestion is brought out by the careful handling of line, rhyme,
and sound patterns. In these closing three lines alone a myriad
associations is created by phonetically interrelated phrases, such as
"noch entsinnen"-"nur nach innen," "Die Jahre sind vertan"-
"noch den wilden Schwan," "Der Worte Wunden"-"Die Zeit der
Wunder," "wilden Schwan"-"Wunder schwand." The miracle
of those bygone years persists in the magical ambiguity of their
passing and in the act of reminiscence by which they are captured.

It is in this poem, too, that Hermlin most perfectly absorbs the
French influence later stamped by critics on all of his early poetry.
If this second stanza of "Die Zeit der Wunder" is juxtaposed with
the corresponding strophe in Aragon's well-known poem, "Les
Lilas et les Roses" (1940), familiar to English readers in Louis
MacNeice's fine translation,[19] it becomes sufficiently clear where
the contemplative, quickly shifting mood of Hermlin's verses
came from, as well as the handling of stanza, line, and rhyme-
scheme:

> Je n'oublierai jamais l'illusion tragique
> Le cortège les cris la foule et le soleil
> Les chars chargés d'amour les dons de la Belgique
> L'air qui tremble et la route à ce bourdon d'abeilles
> Le triomphe imprudent qui prime la querelle
> Le sang que préfigure en carmin le baiser
> Et ceux qui vont mourir debout dans les tourelles
> Entourés de lilas par un peuple grisé [20]

Hermlin learned from Aragon the technique of the loose alexandrine, a verse pattern very rarely used with any success in

19. See *Aragon: Poet of the French Resistance*, ed. Hannah Josephson and
Malcolm Cowley (New York, 1945), p. 34.
20. Louis Aragon, *Le Crève-Coeur* (Paris, 1941), pp. 40–41.

German poetry. In "Die Zeit der Wunder" Hermlin calculates ingeniously, applying the French scheme without a trace of rigidity. The subtle suggestiveness of Aragon's verses also impressed him, the evocation in "Les Lilas et les Roses" of an intensely experienced historical situation by means of unobtrusive allusions and cogent sensual associations. Aragon's poem, too, mourns the loss of two loves, one personal and one historical (his wife Elsa and his beloved France), just as "the time of miracles" which Hermlin's speaker misses corresponds to the days of youth and to a period of confident political activism. Such lines as "Die Schwalben schrien in einem Abend voller Süsse" and "Ich weiss noch heut der blauen Nebel bittren Ruch" have close parallels in Aragon's lines. Hermlin learned from the French poet to lament the disappearance of "l'illusion tragique" and to recall the naïve hopes of former days, with all their ambiguity and touching relevance. Yet despite the many similarities, Hermlin's poem is by no means merely derivative. In this case he adapts masterfully, combining the soft, melodic movement of the French source—the controlled swell of the alexandrine—with the harsh, more abrupt, shocking diction of his earlier poetry and his expressionist heritage, as in the opening lines:

> Die Zeit der Wunder ist vorbei. Hinter den Ecken
> Versanken Bogenlampensonnen. Ungenau
> Gehen die Uhren, die mit ihrem Schlag uns schrecken,
> Und in der Dämmrung sind die Katzen wieder grau. (82)

By sensitively transferring the atmosphere of Aragon's poems in his volume *Le crève-coeur* (1941), which is that of France after the Armistice, to that of 1947 Germany, Hermlin has created a work which belongs among the very best of German political poetry.

It was in the period immediately after the war, then, when his stance was one of pensive remembrance and when his vision was charged through with uncertainty and resignation, that Hermlin developed a tone and technique truly his own. What troubled him at this time, and what gave rise to his skepticism, were the restorative tendencies in postwar German society or, more generally, the apparent failure to come to terms with the immediate past and learn from it in building for the future. But Hermlin does not name this discomforting situation; he evokes it, alludes to it, suggests his discontent in "Die Zeit der Wunder" by associating it with other, less specifically historical frames of reference. For this reason, and because he succeeds in modulating his poetic language to suit the changing directions within the poem, he introduces a subtlety and controlled ambiguity lacking in his earlier works.

"Volkstümlichkeit" (After 1950)

Hermlin's volume *Der Flug der Taube* was published in East Berlin in 1952 and was obviously meant for an East German reading public. Except for two poems from the "Erinnerung" cycle, it contains exclusively texts glorifying events of Communist history, from the October Revolution ("Aurora") to the international youth festivals held in East Berlin in 1951 ("Die Jugend"). The heroes are Soviet and Greek resistance fighters ("Der Granit von Leningrad" and "EPON"), Wilhelm Pieck, and above all, Stalin. In addition to the long biographical hymn "Stalin," the title poem celebrates the Soviet leader as the bringer of world peace.

In this context the poem "Terzinen" (1946–47) from the "Erinnerung" cycle seems strikingly out of place. It is subdued in its emotionality, the terza rimas flowing gently from memory to fading memory:

> Der Regen wäscht aus Tafeln Wort um Wort,
> Rinnt auf Monti-Valerien und Plötzensee.
> Die Schwalben liegen in der Hand des Nord. (63)

This poem opens the "Erinnerung" cycle and, programmatically, sets the tone of the entire group. It sides with the fallen victims of the war in what seems to be their new struggle, against the rushing flood of time. While rain threatens to wash away their legacy, swallows remain fluttering in the wind as reminders of their doomed activity. The dead lie waiting in their graves, and the speaker's words, too, are said to falter and deliberate before finding utterance. In the two opening stanzas the swallows, the dead victims and the words themselves are implicitly identified:

Die Worte warten. Keiner spricht sie aus:
Auf ihren Lidern eine Handvoll Nacht,
Ihr Haar wärmt Nest und Brut der Wintermaus.

Aus ihrem Säumnis ist mein Traum gemacht,
Mein langer Tag aus ihrer Endlichkeit.
Die Schwalben sind vom Winde überdacht. (63)

The poet-speaker's "dream" is made of the victims' patient waiting because he hopes that their example will some day be con-
secrated in the noble aspirations of posterity; until then, as is said
in the third stanza, their name will remain: "Vermächtnis, Schwur
und Mahnmal ungeweiht." These metaphoric nuances—the sense
of the verb "warten," the image of the flight of swallows counter-
acting the pouring rain, and the function of poetic utterance as a
force of recollection and preservation—are all present in the
intriguing final lines of the poem:

Geknebelt mit Gesängen gingen sie
Dahin. Jetzt schmilzt ihr Fleisch vom Rattenbiss

Sechs Fuss tief in des Wartens Euphorie,
Wenn sich die Regensäulen auf sie lehnen.
Der Schwalbensturz allein vergisst sie nie,

Die langsam treiben unter den Moränen. (63–64)

Their illusions were shattered, their flesh is now decaying, and all
nature seems to bear down on them like mighty pillars, or age-
old glaciers. Yet beneath the weight they glide on slowly, patiently,
"euphorically," waiting for future generations to live up to their
name.

West German commentators on Hermlin's poetry have, I think
rightly, singled out "Terzinen" for its outstanding quality.[21]
Marred somewhat by a hackneyed imitation of Rilke in the verses
"Den Blick voll Bläue, Hand und Atemzug, / Die Abende von
lauem Gold wie Tee," it does not stand up to the consistent excellence of "Die Zeit der Wunder." But the mood of melancholy
reminiscence, similar to that in "Die Zeit der Wunder," is mem-
orably evoked in these gentle, skillfully modulated terza rimas.

21. See *Die Zeit*, April 29, 1954, p. 6; *Neue Zürcher Zeitung*, February 8, 1966,
p. 5; *Frankfurter Allgemeine Zeitung*, September 14, 1963; and *Neue Deutsche
Hefte*, *13* (1966), 145.

Even the genitive metaphor—so essential to Hermlin's poetic diction yet so troublesome in much of his earlier poetry—is here handled with some ingenuity, as in "eine Handvoll Nacht" and "des Wartens Euphorie." "Terzinen" is unquestionably one of his most notable achievements, with "Die Zeit der Wunder," "Ballade nach zwei vergeblichen Sommern," and "Die Einen und die Anderen" perhaps the closest he ever came to perfection.

East German reviewers of *Der Flug der Taube*, however, were of a different opinion; the negative reception of "Terzinen" and similar poems in the DDR in 1952 is highly revealing for a study of Hermlin's poetic development. Writing in the East Berlin weekly *Sonntag*, Eduard Zak contrasts "Terzinen" to the long, hymnic poem "Die Jugend" (1951), in which Hermlin has conclusively and happily left behind the "preciosity and obscurity" of his earlier writing. Zak then cites the closing five lines of "Terzinen" ("Jetzt schmilzt ihr Fleisch . . ."), and argues that these victims, who fell in their struggle against fascism, are not sufficiently distinguished from other corpses. By simply asking what the dead victims' "euphoria" means, and why they drift under "glaciers," he believes that he has proven these images to be without any meaning. Zak concludes his interpretation: "In this case the affected form seems to us to have perverted the well-intended theme." [22]

Clearly, "Terzinen" is here considered out of the context of the cycle to which it belongs. Though six of the poems from the "Erinnerung" group are omitted from *Der Flug der Taube*, the other poem which is included, "Die Asche von Birkenau," could hardly be more specific as to the dead who are being recalled:

> Die man ins Gas sandte,
> Waren des Lebens voll,
> Liebten die Dämmerung, die Liebe,
> Den Drosselschlag, waren jung;
> Schwer wie vorm Sturm Wolkengeschiebe
> Ist die Erinnerung. (75)

Still more misleading is the way in which the end of the poem is discussed without reference to what had preceded: the former

22. *Sonntag*, June 7, 1952: "Hier scheint uns die gesuchte Form den richtig gemeinten Gehalt pervertiert zu haben."

enthusiasm of the dead and their effect on the speaker, the careful
identification of the speaker, and particularly his words of remembrance, with the buried victims (the sense of waiting), and
the symbolic interplay between rain and swallows culminating in
the final verses. Nor is mention even made of the "affected form"
itself, the traditional terza rima. All of these components, which
any criticism of the poem must consider, would have helped explain the seemingly problematic words "Euphorie" and "Moränen."

Yet there is plainly another, more urgent reason for the reviewer's objection to these two usages. "Such esoteric language,"
Zak writes, "was unsuitable to the goals of a progressive poet
because it deprives the masses of what they are entitled to." [23] The
reviewer for *Neues Deutschland*, Henryk Keisch, states this criticism in a classic example of an official plea for socialist realism
in poetry: "There are still too many images and similes which fail
to awaken a logical train of thought by corresponding to the
situation and furthering comprehension. All too often the reader
searching for the meaning finds himself guessing, quibbling, and
interpreting. Why? Obviously because Hermlin still underesti-
mates the role due to conscious, constructive rationality, even in
poetry. To let oneself be driven by subjective trains of thought,
that means to neglect the conscious structuring of reality." The
poet's "train of thought," what direction he gives the poem and
what he means by it, should be immediately clear. "If words have
a meaning," Keisch declares, "then it should be accessible to the
reader, indeed to the average reader; if they have none, then why
were they even written down? . . . The larger the circle of
people whose realm of experience provides the poet with his means
of expression, the more popular, the more 'national' is his
poetry." [24]

23. *Sonntag*, June 7, 1952: "Solche Esoterik . . . war ungemäss den Zielen eines
fortschrittlichen Dichters, weil sie den Massen entzieht, worauf sie Anspruch
haben."

24. *Neues Deutschland*, March 9, 1952: "Zu zahlreich sind noch die Bilder und
Vergleiche, die keine dem Zusammenhang entsprechende, das Verständnis för-
dernde Gedankenverbindung wecken. Zu oft muss der nach dem Sinn forschende
Leser raten, deuteln, interpretieren. Warum? Offenbar, weil Hermlin noch immer
die Rolle unterschätzt, die dem gestaltenden Bewusstsein auch in der Lyrik ge-
bührt. Sich von subjektiven Gedankenverbindungen treiben zu lassen, das bedeutet Verzicht auf die bewusste Gestaltung der Wirklichkeit. . . . Haben die
Worte eine Bedeutung, so soll sie dem Leser, und zwar dem durchschnittlichen,

The critical category Hermlin confronted in these founding years of the DDR was literary "popularity"—"Volkstümlichkeit" understood in its narrowest sense. His political position as a Communist in the resistance movement, and thus the ideological content of his poetry, were never questioned. But he was reminded that to become a truly "meaningful" poet his poetic language would have to become more "popular," more generally accessible to the widest reading public. Fighting on the side of the masses is not enough; he has now to find, in Zak's words, "the language which his people can recognize and understand as the expression of its best thoughts." According to Zak, the development evident within the volume *Der Flug der Taube*, from "Terzinen" to "Die Jugend," provides conclusive proof that Hermlin has already found that language, a discovery which is bound to become his "inexhaustible source of poetic power" in the future.[25]

With the introduction of Soviet categories of art in the DDR after 1949, the idea of literary "popularity" and "solidarity with the people" ("Volksverbundenheit") became current. The general tendency of East German cultural politics in the early 1950s was in fact characterized by the pathetically romantic attempt to cultivate a "folk art" in the new socialist society. Published descriptions of the international youth festivals were filled with outbursts of enthusiasm for the folksy simplicity of dances and songs, particularly from the underdeveloped parts of the world.[26] In the

zugänglich sein, haben sie keine, warum wurden sie niedergeschrieben? . . . Je grösser der Kreis der Menschen, deren gemeinsamer Erlebnisbereich dem Dichter seine Ausdrucksmittel liefert, um so volkstümlicher, um so 'nationaler' seine Lyrik."

25. *Sonntag*, June 7, 1952: "Der Band und die Entwicklung, die in ihm sichtbar wird, erbringen den Beweis, dass der hochbegabte Dichter, der schon immer auf der Seite des Volkes kämpfte, nun auch den Weg gefunden hat, der ihn zum bedeutenden Dichter macht: er hat die Sprache gefunden, die sein Volk als den Ausdruck seiner besten Gedanken erkennen und verstehen kann; eine Begegnung, die für den Dichter selbst zum unerschöpflichen Quell poetischer Kraft werden muss." For a full account of Hermlin's development from the official East German point of view, see the book in the series "Schriftsteller der Gegenwart," *Erich Weinert, Stephan Hermlich, Kuba*, edited for use in high schools by the Collective for Literary History at the Verlag Volk und Wissen under the direction of Klaus Gysi (Berlin, 1955), pp. 53–66.

26. See "Erlebnisse und Erfahrungen bei den Weltfestspielen," *Sinn und Form*, 3 (1951), 131–46, reports by Herbert Ihering, Max Schröder, and Maximilian Scheer.

initial declaration of the Kulturministerium in 1954, signed by
Johannes R. Becher, there is a lengthy section on folk art, containing statements of the enormous financial subsidies given by the
government for the fostering of a national folk culture and exclamations painfully reminiscent of National Socialist cultural
decrees of some years earlier: "Where folk art lives and blossoms,
there is no place for antihumanist art. Where German people give
expression to their own national sentiment in their mother tongue,
the influences of American cultural destruction, 'Kitsch,' and trash
will never flourish. Where German folk art lives, so does love
for the great cultural past of our people and reverence for the
works of our masters." [27] This whole programmatic trend culminated as late as the conference at Bitterfeld in 1959; the aim
which Walter Ulbricht then had in view was, in his own words,
"to provide our literature and all of the arts with a new socialist
content and to make them accessible to the entire people. With the
help of writers and artists, as well as the talented workers, we
want to create the culture of the new Germany—that culture
which is national in form and socialist in theme." [28]

    Hermlin himself was not unaware of these political develop-
ments; nor did he publicly resist the pressure for greater "popularity" in literature. Time and again he demonstrated his loyal
commitment to the DDR and the Party, both as a political spokesman and as a national representative at literary conferences.[29] That

27. *Neue Deutsche Literatur*, 2 (1954 supplement), pp. 21–22: "Wo die Volkskunst lebt und blüht, ist kein Platz für eine antihumanistische Kunst. Wo deutsche Menschen in ihrer Muttersprache ihrem eigenen nationalen Empfinden Ausdruck geben, ist den Einflüssen amerikanischer Kulturzerstörung, dem Kitsch, dem
Schund der Boden gezogen. Wo die deutsche Volkskunst lebendig ist, lebt die
Liebe zu der grossen kulturellen Vergangenheit unseres Volkes, lebt die Achtung
vor den Werken unserer Meister der Kunst."

28. Ulbricht, "Fragen der Entwicklung der sozialistischen Literatur und Kultur,"
Zur sozialistischen Kulturrevolution 1957–1959: Dokumente, 2, 457–58: "Es geht
darum, unserer Literatur, der bildenden Kunst, den schönen Künsten überhaupt,
einen neuen, sozialistischen Inhalt zu geben und sie dem ganzen Volke zugänglich
zu machen. . . . Wir wollen mit Hilfe der Schriftsteller und Künstler und der
Talente aus dem arbeitenden Volk die Kultur des neuen Deutschland gestalten,
jene Kultur, die ihrer Form nach national und ihrem Inhalt nach eine sozialistische ist." For an informative, though excessively polemical account of the
cultural situation in the DDR in the late 1940s and early 1950s, see Lothar von
Balluseck, *Kultura: Kunst und Literatur in der Sowjetischen Besatzungszone*
(Cologne, 1952).

29. Even at such delicate moments as the workers' uprising of June 17, 1953,
and the building of the Wall on August 13, 1961, he came through with a show of

Hermlin in his various functions for the Academy of Arts and the German Writers' Union also lent vocal support to the official art policy in the early 1950s is beyond doubt. In a speech before the Writers' Union in 1952, "The Struggle for a German National Literature," he spoke out emphatically for socialist realism and the idea of "Volkstümlichkeit" in the creation and reception of literature. The "Manifesto of the Third German Writers' Congress," published with that speech and evidently also drafted by Hermlin, contains such declarations as: "We derive the power to create our works from the people. To give power to the people is the content and aim of our art. Therefore we use the clear language of the people and call on critics and literary scholars to speak the language of the people as well. Only when those to whom our work belongs are drawn into creative collaboration can poets grow from criticism and create a literature which serves the growth of the people." [30] At the time he published his volume *Der Flug der Taube* (1952), Hermlin openly supported the official move to "popularize" the language of literature. Judging from his own statements, he agreed with the criticism against his earlier, "esoteric" practices, and he was quite willing to adjust his means of expression to meet the Party's wishes.

Many examples illustrate Hermlin's poetic adjustment, his answer to the call for socialist realism in poetry. In *Der Flug der*

loyalty. He responded in 1953 with the story "Die Kammandeuse" in which—perfectly faithful to the official Party version—the atmosphere of discontent is attributed to a neo-Nazi conspiracy; and in 1961, with an immediate answer to the challenging open letter of Günter Grass and Wolfdietrich Schnurre, in which he emphatically proclaims full approval of his government's policy. "Die Kommandeuse" is included in *Erzählungen* (Berlin and Weimar, 1966), pp. 221–36, and the entire open correspondence regarding the Wall appears in Hans Werner Richter, ed., *Die Mauer oder Der 13. August*, (Reinbek, 1961), pp. 62–68. Most recently—in June, 1967—Hermlin again expressed his commitment in a carefully formulated speech delivered during the campaign for the National Front. (*Neues Deutschland*, June, 1967). In the early 1950s Hermlin's attitude was one of unflinching devotion; see, for example, his declaration "Die Republik ist meine Heimat" which appeared in *Neues Deutschland* on September 5, 1954.

30. *Der Kampf um eine deutsche Nationalliteratur* (East Berlin, 1952), pp. 29–30: "Vom Volk empfangen wir Kraft für die Schöpfung unserer Werke. Dem Volk Kraft zu geben, ist der Inhalt und das Ziel unserer Kunst. Darum bedienen wir uns der klaren Sprache des Volkes und fordern die Kritiker und Literaturwissenschaftler auf, ebenfalls die Sprache des Volkes zu sprechen. Nur wenn die, denen unser Werk gehört, in die schöpferische Mitarbeit einbezogen werden, können die Dichter an der Kritik wachsen und solche Literatur schaffen, die dem Wachstum des Volkes dient."

Taube there is "Die Jugend," a long echo of his experiences at the youth festivals; "Aurora," a hymn praising the Russian Revolution; and three poems glorifying the heroes of world peace— "Stalin," "Wilhelm Pieck," and "Der Flug der Taube." Also typical of East German poetry in these years was the *Mansfelder Oratorium* (1950), for which Hermlin was awarded a national prize. This historical "industry oratorio," which ends with choruses of "Vorwärts" and propagandistic platitudes, became compulsory reading for all school children in the DDR, and sections of it appeared in every official anthology of the 1950s. In all of these poems Hermlin's partisanship for the Communist cause is combined with a poetic language immediately accessible to the masses.

Most illuminating of all with respect to Hermlin's own development, however, and to the crucial question of stylistic "popularity," is the poem "Ballade von Henri und Erika," which was first published in *Der Flug der Taube*.[31] In a footnote Hermlin

31. Ballade von Henri und Erika

> Zwei waren, die sich nicht kannten,
> Nicht des andern Land noch sein Gesicht.
> Doch der Name, den beide nannten,
> Den sie sich sandten
> Wie ein Lächeln, wie ein Gedicht,
>
> War der gleiche, war warm wie das Leben
> Oder frisch wie das neue Brot,
> Hell wie Birken, die dem Wind sich geben,
> Wie junger Liebe Beben,
> Brannte tief wie das Abendrot.
>
> Er war von Toulon ein Matrose,
> Er kannte das Meer und den Krieg,
> Er sagte: Wie der Sturm auch tose—
> Rot wie die Rose
> Flammt überall der Völker Sieg.
>
> Überall sind die Herren die gleichen,
> Die Tränen sind überall gleich,
> Der schmutzige Krieg muss weichen,
> das Dollarzeichen
> Schändet Vietnam und Frankreich.
>
> Sie lernte ihre Stadt lieben,
> Die Zerstörte ward mit ihr jung
> Trotz Lügen und Knüppelhieben,
> Als Herzen, Fahnen trieben
> Im Sturm der Begeisterung.
>
> Kann man ein Herz zerschneiden,
> Wenn es weiterschlagen soll?

explains that the heroes of his poem are young peace fighters who were both arrested for their activity: Henri Martin for urging his French comrades in Vietnam "to support the struggle of the Vietnamese people against French imperialism" and Erika Thürmer for banding together with the Free German Youth (FDJ) in West Berlin to fight for peace. Hermlin's theme, therefore, perfectly met the requirements: it was "contemporary" and partisan to the struggle for peace and an end to imperialism in Germany and throughout the world.

The twelve-stanza poem consists of two units, the first containing four, the second two pairs of stanzas. The first unit deals

---

Dachte sie. Die den Krieg leiden,
Den Frieden meiden,
Sind sicherlich feig oder toll.

Sie sagten gemeinsam den Namen,
Sie, die sich niemals gesehn,
Die Botschaften gingen und kamen,
Wie Gewässer und Flammen
Konnte sie jeder verstehn.

Sie waren von Grenzen geschieden,
Die eine war hier, der andre dort.
Der Schlaf hat ihr Herz gemieden,
Sie sagten: Frieden,
Frieden heisst das Liebeswort.

Das Leben hat sie beschworen,
Sie wussten nicht, wie ihnen geschah:
Der Friede sei endlich geboren!
Ich bin verloren
Ohne euch, Henri, Erika!

Mit den Kindern der neuen Epoche
Geht das Leben nicht sanft um. Streng
Ziehn die Tage im Jahresjoche.
Doch jede Woche
Gibts mehr Erika Thürmer, Henri Martin.

Von der Kirschenzeit singen die einen,
Die andern vom Lindenbaum.
Die Tauben auf den Grabsteinen,
Was alle meinen,
Gurren sie. Es ist kein Traum.

Und man befreite die eine,
Den andern muss man befrein!
Deine Lieb ist die meine,
Stärker ist keine
Macht. Sie wird Sieger sein!

Dichtungen, pp. 125–27

with the two youths, Henri and Erika. They do not know one another, but they are mysteriously bound together, despite geographic separation, in the name, which is characterized in the first stanza pair and finally stated at the end of the fourth: "Frieden heisst das Liebeswort." Between the opening and closing sections of this unit each of the youths has a pair of stanzas, strophes three and four for Henri and five and six for Erika. The second unit is less clearly constructed, though it can be seen that the first section—stanzas nine and ten—generalizes the meaning of these two specific youths, showing them to be representative of the new age; and the second—stanzas eleven and twelve—builds up to the assertion of their function in rallying confidence in the final victory of peace and love.

The structural principle of the stanzas, stanza pairs, and units and of the poem as a whole is given in the theme: it is a continual and overall progression from battle to peace, from struggle to victory, from challenge to determination and conquest. In the first unit the magical name is finally found; the second is an assurance that it will triumph. In the first unit the two youths must fight individually and then together before the name can be uttered in stanza eight, where the procedure from challenge to inspiration can best be seen in miniature:

> Sie waren von Grenzen geschieden,
> Die eine war hier, der andre dort.
> Der Schlaf hat ihr Herz gemieden,
> Sie sagten: Frieden,
> Frieden heisst das Liebeswort.

What denies the poem all literary worth is the complete banality of its diction and poetic means. In its conception it was clearly meant as a folk ballad, narrating the strange fate of two separated lovers kept in contact with one another by mysterious messengers (doves?). Linguistically this original intention to revert to a folk tradition is obvious in the opening line, "Zwei waren, die sich nicht kannten," and especially in the lines describing Henri: "Er war von Toulouse ein Matrose, / Er kannte das Meer und den Krieg." Aside from these very artificial leanings on folksy turns of phrase, Hermlin has recourse only to common diction, to which he is entirely incapable of giving any dimension beyond the cliché.

The language is hopelessly bald and colorless, the entire poem containing only three attributive adjectives. Two of them appear in stanza two, which with its heaping of sensual images is plainly a remnant of Hermlin's earlier style. The third of these is "der schmutzige Krieg," a cliché used unfailingly in every East German news report about the situation in Vietnam. In fact, the stanza in which it occurs illustrates well the low level Hermlin has reached:

> Überall sind die Herren die gleichen,
> Die Tränen sind überall gleich,
> Der schmutzige Krieg muss weichen,
> Das Dollarzeichen
> Schändet Vietnam und Frankreich.

These lines contain all that we are told about Henri's struggle. His acts of heroism and subsequent imprisonment are not made physically present by suggestive imagery or subtle indirectness, nor are the evils of the "imperialist" war in Vietnam brought to life. The sloppy handling of rhythm here—with the stress falling on "Frank*reich*"—is not Hermlin's most serious blunder of this kind: the last, triumphant word of his Stalin poem, "STALIN," is made to rhyme with "dahin." The stanza under discussion might conceivably be justified as a quote, as Henri's language and not the speaker's, and the same defense might even be attempted with Erika's line, "Sind sicherlich feig oder toll." But certainly the end of the poem, a statement by the speaker himself, is no less impotent in all its directness.

The poem fails because its formal means do not at any point create a sense of necessity. The technique of allusion and evocation, employed so brilliantly in "Die Zeit der Wunder," here becomes no more than a reference only superficially integrated into the text. The same French folksong, "Le temps des cerises," that was quoted in "Die Zeit der Wunder" is mentioned again here ("Von der Kirschenzeit singen die einen, / Die andern vom Lindenbaum"); but in this case it serves only as a futile reminder of the folksy tone with which the poem began and, as is clear from Hermlin's footnote, as a further response to the call for "popularity": "Two peoples are spoken of here in the names of their most common songs. The French song 'Temps des cerises' corresponds to the German 'Lindenbaum' in popularity and national authenticity." [32] The five-line stanza with a rhyme scheme of abaab ("a" feminine, "b" masculine) is unsatisfactory, not because it is inappropriate to the theme of the poem, but because Hermlin consistently fails to exploit the particular capacities inherent in it as a strophic form.

This technical deficiency becomes most obvious when we compare the "Ballade von Henri und Erika" with the masterpiece which may well have been one of its direct models and which at any rate has exactly the same stanza pattern—Eichendorff's "Zwei Gesellen." [33] Also a verse narrative telling of two lives, each indi-

---

32. *Der Flug der Taube* (East Berlin, 1952), p. 82: "Zwei Völker werden hier mit dem Namen ihrer verbreitetsten Lieder genannt. Dem deutschen 'Lindenbaum' entspricht das französische 'Temps des cerises' (Kirschenzeit) an Popularität und nationaler Gültigkeit."

33. Die zwei Gesellen

Es zogen zwei rüst'ge Gesellen
Zum erstenmal von Haus,
So jubelnd recht in die hellen,
Klingenden, singenden Wellen
Des vollen Frühlings hinaus.

Die strebten nach hohen Dingen,
Die wollten, trotz Lust und Schmerz,
Was Recht's in der Welt vollbringen,
Und wem sie vorübergingen,
Dem lachten Sinnen und Herz.

Der erste, der fand ein Liebchen,
Die Schwieger kauft' Hof und Haus;
Der wiegte gar bald ein Bübchen,
Und sah aus heimlichem Stübchen
Behaglich ins Feld hinaus.

Dem zweiten sangen und logen
Die tausend Stimmen im Grund,
Verlockend' Sirenen, und zogen
Ihn in der buhlenden Wogen
Farbig klingenden Schlund.

Und wie er auftaucht' vom Schlunde,
Da war er müde und alt,
Sein Schifflein das lag im Grunde,
So still war's rings in die Runde,
Und über die Wasser weht's kalt.

Es singen und klingen die Wellen
Des Frühlings wohl über mir;
Und seh' ich so kecke Gesellen,

vidualized and rounded out, Eichendorff's poem begins by speaking of the two together, then treats them separately one after the other, and ends with them back together again, their emblematic significance and their effect on the speaker: "Ach seh' ich so kecke Gesellen, . . . Ach Gott, führ' uns liebreich zu dir!" (The thematic difference that in Eichendorff's poem the two figures are contrasting and only indirectly complementary is not important here.) Yet, as Oskar Seidlin has shown in his penetrating interpretation,[34] Eichendorff makes full use throughout of the five-line abaab stanza. He continually evokes the sense of tension and release, swelling up and final sinking, ritardando and conclusion, so characteristic of the fates of the two "Gesellen" and their relation to one another and so crucial to the theme of the poem. Hermlin, on the other hand, without exception neglects the chance to realize the potential of the stanza: he fails to utilize the mounting, deliberating feature of the fourth line, which might have been of great value to him if he had integrated it with his theme of struggle and eventual triumph. Forms and techniques improperly used inevitably lose that indispensable quality of necessity; particularly such a rare structure as the five-line stanza with this rhyme scheme (more common is aabba) can only justify its use by proving its unique adequacy to the task. A similar case can be made against Hermlin's handling of line and rhythm, which is equally haphazard.

The main issue, though, is the language. All Hermlin's efforts—which might otherwise have gone to chiseling out the pace and direction of the poem—have here been devoted to arriving at a diction cropped clean of all esoteric usages and readily familiar to the widest reading public. As exemplified by the "Ballade von Henri und Erika," Hermlin would be a model case for Hans Magnus Enzensberger's analysis in his controversial essay, "Poetry and Politics," of the destructive influence of political authority on the poetic process. In fact, although Enzensberger does not

---

Die Tränen im Auge mir schwellen—
Ach Gott, führ' uns liebreich zu dir!

  Eichendorff, *Werke* (Stuttgart, 1953) 2, 63–64
  34. "Eichendorffs 'Zwei Gesellen'," *Versuche über Eichendorff* (Göttingen, 1965), pp. 169–92.

specify names or governments, he does refer to Stephan Hermlin and the DDR at one point. Speaking of "Plato's totalitarian pupils," the modern-day censors, Enzensberger observes that they have forbidden not only certain themes and subject matters as dangerous to the state, but even certain stylistic modes and means of expression—"deviations in the poetic language itself." "Only a few years ago," he continues, "the Politbüro of a certain small central European state paid one of its poets the peculiar honor of forcing him to change the punctuation which he had chosen for his poems. For reasons of state he was summarily enjoined to put back the commas and periods which he had formerly omitted."[35] Hermlin's technique of minimal punctuation —a fundamental feature of his style, which assured it an uninterrupted melodic flow—was abandoned in the early 1950s—though, it must be stated, only seldom with detrimental effect on the poems as literary texts.

This change, however, points to the more significant obligatory modifications which signaled the disintegration of his poetic style. It is not that his poetry was suddenly forced into the service of a political ideal or party; even the earliest "ballads" ended with fanfares to the Communist cause. It is not even that he began singing in praise of political rulers such as Stalin and Wilhelm Pieck, trying his hand at the modern *basilikos logos* which Enzenberger finds a poetic impossibility; Henri and Erika, these two well-meaning youths, have served as well in this respect as did Stalin. (In fact, Hermlin contends to this day that, poetically speaking, his hymn to Stalin—nearly interchangeable, down to the details of vocabulary and imagery, with Johannes R. Becher's, the example cited by Enzenberger—is among his finest literary achievements since he moved to the DDR. To some extent, one must admit, he is probably right.) What disqualifies this ballad, and virtually all of the volume *Der Flug der Taube*, as poetry, is rather the effect

35. "Poesie und Politik," *Einzelheiten II* (Frankfurt, 1963), pp. 113–37. Pp. 134–35: "ihre [Platons totalitärer Schüler] Schrifttumskammern haben nicht allein Tendenzen und Inhalte, sie haben, platonisch gesprochen, 'Vortragsweisen' und 'Tonarten', also Abweichungen in der poetischen Sprache selbst als Staatsgefährdung verboten, und noch vor wenigen Jahren hat das Politbüro eines mitteleuropäischen Kleinstaates einem Dichter die makabre Reverenz erwiesen, ihn zu einer Änderung der Interpunktion zu zwingen, die er für seine Texte gewählt hatte: im Namen der Staatsraison ward ihm auferlegt, die Punkte und Kommata, die er fortgelassen hatte, wieder einzusetzen."

of the deliberate interference by political authority with the poetic process itself, its success in regulating and leveling off the poet's means to suit what were felt to be the political needs of the day. This interference, which by no means met with complete resistance from Hermlin at the time, consisted in an appeal to the category of "Volkstümlichkeit," and its effect was the complete banalizing and decoloring of his poetic language.

A few years later, when the cultural climate in the DDR became slightly more conducive to differentiation and critical discussion, the topic of literary experimentation and stylistic accessibility came to concern some of East Germany's most esteemed authors. Anna Seghers and Bertolt Brecht in particular (both of whom had defended a liberal conception of realism in their famous exchanges with Georg Lukács in the 1930s [36]) took issue with the rigid application of the term "Volkstümlichkeit" in the DDR. In her speech in January 1956 before the Fourth German Writers' Congress, in which several of the issues discussed with Lukács occur again, Seghers directly justified formal experimentation and called on writers to search for new forms even if they at first appeal only to small sections of the population.[37]

In the late 1930s Brecht wrote a series of essays entitled "Popularity and Realism" ("Volkstümlichkeit und Realismus"), which contains many explicit warnings against lowering aesthetic standards in order to meet what are falsely conceived of as the base needs of the people. Brecht insisted that the masses are willing and able to understand the boldest, most original and complex means of expression, as long as the work gives voice to their interests. He saw ways of reaching the people other than addressing them directly, and he recognized that to write for small groups may have great value even in revolutionary literature and does not mean an abandonment of the masses. As is clear from one of his favorite mottoes of those years, Brecht was careful not to define "popular" art as a mere duplication of common speech: "To look at the mouths of the people," he would write, quoting Martin Luther ("dem Volk aufs Maul schauen"), "is entirely different from speaking with the mouths of the people" ("dem

36. See "Ein Briefwechsel zwischen Anna Seghers und Georg Lukács," *Internationale Literatur*, 9 (1939), 97–121, and the section "Formalismus und Realismus" in Brecht, *Gesammelte Werke*, 19, 290–338.

37. *Die grosse Veränderung und unsere Literatur* especially p. 30.

Volk nach dem Mund reden"). With such thoughts, Brecht could only be appalled by the primitivism of East German literary politics in the early 1950s. In his contribution to a discussion on cultural politics by the East Berlin Academy of Arts and the Cultural Federation (Kulturbund), published in *Neues Deutschland* on August 12, 1953, he could hardly have been more explicit in his plea for a differentiated art, which must address a socially variegated audience. "The question of quality," he noted, "is politically decisive for a genuine socialist art." Brecht was especially adamant in his condemnation of the anachronistic, romantic longing for modern "folksongs" with their artificial simplicity. In 1952 he remarked: "While the folksong says something complicated in a simple way, the modern imitators say something simple (or simplistic) in a simple way. Besides, the populace does not wish to be popular ('Ausserdem wünscht das Volk nicht tümlich zu sein')." As regards the administrative supervision of the writing of poetry, Brecht made the following unambiguous comment in 1954: "It is not the duty of a Marxist-Leninist party to organize the production of poems like a poultry farm; otherwise the poems will resemble each other just like one egg and another. . . . Popular and bureaucular" ("Volkstümlich und funktionärstümlich").[38]

The narrow-minded insistence on "Volkstümlichkeit" resulted in a vulgarization of poetic language rather than its enrichment. As is illustrated in the tragic case of Stephan Hermlin, literary quality can never be attained by the reduction of stylistic means to the lowest common denominator of popular expression.[39] Herm-

38. Brecht, *Gesammelte Werke*, *19*, 322–34; P. 335: "Dem Volk aufs Maul schauen ist etwas ganz anderes als dem Volk nach dem Mund reden." P. 543: "Die Frage der Qualität wird für eine echte sozialistische Kunst politisch entscheiden." P. 505: "Es ist schwierig, vom Volkslied zu lernen. Die modernen Lieder 'im Volkston' sind oft abschreckende Beispiele, schon ihrer künstlichen Einfachheit wegen. Wo das Volsklied etwas Kompliziertes einfach sagt, sagen die modernen Nachahmer etwas Einfaches (oder Einfältiges) einfach. Ausserdem wünscht das Volk nicht tümlich zu sein." P. 546: "Es ist nicht die Aufgabe der marxistisch-leninistischen Partei, die Produktion von Gedichten zu organisieren wie eine Geflügelfarm, sonst gleichen eben die Gedichte sich wie ein Ei dem andern. . . . Volkstümlich und funktionärstümlich."

39. It is interesting to note that an appeal for caution in the use of the criterion of literary accessibility came even before the tightening of Soviet literary policies in the 1930s. Anatoly Lunacharsky (1875–1933), the Soviet dramatist and first People's Commissar for Education from 1917 to 1929, expressed such a warning in his essay written in 1928, "Theses on the Tasks of Marxist Aesthetics." Recently

lin himself was not blind to the detrimental, or at least delimiting, effects of official policies on poetry. He has never spoken about his own development, but in a speech concerning the Polish national poet Adam Mickiewicz, held in November, 1955, he made the following ambivalent, but highly revealing statement: "When the social struggle becomes most acute, poetry has no choice but to either prostitute itself by commitment to the doomed or, on the side of progress, to restrict its actual domain." [40] By "the doomed" Hermlin meant the modernist, or "formalist," tendencies of poetry in "bourgeois" society, and "progress" refers to the new, socialist world. Indirectly, then, he admits that by aligning himself with the cause of socialism he sacrificed some of the actual domain of poetry; but he insists that this choice was the result of historical necessity. The side of progress, evidently, cannot accommodate the entire domain of poetry.

In 1956 Hermlin published the collection *Dichtungen*, which includes all of the early ballads, the entire "Erinnerung" cycle, and the poems from *Der Flug der Taube*. The book was reviewed, not by a Party-appointed "critic" such as Eduard Zak, but by the poet Günther Deicke. He deliberately centered attention on Hermlin's earlier poetry and sharply denounced the reviewers who had once criticized it. "Uncommon usage can be understood," Deicke ended, "if it is only treated willingly and patiently." [41] The change in emphasis in public statements on Hermlin is also evident in a speech by Peter Huchel, held on the occasion of the awarding of the F. C. Weiskopf prize to Hermlin in 1958. When he praised Hermlin for his meticulous formal craftsmanship,

the unorthodox Austrian Marxist Ernst Fischer referred to Lunacharsky's remarks in attempting to combat the usual, dogmatic interpretation (and application) of Lenin's famous 1905 article on "Party Organization and Party Literature." Fischer, *Kunst und Koexistenz* (Reinbek, 1966), pp. 190–99. See the German selection of Lunacharsky's theoretical writings, *Die Revolution und die Kunst* (Dresden, 1962), pp. 5–18.

40. "Rede über Mickiewicz," *Begegnungen 1954–1959*, p. 256: "In den Zeiten der äussersten Zuspitzung des gesellschaftlichen Kampfes hat die Dichtung keine andere Wahl als sich entweder, für das zum Absterben Verurteilte Partei nehmend, zu prostituieren oder, auf der Seite des Fortschritts, ihre eigentliche Domäne einzuschränken."

41. "'Ich will eine neue Sprache': Einige Gedanken zur Lyrik Stephan Hermlins," *Nationalzeitung* (East Berlin), March 14, 1957: "Das Ungewohnte gibt sich dem Verständnis, wenn man sich ihm willig nähert und sich geduldig mit ihm befasst."

Huchel was not specific, but he was assuredly not referring to the volume *Der Flug der Taube*. "Spring water spilled on the floor has only a dim glow—but when poured into a glass, it is full of light." [42] Though this metaphor, which closes Huchel's speech, is ultimately more revealing about Huchel than about Hermlin, it is a further indication that by 1958 the climate had changed.

Neither the changed political climate and greater receptivity for his best poems nor his own implicit awareness of his compromise at a time "when the social struggle had been most acute," succeeded in salvaging Hermlin's poetic power—or rather, by this time, in bringing it back to life. His last published poem (1958) bears the tragically appropriate title "Der Tod des Dichters: In memoriam Johannes R. Bechers." [43] Like the sonnets also written after 1956 ("Die Vögel und der Test" and "Die Milch"), this Asclepiadean ode unquestionably contains strong lines and even entire sections, such as the eighth stanza:

> Ach, ihn blendet der Tag strömend mit Sommerlicht,
> Und der Atem geht schwer, ringend im Mittagskampf,
> Wenn die feindlichen Stimmen
> Schreckverworren vorüberfliehn.

But as is clear even here, this monumental force is anything but his own, nor could it introduce a new phase of his development. It is entirely in the tradition of the classical ode, demonstrating at its most intolerable moments the stiltedness and stylization of the worst imitation of Hölderlin. Stanza five, for instance, is about the poet and "die Völker":

> Doch dem Weilenden, der fernhin entschwinden sieht,
> Unaufhaltsame, sie, die keine Mühsal schreckt,
> Die den Abgrund nicht fürchten
> Und die Drohung der Wasser nicht, . . .

The thematic progression from struggle to assurance, the images of darkness and light, autumn and spring, the dawning of a new day which had dominated the poems in *Der Flug der Taube*, are again decisive, the difference being that the diction is conspicuously

---

42. Printed in *Sonntag*, April 27, 1958, p. 8: "Quellwasser, auf den Boden geschüttet, hat nur geringen Glanz—in ein Glas gegossen, ist es voll Licht."

43. This poem appears in the selections *Gedichte*, pp. 118–19, and *Gedichte und Prosa*, pp. 37–38.

elevated above the "popular" level. As deliberate as it may have been, however, this change does not constitute an innovation on Hermlin's part; rather, he has simply taken refuge in techniques and conventions borrowed from Hölderlin. Hermlin carefully avoided the clichés of common speech which had entered into his poetry at the beginning of the 1950s but replaced them with clichés from the poetic past. "Der Tod des Dichters" is a swan song in the truest sense; it represents Hermlin's last gasp for breath, his desperate flight from everyday commonplaces into the commonplaces of the lyrical tradition. By 1958 he had made a complete turn since his warnings to the young Hölderlin epigones in his radio speeches immediately after the war.

Most ironic of all is that Hermlin's criticism of Johannes R. Becher in the 1940s applies perfectly to his own poem written in Becher's memory. "It has been proven beyond doubt," he said, "that concern for a new realism has in this instance destroyed the substance and autonomy of poetry: Becher has arrived at neo-classical smoothness and conventional verse concoctions." Becher's (and Hermlin's) deliberate striving for stylistic conventionality does not run counter to the program of literary "Volkstümlich-keit." On the contrary, the two tendencies complement one another, as components of a "new realism." In his notebook of theoretical reflections entitled "Defense of Poetry" (*Verteidigung der Poesie*, 1953), Becher observed: "true novelty expresses itself in traditional forms; innovation makes a formally inconspicuous and conventional appearance and thereby enables itself to be readily understood and to become accessible even to people lacking in literary training." [44] The main thrust of the campaign for literary accessibility, therefore, was directed not so much against "poeticized" forms and diction as against stylistic originality. "Volkstümlichkeit" means general familiarity to all—the familiarity of common speech or the familiarity of recognizable poetic structure. Hermlin could elevate the diction of his poetry above the level of everyday expression only because he knew that the

44. *Verteidigung der Poesie* (Berlin, 1953), p. 109; reprinted in Becher, *Über Literatur und Kunst*, ed. Marianne Lange (Berlin, 1962), p. 239: "das wahrhaft Neue äussert sich in herkömmlichen Formen, das Neue tritt formal unscheinbar und konventionell auf und schafft sich so die Möglichkeit, leichter verständlich zu sein und auch bei denen Zugang zu finden, die literarisch nicht vorgebildet sind."

predictable cadence of classical meters was considered to be just as
"popular" as doggerel about imperialism ("Das Dollarzeichen /
Schändet Vietnam und Frankreich"). The task of poetry, according to these vulgar and thoroughly un-Marxist dictates, is to
placate, by stooping to a crudity felt to be immutably proper to
the masses; what poetry may not do is baffle and challenge, by
virtue of nuance, innovation, or quality.

Hermlin's poem "Der Tod des Dichters" marks the undoing
of its author as a creative poet. Written in memory of Johannes
R. Becher, it illustrates the total convergence of his career with
Becher's: both ended in pseudoclassical "popularity" and pseudo-
popular "classicism." Ten years earlier, when Hermlin had expressed regret over Becher's development, he wrote his most successful poems, in a style combining brilliantly the poetic diction
of early German expressionism and the mood of Louis Aragon's
subtle political verse. But those years after the war (when he wrote
"Die Zeit der Wunder") constitute the brief blossoming of his
talent, when he skillfully harnessed the erratic outbursts of his
early, wartime "Balladen von den Grossen Städten." As exemplified
by the "Ballade von Henri und Erika," his poetry in the early
1950s was written in strict conformity to the category of "Volkstümlichkeit," with the result that his language was depraved to
the level of common speech. As a final, futile escape from this
artificial folksiness, Hermlin had recourse only to the outworn
conventions of the lyrical past: hackneyed imitation of Hölderlin
replaced the feeble "modernizing" of Eichendorff. In both cases—
the "folk tone" of his peace poems from the early 1950s and the
"classicism" of his odes and sonnets written after 1956—the demand for "Volkstümlichkeit" was decisive, since the dominating
impulse was for familiar, unobtrusive means of expression. The
effect in both cases was the complete and irreversible banalization
of poetic language, with the poet taking up refuge first in the
platitudes of political propaganda and then in the commonplaces
of literary history. Since Becher's death in 1958, Hermlin has found
no new techniques, no new starting point or tendencies which
could revitalize his productive talent. In the past decade he has
not published a single new poem, and I think it is safe to assume
that he has not written any.

Yet it has become increasingly clear in recent years that Hermlin has not lost the keen poetic sensitivity which he exhibited in his radio speeches and poems of the period just after the war. Several times in the 1960s he has shown that he is still receptive to new directions in poetry and has publicly admitted his adherence to an understanding of art which runs directly against the grain of official cultural policy. In December 1962, simultaneous with the removal of Peter Huchel from his position as editor in chief of *Sinn und Form*, Hermlin organized an evening of poetry readings at which he himself read countless poems by young authors who had at an earlier date complained that they had been having difficulty getting their works published. Many of the texts were boldly experimental in technique and sharply critical of social conditions in the DDR. The upshot of this event (which was of crucial importance for the wave of new East German poetry emerging at that time) has been related frequently. Hermlin was dismissed from his post as Secretary of the Section for Literature in the Academy of Arts, and he was accused by Kurt Hager of "circulating poems permeated by the spirit of pessimism, ignorant fault-finding and enmity toward the Party"; by Alexander Abusch for not standing up "in the name of the Party against tendencies in some poems which are fundamentally foreign to our socialist ideology and even hostile toward our labor force"; and by Walter Ulbricht for "attempting to use some poems to incite the young people against their elders." [45] The wrath of the entire ideological pantheon was upon him. In response to these charges Hermlin admitted his guilt and agreed that his dismissal was just. But he did not, as is so often the case in such official confessions, ask to be excused for momentary lack of discretion, nor did he assure the authorities that he would never deviate again. Rather, he stated that the errors made on that evening were in full keeping with his character and that his failure to judge the poems in relationship to their immediate political consequences—as the worried officials

45. See, for example, Lothar von Balluseck, *Literatur und Ideologie 1963*, pp. 16–19. P. 18: "Verbreitung von Gedichten, die vom Geist des Pessimismus, der unwissenden Krittelei und der Feindschaft gegenüber der Partei durchdrungen waren" (Hager); "nicht parteilich gegen Tendenzen in einigen Gedichten [aufgetreten], die unserer sozialistischen Weltanschauung wesensfremd, ja zum Teil sogar unserer Arbeitermacht feindlich entgegenstehen" (Abusch); "Bemühungen, mit Hilfe einiger Gedichte die Jugendlichen gegen die Alten zu hetzen" (Ulbricht).

had obviously done—was consistent with his own position toward poetry. "I often appreciate poetry and art, which occupy nearly my whole life, independently of the historical time and setting in which they find expression. I admit that this is a mistake; but I also know that I am not proof against repetition of this error." In the same statement—published in *Neues Deutschland* on April 6, 1963—Hermlin strongly defended Wolf Biermann, against whom a campaign was under way even then. In answer to Kurt Hager, Hermlin noted of Biermann: "I consider him to have a very great talent, and I would therefore like to request that the Party not lose sight of him and continue to further him." [46]

Hermlin also took issue with the ideologues in his speech on "Tradition and Modernity," one of his most recent statements on poetry, which was delivered at a conference in Budapest in 1964. The other representative of the DDR at the conference was Alfred Kurella (b. 1895), whose contribution was no more than a collection of the inevitable clichés identifying "real" modernity with socialist realism.[47] Hermlin, on the other hand, spoke quite openly of the seeming paradox that "the builders of the most modern society show a certain uneasiness at the sight of a modern poem." The latter use of "modern" here clearly refers to the mainstream of European poetry; and Hermlin no longer opposed literary modernity to social "progress" and dismissed it as historically "doomed." It is becoming clear in the post–cold war period, he stated, "that true poets do not wear the uniform of established ideas, so that a cursory glance would make it possible to neatly pigeonhole them in one of two all-embracing schools." [48] Hermlin especially acclaimed the work of Guillaume Apollinaire, whose

46. Balluseck, p. 19: "Das hängt wohl damit zusammen, dass ich Dichtung und Kunst, die mein Leben fast ausfüllen, oft abhängig von Zeit und Ort betrachte, da und wo sie sich äussern. Ich erkenne das als einen Fehler an; aber ich weiss auch, dass ich vor der Wiederholung dieses Fehlers nicht gefeit bin. . . . Ich halte ihn für ein sehr grosses Talent, und ich möchte darum bitten, dass man ihn nicht aus den Augen lässt und dass sich die Partei weiter um ihn kümmert."

47. Kurella's speech was printed in *Sinn und Form*, 17, (1965), 788–91.

48. "Über Tradition und Moderne: Ein Beitrag zur Budapester PEN-Diskussion," *Sinn und Form*, 17, (1965), 786–88; reprinted in *Du/Atlantis*, 7 (1966), 895, and in *Die Zeit*, November 27, 1964. "Die Erbauer der modernsten Gesellschaft [zeigten] ein gewisses Unbehagen beim Anblick eines modernen Gedichts. . . . dass wahre Dichter nicht die Uniform fertiger Ideen tragen, was einem nach einem kurzen Blick gestattet, sie bequemerweise einer von zwei grossen Herden zuzuordnen."

greatness and genuine originality will never be effaced simply because it is condemned, or ignored, for ideological reasons.

Finally, after a rejection of poetry deliberately lacking in all communicative function and intentionally withdrawing itself from human comprehension, Hermlin very poignantly replied to the dogmatic call for immediate literary accessibility. He reminded the audience of an observation by Mayakovsky, "who found it funny that nobody ever boasts of not understanding mathematics or French, while at the same time it is common practice for someone to admit triumphantly that he did not understand this or that poem." Mayakovsky may have found this distinction "funny," but I doubt that Hermlin, who had experienced its consequences when he adjusted his poetry to the simplest arithmetic formula, would say the same for himself. "This saying by Mayakovsky," he ended sadly, "is already thirty-five years old." [49] The threat to literature perceived by the great revolutionary Mayakovsky in 1929 is still present in countries impeded by Soviet cultural policies. The career of Stephan Hermlin, once a gifted political poet, remains truncated, bearing grim testimony to the fatal impact of restrictive ideological demands.

49. "Über Tradition." "Man sollte sich bei dieser Gelegenheit an ein Wort von Majakowski erinnern, der es komisch fand, dass niemand sich damit brüste, Mathematik oder Französisch nicht zu verstehen, während es gleichzeitig üblich sei, triumphierend festzustellen, man habe dies oder jenes Gedicht nicht verstanden. Dieses Wort Majakowskis ist immerhin schon fünfunddreissig Jahre alt."

2

Franz Fühmann: The Dialectics of Fantasy

"Secret Paths into Chaos" (*1940–45*)

"Franz Fühmann, born in 1922 in the town of Rochlitz in the Riesengebirge [Sudetenland], joined the ranks at the age of nineteen: since 1941 he has been a soldier, assigned to the Eastern Front. The corporal writes poems, some of which have been lost on the endless marches, a few of which have been saved. From them emerge the language and inner world of the twenty-year-olds, the pressures and endurance, the harshness and greatness of their destiny." These sentences, introducing Franz Fühmann to German readers, appeared along with three of his poems in Dr. Joseph Goebbels' propaganda weekly, *Das Reich*.[1] Fühmann indeed "wrote poems": he began at fourteen or fifteen, sometimes rattling off as many as five or ten a day; by the time he enlisted, they probably numbered in the hundreds. None of these youthful outpourings, however, have survived, and only a very few of his wartime poems are still available: four were published in *Das Reich* in 1944–45, and five earlier ones appeared in 1942 in a small poetry series entitled *Das Gedicht: Lyrik junger Menschen*. The poet has provided me with four additional texts which he considers typical of his poetry from these years. (All thirteen poems are included in the appendix, pp. 317–24.)

1. *Das Reich*, June 25, 1944: "Franz Fühmann, in Rochlitz im Riesengebirge 1922 geboren, rückte neunzehnjährig zum Heeresdienst ein: seit 1941 ist er Soldat, immer im Osten eingesetzt. Der Obergefreite schreibt Gedichte, ein Teil geht auf den endlosen Märschen verloren, ein kleiner Teil wird gerettet. Aus ihnen steigt Sprache und innere Welt der Zwanzigjährigen auf, Bedrängnis und Bewährung, Härte und Grösse ihres Schicksals."

It may be, as *Das Reich* emphasizes, that the mood expressed in Fühmann's poetry was somehow representative of the sentiments and situation of Hitler's young soldiers fighting on the Eastern Front. It is clear, however, that these poems by the devoted soldier have very little to do directly with the officially sanctioned poetry of National Socialism. They bear no resemblance, in language or temperament, to the flag-waving, drum-beating SA battle cries of such poet-warriors as Heinrich Anacker (b. 1901), Herybert Menzel (b. 1906), and Gerhard Schumann (b. 1911). Nor do they attempt to inspire a sense of "higher community," of supreme mission as "Kameraden," in service of the Führer or the exclusive national Volk. There is also little of the heroizing and mythologizing "Nordic renaissance" strain, present for example in the poems of Johannes Linke (b. 1900), nor the "Blut und Boden" mystique characteristic of nature poetry as it was adapted by such Nazi writers as Hans Baumann (b. 1914) and Gerhard Schumann in his volume *Wir aber sind das Korn* (1936). Also entirely absent from Fühmann's poems is any sense of racial bonds to his "Heimat," the locality of his origin as a component, bound to it by ties of blood and language, of the great German Reich. He does not even write as a German voice from the border area, as would be expected from a young Sudeten German; his poems have no place among those of the spokesmen for his native Bohemia —notably Wilhelm Pleyer (b. 1901) and Hans Watzlik (1879–1948)—in the *Sudetendeutsches Lyrikbuch*.[2] In short, Fühmann is not to be confused with the "proclaimers and warriors" ("Künder und Kämpfer") approved by the Nazis as "poets of the new Germany," nor are his poems in any immediate sense "calls into the Reich" ("Rufe in das Reich," the title of a famous anthology of Nazi poetry [3]). No matter how fanatic a National Socialist believer Fühmann may have been during the war, his loyalty to National

2. *Sudetendeutsches Lyrikbuch*, ed. Adalbert Schmidt (Reichenberg, 1939). See also the anthologies *Wir tragen ein Licht: Rufe und Lieder sudetendeutscher Studenten*, ed. Herbert Cysarz (Munich, 1934), *Kameraden der Zeit: Sudetendeutsche Gedichte*, ed. Franz Höller (Karlsbad, 1936), and *Sudetendeutsche Dichtung der Zeit*, ed. August Friedrich Velmede (Berlin, 1938), as well as Wilhelm Pleyer's volumes *Deutschland ist grösser: Gedichte eines Grenzlanddeutschen* (Weimar, 1932), and *Lied aus Böhmen: Gedichte* (Munich, 1938).

3. *Rufe in das Reich: Die heldische Dichtung von Langemarck bis zur Gegenwart*, ed. Herbert Böhme (Berlin, 1934).

Socialism is not directly evident in his poetry, at least not in the samples available to us.

On the other hand, it would be even more mistaken to classify these verses as a kind of oppositional poetry, expressing protest to war and a skepticism as to the mission of National Socialism. Although war does seem to be portrayed as a horrifying and even mournfully destructive force, and though the sense of defeat is perhaps even more prevalent than the will to conquest, Fühmann never wavered in his devotion to Hitler's youth and military organizations, nor did he question the ultimate justice of the war. He did not associate—as did all the opposition poets, no matter from what perspective—the Third Reich with a general dissolution of human values, and his poetic expression was as different from the brooding, moralistic sonnets of such "inner emigrants" as Reinhold Schneider or Rudolf Hagelstange as it was from the flaming verse of National Socialism.[4] Fühmann wanted nothing more—as he has said in conversation—than to be a good soldier, and he failed at that ambition only because of his own physical clumsiness.

These two distinctions drawn, I would like to survey briefly the thirteen available poems and attempt to define some of their characteristics, with particular emphasis on features which may be most revealing for a comparison with Fühmann's later, Communist poetry. The texts suggest that these poems are written by a believing National Socialist—as we know to have been the case biographically—but that they are so only in an indirect, subtle way. They plainly lack the confessional, nationalistic, and militant aspects by which National Socialist propaganda verse is generally identified.[5] They nevertheless illustrate certain qualities typical of much of the poetry written in the Third Reich according to more basic concepts—concepts less obvious but perhaps more fundamental to the National Socialist idea of poetry than are employed in discussions of the usual verse proclamations of the "German destiny."

4. On poetry of the "inner emigration," see Charles W. Hoffmann, *Opposition Poetry in Nazi Germany* (Berkeley and Los Angeles, 1962).

5. See, for example, Abrecht Schöne, *Über politische Lyrik im 20. Jahrhundert* (Göttingen, 1965), and Rolf Geissler, "Dichter und Dichtung des Nationalsozialismus," in Hermann Kunisch, ed., *Handbuch der deutschen Gegenwartsliteratur*, pp. 721–30.

The earliest is the hopelessly clumsy heroic poem "Griechischer Auszug," with its stiff, uncomfortable handling of the six-dactyl line. (See Appendix, pp. ooo–ooo, for all references.) Here more than anywhere are to be found some of the typical features of Nazi poetry: the toying with heathen mythology, the demonic glorification of defiant military boldness and the sense of comradeship on the battlefront, and the fascination with death and apocalyptic downfall. Were it not for the mention of Greece in the title, this poem could easily be taken for one of the many imitations of Germanic sagas by National Socialist poets. Indeed, the tone, if not the outcome, of this poem is nearly identical with that in the anthology piece "Wikingerfahrt" by that fanatical SS official Kurt Eggers (b. 1905).[6] Other traces of a "Germanic" pseudosaga mood occur in the poem "Finnische Grenze," particularly in the line "Zorn stieg und Hass in die Welt" and in the first stanza:

Nichts war die Trauer mehr
Riesengross hob sich der Brand.
Schweigend und leidend leer
lag Land.

The exaggerated use of alliteration as well as the sense of cosmic doom are deliberate reminiscences of the Edda, and especially the Völuspa—which, as we know from Fühmann's autobiographical narrative, Das Judenauto (1962)—made a deep impression on the

6. Eggers' poem "Wikingerfahrt" appeared as the first poem in his volume Der deutsche Dämon (1942). It was also printed in Das Reich, July 5, 1942, and in the standard anthology Gedichte des Volkes: Vom Jahr 1 bis zum Jahr 5 des Dritten Reiches, ed. Herbert Böhme (Munich, 1938), p. 182.

Wir haben
singenden Herzens
den Anker gelichtet
der unser Schiff
an sichres Ufer band.
Und jubelnd
setzen wir die Segel.
Nun brauset, Stürme,
brandet, Wogen:
Wir kommen übers Meer gezogen.
Der Möwe Schrei
ist Abschiedsgruss,
der Möwe Schrei
sei uns Willkomm.
Was ist des Festlands

fetter Acker
gegen der Meer
sturmaufgewühlte Leidenschaft?
Der Sehnsucht Segel
führt unser Schiff
ins Morgen.
Jubelt, ihr Brüder,
die Wolken der Sorgen
sind Boten der Tat.
Jauchzet, ihr Brüder,
und weitet die Brust
dem Peitschen der Gischt.
Singet, ihr Brüder,
der göttlichen Lust,
der Gefahr!

soldier-poet when he first read it in 1943 or 1944.[7] It is likely that
Fühmann wrote many other poems showing signs of the "Nordic
renaissance" tendency, although I believe that he was not so much
deliberately intent on glorifying the Germanic past as he was
merely fascinated with the language and the dark, fantastic aura
of apocalypse. Also approaching typical National Socialist verse is
the poem "Bauerngebet" with its theme of simple, folksy piousness.
"Bauerngebet" would find its place among the slews of "Heimat"
and "Volkstum" poems, written in romantic praise of the humble,
God-fearing country folk, the mythical "eternal peasant." It is
nearly interchangeable with the poems in the section "peasants and
prayers" ("Bauern und Gebete") of the anthology *Rufe in das
Reich.*[8]

Aside from these, there is a group of four or five poems whose
most striking feature derives from Fühmann's indebtedness to
other poets, each of whom became in one way or another sacred
during the Third Reich. "Cäsar" and "Kupferner Spiegel / Wien"
are such obvious imitations of Rilke's *Neue Gedichte* that they
require no further discussion, and "Nach der Schlacht," although
far more original, also relies heavily on mannerisms from Rilke.
In the latter poem, however, Fühmann copies more than merely
formal, external techniques, such as the vocabulary and the loose
handling of line and stanza. Here a thematic factor, emphasized in the literary credo of National Socialism, seems to have
entered: the idea of what was called an "existential turnabout"
from horror at death to praise of and harmony with nature and
the "Volk." The importance of this influence of Rilke on the
German "war generation" (or at least the parallel between Rilke's
experience and that of patriotic Germans of the 1930s) is presented
in National Socialist terms by Hermann Pongs in his essay "Rilkes
Umkehr und das Erlebnis der Frontgeneration" (1936).[9] In
general, however, it was the "magical power" (Pongs) of Rilke's

7. *Das Judenauto: Vierzehn Tage aus zwei Jahrzehnten* (East Berlin, 1962),
especially the chapter "Völuspa," pp. 111–126.

8. *Rufe in das Reich*, pp. 201–28. For a discussion of exactly this kind of poem
(from Jakob Kneip's volume *Bauernbrot*), see Franz Schonauer, *Deutsche Literatur im Dritten Reich* (Olten and Freiburg, 1961), pp. 84–86. For the National
Socialist treatment, see, for example, Heinz Kindermann, *Die deutsche Gegenwartsdichtung im Aufbau der Nation* (Berlin, 1935), pp. 31–38.

9. *Dichtung und Volkstum*, 37 (1926), pp. 75–97.

world and of his poetic language that attracted Fühmann so strongly (and it was a mania: he wrote literally hundreds of Rilke imitations between 1943 and 1946). The ideological or racist labels fabricated by scholars of National Socialist persuasion (such as Pongs' absurd notion of Rilke's tragic feeling of separation from his "natural racial context"—"sein natürlicher Volkszusammenhang") were, I think, of little or no importance to the young Fühmann.

Two other poems which are primarily derivative are "Jede Nacht erglühen neue Sterne" and "Das Mass." The first of these bears the mark of the other claimed "herald" of the Third Reich, Stefan George. The reliance here is both on the theme of "newness," the announcing of a "new realm," and the rigid "pure" form, with its mechanically regular meter, complete correspondence between thought unit and line, and pure rhyme. Such a line as "Neue Menschen wachsen schön und rank" could be one of George's own. Perhaps most important poetically are the images of light and "glowing" ("erglühen," "erstrahlt," "loht"), which was one of the features of George's poetry most frequently adopted by versifiers for the Third Reich. In "Das Mass" Fühmann was emulating another of his favorites, Josef Weinheber (1892–1945), "the lonely Viennese poet [who] was always my lyrical idol" as he is described by Fühmann's autobiographical persona in *Das Judenauto*.[10] What Fühmann most worshiped about Weinheber were clearly not his humorous, playful moments—as in the volumes *Wien wörtlich* (1935) and *O Mensch, gib acht* (1937)— but rather his "high tone," in which he speculates in austere classical forms on the nature of poetry and its "calling" as the voice of his "Volk" in its supreme mission. Lines such as "uns ist gesetzt mit Mass: / in kargen Worten zu sagen," "Mehr bedarf's nicht, / und es ziemt nicht / tönender Wunder der Worte zur Nacht," and "und versöhnend dem Tag die Nacht" come to Fühmann not directly from Hölderlin, as might seem to be the case, but through Weinheber's books *Adel und Untergang* (1934) and *Späte Krone*

10. *Das Judenauto*, p. 169: "Josef Weinheber, der einsame Wiener Dichter, war seit jeher mein lyrisches Idol." On the National Socialist reception and adoption of George, see Schöne, p. 12, and H. G. Atkins, *German Literature Through Nazi Eyes* (London, 1941), pp. 81–84; also, Hermann Pongs, "Krieg als Volksschicksal im deutschen Schrifttum II," *Dichtung und Volkstum*, 35 (1934), pp. 182–219 (on George, pp. 210–18).

(1936). Even the title "Adel und Untergang" ("nobility and downfall") was clearly a guideline for Fühmann ("dem Adel der Sterbenden"); and the line "Mehr bedarf's nicht" occupies such a central position, not because it repeats the words at the end of Hölderlin's well-known ode "An die Parzen," but because that ode was a well-known favorite of Weinheber.[11] The themes of "moderation and discipline" ("Mass und Zucht"), of stoic humility with regard to pain ("Zucht und Demut vollenden das Leid"), and of the nobility of dying and of the dead, all described as the "proper concern" of poetry: this entire complex of thoughts along with the elevated tone and language is derived by Fühmann directly from his "lyrical idol." (How close these terms stand to orthodox National Socialist ideals need not be mentioned.) In this case, as with George, I suspect that Fühmann imitated mainly because he longed to emulate the poet held in highest reverence at the time, and not because of any deeper relationship with the poet's world. It was Rilke, I think, to whom he felt closest and for whom his mania was more than merely a formal external one.

The remainder of these early poems—"Stunde in April," "Kalter Schnee im Dezember," "Nacht am Peipussee," "Dämmrung" and "Russland"—as well as "Finnische Grenze" give less evidence of either a proximity to typical National Socialist verse or the impact of highly esteemed poets. ("Russland" should perhaps also be excluded from this group, since the explosive language of expressionist poetry is dominant and the characterization of death and other images run through the literature of National Socialism.) It is in this cluster of poems, I believe, that the soldier Fühmann displays his own inclinations and talent most clearly.

The group is unified thematically by the sense of identity or interplay between inner sentiment ("Sehnsucht," "Trauer," "Seele," "Herz") and nature. Poems of the "pregnant moment," they all capture a personal experience at a point when inner and outer worlds are reaching for one another and coming into contact. This contact may be one of harmony, as in "Stunde in April," where the "longings" ("Sehnsucht") of nature and of men seem to intermingle, leaving a feeling of promise and hope in fulfillment.

11. See Weinheber's "Variationen auf eine hölderlinische Ode" (1934), *Sämtliche Werke*, 5 vols., ed. Josef Nadler and Hedwig Weinheber (Salzburg, 1954), 2, 35–42.

But more often the relation is discordant, the inner world confronting inimical nature and becoming smothered by it. This is most clearly the case in "Kalter Schnee in Dezember," the entire poem suggesting the downward, falling movement of the snow, which becomes more and more a huge blanket choking away all life. Only the individual's longing ("Nur meine Sehnsucht") strives momentarily to resist by projecting itself upward against the snow, but it too is eventually enveloped by the cold, white "kisses of death." In "Nacht am Peipussee" the external force weighing down on the individual is the immeasurable vastness of the lake and the long, seemingly endless hours of the night, against which the human heart can only seem like a minute bleeding wound. The same sense of smallness and helplessness over against the terrifying "signs" in nature—moon, clouds, night, and wind—is experienced in "Dämmrung." This time the tone is more that of the folksong ("Sieh den Mond sich erheben, Geliebte"), and the encounter with nature is characterized by a foreboding of evil ("voll Grauen," "voll Schrecknissen") rather than by physical damage or destruction. "Russland" and "Finnische Grenze" are more directly poems of war; the enmity of nature is personified by, or even attributed to, the human passions of hate and anger: "Da ein Misston erstand / Da der Hass auferstand," "Zorn stieg und Hass in die Welt." Indeed, in "Russland" the fatal, oppressive vastness characteristic of the outer world is identified with the endless expanse of enemy territory on the Eastern Front:

> Russland—du Land der verzehrenden Ewigkeiten
> Russland—du Land der vernichtenden Todesweiten.

In all of these poems, then, and particularly in the first four, what is crucial is the confrontation of the speaker's inner longing with a fantastic nature—fantastic in that it is pervaded by forces either of magical harmony or of demonic destructiveness.

This group of poems, again excepting "Russland," is also bound together by stylistic features. In the texts mentioned first ("Griechischer Auszug," "Bauerngebet," and so on), which were dominated by the conventions and which imitated models of typical National Socialist verse, Fühmann's rhythms were either extremely regular or extremely irregular and were in both cases forced. In "Griechischer Auszug" the poet was striving for a dactylic line,

but his verses became hopelessly rigid; in his emulation of Stefan
George, "Jede Nacht erglühen neue Sterne," and his pious "Heimat"
poem, "Bauerngebet," the meter was followed so mechanically as to
result in monotony. Even the poems "Dämmerung" and, to a
lesser extent, "Finnische Grenze" suffer because they are so tightly
bound to a rhythmic motive in the end line (... ′ – – ′ [–]). Yet
the long period and looser line also seem forced in Fühmann's use
—for example in the Rilkean attempts ("Cäsar" and "Kupferner
Spiegel") and in the copy of Weinheber ("Das Mass"). "Nach
der Schlacht," which also contains a loose handling of line and
rhythm, is more successful, perhaps because the personal, emotional
tone is more natural to Fühmann. But he is most at ease formally, I
think, in the poems "Stunde in April," "Kalter Schnee im Dezember," and particularly "Nacht am Peipussee" (in my opinion the
best of these early poems). Here no metrical scheme is followed,
nor is the pattern allowed to be exclusively determined by the
directions and turns of thought and feeling. Fühmann is most
successful where there is no more than a suggestion of regularity, where he has leeway to handle loosely a controlled rhythm
and lines of roughly the same length. "Stunde in April" has basically a four-beat trochaic line, but this pattern is varied in its use
to suit the thematic context. The stresses may be accentuated to
suggest immobility, or the line may be treated less abruptly, more
loosely to evoke a sense of softness and harmony:

> Reglos steht ein Baum.
> Aus den Tälern tönt ein weiches Singen.

The six-beat lines of "Kalter Schnee im Dezember" are a bit too
long for Fühmann, but here too it can be seen that he utilizes well
the various possibilities in a guiding but not ruling rhythm ("Meine
Sehnsucht bäumt sich noch einmal auf und loht, / dann umfängt
auch sie der Tod mit kalten und weissen Küssen.").

It was with irregular lines of three beats, as in "Nacht am
Peipussee," that Fühmann was clearly at his best. Here he had
nearly full control over the poem's movement, bringing out splen-
didly (by modifying his use of the rhythm) both the vastness of
the lake and its heavy, oppressive quality:

> Aus der ungeheuren Weite
> wächst der unendliche See
> schwer und stumpf wie Blei.

At the beginning of the second part (stanza three) the lines are lengthened by a beat to suggest the prolonged hours of the night, and this mixed sense of monotony and bewilderment is suddenly broken by the abrupt rhythm of footsteps:

> Langgedehnter Flug von Vögeln.
> Müd und schwer die Stunden lasten.
> Irgendwo ein Lagerfeuer.
> Hie und da ein harter Schritt.

"Nacht am Peipussee" is not a memorable poem, nor does it show any mark of authentic poetic inspiration. It does, however, prove that Fühmann was capable of skillfully and sensitively capturing subtle personal moods and of handling techniques of expression with some ingenuity. With "Finnische Grenze," "Stunde in April," and "Kalter Schnee im Dezember," it reveals clearly that he had his own creative inclinations as a young soldier-poet—to evoke the tense, haunting atmosphere of the front—and that he was able to control an appropriate stylistic medium. It is this cluster of poems, therefore, on which attention must center to determine the relationship of Fühmann to the codified literature of National Socialism being written in the same years.

Surely it is at first sight surprising that this group of short subjective poems—which seem to have more in common with the lyrics of the young Goethe, or of Eichendorff, than with those of Fühmann's comrades-in-arms—is the work of a committed National Socialist. Indeed, these poems cannot be directly or absolutely construed as tendentious, since the terms generally used to identify current traces of National Socialism in literature (such as "Nordic renaissance" or "Blut-und-Boden" tendencies, or glorification of war, or imitation of poets extolled at the time) are plainly quite irrelevant.[12] The two outstanding features of these short poems—the theme of the confrontation between longing subject and fantastic object and, formally, the loose handling of the regular line—are evident in all of Fühmann's poetry, including the best of his postwar Communist writing. They are not necessarily associated with the poetry of the Third Reich.

12. Some of these characteristics of National Socialist literature are suggested in the titles of the central chapters of Schonauer, *Deutsche Literatur im Dritten Reich:* "Glorifizierung des Krieges," "Die 'nordische Renaissance'," and " 'Blut und Boden'—Mythos und 'Volkhafte' Dichtung."

The distinguishing factor, I believe, is the *irrationality* of this mystical theme, especially when these poems are contrasted to Fühmann's own poetry of the 1950s. I admit that this comparison is not just in any absolute sense, because the later poetry was written in accordance with a program of strict poetic rationalization. Nor do I mean to apply the term "irrationality" as a criterion of literary value, as though mechanical construction is categorically essential to good poetry. Rather, I would suggest that these poems attracted the attention of National Socialist editors and cultural talent scouts and came to be included in a contemporary propaganda journal in large part because they are so totally lacking in rationally discernible direction and a sense of dialectical progression; and, accordingly, I believe that the principal result of Fühmann's remarkable transformation between the war years and the early 1950s, as manifested in his poetry, was the elimination and tempering of this exceedingly irrational, mystical element. "Nacht am Peipussee," "Nacht in April," and the others are fantasies, flashes of personal "experience" entirely and deliberately outside the realm of logical calculation. They pivot exclusively on the longing of an individual soul and the countersentiment of a spiritualized nature.

To repeat, irrationality is obviously not peculiar to the poetry of National Socialism, nor does the expression of an ahistorical, internalized "experience" conflict with the essence of good verse. But to situate Fühmann's short "Erlebnis" poems in the context in which they were written and published, it is of crucial importance to recognize that within the National Socialist literary creed rational clarity was explicitly regarded as a negative aesthetic criterion. Time and again official pronouncements singled out precisely the irrational element of art as the distinctive feature of National Socialist works. In his standard book *Arteigene Dichtung unserer Zeit* (1935), to cite one instance, the official National Socialist ideologue Walter Linden declared that "the true poet works totally unconsciously, out of a superpersonal vision and intimation," and in his assessment of individual works he plainly considered dialectical clarity and "genuine poetry" to be mutually exclusive.[13] For obvious reasons lyric poetry was singled out as

13. Quoted in Schöne, p. 19: "Der echte Dichter arbeitet ganz unbewusst aus überpersönlicher Schau und Ahnung. . . . Selbst eine 'Agnes Bernauer' ist zu

the genre most appropriate to this irrationalist aesthetic. In the officially authorized sketch of literature in his time, *National-sozialistische Dichtung* (1935), Hellmuth Langenbucher observed: "The lyric is the one form which makes possible, in the immediacy of experience, the most concentrated absorption of the spirit of the time and expression of its essential configurative currents." [14] Langenbucher then proceeded to characterize the situation of poetry—how and to what end it is created; in so doing, he approximated very closely a description of Franz Fühmann's wartime poetry, or at least its place in a propaganda organ such as *Das Reich*.[15] Poems were taken to be irrational outpourings of young soldiers at the front, drenched with "the immediacy of experience" and the contemporary *Zeitgeist* in all its "configurative currents." They were to serve as utterances which all the frontline soldiers, and the entire "Volk," would appreciate as expressions of their destiny.

In order to understand the repertoire of National Socialist literature in its full range one must probe deeper than the typical fanfares of the SA poets, rather than direct attention exclusively

dialektisch klar und bewusst, um echter Dichtung vollgültig zugezählt zu werden."

14. *Nationalsozialistische Dichtung* (Berlin, 1935), p. 48: "Die Lyrik ist *die* Form, die die am meisten verdichtete Fassung des Zeitgefühls und Deutung seiner wesentlichen Gestaltungsströme in der Unmittelbarkeit des Erlebens möglich macht."

15. *Nationalsozialistische Dichtung*, pp. 48–49: "A poem might have been jotted down by a soldier of the World War right in the midst of the incessant drumfire, scribbled on any scrap of paper within his reach; or a few poems may have come to him in his off days, they set him free, relieved him of the burden of his impressions and feelings; or a poem was written by the SA man when he came home at night from a day of hard service, he wrote it for his comrades as inspiration and confirmation of their efforts in combat. . . . In a poem the breath of combat lives on in greatest vitality; it may be bound to the day and not last as a work of art, but it fulfills its mission in the day, and even this mission has its higher meaning in times when the day is the only thing that the individual and the community can count on. Although much of what thus burst forth from the day may be but a leaf which is immediately blown into oblivion by the storm of the times, nevertheless it is amid the rushing of time a *force* in which the fighting men believe, which sweeps them along and upward. The poem itself fights; it bears the faith of the marching regiments of the new Germany, and it ascends from their ranks in the people, sweeping tens of thousands; it becomes a kind of magic, embracing with magical power a struggling community and conquering a people."

to drumbeats and waving banners. Even Hellmuth Langenbucher
remarked that a book in which no mention at all is made of the
SA, the Third Reich, or National Socialism could be "a thousand
times more National Socialist than a novel abounding with brown
experiences"; it was, he said, a matter more of attitude and mood
than of external considerations. In a concerned and intelligent essay
on the poetry of National Socialism written just after the war,
Kurt Berger made the same point: "It is not so much stylistic
imitations or the long familiar heroic props—the flag, the sword,
and the drum—which go to determine the essence of National
Socialist poetry. Far more distinguishing are the life forces which
are evoked and celebrated in it. It soon becomes clear that the
sentiments and general climate of this poetry are to a great extent
nourished by elements of the irrational, the instinctive, even the
demonic." In analyzing the various complexes of themes and
imagery in National Socialist poetry (such as blood and earth,
death and destiny, and so forth) Berger illustrated that they are
all bound together by the same tendency to mystify and mythify
and to conjure forces counteractive to any sense of rational clarity.
"All individual stylistic means taken together," he stated, "give
evidence of that deep, dark awe, that mingling of reverence and
fear which is the intention of this entire poetic undertaking."
Berger calls this unifying element "propagandistic mysticism," the
search for "expression of the most internalized flowing together of
individuality and cosmic forces, of the individual and destiny,
blood, earth, death and time." It does not suffice, Berger concluded, to consider as the final explanation "the Prussian-militaristic
element and modern Machiavellianism, either separately or in
their National Socialist synthesis. The deeper reason lies in those
treacherous, dark, and blurred forces, ideas, and images which
gained demonic domination over the spirit of the German
people." [16]

16. Kurt Berger, "Schleichwege zum Chaos," *Die Sammlung*, 2 (1946): 68–81.
Pp. 68–69: "Es sind nicht die stilistischen Imitationen oder die altvertrauten hero-
ischen Requisiten—der Fahne, des Schwertes, der Trommel,—so sehr, die das
Wesen der Lyrik des Nationalsozialismus ausmachen. Viel kennzeichnender sind
die *Lebensmächte*, die in dieser Lyrik berufen und gefeiert werden. Hier zeigt
sich bald, dass das Pathos und allgemeine Klima dieser Dichtung sich besonders
stark aus der Sphäre des Irrationalen, des Instinktmässigen, ja Dämonischen
nähren." P. 73: "Alle einzelnen Stilmittel zusammen aber erzeugen jenen tiefen,

It is in these terms, I think, that the location of such works as Fühmann's little nature poems is to be understood. Slews of poems totally lacking in the well-known trappings of fanatical National Socialist literature, and standing only on the periphery of the codified literary scene, are no less immersed in the ideology of the time. This is true of a good deal of the poetry of such older writers adopted by the National Socialists as Georg von der Vring (b. 1889), Hermann Claudius (b. 1878), and Rudolf Binding (1867–1938) and of many other texts included by Goebbels in *Das Reich*.[17] They may not have been intended to praise the Führer or to accompany military marches or even to provide inspiration or solace to the soldiers at the front or the "Volk" back home. But they are all "secret paths into chaos"—"Schleichwege zum Chaos," a phrase of Nietzsche's used by Berger as the title of his essay. Like Fühmann's wartime poems, they all give evidence of the same flight from rationality into a fantasy world peopled by dark,

---

aus Ehrfurcht und Furcht gemischten dunklen Schauer, der die Absicht dieser ganzen lyrischen Bemühung ist. Hier liegt auch die Wurzel für den in allen nationalsozialistischen Bereichen so oft wiederholten Begriff 'Glauben' oder 'Gläubigkeit,' der im bewussten Gegensatz zu Denken oder Erkennen oder Wissen gesehen wird." Pp. 76–77: "Von hier ist es schliesslich nicht weit zu den eigentümlichen Bildern und Vorstellungen, in denen die nationalsozialistische Lyrik nach dem Ausdruck des innigsten Ineinanderfliessens von Individualität und Kosmos, von Einzelnem und Schicksal, Blut, Erde, Tod und Zeit sucht. Ich möchte dieses Verwischen der Grenzen eine Art propagandistischer *Mystik* nennen." P. 81: "Das preussischsoldatische Element und der moderne Macchiavellismus können weder für sich allein noch in ihrer nationalsozialistischen Synthese die letzten Erklärungen sein. Der tiefere Grund liegt in jenen verhängnisvollen dunklen und verschwommenen Mächten, Vorstellungen und Bildern, die über die deutsche Volksseele eine dämonische Herrschaft gewonnen hatten."

17. The following two poems, which appeared in *Das Reich* in the early 1940s, resemble closely the mood and language of Fühmann's early verse:

Über dem weiten Land

Über dem weiten Land
Singt die Dämmerung
Schwermütig ihr Lied.
Das Auge ertrinkt
Im blauen Dunkel
Der werdenden Nacht.

Von den Hügeln her weht
Lautlos der laue,
Landfahrende Wind.

demonic forces, the same fascination with an inexplicable mingling
of the individual soul and a mysterious cosmos.

"The lyric poet need not be afraid of reason," was the advice of
Bertolt Brecht in a group of essays, written in the 1930s, on the
importance of logic in poetry. After undergoing a full course in
antifascist reeducation, the poet Franz Fühmann became aware of
the way in which dialectical calculation could give direction to
his poetic fantasy. Then, however, the new problem arose that
he had learned his lesson too well: in many—though not all—of
his poems of the 1950s rational clarity has gained the upper hand
to such an extent that little if any room remains for fantasy, and
shallow tendentiousness excludes the enigmatic, mysterious atmosphere of such a poem as "Nacht am Peipussee." But in the best of
his later poems the factor of rationality and historical consciousness contributes to the strength and value of his art and in one
or two cases allows for a truly exceptional intellectual profundity.
There Fühmann's lively fantasy has been successfully rationalized, and the full meaning of Brecht's thought is accounted for.
At the end of his essay "Logic of the Lyric," Brecht remarked that
"it is pretty much the same thing whether one says [of a poem]

Das Jubeln verklingt
Den kleinen Sängern
Im schlafenden Wald.

Matt nur erglänzt der See,
Schweigender Urgrund
Liebender Einfalt.
Der Himmel verschwimmt
Ganz in der Ferne
Im nächtlichen Land.

  Hans Bahrs, May 24, 1942

Auf Posten

Golden steht der Mond im Geäste der Pappel
Und schweigt und ist mein Kamerad,
Sein Zauberlicht dringt tief in die Brust
Und küsset sie wach, die Sehnsucht nach Dir—

Flüsternd säuselt der Wind nun im Busche,
Sanft, dass er das tiefe Schweigen nicht bricht;
Aber wie laut klopft mir das Herz nun,
Da ich dich liebend im Traum umarme.

  Private Hans Friedwieg, February 4, 1944

that it has no force because it is without logic or that it is without logic because it has no force." [18]

"Out of Chaos": The Lessons of Stalingrad (1945-50)

Fühmann described his crucial years of reeducation in the Soviet Union in *Das Judenauto*. The tone throughout the book, until the final paean of praise to the German Democratic Republic, is one of mild self-irony, intended to suggest a sense of distance between the author and his protagonist. *Das Judenauto* is a work of fiction, a socialist "Bildungsroman," and the life of Corporal Fjumann (whose name is revealed only in the closing chapters) is conceived as representative of an entire generation. Nevertheless, certain of the specific experiences that are related did, no doubt, deeply impress the author himself in his own life; historical biography continually overlaps with fictional narrative. One such formative event in Franz Fühmann's development, during his years as a soldier for the German army in Greece, was his study of the *Edda;* another, while in a Russian prison camp just after the war, was his reading of a novel by the Soviet author Ilya Ehrenburg (1891-1967).

Den vtoroi (1933), published in German as *Der zweite Tag* by the Publishers' Cooperative of Foreign Workers in the USSR,[19] was Ehrenburg's first truly socialist realist novel. It depicts frankly and in some detail the severe misery of the workers' lives at an industrial plant in the postrevolutionary Siberian town of Kusnezk. Among the committed workers in Kusnezk is a student and defiant egoist named Volodia. The climactic event in the novel occurs when Volodia meets and exerts his influence on young Tolia Kusmin, a feeble "lost soul" and jilted lover. By filling Tolia with vodka and individualistic ideas, Volodia drives him to acts of which he himself is incapable: Tolia attacks a worker and wrecks a treasured machine, for which acts he is tried and sentenced to five years after his plea for forgiveness is rejected. Volodia him-

18. Brecht, *Gesammelte Werke, 19,* 391: "Der Lyriker braucht die Vernunft nicht zu fürchten. . . . Es ist ziemlich gleichgültig, ob man sagt, es habe keine Kraft, weil es der Logik mangelt, oder es mangele der Logik, weil es keine Kraft habe."

19. Moscow and Leningrad, 1935. English title, *Out of Chaos,* trans. A. Bakshy (New York, 1934).

self, it is clear, is only the "evil spirit" behind counterrevolutionary activity; he is a saboteur only to the extent that he can seduce embittered weaklings to commit to action his antisocial thoughts. Fortunately, since Tolia does not mention the instigator's name at the trial, Volodia is able to leave Kusnezk on his own. Finally though, finding that even such an asocial type as the famous mathematician and scholar Professor Grimm is really "a worker like them all" and believes in the "new spirit," Volodia hangs himself.

Having read *Der zweite Tag* with intense interest, the German war prisoners in *Das Judenauto* think that only an oversight can explain the presence in the Soviet camp library of such a frank, unembellished portrayal of the miseries of postrevolutionary Russian life. Corporal Fjumann, one of the captured soldiers, is also convinced that the author of this book, "a certain Ilya Ehrenberg or Ehrenstadt or something like that," had surely been rewarded for his honesty with the gallows, and that the Russians would confiscate it as soon as they caught wind of its existence (pp. 170–172). He, too, is surprised that the Soviet inspectors can have made such a blunder. The character Volodia is particularly puzzling to him, and his misunderstanding is indicative, I think, of his state of mind at the time (1946). As Corporal Fjumann reads Ehrenburg's novel, Volodia, because of a mistake of some kind ("I didn't figure that out exactly"), was expelled from the Komsomol and ordered to leave work and return to Moscow. "Instead of jumping for joy all the way to the ceiling of his smoky barracks," Corporal Fjumann said, "Volodia began to cry and was unhappy and begged to be allowed to stay there and make up for his misdeed by working, and I simply didn't understand that." [20] Fjumann could not understand how Volodia could be unhappy at being expelled from this hell and how the workers could show such endurance and of their own free will work under the worst of conditions without complaining and without making another revolution—"as they had done so often in the past."

That the soldier-prisoner in *Das Judenauto* did not relate the

20. *Judenauto*, p. 172: "Anstatt vor Freude darüber bis an die Decke seiner verräucherten Erdbaracke zu springen, begann Wolodja zu weinen und war unglücklich und bat, hierbleiben und sich durch Arbeit bewähren zu dürfen, und ich verstand das einfach nicht."

plot correctly (he confused the situation of Volodia and of Tolia) is far less revealing than his failure to understand the theme and purpose of the book. Despite Ehrenburg's obvious fascination with the Dostoevskian Volodia and his journalistic concern with reporting substandard working conditions, these elements in the novel are central only negatively; they are presented only as obstacles to be overcome. Volodia is considered by the author to be an anachronism, a remnant of bourgeois ideology; as Volodia says of himself, he is "condemned by history as an untimely phenomenon," and the miserable conditions are also remnants of an earlier social arrangement. Both elements, ideology and conditions of the past, must be represented, since they persist as factors in the present. But they are only foils, the dreadful night before the coming of the "second day" (a quote from *Genesis*). The book is really directed "out of chaos" (the title of the English translation), it is really about the triumph of the Five-Year Plan and about Kolka Rshanov, the model "positive hero." The passages which had attracted the German war prisoners, including Corporal Fjumann, as confirmations of all they had been made to believe about Russia and Bolshevism, were intended to be of only dialectical importance, completely framed and ultimately canceled out by the main "perspective" of the book.

Another matter baffles the hero-narrator of *Das Judenauto*, who again may be clearly identified with the author. Shortly after his arrival in the prison camp he is called forward for a brief interview. After having answered, in a state of near unconsciousness, questions about himself and his past, he is asked whether he ever belonged to the Nazi Party or a branch of it. He deliberates shortly, hoping for an instant that the authorities might now put an end to him; then he lifts his head and says loudly, "Yes, I was in the SA!" "Of course," is the answer of the Russian Commissar who was interviewing him. " 'It's only natural that you were in the SA, judging from your social background and your youth', . . . and when he said it, I no longer understood anything; I heard his words and didn't understand them." How, the young Fjumann thinks, can this Russian stand there and—knowing of him only his name and age, that he was born and brought up in a town in Sudeten Germany, and that his father owned the local drugstore— honestly tell him that it was "only natural" to have joined the

SA? "The whole world must have gone crazy after this war, or else I have gone crazy myself." [21]

Two years later, in the fall of 1947, Fjumann-Fühmann is sent to an "antifascist" school in Latvia and, having heard the first lectures in political economy, "it was as though the blinders had fallen from [my] eyes." Suddenly everything becomes clear to him; "here was the answer to all the questions that had always concerned me, and once I had plowed through the thick volumes of *Capital* by Karl Marx, all the stages of my life stood like the presence of my desk before my eyes, which could now see freely, down to the very bottom of time." [22] Now, with the help of this "completely new way of teaching history," he understands what the Russian Commissar had meant when he said that it was "only natural" for a young Sudeten German from a bourgeois family to have been in the SA, that it was a "natural stage" in his development. Now, finally, he knows what the war in which he had fought had been about, and he can understand the country for which he fought; he understands that the war was one of "imperialism," which was only the "natural stage" in the development of a social order, the "highest stage of capitalism." It is not his SA past which is ultimately "the key to understanding the phenomenon Fühmann," as Marcel Reich-Ranicki maintains,[23] but that he believes that he has found an explanation of it by means of dialectical materialism.

Implicit in *Das Judenauto*, even in its structure, is that the hero, at first so perplexed by Ilya Ehrenburg's novel *The Second Day*, eventually comes to understand the book in the author's terms—

21. *Judenauto*, p. 155: " 'Das ist doch nur natürlich, dass Sie in der SA waren, bei Ihrer sozialen Herkunft und Ihrer Jugend', sagte der Kommissar, und da er es sagte, verstand ich nichts mehr; ich hörte seine Worte und begriff sie nicht. . . . [ich] dachte, die Welt sei verrückt geworden, verrückt nach diesem Krieg, einfach verrückt, oder war ich verrückt geworden."

22. *Judenauto*, p. 177: ". . . war es mir wie Schuppen von den Augen gefallen. . . . Hier war ja die Antwort auf alle Fragen, die mich immer bewegten, und alle Stationen meines Lebens waren, da ich die dicken Bände des 'Kapitals' von Karl Marx durchgewühlt hatte, wie die Gegenwart meines Schreibpults vor meinen Augen gestanden, die nun frei sehen konnten, hinab bis zum Grund der Zeit."

23. "Kamerad Fühmann," *Deutsche Literatur in West und Ost* (Munich, 1963), p. 422: ". . . wohl wichtigste Schlüssel zum Verständnis des Phänomen Franz Fühmann . . ."

as a reflection of the successful construction of a socialist society, and not as a study in social misery and nihilist decadence. Fjumann is, after all, himself a "positive hero," having come, after many tribulations and stages of human weakness, to a comprehension of the laws of social change and an allegiance to the Communist cause. Along with a sudden clarity of vision about personal and historical development, both Fühmann and his hero attain a totally new conception of literature. Here again Fühmann's antifascist reeducation was crucial, and two sets of texts, one mentioned in *Das Judenauto*, were of particular importance.

Just after he expresses his puzzlement over Ehrenburg's book, Fjumann is advised by one of his companions, Major Hochreiter, to read Lenin's essays on Tolstoy. Although Fjumann shows no interest in the essays at that point, having his own worries and having had enough of "these Russian questions" for the time being, it is absolutely certain that Fühmann himself read them and was very deeply affected by them.[24] With their help he came to view a novel such as *The Second Day* as the realistic reflection, from a socialist standpoint, of the Soviet Union during the Five-Year Plan, just as Tolstoy's works were interpreted by Lenin as the realistic reflection, from a critical standpoint, of Russia in the period between the reforms and the 1905 revolution. (I suspect, incidentally, that Fühmann was also influenced by Plekhanov's writings on Tolstoy, a typical explanation of ideology from class origin. They were published in Germany together with Lenin's, despite the irreconcilable difference in interpretation.[25])

The other source of Fühmann's reeducation in literary theory, never mentioned in his writings, were the complementary essays of Georg Lukács, "Fortschritt und Reaktion in der deutschen

24. That Fühmann himself read and was deeply influenced by Lenin's essays is stated in a recent speech in memory of Louis Fürnberg, *Sinn und Form*, 19 (1967), p. 784: "bei mir waren es die Aufsätze Lenins über Tolstoi gewesen, die mich, den verwirrten, ratlosen Hitlersoldaten von gestern in einem kleinen Lager im Kaukasus überwältigt und auf die Knie geworfen hatten: das also war der verlästerte, verhöhnte, hundertmal totgesagte Marxismus, von dem wir bislang nur ein wüst entstelltes, absurd verlogenes Zerrbild im Kopfe getragen, solche Weltsicht war das, solche Erkenntnis, solches Begreifen des Geistes! Ein erstes Ahnen, ein erstes Angerührtwerden, und das wunderbare Gesetz begann sich im ehemaligen Feindesland hinter Stacheldraht zu vollziehen."

25. N. Lenin and G. Plechanow, *L. N. Tolstoi im Spiegelbild des Marxismus*, ed. W. M. Fritsche (Vienna and Berlin, 1928).

Literatur" and "Deutsche Literatur im Zeitalter des Imperialismus."
Both were written at the end of the war in an extremely popular
and "propagandistic" vein, as Lukács himself admits.[26] Without
going into the intricacies of Fühmann's initial enthusiasm for these
essays, which he described to me in recent conversations, it is
enough to say that in general he was attracted, as in his reading of
Lenin's theories on Tolstoy, by the historical and social interpretations of literature, and the application of moral standards in
the formation of aesthetic judgment. Here for the first time he
encountered a sketch of the history of modern German literature
which endeavored to distinguish between the "progressive" and
the "reactionary" tendencies in specific literary periods, authors,
and works. To his surprise, some of the writers whom he himself
had held in absolute reverence were mercilessly condemned for
their contribution to the "German catastrophe" or were totally
omitted from discussion. Moreover—and of utmost importance
for Fühmann's own creativity—literature, and contemporary German literature in particular, were conceived of as having a social,
didactic task, that of leading the German nation out of its "deepest
political, moral and ideological decay" back to civilized humanity.[27] Literature was not, as it had been for Fühmann, the dark,
melancholy outpouring of a solitary soul, looking inward at itself
or outward at ahistorical, cosmic forces; rather, it was viewed as a
constructive act of communication, a reconciliation with history
and the past, directed at a better future. The stanza by Johannes
R. Becher which Lukács quoted at the end of his second essay
(p. 227) as an expression of the "general mission of German literature" is a precise description of Fühmann's literary concern after
his return to Germany in 1949:

> Grosses, Grosses war mir aufgetragen:
> Meines Irrtums Reste zu zerschlagen

26. The two essays, which first appeared in *Internationale Literatur*, 15 (1945),
have been reprinted together as *Skizze einer Geschichte der neueren deutschen
Literatur* (East Berlin, 1953, and Neuwied, 1963). On page 5 of the recent West
German edition Lukács calls his book "a short, popular and propagandistic
synopsis" ("eine kurze, populäre und propagandistische Zusammenfassung").

27. *Skizze*, p. 226: "das deutsche Volk aus seinem bisher tiefsten politischen,
moralischen und ideologischen Verfall ins zivilisierte, ins menschliche Leben zu-
rückzuführen."

Und mich über mich kühn zu erheben,
Ein gewandelt Bild euch vorzuleben.

Fühmann's antifascist reeducation in the Soviet Union—his reading of Marx, Lenin, Ehrenburg, and Lukács, as well as Becher —resulted in an ideological transformation of the most radical dimensions. Suddenly his entire attitude toward life and literature was altered—as was, inevitably, his work as a creative poet. Unlike the poetic adjustment of Stephan Hermlin, however, the change evident in Fühmann's poetry is not primarily stylistic: since his diction had not been marked by unusual "esoteric" usages, there was no need to significantly adapt it to suit an unlettered audience. Rather, Fühmann's poetic "rebirth" in the DDR was characterized by a complete shift in thematic direction; whereas his wartime poems were dominated by an aura of foreboding and destruction, his writings of the 1950s invariably lead to the unfolding of a brighter future. The soldier-poet of death and apocalypse learned the techniques of socialist realism, and became a poet of the revolutionary "perspective."

Yet I believe that this obvious distinction between pessimism and optimism, between "Götterdämmerung" and "twilight forward" ("Dämmerung nach vorn," to use Ernst Bloch's phrase) may be more meaningfully stated in terms specifically relevant to Fühmann's own poetic inclinations. That is, the thematic difference may be studied in its relation to a feature common to nearly all his verse, from his time as a soldier in Hitler's army through his Communist poetry of the 1950s. Fühmann has consistently been drawn to the fantastic; both before and after his ideological conversion in the Soviet Union his poetic world is surrounded by wondrous, miraculous elements and relationships. In his wartime poems he was attracted to the atmosphere of the sagas and temperamental "gods," and his personal nature poems, such as "Nacht am Peipussee," were haunted by mysterious, demonic forces. In the 1950s, again, all the emotional experiences of Fühmann's protagonists contain something magical and overwhelmingly dreamlike. Stalingrad, which the poet visited in 1953 as a guest of the Soviet government, is felt to loom before him as the great "city of sagas" ("Sagenstadt"), and on his return to the "new Germany" the wreckage of East Berlin strikes him as a dazzling paradise:

> Und wir träumen
> das Morgen: Goldene und silberne Paläste werden wir erbauen
> und regenbogenfarbne Gärten, und wir stecken schon die
> Felder ab,
> auf denen all Frucht und Süsse reifen wird.
> Wir werden reich sein, mit der Sonne werden wir die Städte
> heizen. (93) [28]

Fühmann is never inclined in his verse to remain down to earth
or to temper his impulses with ironic coolness. He sings enthusiastically of a fantasy world, whether it is imminent apocalypse
or the glorious present opening into a magical future.

The real meaning of Fühmann's ideological transformation—
his new awareness of an optimistic historical "perspective"—becomes most readily apparent in its relation to this basic distinguishing sense of fantasy. Imprisonment and reeducation in the Soviet
Union did not detract from his basically mystical leanings. Rather,
as "the giver of meaning to my existence" ("die Sinngebung meiner
Existenz"), the lessons of dialectical materialism made him believe
that he could finally *understand* the mysteries of life. A passage
in his long autobiographical poem "Die Fahrt nach Stalingrad"
reads:

> O Wunder
> dieser Gefangenschaft! Die uns einst Feinde hiessen,
> erkennen wir als unsre wahren Freunde; die
> uns einst die Führer schienen, wir erkennen
> sie nun als Irreführer; die Gefangenschaft
> wird zum Beginn der Freiheit; und die Niederlage
> wird Sieg sein für unser Volk, und wo wir Ende wähnten,
> beginnt das Neue, führt das Leben aufwärts,
> und Stalingrad wird Wende und Errettung, wird der Durch-
> gang
> in einen lichten Tag . . . (87)

Stalingrad, that city Fühmann came to view as the axis of his life,
taught him the sense and ultimate rationality of imaginative fantasy; it taught him, in a phrase which formed the title of his most

28. Quotations from Fühmann's later poetry are from the volume *Die Richtung
der Märchen* (East Berlin, 1962).

famous poem and volume of poetry, "the direction of fairy tales"
("die Richtung der Märchen"):

> Stadt Stalingrad, ich darf dich wiedersehen,
> du Stadt, die mir mein Vaterland errettet,
> und die mich lieben lässt, und die mir Verse zuraunt,
> und die die Märchen mich verstehen lehrte
> und alle Träume, die hinab die Wälder gehn
> zur blauen Zukunft und zu Deutschlands Glück . . . (98)

Communist Fairy Tales (After 1950)

It was in the fairy tale, the märchen, that Fühmann found the
genre—or "simple form" ("einfache Form") to use André Jolles'
term [29]—most appropriate to his rationalized sense of fantasy.
What attracted him was not the air of surreality, of the weird and
the grotesque, which many modern writers find in the märchen in
harking back to their forebears of German romanticism. Fühmann's verse fairy tales have nothing to do with the many "anti-
märchen"—as Kafka's works have been called [30]—by twentieth-
century visionaries of anxiety and the bottomless abyss of existence. He does not pick out the unreal yet spookily real elements
and the technique of "double perception," which seem to be the
only value left in the märchen for most modern writers.[31]

A more accurate explanation of Fühmann's turn to the märchen
is that it was in line with the official program of "folk art"; in
the versified folktale he could not fail to write with the simplicity
needed for "popular" poetry.[32] Fühmann, indeed, never hesitated

29. See André Jolles, *Einfache Formen; Legende, Sage, Mythe, Rätsel, Spruch,
Kasus, Memorabile, Märchen, Witz,* 2nd ed. (Tübingen, 1958).

30. Clemens Heselhaus, "Kafkas Erzählformen," *Deutsche Vierteljahrsschrift,* 26
(1952), 353–76.

31. Cf. Marianne Thalmann, *Das Märchen und die Moderne: Zum Begriff der
Surrealität im Märchen der Romantik* (Stuttgart, 1961). One such use of the "sur-
real" qualities of the "Märchen" by a modern author can be seen in Hesse's *Der
Steppenwolf* (1927); see the discussion of that aspect of the novel in Theodore
Ziolkowski, *The Novels of Hermann Hesse: A Study in Theme and Structure*
(Princeton, 1965), pp. 200–06.

32. Cf. Wolfgang Steinitz, "Lied und Märchen als Stimme des Volkes," *Deut-
sches Jahrbuch für Volkskunde,* 2 (1956), 11–32. The dissertation by Waltraut
Woeller, *Der soziale Gehalt und die soziale Funktion der deutschen Volksmärchen*
(East Berlin, 1955), may also be relevant, although I have not seen it; an excerpt

to meet such policy requirements. When asked to "reflect" developments in the new society, he turned in his prose writing from his usual theme of the Third Reich and the war to playful stories praising the East German People's Police; and after 1959, when industry, the "Betrieb," became the recommended theme for all fiction, he spent some time in a shipyard and came through with the feeble reportage *Kabelkran und blauer Peter* (1962), for which he won the literary prize of the Free German Federation of Unions (FDGB).[33] The bulk of Fühmann's poetry was also written completely in accordance with official wishes, his volumes being dominated by all the shallow commonplaces of the worst socialist-realist verse. This prevailing feature extends from the first poem he wrote on his return from the Soviet Union, "Heimkehr eines Neubauern" (1949), a praise of land reform from the perspective of a gratified peasant (the religious piety of the peasant in "Bauerngebet" is replaced by class consciousness), all the way to one of his most recently published poems. "Der neue Stern" (1959) is a typical Sputnik poem:

> Nun ist diese Angst gewichen
> und liegt Äonen fern.
> Ihr Schreckbild ist verblichen,
> ich sehe einen neuen Stern,
> und dieser Stern wird nicht schwinden . . . (168)

In between appeared the volume *Die Nelke Nikos* (1953), written entirely in the spirit of the youth festivals. It contains such enticing titles as "Songs of Young Tractor Drivers" ("Lieder junger Traktoristen"), "Aufbausonntag," "Chor des Komsomolzen," "Go home," "Westdeutsche Manöverlandschaft," and "Der 1. Mai 1952 in Berlin" and ends with the feeble hymn, "Dank dir, Sowjetunion." The title of the volume refers to Nikos Belojannis, a young Greek partisan who was executed for his struggle against the

---

from that work appears in *Wissenschaftliche Zeitschrift der Humboldt-Universität zu Berlin* (Gesellschafts- und Sprachwissenschaftliche Reihe), *10* (1961), 395–459.

33. On the development of Fühmann's prose, see Marcel Reich-Ranicki, "Der exemplarische Weg des ostberliner Erzählers Franz Fühmann," *Die Zeit*, March 31, 1967, pp. 25–26.

Greek regime and forces of American "imperialism"; Fühmann
composed three songs acclaiming Nikos as a symbolic hero for
the cause of world peace and a brighter future. Here are some of
Fühmann's impotent lines from the early 1950s:

> Ich weiss es: Der Tag er wird kommen!
> Es leben ja schon, die ihn zeugen,
> ihn schauten ja schon die Gefällten;
> o es streckte doch Nikos die Nelke
>
> dem Tag ohne Abend entgegen . . . (35)

In the same volume is the poem "Märchen," and in tone and vocabulary it is perfectly in its place:

> Nie sind die Märchen zu Ende gelesen,
> weil das Leben immer beginnt;
> und zerfallen der bösen Hexen Besen
> raunt noch immer der gute Wind,
>
> und sind alle Drachen geschlagen:
> die Helden haben nicht Ruh.
> Sie wandern den klaren Tagen,
> dem Morgen ohne Abend zu. (39–39)

This fairy-tale poem is socialist realism reduced to the simplest
phrase: our dreams will all come true. At this level the märchen
was for Fühmann no more than a device for conveying in a
slightly varied context the same oversimplified prophecy that can
be found in any of the subpoetry written in the DDR at the time.

Yet I believe that Fühmann's inclination to the fairy tale involves a genuine affinity which runs deeper than the poem
"Märchen" might suggest. He wrote several such poems which
are entirely defensible as literature and go far beyond the verse
platitudes and trivial optimism sanctioned by provincial East
German politics. Fühmann found in the märchen a genre that
allowed him to combine his childlike fascination with fantasy and
the dialectical conception of human development he had acquired
during his Soviet reeducation. Implicit in it he found the structure
appropriate to his new theme, that of the "miracle" of human
regeneration in a state of simultaneous freedom and restriction.

Before coming to Fühmann's verse fairy tales, however, several
other poems must be considered which neither belong directly to
the märchen complex nor consist merely of the clichés of socialist
realism. Most amazing is the short personal nature poem that first
appeared in *Die Nelke Nikos*, "Abend am Fluss":

Lichter, zitternd,
vom Atem des Abendwindes
bewegt, Traumbilder des ruhenden
dunkelkühlen Gewässers—

O wie euch der Fluss hinabträumt:
unwirkliche Monde aus rinnendem
Silber, Spiralen der Sterne,
tonlos schwingende Ufer—

Unsere Herzen
haben die Kuppel des Himmels erschüttert.
Der Fluss
tönt die Akkorde der Sehnsucht

leis wie ein sanft berührtes
gespanntes Tamburin
uralter Abendgefühle. (25)

"Abend am Fluss" is clearly out of place in Fühmann's postwar
verse and bears little resemblance to anything published in the
DDR in the early 1950s. There is no aspect of it that is social,
much less socialist; it is, rather, a brilliant little "Erlebnisgedicht"
in the style of Georg Trakl. The mood is Trakl's, and the most
unmistakable of Trakl's techniques are the word "tönt" and the
departure from the initial isolated noun: "Lichter, zitternd. . . ."
Within Fühmann's opus this expression of the interplay of individual longing ("Unsere Herzen," "Sehnsucht") and nature stands
much closer to such wartime poems as "Stunde in April" and
"Nacht am Peipussee" than to his writings after his training in
Soviet Marxism. "Abend am Fluss" is superior to those early
poems, however, in the more subtle handling of line and syntax
and in the intriguing triangular relationship among sky, river,
and human feeling. The fine use of sound patterns, alliteration
("Silber, Spiralen der Sterne"), and particularly assonance (the

interplay of "a" and "u," as in the last stanza), lend the poem evocative power, as does the slightly exotic usage "Tamburin," which completes the sense of trembling and gentle percussion running through the poem. The place of this tiny gem amid the crude ore of the volume *Die Nelke Nikos* Fühmann himself cannot explain; he feels strongly attracted to it, even though it has little to do with his central theme of socialist transformation.

Also unique, though expressing that very theme, is the long autobiographical narrative poem, "Die Fahrt nach Stalingrad" (1953). It relates the poet's three confrontations with the city Stalingrad: as a soldier in the invading German army, then as a war prisoner, and finally as invited guest from the DDR. An honest and penetrating confrontation with the recent German past and an expression of the will to human regeneration, "Die Fahrt nach Stalingrad" is a poetic feat worthy of highest respect, and as a document it was deserving of the awards it brought its author. At times the strange, nightmarish aura of the Eastern Front is captured with remarkable versatility: "Draussen geht Sturm ums Haus; / zerfetztes Grau von Wolken, fast bis an die Erde / hinabgedrückt, treibt vorbei" (48). That Fühmann's reversal and enthusiasm for the Soviets, his former enemy, was anything but opportunistic is movingly evident:

> Und das warn sie, die auf der anderen Seite
> der Front gestanden, sie, die Unenträtselbaren,
> die Wissenden, die Lächelnden im Sterben noch,
> die Sieger . . .
>   Ja, nun sahn wir sie und lebten unter ihnen.
> Hart war dies Leben. Aber es war *Leben*,
> gemeinsam, denn sie lebten alle Härten mit uns mit,
> den Hunger und die Arbeit, wenn der Frost klirrt, wenn der
>   Regen schiesst,
> die Mühn des Aufbaus: Mit den Händen aus
> den Trümmern Ziegel bergen, hungrig Ziegel schleppen.
> Sie teilten Brot und Ruh mit uns zu gleichen Teilen;
> schon dies war ungeheuer. Aber grösser noch, und nie gewesen
> war, dass sie uns in der Gefangenschaft das Vaterland,
> dass sie uns unsre Seele gaben (77–78)

Aesthetically "Die Fahrt nach Stalingrad" is extremely uneven.
It contains powerful, driving sections under the influence of
Klopstock, Trakl and Rilke,[34] such as the beginning:

> Die Steppe: trockener Acker,
> zitterndes Silbergras.
> Dunkel steht das Gewölk. Es verdichtet sich
> die kochende Luft; wie bitterer Dunst
> umfängt uns der Geruch des Wermuts.
>
> Langsam rollt unser Zug durch die glühende Landschaft der
>   Sagenstadt zu.
> Die Räder singen. Phantastisch gewundene Wege
> steppeneinwärts wie Flüsse aus Staub und Geschichte . . . (43)

But alongside such strong passages there occurs the most trivial
kitsch, as for example in the speaker's pseudocolloquial conversation with his wife after his return to Germany:

> Ich liebe dich. Du trägst ein Kind von mir.
> Wir sitzen oft beisammen, und wir träumen
> von unserm Kind: Wird es ein Norbert, eine Bärbel sein?
> Wir wissen's nicht. Doch ob's ein Junge, ob's ein Mädel wird:
> Ihm wird der Irrgang, den wir beide einst durchlitten haben,
> erspart. Es wird auf graden Wegen gehen. (95–96)

The entire end of the poem, unfortunately, is made unreadable
by those empty socialist realist platitudes about brighter and
happier days which mar the bulk of Fühmann's postwar poetry.
    What is ultimately most objectionable about "Die Fahrt nach
Stalingrad," however, is not its unevenness and sections of unsal-
vageable pettiness, but that in such a long poem the linguistic
means are not developed in accordance with the development and
progression of the narrative. One would expect that, to match the

---

34. The most obvious example of the strong lingering influence of Rilke is in
the poem "Ausbruch eine Gewitters," which ends:

> Noch einmal Schweigen. Die Vögel verhalten im Fluge,
> und einen Herzschlag lang hält die Erde den Atem ein—
> bis es geschieht,—und in der vernichtenden Fuge
> der Blitze erneut sich des Lebens massloses Lebendigsein . . .
>   (*Die Nelke Nikos*, p. 29)

obvious epic technique of flashback and altered perspective, different dimensions of language would be exploited to concretize the difference in attitude of the same person in three stages of life; instead, the change in autobiographical perspective is taken only thematically, and the same style, alternating image-filled enthusiasm and a conversational tone, characterizes soldier, prisoner, and guest alike. This homogeneity I believe to be indicative of Fühmann's own development: he did not, as did Stephen Hermlin, substantially adjust his stylistic means to suit the demands of the new society. His transformation came rather in the mode of thought; his vision was changed from apocalyptic doom to revolutionary understanding. There is, for this reason, a serious discrepancy between thematic intention and thematic realization in a narrative poem which would describe the "great change" by means of perspective; what is missing is a reflection of the experienced transformation of human outlook. It is only in other poems, where there is no attempt to assimilate an earlier mental standpoint, that the theme of human change is expressed satisfactorily. Nevertheless, "Die Fahrt nach Stalingrad" is a challenging, powerful poetic document, the evidence of a mind truly tortured by the past and honestly willing to cooperate in overcoming it.

Two other narrative poems, "Die Seefahrer" and "Der Nibelunge Not," are worth mentioning. They are bound together not only in their thematic direction from darkness and confusion to light and promise, but also technically, in the irregular three-beat line which I consider to be the rhythm used most successfully by Fühmann in his early poems. In the 1950s Fühmann often employed a very loose adaptation of the traditional pattern from the *Nibelungenlied*. He was attracted to this divided six-beat form, I think, because it provided the stylistic moderation and controlled informality of rhythm which seems most appropriate to his poetic inclinations. Narrative poems such as "Die Seefahrer" and "Der Nibelunge Not" contain some quite remarkable passages written in this pattern.[35]

35. The same form occurs in many other poems of this time ("Zum ersten Mal im Theater," "Märchen," "Auf einem alten Friedhof," "Das Kind im Zirkus," "Die Demagogen," and others), and was taken by Fühmann, as he himself has said in conversation, from Theodor Fontane's historical ballads (e.g. "Gorm Grymme") and Gottfried Benn (such poems as "Die Dänin," "Einzelheiten," and "Am Saum des nordischen Meers").

"Die Seefahrer" may be viewed as an answer, from the "perspective" of socialism, to Georg Heym's poem of the same title and, for similar reasons, to Fühmann's war poem "Griechischer Auszug." The sense of foreboding and superhuman dangers is replaced by hope—"ob nicht das furchbare Dunkel, / das ihnen vom Haupt nicht mehr weicht, / einmal das milde Gefunkel / eines Sternes reicht" (106)—apocalyptic shipwreck by the signs of a brightening horizon—"Nächte, die heller werden, / das sind die Zeichen der Zeit" (106–07). The boat is no longer "drunken," as in Heym's Rimbaudlike vision. The sea voyage is made with an end in view, though perhaps not directly in sight; the poem ends, "von der Fahrt, von ihrem Ende, / das keiner, das jeder sieht." Although infinitely more readable than the puerile "Griechischer Auszug," "Die Seefahrer" is linguistically an extremely uninteresting poem, totally lacking in the fascination and richness of Heym's columnar stanzas:

> Die Stirnen der Länder, rot und edel wie Kronen,
> Sahen wir schwinden dahin im versinkenden Tag,
> Und die rauschenden Kränze der Wälder thronen
> Unter des Feuers dröhnendem Flügelschlag.[36]

More successful, and leading to the märchen poems, is "Der Nibelunge Not." As a verse adaptation of the Nibelung saga it cannot compare in psychological subtlety and linguistic finesse to Agnes Miegel's (b. 1879) masterly ballad, "Die Nibelungen" (1905). But it is a fine poem for its own purposes, having been intended as a response to the long line of "heroic" ballads based on this source—from Feliz Dahn's (1834–1912) "Hagens Sterbelied" and Emanuel Geibel's (1815–1884) "Volkers Nachtgesang" through Börries Freiherr von Münchhausen's (1874–1945) "Hagen und die Donau-Frauen" and "Ein Lied Volkers" (both 1920). The last link in this tradition were the many nationalistic variants written during the time of the Third Reich, typified by Hans Henning Freiherr von Grote's (b. 1896) "Das Lied von Siegfried." [37] In his poem Fühmann points to the emptiness of the "great belief"

36. Heym, *Dichtungen und Schriften*, I, 339.
37. Entire poem quoted in the anthology *Deutsche Heldendichtung: Ein Jahrtausend deutscher Geschichte in Liedern,* ed. Mirko Jelusisch (Leipzig, n.d.),

in heroic loyalty and renown, which had filled the hearts of the
invading Nibelungs once they had met their master:

> verweht im Wind sind die Worte
> von Ehre, Treue, Ruhm.
> Was blieb? Um den Hort ihre Morde,
> ihr Heldentum. (111)

He centers attention not so much on the battle itself as on the end
of the "bold knights' combat" ("küener recken strîten," as the
Nibelungenlied puts it at the outset). The scene is plainly his-
toricized in analogy to the defeat of the Germans by the Soviets:

> Sie folgten ihrem Herrn,
> dem Fürsten, der führte, verschworen
> ward ihnen Lehn und Lohn:
> Zu Worms am Rheine geboren
> und verwest am Don.

At the end, of course, winter turns to spring, and the justly tri-
umphant begin to show signs of renewed life: "Die versehrte
Flur grünt wieder, / was zerklafft war, schliesst sich sanft." The
Nibelungs' "Not" is the curse of German war guilt: "Nur als
Fluch durch die Zeiten zu treiben: / das ist der Nibelunge Not."

The poem suffers somewhat from being a too obvious reinter-
pretation of the source, but in compensation there is some quite
powerful handling of the adapted Nibelungen strophe. The opening stanza is an example of Fühmann's ability in the use of language:

---

p. 57. On this tradition in German poetry, see Eberhard Sitte's interpretation of
Miegel's "Die Nibelungen" in *Wege zum Gedicht*, ed. Rupert Hirschenauer and
Albrecht Weber (Munich and Zurich, 1963), 2, 498–99. "Das Lied von Siegfried"
reads:

> Denn wo endlich Männer ehern zusammenstehn,
> Wo die heimischen Winde um Bruderstirnen wehn,
> Wo ein grosser Glaube in allen Herzen schlägt,
> Wo nur Heimatliebe ein Leben trägt,
> Wo gegen finstere Mächte Mannentreue sich wehrt,
> Wo aller Dinge Letztes das makellose Schwert,
> Wo des Volkes Grösse das erste Wort für die Welt:
> Ersteht dem neuen Drachen wieder der neue Held,
> Siegfried, der Deutsche!

Zu Blöcken, schwarzen und roten,
geschichtet, und Schnee darauf:
Verfallend, verfaulend, die Toten,
hier liegen sie zuhauf,
ein ungeheures Verwesen,
von Krähen überschrien;
die ihr Fleisch wähnten auserlesen,
mit dem Schnee nun schmelzen sie hin.

The sight of columns of corpses has its rhythmic correlative in
the first lines by means of the caesura after the first foot, as does
the sense of melting snow and disintegrating flesh in the uninterrupted line, "mit dem Schnee nun schmelzen sie hin." Most
significant, however, is that the fantastic world of the myth—in
the work of earlier adapters containing mysterious, ahistorical impulses—is here rationalized, even moralized, by being brought into
association with historical actuality. The same kind of interpretation occurs in the märchen poems, with the difference that in the
fairy tale Fühmann found a structure in which history and human
nature could be treated as a process of development, and not
merely as an illustration of guilt and of the need for just moral
retribution.

Along with the verse Märchen, Fühmann wrote a number of
poems about children ("Die Kinder," "Zum ersten Mal im Theater," "Das Kind im Zirkus" and others); but unfortunately, like
some of his verse fairy tales, they are not childlike in their simplicity but merely juvenile and simplistic. There can be, in my
opinion, no excuse for such triteness as is evident in the following
doggerel condemnation of private property:

Einen Nachmittag lang hab ich einen Karren
voll Kinder durch die Wiesen gefahren,
querüber durch alles, was bei uns blüht.
Nun bin ich glücklich und müd.
Wie schön doch die Welt sein kann: Schmetterlinge, Schle-
hen, Mohn und mein Kinderkarren!
Allerdings: müsste ich ihn berufshalber täglich fahren,
wären sie etwa eines Grafen Kinder
und ich wäre sein Fuhrknecht, so dächte ich: Schinder,
Ausbeuter, Hund, Henker, hol dich die Pest. (165)

This is simpleminded regression and nothing more, a flight from the genuine complexities of collectivization into an infancy of concocted fun and frolic. The only one of these poems which might vaguely warrant consideration is "Die Kinder am Strand," in which the building of sand castles on the beach is compared with social reconstruction, the raging sea with the terror of National Socialism:

> Aber die Schöpfung soll dauern!
> Das Wunderbare geschieht:
> Nach dem Erschrecken, dem Trauern
> wird wieder die Hand bemüht,
> und sie zwingt die schwierigen Stunden,
> dass die Burg, dass der Berg aufersteh,
> und, wieder überwunden,
> überwindet sic wieder die See. (167)

Here there is at least a semblance of sophistication and not that facile atmosphere of happy endings which generally surrounds the world of Fühmann's second childhood; the sea, after all, is also a part of creation, and the castle walls may again be exposed to a pounding surf. But there is a serious problem in the entire analogy, particularly if it is assessed from a Marxist standpoint: the equation of a negative historical phenomenon (the Third Reich) with a natural force such as the sea suggests that human confrontation with it is without ultimate direction; all that can be hoped for is continual reconstruction. At the end of the poem, therefore, the young castle builders realize not only that the drive to construct is inescapable, but also that destruction is bound to recur with unrelenting horror. The closing stanza reads:

> und tief in der Seele innen
> wird etwas schon bewusst:
> Du kannst ihr nicht mehr entrinnen,
> der süssen fordernden Lust,
> die Berge, die Burgen zu bauen
> mit Brücken und Türmen und Tor,
> und nicht mehr dem Grauen zu schauen
> die Woge des Meeres davor. (167)

Unlike the poem "Die Seefahrer," where the sea was overcome when its perils were braved, the change here can only be in sub-

jective human awareness and not in the immutable objects of
nature. If the Third Reich is like the mighty surf, then opposition
to it must be an experience of eternal recurrence rather than
progress toward eventual triumph.

This conflict of opposition and direction is central to the
märchen poems. The best of these, and most revealing of Fühmann's attraction to the märchen, are not those in which he simply
adapts an individual tale—such as "Aschenputtel," "Dornröschen,"
and "In Frau Trudes Haus." Most of these are rather flat and
facile applications of folk plots to the themes of evil and its ultimate
defeat, so prevalent in the programmatic "antifascist" verse of the
time. His version of Snow White, for instance, ends with the
pathetic lines:

> Mein Volk, mein unsterbliches Volk, deine Zeit wird an-
>   brechen,
> in der nur Wahrheit herrschen wird;
> und Schneewittchen, vieltausendgestaltig,
> gegenwärtig wird sie sein
> in meines Volkes Arbeit,
> in meines Volkes Glück. (133)

In "Die Prinzessin und der Frosch" (147) the desperate heroine
has merely to recognize that she is "human" to convert her bed-
fellow from a slimy frog into a shining prince. Some are not
without their charm, such as the ironic twist given the Rumpelstilz-
kin tale in "Der Müller aus dem Märchen"; the miller looks on
with some astonishment when the king abducts his only daughter,
she who can spin straw into gold. Fühmann's tone is, in this case,
similar to Brecht's:

> "mein Gott, wer soll das verstehen:
> Mein Kind—der Königsthron,
>
> mein Kind—die Kalesche, die Krone,
> die Gnade—was wird aus mir . . ."
> So sehe ich ihn stehen
> vor seiner Eichenholztür,
>
> ein deutscher Müller, bieder und brav,
> den der Keulenschlag der Königsgunst traf. (135)

But for the most part these "modernized" fairy tales are too trite and platitudinous to be taken seriously even by children.

Rather, I should draw attention to the poems in which Fühmann reflects on the nature of märchen, their "wisdom" and "direction" —"Die Weisheit der Märchen" and especially "Die Richtung der Märchen." Here the popular plots themselves appear only in bits and pieces, as allusions illustrating thoughts considered basic to the genre as such:

> Immer sind die geringen Dinge die wichtigen.
> Das schwärenbedeckte Fohlen kann reden.
> Das verrostete Schwert kann Drachen töten.
> Das Aschbrot, in das der Mutter Liebe gebacken ist,
>   gibt der Hexe ein gutes Herz. ("Die Weisheit der Märchen,"
>   p. 148)

Surrounding and framing these interspersed references are gnomes stating the most fundamental wisdom of the märchen: the development from struggle to conquest and happiness, the continual surmounting of external obstacles and arrival at the real "basis" of existence. A passage from "Die Weisheit der Märchen" expresses concisely Fühmann's poetic interpretation of the folktale:

> Die Weisheit der Märchen: Immer
> geht die Reise zum Grund, und immer ist es
> dunkel zunächst am Grund. Der Held
> tastet mit den Händen. Dann sieht er
> ein kleines Lichtlein. Er geht, und am Ziel
> ist das Lichtlein gross wie der helle Tag,
> und im hellen Licht liegt das Drachenschloss
> mit der verwunschenen Prinzessin. (149)

What is important is not the goal itself, "der Grund," but the progressive movement toward it—"die Reise zum Grund." The folk hero is forever on his way; his happiness and fear (even for the one who claims not to know fear) derives from his feeling of incompleteness. Some of his human potential has not yet been realized:

> Die Weisheit der Märchen: Immer
> wächst aus der Mühsal das Glück und aus

dem Wunder das Wirkliche. Immer
hat der Held Angst.

Einer, der das Gruseln nicht kennt,
ist unglücklich; er fühlt, es fehlt ihm
ein Stück Menschentum, und so
zieht er aus, das Gruseln zu lernen. (148)

Of decisive importance to Fühmann were not the plots of individual fairy tales. What he discovered, rather, was the structure
of the genre, märchen, as a philosophical metaphor for the dialectical direction of human endeavor. The poem "Die Weisheit der
Märchen" ends, in lines again reminiscent of Brecht:

Ich verneige mich tief vor der Weisheit des Volkes,
der wir es danken,
dass es im Märchen
dialektisch zugeht. (149)

The "wisdom of fairy tales," their basic metaphorical significance,
is that this popular narrative form embodies the full dialectic
of creative fantasy.[38]

Fühmann's most brilliant poem, in which these thoughts on the
wisdom of the fairy tale are expressed with startling precision and
subtlety, is "Die Richtung der Märchen":

Die Richtung der Märchen: tiefer, immer
zum Grund zu, irdischer, näher der Wurzel der Dinge,
ins Wesen.

Wenn die Quelle im Brunnen nicht springt
und ratlos die Bürger sich stauen:
Held Hans hebt den Stein, der im Wasser liegt,
da hockt eine Kröte darunter,
die Kröte muss man töten,
dann springt der Quell wieder rein.

---

38. Two important East German poets, Georg Maurer and Karl Mickel, have
written about Fühmann's concept of the märchen, and both emphasize the importance of dialectics as a structural principle in his poetry and prose. See
Maurer, "Näher der Wurzel der Dinge: Das Märchenmotiv bei Franz Fühmann,"
Neue deutsche Literatur, 12 (1964), 111–27, and Mickel, "Von der Richtung der
Märchen," *Neue deutsche Literatur*, 10 (1962), 116–20. Maurer's essay was reprinted in his book *Der Dichter und seine Zeit* (Berlin, 1956), pp. 125–38.

Die Spindel fiel in den Brunnen,
das Mädchen sprang in die Tiefe,
unten tat sich ein Pfad auf,
der führte zur weisen Frau,
die lohnte gerecht mit Gold oder Pech
im Lande tief unter dem Brunnen.

Als er gegen den Drachen zog,
musste der Held den Schacht hinab,
den Drachen in der Höhle zu treffen.

Er sagte: "Lasst mich hinunter, und wenn ich
    vor Angst an den Strängen zerre, dann folgt meinem Zerren
        nicht,
    lasst mich noch tiefer hinunter, und je mehr ich zerr, desto
        tiefer lasst mich hinunter." Und
    sie liessen ihn hinunter, und er zerrte, und sie liessen ihn tiefer
        hinab,
    und er kam, zerrend, in die Höhle,
    und er besiegte den Drachen.

Dem Grund zu, die Richtung der Märchen,
dem Grund zu, wir zerrn an den Strängen,
dem Grund zu, wir zerrn an den Strängen,
dem Grund zu: Wir zerrn an den Strängen . . . (125–26)

The actual "plot" of the poem is contained in stanzas two, four, and five; it is framed by an introductory formula and a final chorus and interrupted by a subtheme in stanza three.

The main märchen is simple: the hero, Held Hans, sets out to slay the dragon who is blocking the village well. Yet already in the second line of the second stanza, in the characterization of the troubled "Bürger" ("sich stauen"), a deeper, symbolic level of understanding suggests itself. It is not really the well which is congested, but the bewildered townspeople standing by; the cursed dragon lurks within man, and the hero must descend the shaft of human consciousness to confront it. The descent is bound to be frightful, and the hero will often feel forced to tug at the cords by which he is being lowered. But those above the well must ignore his signals, he himself says, for him to penetrate deep enough and dispel the curse. The choral last stanza ("dem Grund zu, wir

zerrn an den Strängen") brings out again the symbolic significance
of the märchen: society as a whole must act, penetrating deeper
and deeper into its own evils and forcing itself beyond its limits.
(The German expression "an einem Strang ziehen" means to act
in concert, with the same end in view.)

Interpersed within this complex, just after the hero is given his
assignment ("die Kröte muss man töten"), is another little märchen
(stanza three), seemingly unrelated to the fate of Held Hans. A
young girl's spindle fell into the well, she jumped in after it, a
path opened up leading to the wise woman who "rewarded her
justly" for her efforts. The tone here is very gentle, the rhythm
slightly irregular but controlled (the three-beat line again). There
is even a suggestion of symmetry in the stanza's construction: lines
one and six both end with "Brunnen," lines two and five tell of the
activity of the girl and the wise woman respectively, and lines three
and four are devoted to the path and are further linked by the
assonance "auf"-"Frau." The ease and confidence with which this
quest is undertaken and fulfilled and the gentle regularity of the
stanza in which it is related contrast markedly with the remainder
of the poem—the hero's hazardous adventure, the irregular stanzas,
and the generally hard, driving rhythms.

An explanation of the purpose of this interlude is crucial to an
understanding of the poem and of Fühmann's interpretation of
the märchen as a genre. Its function may perhaps best be characterized as emblematic anticipation. Though no causal nexus between
the two tales is explicitly established, it is possible from the very
position of the narrative excursus in the poem to determine its
bearing on the main development. The key factors, I think, are
the word "gerecht" and the completion and roundedness of the
young girl's fate. The ultimate justice of this little märchen teaches
Hans to overcome whatever anxiety and deliberation may impede
him in his own quest. It is as though, before departing, Hans had
gone to visit the village wise man, who inspired him with the story
of the girl who lost her spindle. In their unobstructed symmetry
the adventures of the young girl plainly belong to the unreal world
of miracles. But, as is said of the "wisdom of fairy tales"—"Die
Weisheit der Märchen: Immer / wächst aus der Mühsal das Glück
und aus / dem Wunder das Wirkliche" (148). Once the tale has
been told, the real hero Hans is no longer driven on by subcon-

scious impulses but by a kind of consciousness-in-advance. He knows before he leaves that he will tug on the ropes; but he also knows that his signals of desperation must go unheeded because his destination is justice and wisdom. From the interspersed märchen Hans learns hope.

The poem "Die Richtung der Märchen" might be read in still another context. The similarity of its theme to central strains in the philosophy of Ernst Bloch provides proof that Fühmann's attraction to the märchen is not without ideological and historical associations. Bloch, the philosopher of hope, is also the philosopher of the "real" fairy tale. The point of departure for his voluminous treatise *Das Prinzip Hoffnung* (written from 1938 to 1947 and published in full in 1959) is a reading of the tale about the man who set out to learn fear, in the light of recent history. Bloch begins:

> Who are we? Where do we come from? Where are we going? What do we expect? What awaits us?
>
> Many people only feel confused. The ground trembles, they do not know why or from what. Their condition is anxiety, and if it becomes more specific, it is fear.
>
> Once a man set out to learn to fear. This came more quickly and more easily to him in time just past, this art was horribly mastered. But now, except for the inspirers of fear, a feeling more suitable to us falls due.
>
> The point is to learn to hope.[39]

The fairy tale forms "a constituent part of Bloch's philosophy," as a märchen scholar has noted,[40] referring primarily to the long third section of *Das Prinzip Hoffnung*, "Ideal Images in the Mirror" ("Wunschbilder im Spiegel," pp. 359–519).

39. *Das Prinzip Hoffnung, 1, 1:* "Wer sind wir? Wo kommen wir her? Wohin gehen wir? Was erwarten wir? Was erwartet uns?
Viele fühlen sich nur als verwirrt. Der Boden wankt, sie wissen nicht warum und von was. Dieser ihr Zustand ist Angst, wird er bestimmter, so ist er Furcht.
Einmal zog einer weit hinaus, das Fürchten zu lernen. Das gelang in der eben vergangenen Zeit leichter und näher, diese Kunst ward entsetzlich beherrscht. Doch nun wird, die Urheber der Furcht abgerechnet, ein uns gemässeres Gefühl fällig.
Es kommt darauf an, das Hoffen zu lernen."
40. Hermann Bausinger, "Möglichkeiten des Märchens in der Gegenwart," *Märchen, Mythos, Dichtung: Festschrift Friedrich von der Leyen,* ed. Hugo Kuhn and Kurt Schier (Munich, 1963), p. 21: ". . . das Märchen bildet einen positiven, geradezu konstitutiven Bestandteil der Blochschen Philosophie."

It is also an indispensable component of Bloch's Marxism. At the very end of his work (p. 1621), in discussing the "sober" and "enthusiastic" aspects of Marxism, Bloch again thinks of the märchen: "Marxism, in all its *analyses* the coldest detective, nonetheless takes the *märchen* seriously, the *dream of a Golden Age* practically . . ." The märchen symbolizes for Bloch the prophetic, utopian stream of Marxism which flows in dialectical interplay with the stream of analysis and social critique. It illustrates in a work of human fantasy that element of "illumination forward" ("Vor-Schein") crucial to his conception of art and of human consciousness. Past and present in the märchen are seen to point outward to the future; they are already "pregnant" with the future. The wisdom of the märchen is revolutionary because it is directed beyond the obstacles that it sets up. "Fantastic as the märchen is," says Bloch, "in the overcoming of difficulties it is forever wise. Courage and cunning meet with success in an entirely different way than in life, and not only that: as Lenin says, it is certainly the already present revolutionary elements which here take the story beyond the given limits." The characteristic initial phrase of the märchen, "Once upon a time" ("Es war einmal"), is also expressive for Bloch of the transcending revolutionary quality; it does not indicate, as it does for C. G. Jung, an "archaic-collective regression" of consciousness into a primordial state, but rather "means in the style of the märchen not only a past but also a brighter and more pleasant elsewhere." "The setting of such märchen images in a once-upon-a-time makes the once of the future gleam through the once as past." [41]

Fühmann's "Die Richtung der Märchen" is about a man who sets out to learn hope—the principle required, according to Bloch, to transcend an age of fear. The conditions for anxiety are given in Hans's very undertaking, in the deep darkness of the well, and

41. *Prinzip Hoffnung, 3,* 1621: "der Marxismus, in allen seinen *Analysen* der kälteste Detektiv, nimmt aber das *Märchen* ernst, den *Traum vom Goldenen Zeitalter praktisch.*" *1,* 411: "So phantastisch das Märchen ist, so ist es doch, in der Überwindung der Schwierigkeiten, immer klug. Auch reüssieren Mut und List im Märchen ganz anders als im Leben, und nicht nur das: es sind, wie Lenin sagt, allemal die schon vorhandenen revolutionären Elemente, welche hier über die gegebenen Stränge fabeln." *1,* 410: "Es war einmal: das bedeutet märchenhaft nicht nur ein Vergangenes, sondern ein bunteres oder leichteres Anderswo." *1,* 110: "Auch die Verlegung solcher Märchenbilder in ein Es-war-einmal lässt das Einst als Kommendes in dem Einst als Vergangenes allemal durchschimmern."

in the fearful dragon at its bottom. But structured into the poem, as a story to itself, is the element of "Vor-Schein"; the tale of the young girl who finds justice makes the "once" of Hans's future "gleam through the once as past." The crucial interlude provides the hero with the faculty of anticipation, with that "pre-consciousness" ("Vor-Bewusstsein") which lies at the core of Bloch's Marxism. "Die Richtung der Märchen" is, from this point of view, a poetic expression of *Das Prinzip Hoffnung*.

The last sentences of Bloch's treatise contain his definition of the socialist ideal, and I consider them relevant to the formulaic utterance with which "Die Richtung der Märchen" begins. In his pithy, difficult style, Bloch concludes: "The real genesis is not *at the beginning but at the end*, and it only starts to begin when society and existence become radical—that is, grasp their roots. But the root of history is working, creating man, restructuring and overcoming his conditions. Once he has grasped himself and establishes himself without alienation and estrangement in a real democracy, then something emerges in the world that appears to everyone in childhood and where nobody yet has been: home." [42] The "radical" humanism which forms the basis of Bloch's philosophy is derived directly from the early Marx, and he is brought home in these final words with a reference to the famous passage from Marx' introduction to the "Critique of Hegel's Philosophy of Right": "Theory is capable of seizing the masses as soon as it demonstrates ad hominem, and it demonstrates ad hominem as soon as it becomes radical. To be radical means to grasp the matter by the root. But the root for man is man himself." [43] For Fühmann, the "direction of fairy tales" is "radical," toward the "root of things" and into the essence of humanity:

---

42. *Prinzip Hoffnung*, *1*, "Die wirkliche Genesis ist nicht am *Anfang, sondern am Ende*, und sie beginnt erst anzufangen, wenn Gessellschaft und Dasein radikal werden, das heisst sich an der Wurzel fassen. Die Wurzel der Geschichte aber ist der arbeitende, schaffende, die Gegebenheiten umbildende und überholende Mensch. Hat er sich erfasst und das Seine ohne Entäusserung und Entfremdung in realer Demokratie begründet, so entsteht in der Welt etwas, das allen in die Kindheit scheint und worin noch niemand war: Heimat."

43. *Marx-Engels Gesamtausgabe* (MEGA), Part One, I, 614: "Die Theorie ist fähig, die Massen zu ergreifen, sobald sie ad *hominem* demonstriert, und sie demonstriert ad *hominem*, sobald sie radikal wird. Radikal sein ist die Sache an der Wurzel fassen. Die Wurzel für den Menschen aber ist der Mensch selbst." (The translation is my own.)

Die Richtung der Märchen: tiefer, immer
zum Grund zu, irdischer, näher der Wurzel der Dinge,
ins Wesen.

The märchen represents for him, as for Bloch, the miraculous rationality of socialism, the "wondrous law" of dialectical materialism.[44]

"Die Richtung der Märchen" is a poem of individual and collective regeneration, the revolution, as it were, of human consciousness. Without reading too much philosophy into it, I believe that
there is an undeniable similarity between Fühmann's theme and
Bloch's ideas and that the mode of thought which attracted the
two to the märchen is a definite point of contact. It is probably no
accident that the poem was composed in the later 1950s, just when
Bloch's ideas were having their momentous effect among intellectuals in the DDR. In any event, "Die Richtung der Märchen,"
with its subtle modulation of tone and expressive intensity, is
certainly the finest of Fühmann's poems and one of the best
written in the first decade of the DDR. The dialectic given in its
style and in its image of the cord symbolizing at once man's restrictions and his freedom corresponds to the dialectic tension of the
märchen as a genre. Max Lüthi, the eminent folklorist, has characterized the fairy-tale in an essay on "Freedom and Engagement
in the Folktale" (1963): "Mere wishful thinking is enough; the
ease with which thought is realized is one of the elements of
freedom in the märchen. But at the same time the mechanistic
aspect, the abruptness, the unorganic nature of transformation is
an element of the fairy tale's rigidity which, like freedom, belongs
to the basic traits of the märchen and forms with it a higher unity,
so that each is dissolved in the other."[45] The direction of Füh-

44. "Das wunderbare Gesetz" is the title of the last book of verse by Louis
Fürnberg (1909-52), a poet to whom Fühmann feels closely related. In a speech
(1967) in memory of Fürnberg, Fühmann interprets this phrase and emphasizes its
aptness as an expression of his own conception of socialism. *Sinn und Form,
19* (1967), 784.

45. "Freiheit und Bindung im Volksmärchen," *Märchen, Mythos, Dichtung,* pp.
1–14. P. 4: "Das blosse Wunschdenken genügt; die Leichtigkeit, mit der der
Gedanke sich verwirklicht, gehört zu den Elementen der Freiheit im Märchen.
Aber zugleich ist die Mechanistik, die Plötzlichkeit, das Unorganische der Verwandlung ein Element der Märchenstarrheit, die wie die Freiheit zu den Grundzügen des Märchens gehört und mit ihr zusammen eine höhere Einheit bildet, so
dass jedes im andern aufgehoben ist."

mann's poem aptly reflects the "direction" he feels inherent in the märchen, from awareness of the obstacle through fear and hope to the "higher unity" of freedom and engagement with other men.

In this poem, too, it is clear that Fühmann's poetry of the 1950s gained a quality and challenging intellectual force which were totally lacking in the verse he wrote as a soldier a decade earlier. His conversion to Soviet Marxism did not alter his basically mystical inclinations, his sense of fantasy and attraction to the miraculous, which was the most striking feature of his early writings. As is evident in the emotional chorus in the closing stanza of "Die Richtung der Märchen"—and in the flurries of optimistic exclamations which characterize the bulk of his socialist-realist poetry—Fühmann was never inclined to temper his enthusiasm for whatever impressed him most. As a soldier he conjured an emotional apocalypse which he felt to envelop his "destiny" on the vast, inimical battlefield; as an awakened Communist he sang passionately of a new fantasy world: the bright future and the redemption promised by socialist reconstruction. Nor did his reeducation substantially affect the linguistic and formal techniques of his verse: both before and after his conversion his vocabulary derived from Rilke and German expressionism, and in both periods he favored the rhythm of a loose three-beat line. Fühmann's transition from the war years to the early 1950s was primarily ideological and not—as in the case of Stephan Hermlin—stylistic.

The main difference created by this transition, and the reason for the improvement in his poetry, is dialectical materialism, a teaching that provided Fühmann with a rational intellectual framework for his visions of fantasy. Not that his many partisan Communist hymns of allegiance are any more "rational" than his "Erlebnis" poems written at the front, though they may be more mechanical in their construction; the factor of poetic rationality contributed by Marxism to Fühmann's creativity can be seen, rather, in the function of the dialectic as structure and as metaphor. The dialectical direction of human activity, as he found it embodied in the märchen, became for him a theme with all the intricacy of a mythic dimension. This theme found satisfactory expression very rarely (perhaps only once or twice), but the dimension was present and was made available to him by his crucial education in the Soviet Union. The poetic adjustment of

Franz Fühmann—unlike that of Stephan Hermlin, which proved to have fatal consequences—allowed for a deepening of his vision and the maturing of his talent.

Like Hermlin, however, Fühmann stopped writing poetry at the end of the 1950s. In his turn to prose he has continued as a creative author of some merit: such stories as "Kameraden," "Das Gottesgericht" and "König Ödipus," as well as parts of *Das Judenauto*, are judged by some critical readers to be finer than any of his verse.[46] But he has not published any lyric poetry since his futile Sputnik poem, "Der neue Stern" (1959). Fühmann, unlike Hermlin, adapted himself to the new society to the benefit of his poetic output. But like Hermlin, he was unable to make the adjustment within the society which became essential in the late 1950s. By then the days of enthusiastic optimism and revolutionary fairy tales were over, and a new mood of apprehension and ironic sobriety was in order.

46. On Fühmann's prose, see the essays by Marcel Reich-Ranicki, "Kamerad Fühmann" and "Der exemplarische Weg des ostberliner Erzählers Franz Fühmann." For a discussion of the märchen as the thematic connection between his poetry and his prose, see Georg Maurer, "Näher der Wurzel der Dinge" and Karl Mickel, "Von der Richtung der Märchen."

Part Two: Visions

er redet
zum Sand,
der ihm den Mund füllt—so wird
reden der Sand, und wird
schreien der Stein, und wird
fliegen das Wasser.

Bobrowski, "Antwort"

3

Peter Huchel: The Disenchanted Idyll

> One aged man—one man—can't keep a house,
> A farm, a countryside, or if he can,
> It's thus he does it of a winter night.
> > Robert Frost, "An Old Man's Winter Night"

Peter Huchel is perhaps better known as an editor than as a poet. For fourteen years, from 1949 to 1962, Huchel directed the East Berlin quarterly *Sinn und Form* and almost singlehandedly made it into one of the leading cultural periodicals in postwar Germany. *Sinn und Form* served as a very real bridge between the two parts of the country, a literary forum in which quality and not political orthodoxy was decisive. Here works by Pablo Neruda and Paul Celan, Hans Magnus Enzensberger and Stephan Hermlin, Anna Seghers and Nathalie Sarraute, Bertolt Brecht and Thomas Mann appeared side by side. Though there was clearly a preference for writers of Marxist persuasion, *Sinn und Form* included regular contributions by such different thinkers as Georg Lukács, Ernst Bloch, Jean-Paul Sartre, and Ernst Fischer, all of whom have been condemned by dogmatic East German authorities for ideological heresy. Some of the major Western writers have been published in the DDR only in *Sinn und Form*; furthermore, it was through these pages that such important East German writers as Günter Kunert, Peter Hacks, and Johannes Bobrowski were first made available to German readers East and West. The spirit behind this enterprise was Peter Huchel, and he was guided by a feeling for aesthetic value which made no compromises to fashion or to political decrees.

In the West this courageous undertaking attracted widespread interest, particularly since it was brought to a halt in 1962.[1] When it was discovered in the DDR that walls are safer than bridges and that good fences make better neighbors than do unorthodox intellectuals, *Sinn und Form* was taken from Huchel's hands and came under rigid Party supervision; it became, like *Neue Deutsche Literatur*, an organ devoted more exclusively to East German output and consumption. Huchel was charged with deviationism—in short, with showing more concern for "Form" than for "Sinn." Since the end of 1962, when the last issue under his editorship was published, Huchel has been personally isolated and officially ostracized in East German literary life.

Immediately after his dismissal, however, his volume *Chausseen Chausseen* (1963) appeared in West Germany, and attention was successfully drawn from Huchel the condemned editor to Huchel the poet. Indeed, the poems in this volume and his experiences with *Sinn und Form* are intimately related to one another; some of the texts, especially those at the end of the book, are plainly responses to the repressive measures taken against him. But they are also more than that, as he himself is more than the victim of political witch hunting; poetry speaks for the man and not only for his incidental function, and it must be studied in its development over the years. A study of Peter Huchel's poetic development is, I think, especially rewarding because his career constitutes a sensitive personal reaction to the course of German history over the past forty years. The Weimar period, National Socialist rule and the war, postwar reconstruction and consolidation of East German society—these events of the recent past form the vast canvas on which the delicate strokes of Huchel's verse must be read.

Huchel's poetry has passed through four major phases which, though they obviously overlap, are clearly enough demarcated;

1. On *Sinn und Form*, see the two articles by Marcel Reich-Ranicki, "Ein anderer Sinn, eine andere Form," *Literarisches Leben in Deutschland* (Munich, 1965), pp. 134–36, and "Ohne 'Sinn und Form'," *Wer schreibt, provoziert* (Munich, 1966), pp. 46–50; also Werner Wilk, "Peter Huchel," *Neue Deutsche Hefte, 10* (1963), 81–96.

each of them may be named after a poem.[2] The first group, "Origin" ("Herkunft"), can serve to determine the situation of Huchel's early works in the context of German poetry written in the late 1920s and early 1930s by distinguishing it from both revolutionary proletarian lyrics and the beginnings of modern German nature poetry. In the second section, "Germany's Twelve Nights" ("Zwölf Nächte"), fall the poems written in reaction to National Socialism and the war (between 1933 and 1945). In the third stage of Huchel's career, the brief period of optimism between 1945 and about 1953, the poet set his hopes on the construction of a qualitatively new society in the Soviet Occupied Zone, and especially on "The Law" ("Das Gesetz"), the newly introduced land reform. The poetry of this phase is close to the socialist realism prevalent at the time, and it was considered in the DDR to represent the peak of Huchel's achievement. He has since dissociated himself from it almost completely, but it is essential to a full understanding of the fourth period. The title "Winter Psalm" ("Winterpsalm") characterizes perfectly Huchel's years of profound disappointment and resignation since the mid-1950s, expressed in those magnificent and brooding poems of *Chausseen Chausseen*, in which melancholy reflections alternate with striking images of a nearly frozen landscape.

Huchel's development begins with a kind of intuitive reliance on his actual environment, the rural province Mark Brandenburg near Berlin; his early verse is enchanted by the sounds and sights of natural landscapes. But as a nature poet Huchel was deeply concerned with the fact of social deprivation among the inhabitants of the province, the pronounced stratification between the large landowners and the destitute migrant workers. The poet's response to the unjust conditions took the form of a subtle poetic idyll, an ideal harmony between man and nature. In his "origin" in the late 1920s Huchel was neither a "pure" nature poet nor an agitator for proletarian revolution; rather, he constructed his own "version of pastoral" in the unrealized ideal of productive human labor. With the coming of National Socialism, this idyll becomes haunted and is then burst asunder by the ravages of the war. The linguistic

2. I have organized this chapter according to the periods suggested by Peter Hamm in his useful essay, "Vermächtnis des Schweigens: Der Lyriker Peter Huchel," *Merkur, 18* (1964), 480–88.

assurance and rhythmic musicality of his early verse are broken, as is the serene harmony of his initial ideal. But in the immediate postwar years Huchel returns to his pastoral more resolutely than ever, sincerely hopeful that his vision of social justice will become a reality with the institutionalization of land reform. For a brief time his poetry is hymnic in its confident direction, though rather conventional and empty in its means of expression. Once his hopes are dashed and the final period of bitter disillusionment emerges, the tendencies already evident in his wartime poetry begin to appear again in full, mature development. Hymn gives way to psalm; melodic richness changes to an abstract, cryptic style; and the idyll of self-fulfilling human activity is conclusively disrupted in the face of universal exploitation of man by man.

An analysis of what I consider the best of his poems will show the evolution of this fascinating career from the harmonious idyll of the 1920s to the older man's somber disenchantment. It seems as though worlds separate those early scenes of abundant autumn and the icy muteness of his late poems; but Peter Huchel's masterpieces, the poems "Oktoberlicht" (ca. 1932) and "Winterpsalm" (ca. 1962), belong to one world, unmistakably unified by the same courageous humanity. After decades of brutal hardship, after the idyll is dissipated, it is the same poet's unfailing voice and the same poet's steady hand which make art of the scattered fragments.

Origin (1925–33)

In order to appreciate Huchel's early poetry and his personal political viewpoint, there must be a clearing of the air thick with subsequent distortions. Most illuminating for this purpose is a short autobiographical sketch published in 1931 in Willy Haas' periodical *Die literarische Welt;* there, Huchel said of himself:

> he didn't take part in the mad dash for a place of shelter. His contemporaries sit in Party headquarters and sometimes even they admit that there are bad smells coming from some corner or other. Still, they have a roof over their heads. But because Marxist dignity is not becoming to him, he'll have to go on letting himself be rained on under unpromising skies. They beckon to him from under the ark of the Party, and he under-

stands their call: "We can prove to you from the sub-structure that you'll sink without leaving a trace behind." He can hardly object to that, and has no reply at all. They must know, since they have scientific knowledge. But meanwhile his heart goes on beating privately. And he lives without excuses.[3]

Huchel sympathized with the Marxists and shared their concerns, but he did not join the Party or commit himself to organized socialist institutions. In considering his poetry of these years, East German critics have emphasized the first aspect of Huchel's attitude, his socialist leanings, while the West Germans have completely ignored it, trying to make of him one of those asocial, often mystical nature poets writing in the shadow of Wilhelm Lehmann (1882–1968).

Characteristic of the East German interpretation is the attempt to loosely associate early Huchel with the proletarian literature fostered in the late 1920s by the League of Proletarian Revolutionary Writers. Among the members of this group were Johannes R. Becher, Erich Weinert, Ludwig Renn, and Hans Marchwitza, and its program ("Unsere Front") was stated in no uncertain terms by Becher in the first issue of its organ, *Die Linkskurve* (August 1929): "Revolutionary proletarian literature is not poor people's poetry or literature of pity, it doesn't whimper, teary-eyed, over the misery of the proletariat, it doesn't casually leaf through the war as though it were an album of horror. It is born in drumfire and street fights, it has grown up under the pressure of censorship. Its answer to exploitation and war is a solution of action. Revolutionary proletarian literature sings of

3. *Die literarische Welt*, 7 (1931), 3–4; quoted in Franz Schonauer, "Peter Huchels Gegenposition," *Akzente*, *12* (1965), 404–14:

> Denn er hat sich nicht an dem Start nach Unterschlupf beteiligt. Seine Altersgenossen sitzen im Parteibüro, und manchmal geben sie sogar zu, dass es aus irgendeiner Ecke her nicht gut riecht. Immerhin, sie haben ihr Dach über dem Kopf. Aber da ihm selbst die marxistische Würde nicht zu Gesicht steht, wird er sich unter aussichtslosem Himmel weiterhin einregnen lassen. Sie winken aus der Arche der Partei, und er versteht ihren Zuruf. Der lautet: "Wir können dir an Hand des Unterbaues nachweisen, dass du absacken wirst, ohne eine Lücke zu hinterlassen." Aber dagegen hat er nicht viel einzuwenden, nichts zu erwidern. Sie müssen es wissen, denn sie haben die Wissenschaft. Doch unterdessen schlägt sein Herz privat weiter. Und er lebt ohne Entschuldigung.

class love and class hate."[4] Peter Huchel was also on the side
of the proletariat; as his poems illustrate, he felt closely bound
to the poor servants and exploited farmhands of his native region
—to all those who had to work the soil for somebody else. Even
the roaming beggars and migrant workers are integral images in
his poetry. As Huchel stated later, "What did I care about in
those days? I wanted to make visible in the poem a deliberately
ignored, suppressed class, the class of the people, the maidservants
and coachmen."[5] In the poem "Der polnische Schnitter" he even
expresses solidarity through his persona, the Polish mower, with
the international workers' movement which had begun in the East.
The last stanzas read:

> O Feuer der Erde,
> mein Herz hält andere Glut.
> Acker um Acker mähte ich,
> kein Halm war mein eigen.
>
> Herbststürme, weht!
> Auf leeren Böden
> werden die hungrigen Schläfer wach.
> Ich geh nicht allein
> die helle Chaussee.
>
> Am Rand der Nacht
> schimmern die Sterne
> wie Korn auf der Tenne,

4. Quoted in *Proletarisch-revolutionäre Literatur 1918 bis 1933* (East Berlin,
1965), p. 5: "Proletarisch-revolutionäre Literatur ist nicht Armeleutepoesie oder
Mitleidsdichtung, sie bewimmert nicht tränenbeflissen das Elend des Proletariats,
sie blättert nicht beschaulich in dem Krieg wie in einem Schaueralbum. Im
Trommelfeuer und in Strassenkämpfen ist sie geboren, sie ist unter dem Druck
der Zensur gross geworden. Die Antwort, die sie auf die Ausbeutung und auf den
Krieg gibt, ist eine aktive Lösung. Proletarisch-revolutionäre Literatur singt
Klassenliebe und Klassenhass."

5. Quoted in Eduard Zak, *Der Dichter Peter Huchel* (East Berlin, 1953), p. 32:
"Um was ging es mir damals? Ich wollte eine bewusst übersehene, unterdrückte
Klasse im Gedicht sichtbar machen, die Volksschicht, Mägde und Kutscher." In
his article "Peter Huchel und sein lyrisches Werk," *Neue Deutsche Hefte*, 15
(1968), 11–32, Ingo Seidler expresses his doubts as to the sincerity of this statement,
which was made as a kind of program in retrospect; but there can be no doubt,
as Seidler also notes, about Huchel's sympathy with this deprived social class in
his early verse (see p. 19). Seidler's fine essay was reprinted in *Hommage für Peter
Huchel*, ed. Otto F. Best (Munich, 1968), pp. 90–109.

kehre ich heim ins östliche Land,
in die Röte des Morgens. (S, 14–15) [6]

These lines are singled out by East German commentators as clear evidence of Huchel's "Parteilichkeit," his active siding with the rural proletariat as a class, and are thus linked up with his socialist-realist cycles of the early 1950s, "Das Gesetz" and "Bericht aus Malaya."

There is some validity in such an interpretation, and a good deal can be made of Huchel's continual concern for the landless farmhands of the countryside. But within the context of his poetry this concern is more profound than mere partisanship of specific class interests, and it does not include any proposals for an active social solution. Huchel's poems "Der polnische Schnitter" and "Herbst der Bettler," in which voice is given to the lower strata of society, have little in common with the tendentious verse typical of the League poets. Alexander Roll's "Lied der Arbeitlosen," for example, which appeared in *Die Linkskurve* in 1930, contains an element of revolutionary outrage wholly lacking in Huchel's work.[7] Whereas the organized proletarian writers were guided by

6. Poems are quoted from the volumes *Die Sternenreuse* (Munich, 1967), a republication, with changes, of the volume *Gedichte* which appeared in 1948 in East Berlin and Stuttgart; and *Chausseen Chausseen*. They will be cited as "S" and "CC" respectively.

7. Wir ziehen durch die Städte,
   Kalt bläst der Wind uns an,
   Der Bürger schnarcht im Bette,
   Wir frieren um die Wette,
   Stelln uns zum Stempeln an.

   . . . .

   Die satten Bürger prassen.
   Wir hungern. Sie sind dick
   Und haben volle Kassen.
   Das sind die beiden Klassen
   Der deutschen Republik!

   . . . .

   Wir werden nicht mehr schweigen.
   Hunger hat keine Zeit!
   Wir wollen nicht länger leiden.
   Bald werden wir uns zeigen.
   Wir sind zur Tat bereit!

   In *Die Linkskurve* (December 1930)

the example of Mayakovsky's declamatory style, Huchel's admiration in those years was for the more private, nostalgic Sergey Yesenin (1895–1925); his concern over social deprivation led him not to public proclamation but inward to a vision of unimpeded justice.

Many West German critics, on the other hand, tend to disregard Huchel's sympathy with the exploited lower classes; they emphasize his "pure" nature poetry, his mystical bonds with the forces of nature, and the magical charm of his rhythms. Werner Wilk, for example, defines his place in the tradition by remarking, "Like Loerke and Lehmann, he has his roots in the groundwater of Eichendorff." [8] Almost invariably Huchel's early poetry is neatly grouped with that of the early Lehmann, Oda Schaefer, Horst Lange, Theodor Kramer, the early Günter Eich, Elisabeth Langgässer, and countless other representatives of modern "Naturlyrik" —a term referring to the trend in German poetry since the 1920s away from the rhetorical fervor and abstraction of expressionism and toward an intimacy with the concrete details of nature in all its abundance.

There are reasons for these associations: for some years Huchel was a regular contributor to the periodical *Die Kolonne*, which specialized in that kind of nature poetry, and in 1932 he was awarded the *Kolonne* Prize for his volume *Der Knabenteich* (which Huchel withheld from publication in 1933 for political reasons). Indeed, although there is in Huchel's poetry none of the pantheistic mythologizing of Loerke and Lehmann—whose verses are inhabited by Pan, Oberon, and Merlin—and of course none of the fervent religiosity of Elisabeth Langgässer, some of his poems clearly belong to the repertoire of modern "Naturlyrik." "Löwenzahn" is an example, as is "Sommer" ("Dich will ich rühmen, / Erde, / noch unter dem Stein, / dem Schweigen der Welt / ohne Schlaf und Dauer"), as well as the fine poem "Die schilfige Nymphe":

> Die schilfige Nymphe,
> das Wasser welkt fort,

8. Wilk, "Peter Huchel," p. 82: "Wie Loerke und Lehmann hat er seine Wurzeln im Eichendorffschen Grundwasser." Cf. also Curt Hohoff, "Moden und Masstäbe zeitgenössischer deutscher Lyrik," *Welt und Wort, 14* (1959), 135; and Wilhelm Lehmann, "Mass des Lobes," *Deutsche Zeitung und Wirtschaftszeitung*, February 8, 1964, p. 17.

der Froschbauch der Sümpfe
verdorrt.

Am Mittagsgemäuer
der Schatten stürzt ein.
Der Hauch tanzt aus Feuer
am Eidechsenstein.

Im Mittag der Kerzen,
im Röhricht, das schwieg,
ist traurig dem Herzen
Libellenmusik.

Die dunkle Libelle
der Seen wird still.
Es tönt nur das grelle
herzböse Geschrill.

Es neigt sich die Leuchte
ins Röhricht hinein.
Der ödhin verscheuchte
Wind kichcrt allein. (S, 65)

The landscape here is a closed organism in and for itself, and flora and fauna seem to flourish without human participation. Nature is animated to such an extent that the poem has the effect of describing human moods and actions when it really aims only at reconstituting the interplay of sights and sounds in the swamp. In this respect, although not in vocabulary, it is similar to Wilhelm Lehmann's early poem "Über die Stoppeln," from his first volume *Antwort des Schweigens* (1935):

Die Eiche spielt wie ein Dudelsack,
Vom Sturm der jungen Stare geschwellt.
Huflattich schlängelt den weissen Hals,
Wenn Wind über seinen Rücken wellt.

Die Iris plattet die längliche Frucht
Wie die Eidechse sparsamer Glut,
Als grüne Hode schwankt sie und schwillt
Vom schlafenden Zeugungsmut.[9]

"Nature magic" ("Naturmagie") characteristically involves a depersonalization of the landscape, a shift from concern with na-

9. Wilhelm Lehmann, *Sämtliche Werke*, 3 vols. (Gütersloh, 1962), *1*, 450.

ture's effect on the individual temperament to copious attention
to the precise details of a natural scene. Lehmann, Krolow, Langgässer, and others often go so far in their precision that their poems
are little more than catalogues of plant names; and surely few
readers can understand some of Lehmann's verses without the
help of a botanical dictionary: "Mit Feuerschröter, Weidenboh-
renraupe dauern, / Ihr Leib ein Mochusduft, kastanienrot sein
Rücken von Chitin." [10] Huchel never displays his biological erudition in this way, but the element of depersonalization is present
in some of his short poems, which seem almost imagistic in their
descriptive concentration. "Wintersee" is an example:

> Ihr Fische, wo seid ihr
> mit schimmernden Flossen?
> Wer hat den Nebel,
> das Eis beschossen?
>
> Ein Regen aus Pfeilen,
> ins Eis gesplittert,
> so steht das Schilf
> und klirrt und zittert. (S, 66)

Social concern, then, plays no part in some of Huchel's early
poetry, where his preoccupation is exclusively with certain particular impressions and phenomena in nature.

His finest achievement as a poet of "Naturlyrik"—sometimes
pejoratively referred to as "village-pond poetry" ("Dorfteich-
poesie")—is "Der Knabenteich" (published 1932). The first stanza
demonstrates the linguistic richness and masterful control of
rhythm and sound patterns maintained throughout the poem:

> Wenn heisser die Libellenblitze
> im gelben Schilf des Mittags sprühn,
> im Nixengrün der Entengrütze
> die stillen Wasser seichter blühn,
> hebt er den Hamen in die Höhe,
> der Knabe, der auf Kalmus blies,
> und fängt die Brut der Wasserflöhe,
> die dunkel wölkt im Muschelkies. (S, 22)

10. Lehmann, p. 490.

The dreamy noontime setting at the verdant pond, so abundant
in sensual impressions, becomes more and more enchanted; the
distinction between sound and sight becomes increasingly blurred;
and finally the boy, seeking his image on the surface, seems completely hypnotized by the water sprite. It is the sprite's "wild,
animallike gaze" that finally shakes the speaker out of his in-
toxicated reverie; he appears to have been suddenly reminded, in
the words "the same as once before" ("derselbe wie einst"), that
the boy's experiences are really his own. The magnificent third
stanza implies all of these associations:

> Verzaubert ist die Mittagshelle,
> das glasig grüne Algenlicht.
> Der Knabe kennt die Wasserstelle,
> die anders spiegelt sein Gesicht.
> Er teilt das Schilf, das splittrig gelbe:
> froschköpfig plätschert hoch der Nick—
> und summt und sprizt und ist derselbe
> wie einst mit tierhaft wildem Blick.

Yet even the last stanza, in which the speaker addresses himself
and would seem to clear up all the confusion as to time relationships and symbolic meaning, does not really unveil the mystery
but retains a certain ambiguity and refuses to break the spell:

> Und auch der Teich ist noch derselbe
> wie einst, da dein Mund Kalmus blies,
> dein Fuss hing ins Sumpfdottergelbe
> und mit den Zehen griff den Kies.
> Wenn dich im Traum das teichgrüntiefe
> Gesicht voll Binsenhaar umfängt,
> ist es als ob der Knabe riefe,
> weil noch dein Netz am Wasser hängt.

There can be no certainty, we are perhaps told, regarding our
memory when our presence now is so attached by the concreteness
of experience—a calamus reed or a fishnet—to an earlier state.
Boyhood adventures and the reflections of later days converge, as
though the child's cry could still be heard through the years.

Accompanying this thematic intermingling of past and present,
man and landscape, there is an unbroken musicality and ingeniously

calculated cadence that sweep the reader into the poem's compelling flow. Sound and sense are perfectly integrated, since full use is made of subtle sensual associations and variations. Stanza two, for instance, begins with a visual evocation of the pond ("Rot um ihn blüht die Hexenheide, / fischäugig blinkt der Teich im Kraut"), but the striking *au* sound brings a gradual shift to the audible spirit of the setting ("Der gr*au*e Geist der Uferweide / wird über Sumpf und Binsen l*au*t"). It is here the sound of the pond that bewitches the young boy ("wie ein Mund der Z*au*berei") and then, in stanza three, the hypnotizing green of midday reflected in the stagnant water ("Verz*au*bert ist die Mittagshelle, / das glasig grüne Algenlicht"). In the closing lines of the poem, the *au* sound (in "Traum") is again crucial as visual imagery is finally identified with the sounds surrounding the pond. In this concluding "dream" the pond appears as the boy himself, its shiny green surface being his face and its magical tones his voice. The boy, once enchanted by the setting, is now one with the pond's enchanting presence. The final dream is literally the vision of a "Knabenteich."

This brilliant poem unquestionably stands in proximity to the work of Wilhelm Lehmann, Karl Krolow, and other modern "nature poets." But, in my opinion it would be more accurate to speak of a shared tradition rather than a mutual interdependence. Such poems as "Die schilfige Nymphe" and "Der Knabenteich" actually bear greater similarity to the verses of Annette von Droste-Hülshoff (1797–1848), that great forebear of modern "Naturlyrik," than to the work of her twentieth-century followers.[11] Moreover, although such poems give clear evidence of Huchel's talent, they do not in my view express the core of his concern during those years. The natural settings presented here generally serve as the background for active human presence, as one component of his idyll.

The divergence between the characteristic East German and West German interpretations of Peter Huchel's early poetry

11. For an acknowledgment of this heritage, see the essays by Karl Krolow, "Möglichkeiten und Grenzen der neuen deutschen Naturlyrik," *Aspekte zeitgenössischer deutscher Lyrik* (Munich, 1963), pp. 28–51, and "Lyrik und Landschaft," *Schattengefecht* (Frankfurt, 1964), pp. 7–38.

could hardly be more extreme; "proletarian art" and asocial "Naturlyrik" seem, in fact, to be mutually exclusive categories. Yet, as William Empson would assure us in the first chapter ("Proletarian Literature") of his book *Some Versions of Pastoral*, "two people may get very different experiences from the same work of art without either being definitely wrong." As I have shown, there is good reason for pointing out the sympathy with the lower strata of society expressed in Huchel's poems, and at the same time it is no complete distortion to associate them with the verse of other contributors to the periodical *Die Kolonne*. But I believe that both of these categorizations, when pushed too far, miss the particular quality of Huchel's poems. For while the Western interpretation does not take account of the social concern which is unquestionably there, East German commentaries suffer from their failure to consider the private, personal attitude or the aesthetic subtlety not to be found in the poems by members of the League of Revolutionary Proletarian Writers. The solution to this ideological dilemma proposed by William Empson can, I think, be applied to Huchel. Good proletarian art, according to Empson, is usually "Covert Pastoral." When proletarian literature "comes off," he remarks, "I find I am taking it as pastoral literature; I read into it, or find that the author has secretly put into it, these more subtle, more far-reaching, and I think more permanent, ideas." [12] Huchel's poems expressing concern for the poor and disinherited "come off" as literature in a way that the fist-swinging outcries in *Die Linkskurve* do not. They voice a class-consciousness which is at the same time consciousness of a more fundamental relationship between man and his environment.

I will now attempt to analyze, as a "version of pastoral," a kind of personal idyll, that complex of poems which constitutes the best of Huchel's early verse and is most indicative of his overall intentions in these years. I do not mean to suggest that Huchel wished to appeal in any conscious way to the age-old pastoral tradition in Western literature; his poetry can conveniently be treated as "pastoral art" without any specific reference to Theocritus, Vergil, or Edmund Spenser. (The work of Robert Frost, a poet with whom Huchel feels close ties, has been perceptively

12. New York, 1950, pp. 3, 21.

interpreted in the same terms.[13]) Nor do I wish to identify his "pastoral" with the many "embittered idylls" ("erbitterte Idylle") —still another name for the demonized bucolics of Lehmann, Eich, Horst Lange, and others. Rather, having already mentioned Huchel's connections with those poets, I would like to specify the element peculiar to Huchel's "pastoral," linking his social concern with his apparently asocial landscape images.

The best point of departure, in which many of the components of Huchel's idyll are introduced in clear interrelation, is the poem "Herkunft" (ca. 1926). The first two of six stanzas suggest the speaker's arrival at a setting intimately familiar to him but from which he seems to have been absent for many years, a kind of physical remembrance:

> Dass ich kam im Schattenwind,
> weiss davon das Haus?
> Birnen duften mürb im Spind
> alten Sommer aus.
> Wo der Flegel sausend drosch,
> fliegt das Korn zuhauf.
> Wo am Bett das Öl erlosch,
> liegt das Laken auf.

> Als ich mit verharztem Haar
> in die Kiefern kroch,
> klangen laut vom Schwalbenjahr
> Dach und Kammer noch.
> Nachtgeläut umweht das Haus.
> Und durchs kalte Tor
> gehn die Freunde still hinaus,
> die ich längst verlor. (S, 9)

Peculiar to this childhood memory is that the natural and domestic situation appears not as something lost in the distant past, but persisting undisturbed, in its original order, in the present. This quality of endurance from past into present is stressed even grammatically, with the shifting verbal tenses in three of the four sentences in

13. See the book by John F. Lynen, *The Pastoral Art of Robert Frost* (New Haven and London, 1960), especially chapters one and five. Peter Huchel told me of his feeling of artistic kinship with Frost in private conversation.

the first stanza, dependent clauses being in the past tense ("kam," "drosch," "erlosch") and main clauses in the present ("weiss," "fliegt," "liegt"). The continuing alternation in temporality is then contrasted by the second stanza, ending in an elegiac note, a clear statement of loss: "Und durchs kalte Tor / gehn die Freunde still hinaus, / die ich längst verlor."

These last lines, however, lead directly into the second part of the poem (stanzas three through five), where certain of the long-lost "friends" are recalled, one after the other. To each of them is devoted one stanza—first the tinker ("Kesselflicker"), then the maidservant ("Magd"), finally the servant ("Knecht"). Common to all these little portraits is the same movement from past into present that can be observed in the first stanza, with the difference that here the temporal transition is made in connection with the productive activity of the described figure. Each "friend" is, literally, "made present" when he is recalled at work, serving his social function. The first of these stanzas, about the tinker, offers the clearest example:

> Und der Kesselflicker auch,
> der am Feuer sass,
> hämmernd und im Küchenrauch,
> den ich lang vergass,
> vor mir hockt er krumm und alt
> und zigeunerisch,
> kam nachts aus dem Krähenwald,
> suchte Herd und Tisch.

First it is recalled how the tinker "sat" at the fire; he is then seen "hammering" in the smoke-filled kitchen, the present participle "hämmernd" already suggesting that his presence is now being recaptured. Then the speaker sees him squatting before him, the present "hockt" used in marked contrast to "sass" of three lines above. Once his activity is recalled, his busy hammering over the smoky fire, the tinker is no longer a figure of the past but is there again, in the room in which he worked long ago. What was in the first stanza only the grammatical interplay of tenses, becomes here a kind of transcendence of temporal separation. Yet the tinker does not return for long: he is "zigeunerisch," "gypsy-like," just as the memory of his productive activity is fleeting. When the speaker's recollection turns to the situation of the poor man, his reason for coming to the house, there is a reversion to the past tense: "kam nachts aus dem Krähenwald, / suchte Herd und Tisch." There is in these lines, I believe, an implicit social comment, the expression of the speaker's (and poet's) awareness of social injustice. The migrant tinker, like the menial servants ("Magd" and "Knecht"), are intended, despite their individuality, to stand for a specific stratum of society, which might generally be termed the "unprivileged." The tinker does not have the privilege of his own place of shelter but must wander, sometimes coming in from the dark woods to earn some warmth and food. The faithful maidservant must rush out in the early morning hours to work a field, serving ("dienend") the master who is privileged to reap the fruit of her labor.

The stanza about the servant ("Knecht") is somewhat different:

> Und der Knecht, der grübelnd sann,
> war der Tag kaum hell,
> forschend, was die Spinne spann,
> lief im Netz sie schnell,
> seilte sie die Fäden fest,
> zog ein Sturm herauf,
> Regen blieb lang im Geäst,
> war sie träg im Lauf.

Here the figure is not seen at physical labor, but is doing some practical investigation ("forschend," which in its contrast to the past tense "sann" again suggests a passing into the present moment): he is trying to determine what the day's weather will be like by observing the actions of a spider. As is suggested by the rhyme "sann"-"spann," the activity of the spider is meant to parallel, or forecast, the servant's work, though the precise implications of this "correlative" are left unclear. In any case, the stanza does point to the practical everyday wisdom of the simple man, and I detect also a subtle analogy between the activity of the working man and the processes of nature. The factor of social deprivation is not emphasized here, although a sense of discontent is suggested in the word "grübelnd."

In the stanza about the tinker there was a connection, and perhaps even a partial identification, between the speaker and the friends he calls to memory. Its last two lines—"kam nachts aus dem Krähenwald, / suchte Herd und Tisch"—remind the reader of the beginning of the poem—"Dass ich kam im Schattenwind, / weiss davon das Haus?" This sympathetic relationship, ultimately more than "friendship," is the subject of the final stanza—which, significantly, is entirely in the present tense:

> Alle leben noch im Haus:
> Freunde, wer ist tot?
> Euern Krug trink ich noch aus,
> esse euer Brot.
> Und durch Frost und Dunkelheit
> geht ihr schützend mit.
> Wenn es auf die Steine schneit,
> hör ich euern Schritt.

Here all the friends are felt to be present in the house together, as a kind of community, and the elegiac lines of the second stanza ("Und durchs kalte Tor / gehn die Freunde still hinaus, / die ich längst verlor") are answered in these final words, spoken out of awareness and conviction. By recalling this group of people in their productive activity and their unprivileged situation, the speaker senses a continuity between past and present, between their earlier presence and his own reflections. Clearly the poem contains more than merely a "general mood of transitoriness and autumn" ("eine allgemeine Vergänglichkeits- und Herbststimmung"), which is, significantly, all that Wilhelm Lehmann sees in it ("Mass des Lobes").

The same idea of a continuity and identification of interests between the speaker and members of this socially unprivileged class is central to the poem "Der polnische Schnitter," as well as the closely related poems "Der Ziegelstreicher," "Alte Feuerstelle," and "Letzte Fahrt" (all written in the late 1920s and early 1930s). They all tell of an old workingman who wanders the countryside, and all end with the speaker's awareness of his ties with the old man who is now no longer there. Only "Der polnische Schnitter" explicitly names the social evil ("kein Halm war mein eigen") and suggests an appeal to the proletarian movement, and it is also unique among these poems, and rare in Huchel's work as a whole, in that it speaks through a persona. The others are third-

person narrative poems, and the sense of final assurance is not a
confident procession into the rosy Eastern sunrise, as in "Der
polnische Schnitter" ("kehre ich heim ins östliche Land, / in die
Röte des Morgens"), but rather an awakened awareness on the
part of the speaker similar to that in "Herkunft." "Der Ziegelstreicher," for instance, begins "Es kommt der graue Ziegelstreicher, / ich hör im Ahorn seinen Schritt" and ends with the old
man's continued presence in the speaker's memory:

> Es knien im Stall die Kälber nieder,
> die Ochsenglocke schwingt die Nacht.
> Ich hör im Hof den Alten wieder,
> der noch am Rand des Brunnens wacht. (S, 31)

Even more like the figure of the tinker in "Herkunft" is the old
migrant in "Alte Feuerstelle." He too is seen still squatting by the
fire and at work in the farmhouse, and here again the speaker
identifies closely with his suffering (S, 58). The sense of continuity is evoked in the image of the speaker wandering in the
old man's path. The poem ends:

> Er stösst ins Zwielicht mich hinaus,
> dass ich sein Leben finde.
> Ich gehe arm aus meinem Haus
> im bittern Morgenwinde.
>
> Und wo er nachts am Feuer sass,
> steh ich am Distelstrauche.
> Und wandre seine Spur im Gras,
> versengt vom Zackenrauche.

The speaker also retraces a trail at the end of the ballad "Letzte
Fahrt," which, like "Der Knabenteich," is one of Huchel's early
masterpieces. The language is simple, almost sparse, with its short
sentences and the scarcity of rich sensual adjectives. This plain,
"balladesque" style lends itself well to the compact narrative and
characterizes the simple speaker, who is here to be clearly distinguished from the poet. (The old fisherman described as "Mein
Vater" is not Huchel's father.[14]) Despite all the stylistic simplicity

14. Contrast Hamm, "Vermächtnis," p. 482, and Hans-Jürgen Heise, "Peter
Huchels neue Wege," *Neue Deutsche Hefte*, 11 (1964), 104–11; p. 107: "Und so
wird der Weg, der Binsenweg, auf dem einst der Vater ging, schliesslich zum
Weg auf dem nun . . . der Dichter selber zu gehen hat."

and sparsity, the stanzas are uniformly vivid, full of movements, tensions, and nuances. The poem begins:

> Mein Vater kam im Weidengrau
> und schritt hinab zum See,
> das Haar gebleicht vom kalten Tau,
> die Hände rauh vom Schnee.

> Er schritt vorbei am Grabgebüsch,
> er nahm den Binsenweg.
> Hell hinterm Röhricht sprang der Fisch,
> das Netz hing nass am Steg. (S, 27)

In these lines, describing the fisherman making his way to his boat, the man's fate already seems sealed, and the title is hardly needed to indicate that it will be his last outing. Everything he had confronted in his everyday occupation—the dark lake, the sandy, rush-grown path, the hungry fish, his old, wet fishnet, and then his boat ("Der schwarze Kahn, von Nacht beteert")—seems to participate in his death, which is narrated magnificently, with the same calm excitement. Yet it also ends with the image of the path ("Weg"):

> Die Algen kamen kühl gerauscht,
> er sprach dem Wind ein Wort.
> Der tote Hall, dem niemand lauscht,
> sagt es noch immerfort.

> Ich lausch dem Hall am Grabgebüsch,
> der Tote sitzt am Steg.
> In meiner Kanne springt der Fisch.
> Ich geh den Binsenweg.

To read class-consciousness, or even explicit social concern, into this ballad, in which the theme is as generally human as in Goethe's "Der Fischer" or C. F. Meyer's "Im Spätboot," would of course be entirely missing the mark, and even East German critics generally omit it from discussion. Nevertheless, when read in the context of the group of poems which I see as related ("Der polnische Schnitter," "Der Ziegelstreicher," and "Alte Feuerstelle"), "Letzte Fahrt" does perhaps receive this additional dimension, and such lines as "sein Traum und auch sein Leben fuhr / durch Binsen hin und Sand" and "Der tote Hall, dem niemand lauscht" may be interpreted as more than a mere commentary on the neglected life and death of this individual fisherman. At any rate, the notion of continuity between the activity of a man now departed and the concerned awareness of the speaker is there, and it is central to the poem's impact; to this extent the fisherman is still another variant of the tinker in "Herkunft."

The figure of the maidservant ("die Magd") also recurs frequently in Huchel's early poetry. She appears in the poems "Damals," "Am Beifusshang," "Oktoberlicht," "Wilde Kastanie," and "Der glückliche Garten," and in variation in some of his later wartime poems (as "eine Frau aus wendischem Wald," for example, in "Heimkehr"). The presence of the maid is always implied in Huchel's regional landscape; like the tinker and his variants, she forms a constituent part of his pastoral. Her significance can best be studied in the poem which is still perhaps Huchel's best known, the one which is generally felt to be most typically and unmistakably Huchel, "Die Magd" (1926). Here the atmosphere of his province comes alive to all the senses, and hints of his local idiom are masterfully elevated to poetry. The first stanzas read:

> Wenn laut die schwarzen Hähne krähn,
> vom Dorf her Rauch und Klöppel wehn,
> rauscht ins Geläut rehbraun der Wald,
> ruft mich die Magd, die Vesper hallt.
>
> Klaubholz hat sie im Wald geknackt,
> die Kiepe mit Kienzapf gepackt.
> Sie hockt mich auf und schürzt sich kurz,
> schwankt barfuss durch den Stoppelsturz. (S, 12)

The poem tells of the maid's returning to the house with a very young boy, the master's son, after having chopped wood in the forest; her selfless devotion to her chores, and the way in which the boy becomes fully enchanted by her presence. There is throughout something magical and mythic about her: in the beginning her calling to the boy is identified with the toll of the evening churchbells ("ruft mich die Magd, die Vesper hallt"); when she is preparing the boy's supper, she is closer to him than a mother ("Die Magd ist mehr als Mutter noch"); and at the end,

as the boy is falling asleep and she sits knitting by the oil lantern,
she seems a prophetess ("Ihr Strickzeug klirrt und blitzt dabei, /
sie murmelt leis Wahrsagerei").

From a first superficial reading, such as Wilhelm Lehmann's,
"Die Magd" might be thought to be identical in theme and outlook with a poem written in the same years and well known at
the time. In Richard Billinger's (b. 1893) "Die treue Magd," as in
Huchel's poem, the servant-girl is admired for her unflinching
devotion to everyday domestic chores, and her perseverance and
uncomplaining steadfastness seem to give evidence of a nearly
supernatural power.[15] But for Billinger—and this difference is
crucial—the maid's toiling is seen as ultimately justified as part of
the unchanging order of things, and her ability to keep the house-
hold tidy derives from the speaker's conventional sentimental
piety; her loyalty to such matters is considered only natural to
her kind, and as her subsistence now is in the hands of the master
of the house, so her final reward will be meted out by the good
Lord. Another poem by Billinger, "Der alte Knecht," begins and
ends with the same thoughts:

> Ich gehe müde durch das Dorf.
> Ich reinige den Baum vom Schorf.

15. Wie sorgtest du für Hof und Haus!
Du bücktest dich um jeden Span.
Du hobst mit Gott dein Tagwerk an
und löschtest spät dein Lämplein aus.

Was gab dem schwachen Herzen Mut?
Oft staunte ich, wie fröhlich du
die Nacht hingabst der kranken Kuh,
dich sorgtest um der Entlein Brut.

Kein Halm war dein. Und doch, wie stolz
hieltst du vorm Ruf des Hauses Wacht.
Du gabst auf jeden Pfennig acht,
du wuschest, nähtest, sägtest Holz,

du bukst das Brot, du fingst die Maus,
du zogst uns Kinder an die Schuh,
du fandest keine Stunde Ruh,
du gingst ins Feld trotz Sturmgebraus.

Du standst wie in geheimer Haft.
Du klagtest kaum. Du murrtest nie.
Es war, als ob all seine Kraft
der Herrgott deinen Armen lieh.

Billinger, Gedichte (Leipzig, 1929), p. 13

Ich bettle nicht. Ich klage nicht.
Ich tat ja lange schon Verzicht.

. . . .

Das Leben rollt den Sonnenlauf.
Gott hebet all Toten auf
und zeiget schön ein andres Licht.
Ich bete und verzage nicht. (*Gedichte*, p. 81)

"Die treue Magd" is typical "Heimat" poetry, identical in outlook
to all "Blut-und-Boden" literature, and there can be no wonder
that it found its place a few years later in such anthologies of
National Socialist verse as *Rufe in das Reich* (1934) and *Die
Ernte der Gegenwart* (1940).[16]

As a social poet of rural settings, Huchel felt isolated in the
late 1920s. He remarked later that the other socially oriented poets
of the time, with their exclusively urban concern, fatally overlooked "an entire province which Hitler's 'blood-and-soil' poets
later occupied with drum rolls and trumpet fanfares."[17] Yet in his
own poem "Die Magd" Huchel does not suggest any political
solution, nor does he imply that the maid is meant to stand for a
socially exploited class, although this connection is unquestion-
able when the text is read in the context of Huchel's early work
as a whole. She is not presented as a poor girl who suffers because
of her social station, as is the case in an explicitly political poem
with the same title written some eighty years earlier. Moritz Hartmann (1821–72), political poet and journalist at the time of the
revolution of 1848 and after, also wrote a poem entitled "Die
Magd"; in it the servant-girl's activities and frame of mind are
entirely determined by her lowly social status. She addresses the
master's son, whom she secretly loves and who has just left for a
fancy-dress ball, with the words:

"Such eine schöne Braut dir aus
Und nimm auch meinen Segen—

16. *Rufe in das Reich*, p. 220; *Die Ernte der Gegenwart: Deutsche Lyrik von
heute*, ed. Will Vesper (Munich, 1940), p. 229.
17. Quoted in Zak, *Peter Huchel*, p. 32: "Die sich urban gebärenden Literaten
liessen in den zwanziger Jahren eine ganze Provinz unbesetzt, in die später Hitlers
Blut-und-Boden-Poeten mit Pauken und Trompeten einmarschierten."

Ich bin ja nur die Magd vom Haus,
Ich will sie treulich pflegen." [18]

The maid in Huchel's poem, unlike this pining yet resigned crea-
ture, is not plagued by her servile position; yet, unlike Richard
Billinger's trusty housekeeper, she does not go about her business
comforted by the knowledge that her place was ordained by God.
Rather, her very activity and nearness to nature seem to make the
question of class distinction irrelevant. Huchel never condones
an unjust social structure or proposes an ultimate justification for
it; nor does he in this poem and in many others directly attack
class society for the exploitation it brings about. Without idealiz-
ing or sentimentalizing, he shows the transcendence of this conflict in a harmony of productive human activity and the processes
of nature.

The maid's presence is blended with nature throughout the
poem. In the first stanza the sound of her call is not only identified
with the tolling evening bell but also seems to chime in with the
"fawn-colored" rustling of the forest: "rauscht ins Geläut rehbraun der Wald, / ruft mich die Magd, die Vesper hallt." In the
passage about the return home there is a parallel between the
maid laden down with the basket full of kindling wood, the fruits
of a day's labor, and the shaggy goat dragging her teats heavy
with milk:

Klaubholz hat sie im Wald geknackt,
die Kiepe mit Kienzapf gepackt.
Sie hockt mich auf und schürzt sich kurz,
schwankt barfuss durch den Stoppelsturz.

. . . .

Die Geiss, die zottig mit uns streift,
im Bärlapp voll die Zitze schleift.

The identical placement in the stanzas of the words "barfuss"
and "Bärlapp" is further evidence of this implied similarity. Further, the image of the goat's milk-filled mammaries is continued
in the warm, milky smell surrounding the maid as the young boy
grows sleepy in her arms:

18. Hartmann, *Gesammelte Werke*, 10 vols. (Stuttgart, 1874), *1*, 81-82.

> Ich frier, nimm mich ins Schultertuch.
> Warm schlaf ich da im Milchgeruch.
> Die Magd ist mehr als Mutter noch.

Her nearness to nature is again illustrated by the little trick she plays on the way home, the way that she rubs a nut leaf and, as though by magic, the "green" fragrance clings to the boy's hair: "Ein Nussblatt wegs die Magd zerreibt, / dass grün der Duft im Haar mir bleibt." Actually, it is not the fragrance that is "green," but the way in which it "remains" in his hair (the line does not read, "der grüne Duft im Haar mir bleibt"). This adverbial usage is a stylistic technique employed in almost every stanza, eight or nine times in all, and I believe it to be in accordance with the general theme: action and the state of natural phenomena are merged together. Other occurrences of this method are, "rehbraun rauscht . . . der Wald" (twice), "Die Geiss, die zottig . . . streift," "voll die Zitze schleift," "Riedgras saust grau," "kräht müd das Hühnervolk," "die Kruke heiss ins Bett mir schiebt," and "strickt weiss im Petroleumlicht." More than synesthesia, the deliberate confusion of noun and verb, between the state of things and their action, is important here.

The poem as a whole, in fact, deliberately emphasizes the harmony between the maid's activity and the changing state of nature. This intention is made graphically clear by the frame of the poem; the first and last stanzas are:

> Wenn laut die schwarzen Hähne krähn,
> vom Dorf her Rauch und Klöppel wehn,
> rauscht ins Geläut rehbraun der Wald,
> ruft mich die Magd, die Vesper hallt.
>
> Im Stroh die schwarzen Hähne krähn.
> Im Tischkreis Salz und Brot verwehn.
> Der Docht verraucht, die Uhr schlägt alt.
> Und rehbraun rauscht im Schlaf der Wald.

The maid's chore is to bring the young boy of the house home and tuck him in to sleep. The forest is at first filled with the bustling activity of dusk and at the end its rustling is dark and hushed, as though it too had reached a state of slumber. As the maid, she does her job by seeing to it that the little boy is properly tucked in for the night. But she also seems to be more than a maid—she seems to have bewitched all of nature to sleep as well.[19]

This central element of Huchel's idyll, the accordance between productive human activity and the course of nature, is also present in his masterpiece of these years, and one of the finest poems on autumn in the German language:

Oktoberlicht

Oktober, und die letzte Honigbirne
hat nun zum Fallen ihr Gewicht,
die Mücke im Altweiberzwirne
schmeckt noch wie Blut das letzte Licht,
das langsam saugt das Grün des Ahorns aus,
als ob der Baum von Spinnen stürbe,
mit Blättern, zackig wie die Fledermaus,
gesiedet von der Sonne mürbe.

Durchsüsst ist jedes Sterben von der Luft,
vom roten Rauch der Gladiolen,

19. The same idea occurs at the end of the brilliant poem "Damals," which views the situation described in "Die Magd" from the perspective of the boy after he has grown up:

Damals ging noch am Abend der Wind
mit starken Schultern rüttelnd ums Haus.
Das Laub der Linde sprach mit dem Kind,
das Gras sandte seine Seele aus.
Sterne haben den Sommer bewacht
am Rand der Hügel, wo ich gewohnt:
Mein war die katzenäugige Nacht,
die Grille, die unter der Schwelle schrie.
Mein war im Ginster die heilige Schlange
mit ihren Schläfen aus milchigem Mond.
Im Hoftor manchmal das Dunkel heulte,
der Hund schlug an, ich lauschte lange
den Stimmen im Sturm und lehnte am Knie
der schweigsam hockenden Klettenmarie,
die in der Küche Wolle knäulte.
Und wenn ihr grauer schläfernder Blick mich traf,
durchwehte die Mauer des Hauses der Schlaf. (S, 18)

Here the idyll is recalled, the tone is elegiac, and the reader no longer hears the excited voice of the youth relating the events as they happen. But the poem conveys the same notion that the servant-girl is more than her domestic function, that in all her humility she sits like a mighty demiurge, in magical harmony with, and even control over, the processes of the natural world.

bis in den Schlaf der Schwalben wird der Duft
die Traurigkeit des Lichts einholen,
bis in den Schlaf der satten Ackermäuse
poltert die letzte Walnuss ein,
die braun aus schwarzgrünem Gehäuse
ans Licht sprang als ein süsser Stein.

Oktober, und den Bastkorb voll und pfündig
die Magd in Spind und Kammer trägt,
der Garten, nur von ihrem Pflücken windig,
hat sich ins müde Laub gelegt,
und was noch zuckt im weissen Spinnenzwirne,
es flöge gern zurück ins Licht,
das sich vom Ast die letzte Birne,
den süssen Gröps des Herbstes bricht. (S, 24)

In each of these superb stanzas one motif or impression—or rather,
one aspect of the autumn setting—dominates: in the first, dying
and decay; in the second, sweetness; in the third, harvest. Yet all
three stanzas are intricately interrelated, the whole giving a sense
of rounded perfection and, at the same time, progressive development. Sweetness is forecast in the first stanza in the "honey pear"
and in the way the gnat "tastes" the autumn light; and the image
of the walnut emerging brown from its dark-green shell in the
latter part of the second stanza is already suggested in the corresponding lines of the first, where the green of the maple tree is
slowly drained by the last traces of sunlight. The power of the
mellow light to make everything dry and near to death in the first
stanza is countered in the lines that follow by the fragrant sweetness in the air, while sadness and arid dormancy are balanced by
the almost liquid aromas of the garden. Then, in the lines about
the "last walnut," the sense of a resolution is introduced, light and
sweetness merge in their positive qualities with the thought of
harvest.

The first two stanzas deal exclusively with phenomena of
nature—the ripening of fruit, the thick fragrance of plants, insects
dying, and tiny animals settling down to their long, winter sleep.
With the idea of reaping the autumn's harvest, however, attention
turns in the third stanza to human activity and participation. No
longer is the emphasis on the weight of the juicy pear about to

fall from its branch, but on the heaviness of the servant-girl's basket, filled with fruit, which she is busy carrying into the storageroom. The openings of the first and last stanzas stand in clear thematic and rhythmic reference to one another:

> Oktober, und die letzte Honigbirne
> hat nun zum Fallen ihr Gewicht

> Oktober, und den Bastkorb voll und pfündig
> die Magd in Spind und Kammer trägt

Only in the branches of the fruit tree, shaking from the maid's last-minute plucking, is there still movement in the now barren garden. Then, in the closing four lines, comes the final synthesis, and this passage must again be read with reference to the beginning of the poem. The poem's first and last half-stanzas have precisely the same rhyme, and speak of the same phenomena:

> Oktober, und die letzte Honigbirne
> hat nun zum Fallen ihr Gewicht,
> die Mücke im Altweiberzwirne
> schmeckt noch wie Blut das letzte Licht

> und was noch zuckt im weissen Spinnenzwirne,
> es flöge gern zurück ins Licht,
> das sich vom Ast die letzte Birne,
> den süssen Gröps des Herbstes bricht.

In both cases the ripe pear is seen about to fall from the tree, and a tiny insect desperately makes its last effort to free itself from a fatal web. In both cases the element relating the two images is light: the sunlight ripens the fruit and makes it ready to fall, and the gnat struggles to partake of the light, his last lifeblood. But whereas light at the beginning of the poem is a negative force, bringing death (as though by spiders, spinners of the gnat's doom) to nature ("das letzte Licht, / das langsam saugt das Grün des Ahorns aus, / als ob der Baum von Spinnen stürbe"), at the end it serves a useful purpose, bringing autumn's sweetness to the ground to be gathered. The reason for this difference in emphasis regarding the quality of light is the speaker's awareness of harvest, of the maid's productive activity in nature as she culls the ripened fruit. The effects of light and human labor are identical; nature and man collaborate in giving continuity to existence, in drawing further life from death.

Thus, what would seem a melancholy rumination about the cosmic decay of all things in the fall turns out to be the opposite—a praise of the dialectical processes of nature and man's undertakings in their mutual harmony. Again, Wilhelm Lehmann misses the point when he labels the poem an evocation of an autumnal mood of general transience. Huchel's own thematic concern in his early poems might be clarified in their contrast to the verse of Georg Trakl, a poet to whom he feels particularly indebted.[20] The poem "Die Magd," for instance, differs from Trakl's "Die junge Magd" in that it presents an affirmative view of the maid's activity and her magical control over nature instead of rendering a terrifying scene of the young girl's complete disintegration and death in inimical surroundings. Similarly, "Oktoberlicht" is unlike all of Trakl's dismal poems on autumn ("Verfall," "Im Herbst," "Ein Herbstabend," "Herbstseele," "Der Herbst des Einsamen," and the like) in that it leads to an affirmation of autumn as the fruit-bringing season, the time when life is salvaged from all decay. Elegy is answered, perhaps deliberately, by idyll, vision of universal deterioration by a feeling of unity between man at work and nature taking its course.

In order for an idyll, in which fulfillment is reached, to exist, there must be a reality to which it is opposed, in which fulfillment is thwarted. For Huchel this reality lies in existing social conditions, as was perhaps more obvious in the poem "Herkunft" and in the figure of the tinker and its variants. Reality is the miserable social situation of the old man and the passing of his existence into oblivion; the pastoral fulfillment is the sympathetic recollection of the speaker and his feeling of continuity with the departed man's activity. The figure of the maid, too, and particularly the poem "Oktoberlicht," have their counterpart in imperfect reality. The negative complement of "Oktoberlicht" and the idyll of man's unity with nature is "Herbst der Bettler":

20. For Huchel's connection with Trakl, see the introduction to the Czech translation of *Gedichte* (entitled "Twelve Nights") by Ludvik Kundera, *Dvanáct Noci* (Prague, 1958), p. 133.

Das spröde Holz am Brombeerzaun
trug auswärts Früchte viel,
ganz erdige, von Sonne braun
und Regen innen kühl.

Die nachts auf blachem Felde ruhn,
sie kämmten aus das Laub,
eh sie auf drahtgeflickten Schuhn
fortzogen unterm Staub.

Oktoberbüsche, kahl und nass,
verfaulter Nüsse Riss,
im rauhreifübereisten Gras
des Nebels kalter Biss.

Wie eine Wabe, ausgeleert,
die Sonnenblume starrt.
Der Wind, der durch die Dornen fährt,
klirrt wie ein Messer hart. (S, 17)

Here, clearly, the harvesters do not really reap the fruits of autumn, described in the first stanza. Rather, they do their stint of work and move on, drearily and soon forgotten, with their miserly earnings. What autumn leaves them is not bushels of stored fruit, but a nature "bare and wet"; cold, biting mist; and empty, staring sunflowers. The wind seems to clatter like a knife as it blows through the frozen briers. The syntax here grows increasingly choppy; the language is sparse, not rich and abundant as in "Oktoberlicht"; and the alternating rhymes are all masculine, conveying the sense of harsh finality. The "autumn of the beggars," then, autumn seen as social reality, is cruel and unjust, since it negates the potential harmony between man's efforts and the offerings of nature and severs the continuity between dying and further life.

Yet despite occasional directness in his attack on social injustice, Huchel in his early verse is primarily concerned with realization of that harmony and continuity. He writes more of fulfillment than of the frustration of fulfillment; rather, he characteristically answers the facts of social deprivation not with a straightforward accusation but with images of attained justice. These images constitute what I have termed Huchel's idyll. Its two major components are, again, the sense of continuity, dominating the speaker's recollection and awareness, between past, present and future activity (the figure of the tinker and the image of the path, "der Weg"); and the seemingly magical harmony between productive human activity and the processes of nature (the figure of the maid and the image of light, "das Licht"). Huchel expresses this theme, as is clear from the cited examples, in rather conventional forms: generally regular four-line or eight-line stanzas with alternating masculine-feminine rhymes and four or three beats. His poetic vocabulary—characterized by such usages as "Kiepe," "Gröps," "Stake," and "Stoppelsturz"—is firmly rooted in his native province. But over the years Huchel's thematic idyll breaks and, accordingly, stylistic regularity and regional language are gradually abandoned.

Germany's Twelve Nights (1933–45)

Except for some apolitical radio plays and a few unimpressive nature poems which appeared in the periodical *Das Innere Reich* (1935–36), Huchel published nothing during the years 1933–45. He even withheld the equivalent of an entire volume of his earlier poetry, lest it be associated with the kind of nature verse approved by National Socialism. His practical answer to those twelve years of terror was silence and noncooperation. Although he never joined an active resistance organization, he remained as untainted by the barbarism surrounding him as anyone could have who survived without going into exile.

As his friend Alfred Kantorowicz recalls in his book *Deutsche Schicksale* (1949), Huchel wrote many poems in these years of outward silence, but most of them were destroyed and lost during a bombing attack.[21] Only a few have survived or were reconstructed from the author's memory, and these were first published in 1948 in Huchel's first volume, *Gedichte*, which consisted mainly of his early poems. *Gedichte* was republished, with some changes, as *Die Sternenreuse* in 1967. For the most part the works of these years ("Späte Zeit," "Zwölf Nächte," "In memoriam Hans A. Joachim," "Deutschland," "Der Rückzug," "Der Vertriebene,"

21. Vienna, 1964, p. 79.

"Griechischer Morgen," and "Heimkehr") constitute a marked artistic decline from his output of the period 1926–32, as Huchel himself is well aware. Despite their bitterly plaintive tone, these poems are rather feeble as reactions to the historical catastrophe of the time; confronted with events of universal significance, Huchel was forced to relinquish his idyllic province, and, like so many of the "inner emigrants," he had recourse only to a rather vague, moralizing humanism. The concrete detail is lost, and with it the rich local color of his vocabulary. What remains is often no more than a futile appeal to the enduring "Geist":

> Späteste Söhne, rühmet euch nicht,
> einsame Söhne, hütet das Licht.
> Dass es von euch in Zeiten noch heisst,
> dass nicht klirret die Kette, die gleist,
> leise umschmiedet, Söhne, den Geist. (S, 79)

In the poem "Zwölf Nächte" (written in 1938; the numerical correspondence with the twelve years of National Socialist rule is coincidental) Huchel again warns his partners against the murderers' darkness; but his final optimism, with its reference to "the soul's silent light," could hardly have been very encouraging (S, 77). Despite their admirable intention, poems like these were totally helpless as expressions of resistance and hope because of the vagueness and abstractness of their language and imagery. Huchel's truly significant poems about the period of National Socialism, and particularly about the war, were written later, in the 1950s. They were originally included in the chronicle "Das Gesetz," and they will be discussed in the section on "The Law."

Nevertheless, a brief study of the poems from these years is crucial to an understanding of Huchel's development from those idylls of social concern in the 1920s to his short-lived flash of faith in East German land reform in the postwar years. Indeed, some of these poems and stanzas are, I think, outstanding when compared with other oppositional poetry written within Germany at the time. Such a poem as "Späte Zeit" (1933), for example, compares favorably with any German verse "written to the wind" ("An den Wind geschrieben," the title of an anthology of "lyrics of freedom, 1933–1945" [22]):

22. Manfred Schlösser, ed., *An den Wind geschrieben: Lyrik der Freiheit 1933–1945* (Darmstadt, 1960).

Still das Laub am Baum verklagt.
Einsam frieren Moos und Grund.
Über allen Jägern jagt
hoch im Wind ein fremder Hund.

Überall im nassen Sand
liegt des Waldes Pulverbrand,
Eicheln wie Patronen.

Herbst schoss seine Schüsse ab,
leise Schüsse übers Grab.

Horch, es rascheln Totenkronen,
Nebel ziehen und Dämonen. (S, 75)

The tranquil, plaintive natural setting becomes infested with deadly firearms; acorns falling from the trees are like autumn's ammunition trained on the landscape. The whole is like a "late-hour" intimation of imminent evil, sorrow giving way to horror, demonic death masks penetrating all of nature. Most interesting, particularly for Huchel's development, is the way in which the formal regularity begins to break down. The four-line stanza with alternating rhyme scheme, characteristic of his earlier "landscapes," is still present at the beginning of the poem but immediately dissolves into a three-line form with a dangling rhyme (aab) and ends with two rhymed couplets. It is as though the impressions strike the speaker with such force that he is no longer able to sustain them.

A disintegration of poetic conventions is only forecast in "Späte Zeit"; rhyme is still retained, and a perfectly regular four-beat trochaic meter prevails. This process, here only hinted at, first becomes fully manifest in the poetry written after the war, in the 1950s. Other poems of the period 1933–45 generally remain regular in form. More characteristic for these years is that nature—in his early poems the site of a magical harmony between man and his surroundings, a kind of "intact world" ("heile Welt")—is now wounded, shot through with images of destruction and horror. Ashes, blood, and howling corpses now fill Huchel's landscape, replacing the lively frogs and water sprites. The season is winter, and the trees are stripped bare of their foliage.

This scenery appears most powerfully in the poems written

during the war, which Huchel was forced to experience at first
hand. (He was drafted into service in 1940 and sent to the Eastern
Front.) He relates what he saw in a little poem in the style of
the German baroque lyric; it stands at the beginning of the cycle
"Der Rückzug," as a kind of motto:

> Ich sah des Krieges Ruhm.
> Als wärs des Todes Säbelkorb,
> durchklirrt von Schnee, am Strassenrand
> lag eines Pferds Gerippe.
> Nur eine Krähe scharrte dort im Schnee nach Aas,
> wo Wind die Knochen nagte, Rost das Eisen frass. (S, 81)

At the center of the poem, and of nature, lies the horse's carcass
on the snowy roadside, the horror of the scene underlined by the
two long, rhymed lines which follow. What opens as a praise of
"war's glory" ends with the image of nature feeding on its own
death, a lone crow and the winter wind gnawing on the corpse's
bones. Even the bones seem like rusty iron, like the ribs of a
discarded saber case.

The same setting, the wayside on the retreat homeward, is
presented in the third poem of the cycle, and here more than
anywhere else, I think, style and tone anticipate the poems in the
volume *Chausseen Chausseen* (1963). The wartime poem begins:

> Am Bahndamm rostet das Läutwerk.
> Schienen und Schwellen starren zerrissen,
> zerschossen die Güterwagen.
>
> Auf der Chaussee;
> den Schotter als Kissen,
> vom Sturz zersplitterter Pappeln erschlagen
> liegt eine Frau im schwarzen Geäst.
>
> Noch klagt ihr Mund
> hart an der Erde.
> In offene Augen
> fällt Regen und Schnee. (S, 83)

Image quickly follows image, leading from a landscape strewn
with wreckage to the futile weeping of women trampled in chaotic
flight. Huchel is here still bound to the complete sentence, and

he does not yet depart too far from the four-line stanza. But it is clear that the direction is away from both conventions; verbs receive less emphasis syntactically (especially "liegt" and "fällt"), and rhyme and regular rhythm are abandoned. There is only one further step in development (rather than a sudden stylistic break) in the text to the magnificent title poem of *Chausseen Chausseen*, first published in 1950:

> Erwürgte Abendröte
> Stürzender Zeit!
> Chausseen. Chausseen.
> Kreuzwege der Flucht.
> Wagenspuren über den Acker,
> Der mit den Augen
> Erschlagener Pferde
> Den brennenden Himmel sah.
>
> Nächte mit Lungen voll Rauch,
> Mit hartem Atem der Fliehenden,
> Wenn Schüsse
> Auf die Dämmerung schlugen.
> Aus zerbrochenem Tor
> Trat lautlos Asche und Wind,
> Ein Feuer,
> Das mürrisch das Dunkel kaute.
>
> Tote,
> Über die Gleise geschleudert,
> Den erstickten Schrei
> Wie einen Stein am Gaumen.
> Ein schwarzes
> Summendes Tuch aus Fliegen
> Schloss ihre Wunden. (CC, 59)

The images and poetic situation are essentially the same here as in the earlier poem, just as the most striking stylistic features— varied short lines and incomplete syntax—are already present in the cycle "Der Rückzug." Huchel does not suddenly emerge with a totally "new style" in the 1950s, abbreviated, lapidary verses replacing as though overnight the songlike conjurings of more innocent years.[23] Rather, as the idyll of the prewar period was

23. Cf. Rino Sanders, "Peter Huchel: Chausseen Chausseen," *Neue Rundschau*, 75 (1964), 324–29.

wounded and disrupted with the poet's experience of the terror and nightmarish havoc of National Socialism and war, his reliance on poetic conventions had to give way, and his style, too, became gradually more fragmented.

In addition to the disintegration of stylistic regularity, there is also evidence in the wartime cycle "Der Rückzug" of the disruption of Huchel's thematic idyll. The two emblematic figures who had inhabited his early landscapes, the maidservant and the tinker, appear again here. Both, however, have been divorced from their productive activity and their idyllic significance. The female figure who had embodied perfect harmony with nature, sometimes even seeming to magically control its processes, has now become nature's victim crushed by the fall of splintered poplars ("vom Sturz zersplitterter Pappeln erschlagen / liegt eine Frau im schwarzen Geäst"). The old man wandering through the countryside and squatting over smoky fires (the variant of the tinker figure) appears in the wartime poem "Der Vertriebene" (S, 90); here, however, he is seen without any productive function, an outcast roaming in aimless bewilderment through dark forests. In contrast to the early poems "Der polnische Schnitter," "Der Ziegelstreicher," "Alte Feuerstelle," and "Letzte Fahrt," the migrant's path here is endless, the poem containing no final sense of continuity between the figure's former activity and the speaker's vivid recollection of his presence. Thus, the poet's concern for social deprivation has been overshadowed by the fact that nature itself, gravely wounded by the war, has become inimical to man, no longer the site of that harmonious human activity by which the worker could transcend the injustices of the social order.

The haunting, threatening presence of war and death in the pastoral landscape so familiar to the poet in his youth (as, for example, in "Der Knabenteich") may be seen in the poem "Die Schattenchaussee" (S, 84), the fourth in the cycle "Der Rückzug." (Alfred Kantorowicz included this poem in his anthology *Verboten und verbrannt*, 1947.) Here again the speaker is lying at the reedy lakeside, taking in the smells and sights of the marshy setting ("Ich lag zwischen Weiden auf moorigem Grund / im Nebel verschilfter Seen"). But, as the first line suggests ("Sie spürten mich auf. Der Wind war ihr Hund"), the scene is now haunted; it is really a hiding place from pursuing shadows, lined with barbed wire, the worked soil charred by oily flames. A frightening procession of dead men darkens the skies.

Yet here, in this fine example of rural "rubble poetry" ("Trümmerlyrik"), there shines at the end the light of hope. The speaker, washing the taste of blood and sand from his mouth, sees the rising sun reflected on the murky water. The great retreat, filled with such horrifying visions of death and destruction, leads to a final redemption, with the light of morning breaking through the darkened clouds. The next poem (as the group "Der Rückzug" appears in the volume *Die Sternenreuse*) tells of springtime showers ("des Frühjahrs Regengüsse"), and the cycle ends with two hymnic stanzas about the April "night of mourning": "O Nacht der Trauer, Nacht April, / die ich im Feuerdunst durchschwamm" (S, 89). It is the time of rebirth, the plow again set to tilling the grave-studded field:

> O Grund der Welt, noch ungebunden,
> o Pflug, der Gräber nicht verletzt,
> o Mensch, verloren und gefunden

The poet can once again praise the immortal earth and nature's processes. In "Griechischer Morgen" the speaker asks,

> zarteste Kraft des Halms,
> der die Erde durchstösst,
> darf ich euch preisen,
> eh nicht der Mensch den Menschen erlöst? (S, 91)

The question is reminiscent of Brecht's famous lines in his poem "An die Nachgeborenen" (1939), "Was sind das für Zeiten, wo / Ein Gespräch über Bäume fast ein Verbrechen ist / Weil es ein Schweigen über so viele Untaten einschliesst!" For Huchel, however, times had changed by 1946, and the Greek captive in his poem can praise nature even at the moment of his execution ("sein Auge preist / unsterbliches Land, / das Freiheit heisst, / atmende Erde, Feuer der Frühe, / ehe ins Dunkel / die Kugel ihn reisst").

Some of the poems at the end of the volume *Gedichte*, including parts of the cycle "Der Rückzug," "Griechischer Morgen" and "Heimkehr," were written immediately after the war, and in them the general mood and themes of the chronicle "Das Gesetz" are already present. In the very last poem, "Heimkehr," the continuity from the idyll in Huchel's early poetry through destruction to the sense of regained unity between man and nature after the war is clearly evident. In the first stanza the speaker returns to familiar rural surroundings:

> Unter der schwindenden Sichel des Mondes
> kehrte ich heim und sah das Dorf
> im wässrigen Dunst der Gräben und Wiesen. (S, 92)

It is not the same anymore, though—the walls of the houses are crumbling and, as is emphasized through the entire stanza, there has been no harvest. The fruit-giving plants have been choked off by a freezing rain and lack of summer sunshine:

> Soll ich wie Schatten zerrissener Mauern
> hausen im Schutt, das Tote betrauern,
> soll ich die schwarze Schote enthülsen,
> die am Zaun der Sommer vergass,
> sammeln den Hafer rissig und falb,
> den ein eisiger Regen zerfrass?
> Fauliger Halm auf fauligem Felde—
> niemand brachte die Ernte ein.
> Nessel wuchert, Schierling und Melde,
> Hungerblume umklammert den Stein.

But in the frosty morning new signs of life begin to appear as a female figure, the same maidservant known to him in his boyhood ("eine Frau aus wendischem Wald"), emerges from the dark forest to resume tilling. She knows that there will be a harvest this year, even though soil and plow have stood untouched for so long ("Sah sie schon Schwalbe und Saat? / Hämmernd schlug sie den Rost vom Pflug"). Once again she is given mythical import at the end, seen as the mother of the rising morning and of the survivors climbing out from the heaps of rubble ("Mutter der Frühe," "Mutter der Völker"). Sky, mist, and wind are unchanged as she takes to plowing the long-neglected field. This flat and rather sentimental poem cannot compare in richness and simplicity to Huchel's early verse. It is not entirely unsuccessful as a suggestion of the wreckage done to the poet's native terrain and the rebirth of hope as the work of reconstruction begins. But the optimism seems on the whole unconvincing, and the linguistic wealth of earlier years is not recovered. Huchel does not really return to his home ground but to an illusion of continuity growing out of his desperation at the sight of irreparable loss.

But the poem "Heimkehr" is important in a study of Huchel's development because it anticipates the subject of his poetic concern in the 1950s. It illustrates that, simultaneous with the official legislation of land reform of 1945 in what was then the Soviet Occupied Zone, and even before the general collectivization of 1952, the poet had high hopes for the establishment of social justice in the rural areas of his wartorn country. Even in Huchel's early poems, where the idyll of human harmony with nature's processes was drawn in contrast to a social reality in which harmony was blocked ("Oktoberlicht" and "Herbst der Bettler"), the call for institutionalization of social justice was at least implicit. The poet's later praise of the "law" of land reform is not to be viewed as a sudden sacrifice in answer to official decrees, an unwilling turn to a theme totally incongruous with all earlier poetic concerns. Rather, the cycle "Das Gesetz" was the logical continuation and in a way, the culmination of his sympathy for the unprivileged classes inhabiting the countryside of his origin.

However, as mentioned, this theme is only one aspect of Huchel's poetry in its later development. Experience of the terror of National Socialism and the war's destruction had shattered the poet's image of a nature in which any harmony is conceivable and fragmented his poetic means. Literary conventions could no longer be relied on to express the horror and chaos which penetrated his world, and even the sense of security offered by syntactic regularity was already dwindling. In poems set on the rubble-lined trek homeward, mere associations and rows of abbreviated signs and images began to determine course and direction. Thus, while "Heimkehr" and "O Trauer der Nacht, Nacht April" lead to the optimistic passages of Huchel's poetry of the early 1950s, which approximate closely the socialist-realist verse of the time, the poem "Am Bahndamm rostet das Läutwerk . . ." sets the style and tone for much of the volume *Chausseen Chausseen*. It is this latter aspect —the enduring feeling of pessimism and uncertainty and the "splintered," cryptic poetic technique—with which Huchel has continued to identify over the past decade; whereas he has consciously dissociated himself from the songs of praise and images of hope in which language seemed to have regained its full richness but had in fact become feeble and empty. Both these aspects—the dark, fragmented verse and the light, hymnic style—reveal elements which figure in the poet's final disillusionment in the later 1950s.

The Law (1945–53)

On September 3, 1945, a plan for thoroughgoing land reform was declared in Saxony. The announcement, which was shortly echoed in the other provinces of the Soviet Occupied Zone, began: "Democratic land reform is an urgent national, economic, and social necessity. The land reform must insure the liquidation of feudal Junker estates and put an end to the domination by Junkers and great landowners in the village, because this domination has always represented a bastion of reaction and fascism in our country and was one of the main sources of aggression and wars of conquest against other peoples. Through land reform the centuries-old dream of landless and land-poor peasants is to be fulfilled by the transfer of extensive landed property into their hands."[24] Practically, this rural reform—which was soon followed by similar measures in the area of industry—involved the confiscation without compensation of all estates of more than 250 acres, as well as land owned by those considered former Nazis or Junkers or used by officials and organizations of National Socialism. Existing farms of under 12.5 acres were enlarged and the expropriated holdings were parceled out to landless peasants, refugees, agricultural workers, and small tenants. This initial step was followed on Octo-

24. *Volks-Zeitung*, September 8, 1945; quoted in *DDR*, ed. Ernst Deurlein (Munich, 1966), p. 51: "Die demokratische Bodenreform ist eine unaufschiebbare nationale, wirtschaftliche und soziale Notwendigkeit. Die Bodenreform muss die Liquidierung des feudaljunkerlichen Grossgrundbesitzes gewährleisten und der Herrschaft der Junker und Grossgrundbesitzer im Dorfe ein Ende bereiten, weil diese Herrschaft immer eine Bastion der Reaktion und des Faschismus in unserem Lande darstellte und eine der Hauptquellen der Aggression und der Eroberungskriege gegen andere Völker war. Durch die Bodenreform soll der jahrhundertealte Traum der landlosen und landarmen Bauern von der Übergabe des Grossgrundbesitzes in ihre Hände erfüllt werden."

ber 20 in Brandenburg by the formation of Committees for Mutual
Peasants' Assistance, which were merged in early 1946 into the
Union of Mutual Peasants' Assistance (Vereinigung der gegen-
seitigen Bauernhilfe—VdgB). Through this association new land-
owning farmers received help and guidance from factory workers,
unions, experienced farmers, and "knowledgeable advisers" (often
totally inexperienced Soviet functionaries).

From these steps it is clear that the tendency toward collectivization was already present in the period immediately after the war.
The objective of collectivizing agricultural production was not
declared, however, until the Second Party Congress in 1952, when
the establishment of cooperatives, "landwirtschaftliche Produk-
tionsgenossenschaften" (LPG), was announced. What happened
in the time from the initial land reform in 1945 to collectivization in
1952 is explained in official East German sources as an indispensable stage in the process of revolutionary social transformation:
only by first distributing the land among the formerly landless
classes could the way be prepared for agricultural cooperatives
whereby local administrative organs would eventually govern
productive procedures.[25]

The "law" which inspired Huchel's postwar hopes was the
initial land reform, and the period in which these hopes lived were
the years of transition—that is, the years after the exploited agricultural laborers were given the land they worked and before the
founding of officially regulated collectives. In the early 1950s
Huchel described his verse chronicle "Das Gesetz"; it is clear that
his enthusiasm was only for the earliest phases of the rural transformation: " 'The Law' is life itself. . . . With the law the real
day dawns. Out of the grave of a rotten epoch it ascends as the
living word. It means nothing but man. It takes form in the exploited man who becomes free, in the landless who find their
farms and their homeland. The law sows and grows with the seed,
it reaps and places bread on our tables. It is the sustaining reason
for everything that happens, making real the dream of centuries." [26]

25. See Doernberg, *Kurze Geschichte der DDR*, pp. 51–52.
26. Quoted in Zak, *Der Dichter*, pp. 56–57: "Das Gesetz ist das Leben selbst.
. . . Mit dem Gesetz hebt der wahre Tag an. Aus der Gruft einer verfaulten
Epoche fährt es als lebendiges Wort. Es meint nichts anderes als den Menschen.
Es nimmt Gestalt an in dem Geknechteten, der frei wird, in den Landlosen, die
Hof und Heimat finden. Es sät, erntet und legt uns das Brot auf den Tisch. Es

Huchel was not at all unfriendly toward the first impulses of social change in the Eastern part of Germany, and he did not have to be directed to concentrate his poetic energies on the difference made by what seemed the institutionalization of social justice.

Land reform meant for Huchel the accordance of civil law and the laws of nature; he saw it as an act of legislation inscribed in the cornfields as they were tilled. The hymnic section which forms the resolution of his chronicle begins:

> O Gesetz,
> mit dem Pflug in den Acker geschrieben,
> mit dem Beil in die Bäume gekerbt!
> Gesetz, das das Siegel der Herren zerbrochen,
> zerrissen ihr Testament! [27]

Here for the first time—and the only time in Huchel's poetry—the tone is all enthusiasm, a praise of life and nature in full voice, without the elegiac suggestions formerly pervading his verse: "O Stunde des ersten Tags, / der die Tore der Finsternis sprengt! / O Licht, das den Halm aus der Wurzel treibt!" These exclamations, I believe, are sincere, but the language and imagery have become hopelessly conventional and obvious. Such phrases are "Tore der Finsternis" and dark-light metaphors belong to the most common clichés of poets imitating the platitudes of Johannes R. Becher; they dominated, for example, the poetry of Stephan Hermlin and Franz Fühmann from the same years. Yet there is no denying the genuineness of Huchel's affirmation. Land reform was not only an act of social legislation, but a reform of the land itself. By becoming the property of the people, the soil itself was transformed from what it had been—an inimical, devouring element—into something personal and intimate:

> Dein ist mit schwarzen Kiemen die Erde,
> wenn sie in rauher Furche liegt,
> tief gelockert und atmend im Schnee.
> Nicht Maul mehr,
> Fleisch von den Knochen zu zerren,

---

ist der tragende Grund für alles, was geschieht, indem es den Traum von Jahrhunderten wirklich macht."

27. Most of the fragments of "Das Gesetz" appeared in *Sinn und Form, 2* (1950), 127–36.

nicht länger auf Wucher ausgeliehen,
nicht Distelbrache,
nicht Hungeracker der Armen.

Alternating and mingling with the image of the earth as parasitic
jaws is the factor of social deprivation ("auf Wucher ausgeliehen,"
"Hungeracker der Armen"), the suggestion being that the field
itself was sapping the harvest from the exploited farmhands.

With land reform, of course, Huchel considered this situation
overcome once and for all. Yet, interestingly, Huchel does not
describe social justice after it has been realized, the positive results
of land reform, but rather concerns himself with the act of exe-
cuting the law. The remainder of the section beginning "O
Gesetz" takes the form of mild imperatives, the speaker appealing
to the people to take over the land given to them, to work it and
reap the produce of their labors. The legislated reform, in fact, is
made to resemble a kind of popular uprising:

So leg den neuen Grund!
Volk der Chausseen,
zertrümmerter Trecks!
Reiss um den Grenzstein des Guts!

All seems spontaneous, the law is put into effect by the sheer will
and productive activity of the masses, a reflection of events fully
in line with the official Party explanation.[28] One wonders whether,
for the sake of historical accuracy, some mention should not be
made of the Soviet army, which was always ready at hand to meet
any resistance to the confiscatory measures. What interests
Huchel, though, is not so much the technical implementation of
the law, but that the new land-holders make real the potential
benefits by gathering an abundant harvest. In his poem he calls on
them, no longer servile, to break the soil and cultivate it, for the
harvest too will be their own. In this way "Das Gesetz" is directed
toward the future. The speaker's enthusiasm derives, not from a
sense of fulfillment, but from his optimistic hope in a glorious
reality to come.

Huchel's other verse cycle of these postwar years, "Bericht aus
Malaya," is also art dedicated to a brighter future; in fact, here the

28. See Doernberg, Kurze Geschichte, pp. 48–57 ("Die demokratische Bodenreform").

forward-looking tendency is proclaimed programmatically. The
"report," composed as a dramatic dialogue for six voices, tells of
the battle of the Malayans against Japanese domination. A young
Malayan soldier loses confidence in the struggle but symbolically
regains assurance and commitment as the artist Wei Dun learns
from the old masters how to paint "images of hope." Here Huchel
is at his low point aesthetically, in part at least because the Asian
setting is so obviously unfamiliar to him, and the work is hardly
worth discussion. One brilliant section has remained part of
Huchel's opus, the poem "Wei Dun und die alten Meister," in
which the young painter studies the works of the masters and discovers only scenes of horror. The version included in *Chausseen
Chausseen* contains the powerful stanza:

> O alte Meister, ich schabte den Tuschstein.
> Ich wusch die Pinsel aus Ziegenhaar.
> Doch als ich streifte im Rücken des Feindes,
> Sah ich die unbewässerten Felder,
> Das Schöpfrad zerschossen, im harten Geschirr
> Starr hängen den Ochsen am Göpel,
> Die Tempelhalle, ausgeplündert,
> Wo auf dem Schutt lasierter Kacheln
> Im weissen Mittag die Schlange schlief. (CC, 34)

Following on this section in the original context, however, was the
poem "Die Bilder der Hoffnung," which constitutes a direct proclamation of socialist realism expressed through the persona of Wei
Dun's teacher. The relevance of this passage to "Das Gesetz" is
obvious:

> "Nicht male den Bauern Deng Ling-ban,
> Wie du ihn siehst, im Dunst der kalten Strasse,
> Wenn er von Hütte zu Hütte schleicht
> Und wässrigen Reis erbetteln muss.
>
> Male Deng auf eigenem Acker,
> Den er doch bald bestellen wird.
>
> . . . .
>
> Denn Saat und Ernte gehören ihm
> Und Licht und Dunkel und Wind und Regen.
> Er trägt auf seinen Schultern das Jahr.

Nicht immer male, was du siehst.
Male die Bilder der Hoffnung!"
Und langsam kam das Wissen zu mir. (72) [29]

Wei Dun (and Huchel) has learned to describe reality not only
as it is, in all its unconsoling horror, but also it can and will be
when it is changed by human activity. When it is viewed with
socialist knowledge ("das Wissen"), this improved future condition already exists in the present.

The poem "Chronik des Dorfes Wendisch-Luch," intended to
be incorporated into "Das Gesetz" and actually constituting a
miniature of that entire chronicle, provides a sample of Huchel's
socialist realism and illustrates the relationship between his awakened hope in agricultural reform and the idyll of his early poetry.
It first appeared in *Sinn und Form* in 1951 and was included in
many East German anthologies of the 1950s.[30] In this poem, dedicated "to the pioneers of all reconstructed villages," language and
setting are unmistakably Huchel's own, but the techniques and
direction are typical of prescribed socialist realism. At the beginning of the poem an old woman is seen returning to the village
after a day's hard labor in the fields. She is clearly to be identified
with the maid figure in Huchel's early poems:

Am Fahrweg, hinter Wendisch-Luch,

.   .   .   .

seh ich die Alte heimwärts gehn,
holzschleppend durch den Regenschauer,
geduckt ins grobe Schultertuch.

The time historically is after the land reform ("Sie kann dem
Licht des Dorfs vertrauen," "Sie findet ihre Milche im Krug"),
but because she is thinking of earlier conditions ("Denkt sie an
das, was längst versank? / An Brand und Qual und Hunger-
wochen?") the surroundings seem still desolate and unfriendly.
Nothing appears to have been realized yet:

29. Sections of the chronicle, which was written in the late 1940s, appeared in
Neue Deutsche Literatur, 4 (1956), 65–74.
30. For example, Günther Deicke, ed., *Im werdenden Tag* (Leipzig, 1958), pp.
54–57; *Menschen und Werke*, ed. "Deutscher Schriftsteller-Verband" (East Berlin,
1952), pp. 124–27; and *Wir, unsere Zeit: Gedichte aus zehn Jahren*, Christa and
Gerhard Wolf, ed., (East Berlin, 1959), pp. 68–71.

Unwirkliche Stunde,
da regenflötend
die Amsel huscht
aus sinkendem Tag,
das letzte Licht im Nebel tötend
mit einem schwarzen Flügelschlag.

The long middle section is a flashback to the misery of former years, first the war and before, then the very beginning of rebirth. With continuing activity and struggle among the rubble heaps, past gives way to present, and the legislated land reform, not directly mentioned here, appears as the natural result of productive labor. The crucial day, presumably when the law was declared, is described:

Windstiller Tag,
ich sah die Männer säen
Breitsaat von Hand das letzte Korn.
Heuheisser Tag
und spätes Grummetmähen;
die Hungerharke klirrte durch den Dorn.

At the end is a hymn of praise to all nature and human productivity ("O Mensch und Himmel, Tier und Wald, / o Acker, der vom Wetzstein hallt"), and the figure of the peasant woman is generalized to stand for all of the "pioneers" who have overcome exploitation.

The idyll of the maidservant, her magical harmony with nature, by which she seemed to transcend the fact of social injustice, is here realized in society. The legislation of agricultural reform meant for Huchel the institutionalization of the harmony between man and nature in social reality. Autumn is no longer the season when slaving migrants are tragically deprived of the fruit of their labor, as it was in "Herbst der Bettler"; the harvest is now their own. The last lines in the poem, which sing of this realized idyll, are obviously meant to contrast with the dismal earlier times:

O wirkliche Stunde,
da laubkühl flötend
die Amsel huscht
im werdenden Tag,

die eisengraue Frühe rötend
mit einem leisen Flügelschlag.

What began with rather strong language and concrete imagery, rooted in the local setting of the province Brandenburg, ends with the "fluttering wings of sunrise," the most inevitable of all socialist-realist clichés. All subtlety and concreteness vanish and give way to the empty phrases of a schematic optimism. The image of "die eisengraue Frühe" may be impressive, but generally when Huchel glorifies institutions and a predetermined future his language tends to become "popular" and "generally accessible" in the lowest sense. Vocabulary and imagery are most often "common" and outworn.

Huchel was fully aware of the debasing effect on poetic language of the narrowly conceived criterion of "Volkstümlichkeit," as is clear in a statement he made in the early 1950s. East German critics generally cite only the first sentences, in which Huchel sees the beauty of much poetry to lie in its absorption of the language of the people and in which he condemns as artificial a poetic language divorced from life. But he goes on, the main thrust of his argument being directed against the demands for "comprehensibility" and common language "by 'critics' who do not know what popular language is, not to speak of its richness. This trivial demand is an insult to the people, . . . who do not fish lazily in the mud hole of a stale language. Then why should we? The people have more imagination and are more poetical than unimaginative and unpoetic minds can conceive of." [31] It is no wonder that Huchel placed Brecht's essay on "Volkstümlichkeit und Realismus" at the beginning of one issue of *Sinn und Form* (1958).

Huchel was also conscious of the inferior quality of his poetry affirming the "law" and "images of hope": he now dissociates himself completely from "Chronik des Dorfes Wendisch-Luch" and

---

31. Quoted in Zak, p. 28: "Aber schreiben aus dem Lebensgefühl des arbeitenden Menschen heraus heisst nicht, die auf den Hund gekommene Sprache der Kleinbürger benutzen, um sich 'verständlich' zu machen, was von einigen 'Kritikern', die nicht die Volkssprache kennen, geschweige deren Reichtum, manchmal gefordert wird. Diese platte Forderung ist eine Beleidigung für das Volk! . . . Das Volk fischt nicht träge im Teich der abgestandenen Sprache. Warum sollen wir es tun? Das Volk ist phantasievoller und musischer, als phantasielose und unmusische Köpfe sich vorstellen können."

from most other parts of the cycles "Das Gesetz" and "Bericht aus Malaya." I have considered them in some detail because they are revealing as to the evolution of Huchel's pastoral treatment of man and nature. The idyllic harmony, which in the early poems was juxtaposed to a social reality in which this harmony was denied, was seen with land reform to have been realized, or at least potentially realized, in the social order itself. Society itself became a pastoral on the verge of fulfillment, and it is the object of the poet's hymnic praise.

Yet Huchel's poetry from the first decade after the war is not all affirmative and resolutely optimistic. In the verse "report" from Malaya the painter Wei Dun has to see scenes of horror ("Bilder des Schreckens") before he can learn of the "images of hope," and in the chronicle about land reform the redeeming law necessarily follows from a state of lawlessness and chaos. Significantly, Huchel retained in his opus only the poem "Wei Dun und die alten Meister" and, from the cycle "Das Gesetz," only those sections about the period preceding the land reform. He recognized, therefore, the uniformly perishable nature of his socialist-realist verse expressing approval of social changes in East Germany. He was also clearly aware that he had maintained high poetic quality only in the poems (such as "Wei Dun und die alten Meister," "Chausseen," "Dezember 1942," and "Bericht des Pfarrers vom Untergang seiner Gemeinde") in which he attempted to recapture the atmosphere of the war's end and the chaotic retreat amid the scattered wreckage. Together with the hymnic and hope-filled strain of Huchel's writing from the period 1945–55, a mood of uncertainty and a corresponding stylistic fragmentation are also present in his verse of these years.

The style of the fine poem "Chausseen," which originally appeared toward the beginning of "Das Gesetz" (1950), is characteristic of Huchel's "Trümmerlyrik." Syntax is reduced to noun phrases, blurted out between gasps of breath:

Erwürgte Abendröte
Stürzender Zeit!
Chausseen. Chausseen.
Kreuzwege der Flucht.

The entire dusky setting seems to be choking, along with the throngs in desperate flight: "Nächte mit Lungen voll Rauch, / Mit hartem Atem der Fliehenden." The landscape appears unreal in its dreadful reality, the trampled fields staring at flaming skies "with the eyes of murdered horses." Finally, there are the victims fallen by the wayside, their last screams caught in their throats:

> Tote,
> Über die Gleise geschleudert,
> Den erstickten Schrei
> Wie einen Stein am Gaumen.

To close the poem, even their wounds are closed off by swarming flies, "Ein schwarzes / Summendes Tuch aus Fliegen." The images are consistently powerful and richly evocative, and their quick sequence and the staccato two- and three-beat rhythm are perfectly appropriate to a speaker too frightened and horror-stricken to even contemplate the gruesome scenery. Appropriately, this chaotic scene is presented in a totally alogical, associative sequence; but the poet never loses control, and the complex texture at no point appears disparate or arbitrary. Each stanza is masterfully calculated, as is the progression of stanzas, from the nightmarish landscape to the terrified men fleeing breathlessly from incessant gunfire to dead victims abandoned to the flies. The poem is lacking in all consolation, at least in its final version in *Chausseen Chausseen*.[32] The tone is never sentimental or overheated but remains one of chilled, almost calm excitement. The speaker's sullen mood resembles the nighttime fire, "ein Feuer, / das mürrisch das Dunkel kaute."

The same style characterizes the somewhat more comforting poem "Der Treck," with the magnificent opening stanza:

> Herbstprunk der Pappeln.
> Und Dörfer
> Hinter der Mauer
> Aus Hundegeheul,
> Am Torweg
> Eingekeilt der Riegel,

---

32. Significantly (and fortunately) the feeble last lines of the text as it appeared in "Das Gesetz" were later discarded: "Während in heller Sonne / das Dröhnen des Todes weiterzog."

Das Gold verborgen
Im rostigen Eisentopf. (CC, 62)

Here villages are hidden away, closed off from the frigid, cruel
surroundings; and a child knows nothing of the night which comes
limping by on "crutches of bare poplars" ("Auf Krücken kahler
Pappeln / kam die Nacht"). The child's innocence brings a note
of hope to the end of the poem:

Das Kind sah nicht
Die gräberhohle Erde.
Und nicht den Mond,
Der eine Garbe weissen Strohs
Auf Eis und Steine warf.
Das Kind war nahe dem Tag.

The structure of this poem is not quite as firm as in "Chausseen,"
and the linguistic techniques, though brilliant in spots, are not as
uniformly convincing. One of Huchel's major weaknesses, excessive and often unclear genitive metaphors, is present here, as in the
successive lines, "In den kältesten Winkel der Stunde, / Aus der
Höhle des Bluts / Ans Licht zersplitterter Fenster." Further, the
compound adjective, which Huchel generally handles with great
ingenuity, is used too generously (four times in eleven short lines:
"schneeverkrustetem Vieh," "graubemörtelte Mauer," "krähen-
treibenden Nebel," "gräberhohle Erde"). When at his best Huchel
successfully avoids such mannerisms.

A different form, though the same abbreviated style, may be
seen in the poem "Dezember 1942" (originally entitled "Chausseen, Chausseen. Chronik: Dezember 1942"). In his use of four-
beat closed couplets Huchel is following the tradition of artistic
plebeian doggerel sometimes employed in chronicle ballads. "Dezember 1942" reads:

Wie Wintergewitter ein rollender Hall.
Zerschossen die Lehmwand von Bethlehems Stall.

Es liegt Maria erschlagen vorm Tor,
Ihr blutig Haar an die Steine fror.

Drei Landser ziehen vermummt vorbei.
Nicht brennt ihr Ohr von des Kindes Schrei.

Im Beutel den letzten Sonnblumenkern,
Sie suchen den Weg und sehn keinen Stern.

Aurum, thus, myrrham offerunt . . .
Um kahles Gehöft streicht Krähe und Hund.

. . . quia natus est nobis Dominus.
Auf fahlem Gerippe glänzt Öl und Russ.

Vor Stalingrad verweht die Chaussee.
Sie führt in die Totenkammer aus Schnee. (CC, 64)

There has been in recent years some basic disagreement as to the aesthetic value of this poem. Walter Jens, in his controversial *Deutsche Literatur der Gegenwart,* considers it one of the great accomplishments of postwar German literature, capturing in pithy form the entire spirit of the war. "Fourteen lines," he maintains, "suffice here to give, without clichés, an allegoric image of the Second World War. What novelist . . . can contend that he has rendered even a suggestion of the symbolic level evoked by Huchel? Strange that precisely the lyricists, these poets supposedly alienated from the times, offer in tropes and images much more valid utterances about our present day than the novelists in their thick volumes: where are the epic pendants to Celan's 'Todesfuge' and to Huchel's 'Gesetz'?" [33] Hans Egon Holthusen, on the other hand, regards "Dezember 1942" as an example of Huchel at his weakest, as "the false simplicity, the attitude of an affected almanac writer." [34] The lapidary style is for him affected; in reality the poem is empty sentimentality. Both of these judgments seem to me exaggerated. Jens was perhaps misled into unduly high praise by his close personal friendship with the poet, and perhaps even,

33. Jens, *Deutsche Literatur der Gegenwart* (Munich, 1962), p. 107: "Vierzehn Zeilen reichen hier aus, um, fern aller Klischees, ein gleichnishaftes Bild des Zweiten Weltkrieges zu geben. Welcher Epiker . . . könnte von sich behaupten, er habe die von Huchel evozierte Symbol-Ebene auch nur erahnbar gemacht? Seltsam, dass gerade die Lyriker, diese angeblich doch zeitentfremdeten Poeten, in Gleichnis und Bild so viel Gültigeres über unsere Gegenwart aussagen als die Romanciers in dickleibigen Büchern: wo sind die epischen Pendants zu Celans 'Todesfuge', zu Huchels 'Gesetz'?"

34. *Frankfurter Allgemeine Zeitung,* February 29, 1964: "die falsche Einfachheit einer manierierten Kalendermann-Attitüde." Holthusen expresses a more sympathetic understanding of Huchel's poetry in his essay "Natur und Geschichte in Huchels Gedicht," *Hommage für Peter Huchel* (Munich, 1968), pp. 72–77.

as a professor of classics, by the Latin quotations, and Holthusen appears to be projecting his own temperament when he speaks of Huchel's "basically ultraconservative pattern of understanding the world" ("das im Grunde erzkonservative Muster seines Welt-verstehens").

"Dezember 1942" is, I think, a fine, though not an extraordinary, achievement. It may not really be quite as impressive as Celan's "Todesfuge," and the parabolic technique may not come as naturally to Huchel as did the early landscape poems in which Holthusen sees his strength.[35] But the concision and method of slashing contrast are brilliantly conceived, the Bethlehem scene and tight form being a kind of negative "correlative" to the chaotic destruction of wartime Stalingrad. The absolute horror of the historical situation comes close to finding its adequate evocation when this distance is established, real events intermingling with the tranquil, static biblical scenery. The Latin lines signaling the birth of the Child Jesus seem to smash against lines sketching death and the war's desolation. By the final couplet, as Jens correctly points out, the counterimage of Bethlehem fades out, allowing the historical moment and the setting to "speak for themselves" and to close the ringlike complex of imagery. The "death chamber" at Stalingrad remains as a glaring contrast to "Bethlehems Stall," and the winter storm, which was only a simile at the beginning ("Wie Wintergewitter"), is by the last line very real, drifting snow smothering whatever life is left. Even the "Chaussee"—that sign central to Huchel's poetry and standing for flight, for pro-found fear, but also for the way potentially out of destruction— is now covered over, leading only one way. The poem is not sentimental; on the contrary, the deeply felt horror is consciously estranged from the speaker by means of an objective pattern of imagery, a rigid poetic form, and unemotional, scanty language and rhythm ("Ihr blutig Haar an die Steine fror," "Sie suchen den Weg und sehn keinen Stern"). The danger, I think, lies in the other direction: the simplicity seems slightly forced, distance is established to such an extent that much of the concreteness and physical presence of the scene is lost. The allegoric woodcut

35. Huchel's poem is far superior to a comparable text by Holthusen himself, "Ein Mann vor Stalingrad 1942." See Holthusen, *Hier in der Zeit* (Munich, 1949), pp. 31–32.

(which is what this poem seems to be) is here not quite adequate
to the total historical period it is trying to evoke. The method of
richly potent cross-sections and selected visions, as in "Chausseen," is in my opinion more forceful.

The war is also seen in a religious context in the powerful poem
"Bericht des Pfarrers vom Untergang seiner Gemeinde" (CC,
61); here the sense of distance is at a minimum. Rhyme is still
present, but it is loose (in the first stanza, for example, the pattern
is abcbdedfafe), and the basically four-beat rhythm ranges from
the long six-foot line at the beginning ("Da Christus brennend
sank vom Kreuz—o Todesgrauen!") to the exclamation, "O Stadt
in Feuer!" of only two stresses. The pace of the emotional "report"
is for the most part determined, not by these conventions, but by
the preacher's impressions and the intensity of his apocalyptic
vision. For example, as the moment of doom approaches, his voice
seems most excited, and image is heaped on image in quick succession:

> Denn wieder warf die Nacht
> Aus kalten Himmeln feurige Schlacke.
> Und Wind und Qualm. Und Dörfer wie Meiler angefacht.
> Und Volk und Vieh auf enger Schneise.
> Und morgens die Toten der Typhusbaracke.

The tempo slackens at the end, in the hour of downfall, and the
vision of a perishing congregation is sustained over the entire
section:

> O öde Stadt, wie war es spät,
> Es gingen die Kinder, die Greise
> Auf staubigen Füssen durch mein Gebet.
> Die löchrigen Strassen sah ich sie gehn.
> Und wenn sie schwankten unter der Last
> Und stürzten mit gefrorener Träne,
> Nie kam im Nebel der langen Winterchausseen
> Ein Simon von Kyrene.

The speaker, then, is in the thick of the horror, charged with emotional reactions which govern the poem's movement, to a large
extent against the dictates of loosely maintained formal convention. There is little of the parabolic detachment and deliberately

dampened sentiment of "Dezember 1942"; the speaker here appears in terrified involvement with the massive destruction. His quivering voice "reports" in greater fullness the thundering havoc of the time and the desecration of everything holy, as in the description of the attacking squadrons:

> Es schwenkten dröhnend die Geschwader.
> Durch roten Himmel flogen sie ab,
> Als schnitten sie des Mittags Ader.
> Ich sah es schwelen, fressen, brennen—
> Und aufgewühlt war noch das Grab.
> Hier war kein Gesetz! Mein Tag war zu kurz,
> Um Gott zu erkennen.

"Here there was no law"—"Hier war kein Gesetz!": this exclamation occurs three times in the poem, and situates it, along with other poems about the war, in the chronicle "Das Gesetz." Significantly, this chronicle contains two different conceptions of "law" and its opposite. The sections set in the years 1945–47 praise "law" as legislated land reform, and "lawlessness" refers to a condition of social deprivation resulting from an unjust distribution of rural property. In such poems as "Chausseen" and "Bericht des Pfarrers vom Untergang seiner Gemeinde," however, where the setting is the war, "lawlessness" is far more general, corresponding to a state of chaos, hopelessness, and impending doom of the entire human race. The question of man's suffering and the disruption of natural order is conceived of more universally, removed from the specific context of societal injustice which had formed the basis of Huchel's pastoral complex.

Now this divergence in the notion of law and injustice reflects the major tendency in his poetic development. Huchel's idyll, which culminated in his glorification of the "law" as agricultural reform, becomes only one element in his poetry. Ultimately, as the poet grew increasingly discouraged by further developments in East German society, this pastoral element loses its relevance, and the hymnic, confident style and the conventions of socialist realism are abandoned. More and more, emphasis shifts from the problem of productive human activity in nature, and its relation to the social order, to a concern for the enduring misery of all men, regardless of the structure of society. Huchel's poetry comes to

be characterized less by sympathy ("Mitleid") with those denied
the privileges and rights due them than by meditations on the pain
("Leid") and uncertainty which permeate all of human existence.
His tone becomes somber and melancholy, his poetic diction
cryptic and abstract. After enthusiastically proclaiming for a short
time a vision of brightness and oncoming justice, the speaker is
shrouded in darkness and seems to struggle desperately for each
image and each particle of meaningful utterance. Two lines in
"Bericht des Pfarrers vom Untergang seiner Gemeinde" suggest
the poet's preoccupation once he saw that the social institution
on which his hopes had rested was no longer worthy of his praise:

> Hier war kein Gesetz. Es schrieb das Leid
> Mit aschiger Schrift: Wer kann bestehn?

Winter Psalm (After 1953)

After the Second SED Party Congress in 1952, resulting in the
decree to collectivize agricultural production, and particularly
after the popular uprising in June of the following year, when it
became clear that the "toiling masses" remained as exploited as
they had ever been, Huchel's attitude toward East German society
could no longer be one of approval. By that time he had ceased
writing affirmative poetry, and the few subsequent poems still conceived of as forming part of the cycle "Das Gesetz" ("Dezember
1942" and "Winterquartier") dealt with the war and a state of
general "lawlessness," thereby continuing the thematic and stylistic concerns evident in sections of "Der Rückzug" and such postwar poems as "Chausseen," "Der Treck," and "Bericht des Pfarrers
vom Untergang seiner Gemeinde."

From them a direct line may be drawn to the poems of the
decade 1953–63, dominated by the poet's profound sense of resignation and isolation. The other tendency—Huchel's enthusiastic
praise of the land reform, which had culminated his pastoral vision
of man's unity with nature—disappeared with his loss of enthusiasm
and certainty. Alongside the hope-filled idyll and panegyric hymn
there had long been evident in Huchel's poetry a suggestion of
the elegy and the plaintive psalm, as an alternative to the fulfillment
of his ideal. By the middle of the 1950s the idyll comes to a con-

clusive end, and winter night descends on ripened harvest and morning sunrise alike.

Huchel's poetry of disenchantment is dominated by embittered reflections; an abstract, fragmented style; and images of an icy, static landscape. Just when proclamations of a general "thaw" could first be heard, this aging poet's vision was drawn to the frozen features of the human community. In the years of "peaceful coexistence" and a "critical dialogue" his concern has been with the feasibility of further existence and the problem of individual communication. Poetic expression, he senses, is severely threatened by the prolonged inhumanity of social conditions. Huchel's final recourse, therefore, has been to the poem itself; his calm, patient utterances of the past decade are intended to salvage the poem, thereby to preserve a testament to the calculated destruction of spiritual activity. The poems are both self-reflective and self-defensive, bearing witness to their own imperiled situation.

The first poem in which Huchel expressed his resignation was dedicated to his favorite author, the Marxist philosopher Ernst Bloch, on his seventieth birthday (1955):

Widmung

Herbst und die dämmernden Sonnen im Nebel
Und nachts am Himmel ein Feuerbild.
Es stürzt und weht. Du musst es bewahren.
Am Hohlweg wechselt schneller das Wild.
Und wie ein Hall aus fernen Jahren
Dröhnt über Wälder weit ein Schuss.
Es schweifen wieder die Unsichtbaren
Und Laub und Wolken treibt der Fluss.

Der Jäger schleppt nun heim die Beute,
Das kiefernästig starrende Geweih.
Der Sinnende sucht andre Spur.
Er geht am Hohlweg still vorbei,
Wo goldner Rauch vom Baume fuhr.
Und Stunden wehn, vom Herbstwind weise,
Gedanken wie der Vögel Reise,
Und manches Wort wird Brot und Salz.
Er ahnt, was noch die Nacht verschweigt,

Wenn in der grossen Drift das Alls
Des Winters Sternbild langsam steigt. (CC, 45)

It is tempting to interpret this poem with reference to the world
of Bloch's philosophy; immediately following this verse dedication
in its original publication in *Sinn und Form* (1955), Huchel printed
a thirty-two-page essay by Hans Heinz Holz on "Der Philosoph
Ernst Bloch und sein Werk 'Das Prinzip Hoffnung'," and many
of the points discussed therein, particularly the nature and function of symbols and images, seem relevant to a consideration of
Huchel's poem. The line "Der Sinnende sucht andre Spur" suggests the title of Bloch's only explicitly fictional book, *Spuren*
(1930; second, enlarged edition, 1959), and the thinking of a
philosopher who is also an avid reader of detective novels and
stories about the American Indian—his method of seeking "traces"
of the future in past and present. Since in the original version of
the poem the word "Alter" stood in the sixth line of the second
stanza instead of "Herbstwind," the poem's conception might have
had reference to Bloch's thoughts about old age in *Das Prinzip
Hoffnung*. Bloch distinguishes between the old man of bourgeois,
capitalist society, who characteristically scurries about in height-
ened greed for material acquisitions and satisfactions ("Wein und
Beutel"), and the socialist reaching later years and a sense of
spiritual fulfillment and reflective tranquility.[36] The first may
correspond to the hunter and his prey, the second to the contemplative old man ("der Sinnende"), whose interests lie in other
directions. There are several elements in Bloch's philosophy of
hope, therefore, to which the poet may have been alluding when
he dedicated eighteen lines to the aging thinker.

Still more relevant, however, are political facts. By 1955 Bloch,
a member of the SED, had already fallen into Party disfavor.
Even then the philosopher had begun to realize that in the DDR
the "cold stream" of Marxism was blocking off the "warm stream";
more than ever he was becoming aware that hope must include
within itself the possibility of disappointment. He did not elaborate
on this thought while still in the DDR, but on arriving in West
Germany, in his opening lecture at the University of Tübingen in

36. See the section, "Was im Alter zu wünschen übrigbleibt," *Das Prinzip
Hoffnung*, *1*, 37–44.

1961, he spoke with his usual brilliance on the topic, "Can hope be disappointed?" ("Kann die Hoffnung enttäuscht werden?"). While refusing to give up his lifelong ideal of humanistic socialism, Bloch describes with greater precision than before the uncertainty and disillusionment latent in even the firmest hope. In the terms of this lecture, hope remains as a measure of the relatively successful or unsuccessful realization of the constant humanistic aim, and because of its transcending quality, it can best determine how fatally dreams can be turned into nightmares. At the end of his speech Bloch resorts to what is almost a Manichean dualism, incorporating into his thought the absolute negation as a separate entity. "Nothing is more human than to go beyond existing conditions. That incipient dreams rarely mature has long been known. Tested hope knows that better than anyone; in this respect, too, it is not certainty. It also knows above all—by definition, as it were—not only that where danger grows there is redemption, but also that where redemption grows so does danger. Hope knows that frustration lurks as a function of nothingness in the world, that disappointment is latent in objectively real possibility, which bears both salvation and disaster unresolved within itself." [37] Ernst Bloch is like that pensive man in Huchel's poem who must cling to a glare of light in the darkening skies, who had a foreboding of what was still the night's secret and amid proclamations of a "thaw" could see the constellation of winter ascending steadily.

Yet, because of the (fortunate) change from "Alter" to "Herbstwind" and the omission in the final version of the words "for his

---

37. Bloch, *Verfremdungen* (Frankfurt, 1962), 5, 211–19; also in Bloch, *Auswahl aus seinen Schriften*, ed. Hans Heinz Holz (Frankfurt, 1967), pp. 176–81. P. 180: "Nicht nur die eigene, nie still haltende Enttäuschung qua Offenheit, die nur erst partiale Determiniertheit jeder Tendenz-Latenz-Aussage und ihres Gegenstandes selber gehört zur Hoffnung. Sondern auch die umsichblickende, echt orthodoxe Enttäuschung am rückfälligen, bis zur Unkenntlichkeit oder gar bis zu Kenntlichkeit veränderten Produkt gehört zur Hoffnung; qua Unnachlasslichkeit, qua ihrer Pflicht, Masstab zu sein, gemäss dem Zielinhalt, der Reich der Freiheit heisst." P. 181: "Nichts ist menschlicher als zu überschreiten, was ist. Dass Blütenträume fast selten reiften, ist lang bekannt. Die geprüfte Hoffnung weiss das besser als irgendwer; auch darin ist sie ja keine Zuversicht. Sie weiss vor allem auch, sozusagen per definitionem ihrer, dass nicht nur, wo Gefahr, auch das Rettende, sondern wo das Rettende, auch Gefahr wächst. Sie weiss, dass das Vereitelnde als Funktion des Nichts in der Welt umgeht, dass auch ein Umsonst in der objectiv-realen Möglichkeit latent ist, das Heil wie Unheil unausgemacht in sich trägt."

seventieth birthday," Huchel was clearly concerned with remov-
ing his dedication from such specific frames of reference. The
poem contrasts two kinds of human endeavor—that of the hunter
to that of the contemplative man. The first three and the final two
lines may be regarded as setting, with seven lines devoted to each
figure. The hunter's domain is around the ravine ("Hohlweg"),
he is in pursuit of the quickly migrating deer which he ultimately
drags home as booty; the ravine resounds with the hunter's shot,
and above the scene "invisible" stars roam. Characteristic of the
world of the hunter is the shot which "booms like a sound from
distant years" ("Dröhnt . . . wie ein Hall aus fernen Jahren"),
perhaps from that "late hour" when all nature seemed penetrated
by gunshots. (See also "Späte Zeit.") In any case, his activity is
associated with the past, and it ends with fulfillment. The description of the slain deer—actually the antlers, "Das kiefernästig starrende Geweih"—also serves to characterize the hunter's realm.
Walter Jens objects to this line, seeing no sense in the "frosty
isolation" of this one five-beat line among so many four-beat
ones.[38] Yet I think it is clear that only four stresses were intended:
"Das kiéfernästig stárrende Gewéih." What is "strange" (Jens)
about the line are the three unaccented syllables before the end
rhyme, but they can, in my opinion, be justified. The function of
this line is to draw attention to the rigid and inflexible nature of
the hunter's activity by showing its effect on the object of his
pursuit: the deer, first seen dashing quickly across the ravine, is
now all unbending antlers ("kiefernästig starrend"). Rather than
using a strictly regular meter, Huchel chose to evoke this sense
rhythmically by means of a slow, stubborn movement, which contrasts perfectly with the somewhat prancing tempo of the line,
"Am Hohlweg wechselt schneller das Wild." A more valid objection would be to the stanza break, which might have more sensibly
fallen between the passage about the hunter and that devoted to the
man meditating. But perhaps the poet wished to juxtapose directly
the participle forms, "starrende" and "Sinnende."

    The pensive man, we are told, follows other paths; he silently
passes by the resounding ravine, where gunsmoke rises from the
trees. In his pursuit he is armed with "thoughts" which, significantly, do not prevent autumn migration but seem a part of it:

38. In a review of *Chausseen Chausseen, Die Zeit*, December 6, 1963.

"Gedanken wie der Vögel Reise." Yet his booty, the expression of his wisdom ("vom Herbstwind weise") in the word, is not juicy venison but dry bread and salt. The reflective man is characterized by transcending vision; his activity is associated with the future—or rather, with intimation of the future—and the significance of heavenly movements is visible to him.

Directly relevant to this portrait of "der Sinnende" is Huchel's fine poem "In memoriam Paul Eluard" (originally dedicated to Arnold Zweig):

> Freiheit, mein Stern,
> Nicht auf den Himmelsgrund gezeichnet,
> Über den Schmerzen der Welt
> Noch unsichtbar
> Ziehst du die Bahn
> Am Wendekreis der Zeit.
> Ich weiss, mein Stern,
> Dein Licht ist unterwegs. (CC, 79)

The fiery image which must be preserved ("Du musst es bewahren") in the Bloch poem is the "realm of freedom," that ineradicable goal of humanistic striving. But whereas the speaker in the lines for Eluard knows that his star is rising, the wise man ("Der Sinnende") can tell from the constellations only that winter is near. In both cases, however, the transition to freedom has not yet occurred; the world is still filled with pain ("Schmerzen der Welt") and the earth is traversed by hunters and the hunted. The speakers in Huchel's poems and the personages with whom he identifies are isolated from the events, forced outside them and often interpreting them.

Another aspect of this separation of the individual from more common activities may be seen in the "Dedication" ("Widmung," 1957) to the dramatist and novelist Hans Henny Jahnn (1894–1959), also a long-admired friend of Huchel's. Noteworthy here is the idyllic setting toward which the speaker is drawn but which he is forced to abandon.

> Singende Öde am Fluss: wer rief?
> Da mit dem rudernden Fuss des Schwans

Die Nacht nun über dem Wasser naht,
Gehn Feuer dunkel hinab den Pfad,
Wo einmal der Knabe, im Schatten des Kahns,
Den Mittag neben den Netzen verschlief.
Wer aber wollte, wenn eisige Ferne weht,
Mit ihnen dort oben am Hügel nicht leben,
Die melken und pflügen
Und richten Gemäuer
Und Balken an Balken sicher fügen?
Wo sich das wasserhebende Windrad dreht,
Wohnen sie nahe am Korn. Ihr Tagwerk ist gut.
Dich aber rief es, aus feuer-
Brennender Tiefe zu heben
Die leicht erlöschende, ruhlose Glut. (CC, 46)

To a great extent, as Hans Mayer has convincingly pointed out, this poem addresses and refers personally to Hans Henny Jahnn; the whole is really a poetic call and warning from a friend to a friend two years before his death. On Jahnn's death two years later, Huchel repeated in a eulogy the substance of his verse dedication. "All of us who knew him," he said, "have in recent years followed his restless life with consternation, often even with fear. . . . And sometimes it seemed as if he were condemned to tear the ground he had just gained from under his feet. . . . The manysidedness of his endeavors often turned into his undoing." [39] In fact, as Mayer also mentions, the poem constitutes a kind of confrontation between two very different personalities—that of the poet Huchel, whose world is characterized by the tranquil, idyllic setting (suggested at the end of the first stanza and the first seven lines of the second), and that of Jahnn, who tended toward more violent landscapes, mountains and stormy seas, "rivers without shorelines" ("Fluss ohne Ufer," the title of his most famous work, an uncompleted novel trilogy, 1949). The rhyme technique, each line ending answered as though from a distance by a similar

39. Hans Mayer, "Zu Gedichten von Peter Huchel," *Zur deutschen Literatur der Zeit*, pp. 178–88; on the Jahnn poem, pp. 182–85. Huchel eulogy quoted pp. 183, 185: "Wir alle, die wir ihn kannten, haben in den letzten Jahren mit Bestürzung, ja oft mit Angst sein rastloses Leben verfolgt. . . . Und manchmal schien es, als sei er verurteilt, sich selber den Boden, den er eben gewonnen hatte, unter den Füssen wegzureissen. . . . Die Vielseitigkeit seiner Unternehmungen wurde ihm oft zum Fallstrick."

sound, also illustrates this duality and unmatched understanding between two contrasting temperaments.

Yet despite these revealing biographical considerations, I believe that the poetic statement has more general application and that it implies a marked change in the attitude of the speaker himself. Surely the lines, "Wo einmal der Knabe, im Schatten des Kahns, / Den Mittag neben den Netzen verschlief," are reminiscent of Huchel's early nature poems, in particular "Der Knabenteich." But the situation has changed: along with the peaceful swans, night is descending on the water ("Die Nacht nun über dem Wasser naht"), and blazing flames are approaching down the familiar path. The waterside is still musical ("singend"), but its enchantment is now eerie, one of foreboding desolation ("Öde," a key word in Huchel's later poetry) and pierced by a mysterious call. The scene in stanza two, "up on the hill," where the constructive chores of the day are being done, also recalls Huchel's pastoral landscape, housed by hardworking servants and manual laborers. It too, however, is threatened, surrounded by breezes from the "icy distance." The speaker distances himself from the setting, first by phrasing as a question the possibility of finding refuge in such productive tranquility, then by interpreting and evaluating the existence of the hill dwellers: "Wo sich das wasserhebende Wind-rad dreht, / Wohnen sie nahe am Korn. Ihr Tagwerk ist gut." The speaker of the poem, as well as the person to whom it is dedicated, is unable to participate in the harmonious pastoral. He stands outside it, reflects on it, and condones it, but he must recognize that his path does not lead up the gentle hillside. He is called, rather, down into the depths, to salvage as though from a volcanic crater one flickering torch of light.

A stanza in another poem, "Schlucht bei Baltschik," suggests what this action might signify. In that work an old gypsy woman also "lifts" a torch from the fire:

Nachts hebt sie aus dem Feuer
Ein glimmendes Scheit.
Sie wirbelt es über den Kopf,
Sie schreit und schleudert
Ins Dunkel der Toten
Den rauchenden Brand. (CC, 30)

For the lone individual, separated by his calling from the "life" of normal activities (it is significant that in the Jahnn poem the word "heben" rhymes with "leben," reference for the sake of contrast), death has become a central concern, giving meaning to all existence. Death, or nearness to it in old age, was implicitly the bringer of prophetic wisdom and a pursuit more far-reaching than the hunter's in the poem for Ernst Bloch, "vom Herbstwind weise" ("vom Alter weise"); and in this dedication to the sixty-three-year-old Hans Henny Jahnn the decisive contrast is between the naïve, secure vitality on the hill and the individual's impulsive, Empedoclean delve into the underworld. Formal reminiscences of Hölderlin are particularly strong in the second stanza, in such lines as "Wer aber wollte, wenn eisige Ferne weht" and "Dich aber rief es." The suggestion is that death provides a meaning beyond that of life, and that life itself can be judged only with the help of an understanding of the dead.

These ideas are more directly expressed in the poems at the beginning of *Chausseen Chausseen* (1963), especially in the opening poem, "Das Zeichen," which sets the tone for the entire volume. In the poetry of *Chausseen Chausseen*, written mostly in the decade 1953–63, Huchel employs, and masters, a great variety of forms and tones: hymnic, conversational, narrative, epigrammatic, elegiac, and descriptive. Most characteristic is that in many of the best poems these forms are intermingled; the speaker passes from one mood to the other, as for example in the dedication to Jahnn, where nature description was blended with markedly hymnic and elegiac lines.

In the poem "Das Zeichen" a variety of these poetic and linguistic modes functions in quick succession. Nowhere can the wide range of his style and diction (despite a rather limited vocabulary) be better analyzed than here. The poem begins with an evocation of an autumnal scene, rendered in a short sequence of images:

Baumkahler Hügel,
Noch einmal flog
Am Abend die Wildentenkette
Durch wässrige Herbstluft. (CC, 9)

The stanza seems to present a specific condition of nature, and the speaker reflects it as precisely as possible without personally intruding. But with the words "Noch einmal" he does enter, as the strictly spatial, almost static scene is penetrated by the element of a personally experienced time. The imagist snapshot means something to the speaker, although he is not at all sure what, as is clear from the first line in the next stanza, "War es das Zeichen?" In fact, he seems not even to be sure if it really does have a meaning. After this question he reverts again to pure imagism, as though to make sure of the image before renewing the search for its meaning:

> Mit falben Lanzen
> Durchbohrte der See
> Den ruhlosen Nebel.

Because of the position of the question there is a suggestion that the "sign" ("Zeichen") refers to both descriptions—that of the first stanza and that of the second. But what can be the similarity between the sight of a flock of birds flying over a hill and a lake penetrating the mist "with pale-yellow lances" ("mit falben Lanzen," surely the reeds growing upright in the water)? The answer, I think, is suggested in the preposition (or prefix) "durch" and in the metallic quality of the metaphors, "Wildenten*kette*" and "mit falben *Lanzen*." In both cases the atmosphere is pierced "through" by a metallic substance; both scenes, totally visual, seem nevertheless to clang; an interference seems to arise from the rigidity and incompatibility of the elements. Earth, air and water are out of joint with one another, they irritate and interfere with one another. These impressions are, however, only suggested, and their meaning is not at all determined. The question, "War es das Zeichen?" remains, to be raised again, still not fully answered, toward the end of the poem.

In the third stanza the mode changes. The speaker enters, reports a rural setting ("Ich ging durchs Dorf / Und sah das Gewohnte"); and, in the middle six lines of the stanza, unfolds the harmonious pastoral:

> Der Schäfer hielt den Widder
> Gefesselt zwischen den Knien.
> Er schnitt die Klaue,

> Er teerte die Stoppelhinke.
> Und Frauen zählten die Kannen,
> Das Tagesmelk.

Here business is performed with assurance. The people know what they are doing, without confusion or hesitation. This is the daily routine of earthly life, simple but prescribed, without transcendent significance. The stanza ends with two lines in which the tone is again different, the narrative report becoming gnomic statement:

> Nichts war zu deuten.
> Es stand im Herdbuch.

There is no "sign" in this naïve routine; harmonious though it is, there is nothing to interpret in it.

Only with the fourth stanza does a deeper insight finally come, and the tone becomes first hymnic and then cryptic and psalm-like:

> Nur die Toten,
> Entrückt dem stündlichen Hall
> Der Glocke, dem Wachsen des Epheus,
> Sie sehen
> Den eisigen Schatten der Erde
> Gleiten über den Mond.
> Sie wissen, dieses wird bleiben.
> Nach allem, was atmet
> In Luft und Wasser.

What is special about the dead is that they are exempt from the temporal limits and routine categories dictated by earthly activity, from "das Gewohnte" and "das Herdbuch." They even stand outside the processes of nature, being "entrückt . . . dem Wachsen des Epheus." They are, however, granted vision and knowledge of what remains, what outlasts all of earthly creation. The reference of "dieses," the object of their special knowledge and vision, is not at all clear—I think, intentionally. From the lines preceding—"Sie sehen / Den eisigen Schatten der Erde / Gleiten über den Mond" —it would seem to be an ethereal order transcending all of earthly life. Perhaps this is the "sign" in question. But the quotation from St. Augustine serving as the motto for *Chausseen Chaus-*

seen (and appearing on the page preceding this poem) must also be taken into consideration: "im grossen Hof meines Gedächtnisses. Daselbst sind mir Himmel, Erde und Meer gegenwärtig." Also encompassing all of the cosmos, and transcending cycles of temporality and natural processes, is human recollection, or poetic consciousness; and in this connection I do not think it too far-fetched to refer to those often mishandled lines from the end of Hölderlin's poem "Andenken":

> Es nehmet aber
> Und gibt Gedächtnis die See,
> Und die Lieb auch heftig fleissig die Augen,
> Was bleibet aber, stiften die Dichter.

Without pressing the issue, there seems a potential identification of the situation of the dead with the function of the poet. In this respect, too, the poem "Das Zeichen" establishes the keynote for the volume.

The fifth stanza ends with the repetition of the question, "War es das Zeichen?," and begins with a question about the mysterious sign: "Wer schrieb / Die warnende Schrift, / Kaum zu entziffern?" The speaker only knows where he has found it, as he reports in the fourth and fifth lines, "Ich fand sie am Pfahl, / Dicht hinter dem See." In the last stanza he returns to the four-line image of a brittle, frozen nature:

> Erstarrt
> Im Schweigen des Schnees,
> Schlief blind
> Das Kreuzotterndickicht.

To understand this complex of associations, the final stanza of another poem, "Thrakien," may be of help:

> Ein Messer
> Häutet den Nebel,
> Den Widder der Berge.
> Jenseits des Flusses
> Leben die Toten.
> Das Wort
> Ist die Fähre. (CC, 14)

Wilhelm Lehmann is right in objecting to the banality, abstraction, and unconvincing sentiment of this poem, which is one of Huchel's weakest. It is useful, however, as a point of reference to elucidate some of the obscure passages in his more successful works. The clue is found on the other side of the water, where the dead "live." Whether the "word" transports the speaker to the dead or is found among them, the implication is that poetic utterance is inspired by the realm of the dead. In the same passage of "Thrakien" the image of a metallic substance penetrating the atmosphere recurs: "Ein Messer / Häutet den Nebel." Thus, both poems suggest a relationship between this particular "sign" and the situation of the "word," the "script" among the dead. The frozen, muted landscape at the end of "Das Zeichen" and the blindly dormant "thicket of vipers" ("Kreuzotterndickicht") constitute an intensified variant of the scenes at the beginning of the poem. Nature itself is dead ("Kreuz" in "Kreuzotterndickicht" may be significant), leaving only silence, blindness, and icy treachery. Poetry, the "warning script," still lives in nature, as though communing with the dead, drawing utterance from its silence and vision from its blindness, and announcing the lurking danger to all who read.

This drastically altered conception of nature and the situation of poetry lies at the root of the profound sense of melancholy and resignation which has dominated Huchel's verse since the later 1950s. Despite its subtle play of themes and masterfully modulated style, I do not think that the poem "Das Zeichen" is one of Huchel's very best. It does not suffer from unevenness, like the overrated [40] "Elegie," which after a majestic beginning contains in its final stanza the overdone metaphor: "Am Kap einer Wolke / Und in der Dünung des Himmels schwimmend, / Weiss vom Salz / Verschollener Wogen / Des Mondes Feuerschiff." "Das Zeichen," however, is too disparate; the whole, although never entirely fragmented, is not sufficiently integrated and ultimately leaves a rather disjointed impression. But the theme and style are truly representative of the volume the poem introduces, and they are employed with greater perfection in other poems, particularly

40. It was included in Hans Bender, ed. *Widerspiel* (Munich, 1962), pp. 71–72, and Walter R. Fuchs, ed., *Lyrik unserer Jahrhundertmitte* (Munich, 1965), pp. 63–64.

those included in Huchel's last issue of *Sinn und Form*—"Der Garten des Theophrast," "Verona," "Traum im Tellereisen," "Winterpsalm," "Hinter den weissen Netzen des Mittags," and "Soldatenfriedhof."

These poems are his words of farewell to literary life in the DDR, and the statement of his "counterposition" to what was still being extolled as the "construction of socialism." As Franz Schonauer has correctly asserted in his essay, "Peter Huchels Gegenposition," they are not the expression of a direct opposition or political protest; Huchel has not suddenly become an arch-enemy of socialism. Rather, they are the result of poetic development, the loss of confidence in a harmonious nature and the linguistic richness derived from it, which had already begun in his wartime poetry and which mounting political pressure only fostered and intensified. They are a total rejection of the vulgar Marxist demand that poetry be "positive" in its statement and fulfill a clearly recognizable social task. They stand in extreme, uncompromising opposition to that flat optimism in East German verse (including his own) of the early 1950s and maintained in later years only by the most meager talents.[41]

Of particular beauty among these farewell poems is "Verona":

> Zwischen uns fiel der Regen des Vergessens.
> Im Brunnen verdämmern die Münzen.
> Auf der Mauer die Katze,
> Sie dreht ihr Haupt ins Schweigen,
> Erkennt uns nicht mehr.
> Das schwache Licht der Liebe
> Sinkt auf ihre Augensterne.
>
> Es rasselt das Räderwerk im Turm
> Und schlägt zu spät die Stunde an.
> Die Erde schenkt uns keine Zeit
> Über den Tod hinaus.
> Ins Gewebe der Nacht genäht
> Versinken die Stimmen
> Unauffindbar.
>
> Zwei Tauben fliegen vom Finstersims.
> Die Brücke behütet den Schwur.

41. Schonauer, "Peter Huchels Gegenposition," p. 413.

Dieser Stein,
Im Wasser der Etsch,
Lebt gross in seiner Stille.
Und in der Mitte der Dinge
Die Trauer. (CC, 15)

Two slow-moving stanzas announce and evoke the sense of loss, first of communication and intercourse with other beings, then of time and existence itself. At the beginning and end of the poem are metaphors for abstractions: "der Regen des Vergessens" and "in der Mitte der Dinge die Trauer." Otherwise the images remain concrete, except for the epigram, "Die Erde schenkt uns keine Zeit / Über den Tod hinaus." Just as sadness stands "in the middle of things," so this sad truth has its place in the middle of the poem.

But perhaps it is not so absolutely unconsoling to the speaker after all. The last stanza tells of what remains: there is the bridge, which "preserves the oath"; we are made to think of the bridges of Verona, linking the imperishable cultural landmarks of that city.[42] But there was another important bridge in Huchel's life: he conceived of the result of his endeavors, the periodical *Sinn und Form*, as a cultural "bridge between East and West," and it was just this conception which ultimately cost him the editorship and brought him condemnation from East German policy makers.[43] *Sinn und Form*, then, Peter Huchel's forum for all Germany, is perhaps the "bridge" which does not give up the sacred "oath" of cultural openness. And what of "this stone," living on in the water, "huge in its silence"? It seems to be a further mention of the bridge, or of the oath which it preserves. In other poems, however, the stone has other functions. In "Thrakien," for ex-

42. One is reminded of the bridge symbolism in the ninth of Rilke's *Duineser Elegien:* "Sind wir vielleicht *hier,* um zu sagen: Haus / Brücke, Brunnen, Tor, Krug, Obstbaum, Fenster." On the importance of the bridge in Rilke's poetry as an image for "the complete, total and sacred word" and the element of mediation and communication, see Jacob Steiner, *Rilkes Duineser Elegien* (Bern, 1962), pp. 220–22.

43. The statement by Kurt Hager condemning Huchel and *Sinn und Form* is quoted in Schonauer, p. 406: "In dem Bestreben, eine gesamtdeutsche Zeitschrift zu sein, eine Zeitschrift, die auch in Westdeutschland gefällt, eine 'Brücke zwischen Ost und West', wich die Zeitschrift, der man ein hohes literarisches Niveau zugestehen muss, jahrelang sorgfältig einer entschiedenen Parteinahme für die sozialistische Entwicklung in der DDR aus. . . .'"

ample, it is a keeper of "silence," preventing the intrusion, or awakening, of frightening "time": "Hebe den Stein nicht auf, / Den Speicher der Stille. / Unter ihm / Verschläft der Tausendfüssler / Die Zeit." The "silence" in which the stone lives is outside of time, even spiting time; and according to the epigram in "Verona," "Die Erde schenkt uns keine Zeit / Über den Tod hinaus," it lives beyond earthly existence, in death. The stone, then, is reminiscent of the situation of the poetic word in the poem "Das Zeichen"; and in another representative text from the same period, "Unter der Wurzel der Distel," the image of the stone explicitly refers to language, outlasting the passage of time:

> Unter der Wurzel der Distel
> Wohnt nun die Sprache,
> Nicht angewandt,
> Im steinigen Grund.
> Ein Riegel fürs Feuer
> War sie immer.
>
> Leg deine Hand
> Auf diesen Felsen.
> Es zittert das starre
> Geäst der Metalle.
> Ausgeräumt ist aber
> Der Sommer,
> Verstrichen die Frist. (CC, 83)

What remains with melancholy after all the loss is whatever transcends time in artistic activity—for Huchel, his refusal to succumb to ideological demands as an editor and as a poet his unrelenting preservation of the poetic word.

Even more revealing with respect to my decipherment of "Das Zeichen" and association of it with Huchel's disillusionment is the poem "Traum im Tellereisen":

> Gefangen bist du, Traum.
> Dein Knöchel brennt,
> Zerschlagen im Tellereisen.
>
> Wind blättert
> Ein Stück Rinde auf.
> Eröffnet ist

Das Testament gestürzter Tannen,
Geschrieben
In regengrauer Geduld
Unauslöschlich
Ihr letztes Vermächtnis—
Das Schweigen.

Der Hagel meisselt
Die Grabschrift auf die schwarze Glätte
Der Wasserfläche. (CC, 82)

The hope of human fulfillment—that "dream" which Huchel had carried within himself since his earliest poems and which had seemed so near realization a decade before—is now fatally trapped, its burning knuckles clamped between jaws of iron. His poem is now born of felled trees, the indelible "testament" of a mortally wounded nature, and composed of the "last legacy" of its death, "silence." During these wintry years the poem is (as is clear from the other texts discussed) about itself or about the possibility of its own survival. Directly in the center, taking up a line by itself, is the word "Geschrieben," and it is followed two lines later by the one-word line, "Unauslöschlich." Poetry has turned completely inward, having as its themes death and silence, with which it is itself identified. The closing image of the poem is a more precise variation of those scenes in "Das Zeichen" in which one part of nature pierces like metal another substance (the "chain" of wild ducks flying through the autumn air and the lancelike reeds penetrating the mist). Here the connection with death is more explicit: the hailstones carve inscriptions into the water's surface as though it were a tombstone.

It is in this poem, I think, and in the pair of poems that go with it—"Winterpsalm" and "Der Garten des Theophrast"—that the later Huchel is at his very best. The text's entirety is not so long as to get out of hand, the images are developed just enough to become truly penetrating, and the very concrete references are perfectly, inextricably merged with flashes of abstraction. I can think of no more adequate description of this poetry, and of Huchel's situation in the 1960s, than is contained in the three short lines,

> Das Testament gestürzter Tannen,
> Geschrieben
> In regengrauer Geduld

Nor, to be sure, does such a metaphor characterize only this poetry, or only Huchel's situation at this time. Wilhelm Lehmann is, I think, quite mistaken in calling this metaphor "conventional." The disappointing aspect of Lehmann's criticism is that he would really prefer Huchel to write a different kind of poetry, more like his own. He totally fails to take into account the great difference between Huchel's position as a poet and his own. The statement at the center of his critical commentary is surely less revealing about Huchel than about Lehmann himself. "Poetry as resistance against contemporary political conditions," he contends, "must of necessity be deprived of the genuinely lyrical as a timeless element." [44]

The three stanzas of "Winterpsalm" (CC, 80), dedicated to Hans Mayer, constitute a monologue interrupted first by an apostrophe spoken by the wind, then by a psalm (stanza two), and finally by the question closing the poem.[45] The first lines are a report of the speaker's walk through a winter landscape:

> Da ich ging bei träger Kälte des Himmels
> Und ging hinab die Strasse zum Fluss,
> Sah ich die Mulde im Schnee,
> Wo nachts der Wind
> Mit flacher Schulter gelegen.

44. Lehmann, "Mass des Lobes," p. 17. "Lyrik als Widerstand gegen zeitgenössische politische Verhältnisse wird von vornherein auf das eigentlich Lyrische als zeitloses Element verzichten müssen." Lehmann would attribute the literary prizes awarded to Huchel not so much to "artistic reasons," but to "bad conscience" on the part of the donors; as if the talent to significantly awaken "bad conscience" in postwar Germany, in the time of Bertolt Brecht, has nothing at all to do with "artistic reasons"! Huchel's major accomplishment, according to Lehmann, may be that he directs the reader back to the great predecessors on whose shoulders he stands. Paul Valéry is quoted: "Place aux vieux!" Surely Lehmann does not mean himself? Nevertheless, references to Gryphius, Mörike, or Trakl, as is the tendency of some overenthusiastic reviewers, do not necessarily testify to the classical grandeur, and the modernity, of Huchel's best verse.

45. In my interpretation I follow the hints given by Huchel and Hans Mayer's analysis, both included in Hilde Domin, ed., *Doppelinterpretationen* (Frankfurt and Bonn, 1966), pp. 96–100. Mayer's essay also appears in *Zur deutschen Literatur der Zeit*, pp. 185–88.

The wind has a voice, a "fragile" one, which becomes audible when
it comes into contact with light. Huchel reverses the natural order
of things, according to which the wind nourishes the flame. More
important, the wind is really deceived, and the light is only a
mirage:

> Seine gebrechliche Stimme,
> In den erstarrten Ästen oben,
> Stiess sich am Trugbild weisser Luft: . . .

Unaware of the illusion, the wind speaks. In its apostrophe it notes
the smothered scene around it, but it is afraid to report that of
which it is witness. In his comment on the poem Huchel calls the
wind's attitude "all creatures' fear of force" ("kreatürliche Angst
vor der Gewalt"):

> "Alles Verscharrte blickt mich an.
> Soll ich es heben aus dem Schutt
> Und zeigen dem Richter? Ich schweige.
> Ich will nicht Zeuge sein."

The wind falls silent; there was no real flame to ignite it: "Sein
Flüstern erlosch, / Von keiner Flamme genährt." But, as Huchel
notes, the wind's voice "evokes the counterstanza, four lines of a
psalm":

> Wohin du stürzt, o Seele,
> Nicht weiss es die Nacht. Denn da ist nichts
> Als vieler Wesen stumme Angst.
> Der Zeuge tritt hervor. Es ist das Licht.

The appeal is made in that wintry setting characteristic of all
Huchel's late poetry, which he describes in this single interpretation of his own work as "a benumbed, oppressive landscape" ("eine
erstarrte, beklemmende Landschaft"). The two voices, in the
apostrophe and in the psalm, are juxtaposed to suggest a dialogue;
in the middle of the text the isolation is broken. But all creation is
muted and oppressed, in a state of bitter fear, so that the monologue, "untouched by the voice of the wind and by the appeal,"
returns at the end to its beginning, the "final, invulnerable position" (Huchel):

Ich stand auf der Brücke,
Allein vor der trägen Kälte des Himmels.

The monologue can offer no prophecy; it has only a question, which remains unanswered:

Atmet noch schwach,
Durch die Kehle des Schilfrohrs,
Der vereiste Fluss?

Such is the "magnetic field" of the poem (to use the metaphor of Huchel's commentary), the thematic pattern arrived at after the "iron filings" (the various images and sounds in their original conception) have found their proper place and sequence. The text stands for itself and resists intrusive speculations on the part of the interpreter. But, as Huchel also admits, the fact that experience is communicated only "at the outermost edge" of the finished poem is affected by the "situation" and does not comprise merely manneristic obscurity. The "situation" of this poem is best reflected in the attention it received on its first publication: it was this text, more than anything else in Huchel's last number of *Sinn und Form* (1962), that angered East German authorities. "Winterpsalm" was for them more objectionable than the printing of poems by Günter Eich and Paul Celan or publication of speeches by Louis Aragon and Sartre calling for a liberalization of cultural policies in the socialist countries, even more than the placing of Brecht's "Rede über die Widerstandskraft der Vernunft" at the beginning of the issue.

In a way the poem represents the act of indirect protest which was the entire issue. Two statements included by the outgoing editor help determine more precisely what may be the "situation" of Huchel's "Winterpsalm." The first consists of the issue's opening words, the beginning of Brecht's speech:

In view of the very strict measures taken these days in fascist countries against reason, measures as methodical as they are brutal, it is permitted to ask whether human reason will be at all able to resist this violent assault. Such general, optimistic assertions as "reason always wins out in the end" or "the mind never grows more freely than when force is applied to it" are meaningless here. . . . The human capacity to think can be truly damaged in a most astonishing way. This is true both of individual reason and that of entire classes and peoples. The history of the human capacity to think reveals long periods of partial or complete sterility, examples of horrifying reversions and atrophies.[46]

The second revealing statement is the very end of Sartre's speech (held at an International Peace Conference in Moscow and translated for *Sinn und Form* by Stephan Hermlin) on the "Disarmament of Culture." Sartre said of intellectuals: "We are forced to swim against a mighty current: the cold war resulted in only a few deaths, but it caused the world's culture to congeal. But if for the first time in history the cultural creators were truly to unite we could, I am convinced, quickly enter into a period of thaw. And by its very existence, but also because of its deepest concerns, this new power would contribute significantly to the maintenance of peace." [47] In both speeches the human intellect is at stake, and its power of resistance against an oppressive force is in question. Both speak of a period in which reason, culture, and all life are brutally damaged and in a frozen, motionless state.

Huchel's poem "Winterpsalm" is also about "damaged life" ("beschädigtes Leben"), describing a "benumbed, oppressive landscape" in which all creatures are in a condition of mute

46. *Sinn und Form*, *14* (1962), 663: "Angesichts der überaus strengen Massnahmen, die in den faschistischen Staaten gegenwärtig gegen die Vernunft ergriffen werden, dieser ebenso methodischen wie gewalttätigen Massnahmen, ist es erlaubt, zu fragen, ob die menschliche Vernunft diesem gewaltigen Ansturm überhaupt wird widerstehen können. Mit so allgemein gehaltenen optimistischen Beteuerungen wie 'am Ende siegt immer die Vernunft' oder 'der Geist entfaltet sich nie freier als wenn ihm Gewalt angetan wird' ist hier natürlich nichts getan. . . . Tatsächlich kann das menschliche Denkvermögen in erstaunlicher Weise beschädigt werden. Dies gilt für die Vernunft der einzelnen wie der ganzer Klassen und Völker. Die Geschichte des menschlichen Denkvermögens weist grosse Perioden teilweiser oder völliger Unfruchtbarkeit, Beispiele erschreckender Rückbildungen und Verkrümmerungen auf."

47. *Sinn und Form*, p. 815: "Wir haben gegen einen sehr mächtigen Strom zu schwimmen: der kalte Krieg hat nur wenige Tote verursacht, aber er hat die Weltkultur erstarren lassen. Wenn aber wirklich zum ersten Mal in der Geschichte die Kulturschaffenden sich vereinigen würden, könnten wir, davon bin ich überzeugt, schnell in eine Zeit des Tauwetters eintreten. Und diese neue Kraft würde allein durch ihre Existenz, aber auch durch ihre tiefsten Interessen zur Erhaltung des Friedens machtvoll beitragen."

anguish. (Significant in this respect is that in still another famous speech included in the same issue of *Sinn und Form*, Louis Aragon appeals to Communist literary critics to finally study the works of Kafka.[48]) But "Winterpsalm" also deals with, or at least appeals to, the power of resistance of reason and culture. At the end of the second stanza (the psalm itself) occurs the line, "Der Zeuge tritt hervor. Es ist das Licht," which is then followed by a return to the monologue form, that "final, invulnerable position." Who is this witness who dares step forward; what is the "light"? The answer, I think, lies in the monologue itself. Both at the beginning and at the end the speaker notices in the winter setting a kind of form, vessel, or container. First it is only a trough ("die Mulde") perched uselessly in the snow: "Da ich ging bei träger Kälte des Himmels / Und ging hinab die Strasse zum Fluss, / Sah ich die Mulde im Schnee." In the last stanza, however, the enclosed vessellike object is the "throat of the reed" ("Die Kehle des Schilfrohrs"), through which the frozen river may still be breathing:

Ich stand auf der Brücke,
Allein vor der trägen Kälte des Himmels.
Atmet noch schwach,
Durch die Kehle des Schilfrohrs,
Der vereiste Fluss?

For an understanding of this metaphor, which frames the poem, a statement in another speech is revealing—Huchel's own, held on the occasion of the awarding of Stephan Hermlin with the F. C. Weiskopf prize in 1958. Huchel's final words were: "The creative, even the eruptive, element in lyric poetry only rarely exists without rules, it needs a container, a form, so as not to disperse. Spring water spilled on the floor has only a dim glow— but when poured into a glass, it is full of light."[49] It is possible, then, that the vessel seen by Huchel's speaker in the frozen landscape is the poem itself; the "witness" who dares give testimony may be the "light" of poetry, and the monologue on which he

---

48. *Sinn und Form*, pp. 922–29.

49. *Sonntag*, April 27, 1958, p. 8: "Das Schöpferische, ja selbst das Eruptive in der Lyrik lebt nur selten ohne Regel, es braucht ein Gefäss, eine Form, um nicht zu zerfliessen. Quellwasser, auf den Boden geschüttet, hat nur geringen Glanz—in ein Glas gegossen, ist es voll Licht."

falls back, the "invulnerable" power of resistance of poetic form. The poem "shows to the judge" what nature itself, the wind, was too frightened to bear witness to—the "mute anguish" of nature. As the outspoken witness of death, it may also be the preserver of whatever life is left, the "throat of the reed" through which the frozen river may still be faintly breathing.

The "situation" is similar in "Der Garten des Theophrast," which, according to Hans Mayer, seems the complementary poem to "Winterpsalm," belonging to it like the South to the North or the summer sun to winter ice: [50]

Der Garten des Theophrast

Meinem Sohn

Wenn mittags das weisse Feuer
Der Verse über den Urnen tanzt,
Gedenke, mein Sohn. Gedenke derer,
Die einst Gespräche wie Bäume gepflanzt.
Tot ist der Garten, mein Atem wird schwerer,
Bewahre die Stunde, hier ging Theophrast,
Mit Eichenlohe zu düngen den Boden,
Die wunde Rinde zu binden mit Bast.
Ein Ölbaum spaltet das mürbe Gemäuer
Und ist noch Stimme im heissen Staub.
Sie gaben Befehl, die Wurzel zu roden.
Es sinkt dein Licht, schutzloses Laub. (CC, 81)

Once again, culture is threatened and destroyed by brute force. Nature again is defenseless ("schutzloses Laub"), afraid to resist higher authority ("Sie gaben Befehl, die Wurzel zu roden"). But there are differences from "Winterpsalm." Not only is the scene warmer, more summery, but the whole poem is addressed to a human being—the speaker's and poet's son. Three times the son is appealed to, and is therefore the grammatical subject of the first eight lines. Further, there is assurance here that the "voice" of poetry is still alive, the "olive tree" is still upright among the ruins. On the other hand, the poem does not end with an open question concerning the survival of a breath of life under the ice, but with

50. *Zur deutschen Literatur*, p. 187.

a declaration that the fatal command has been given and that the "light" of survival is steadily sinking.

Most important, however, is that the "situation" is conceived of historically and culture is seen as tradition. Poetic conventions—rhyme and a regular four-beat rhythm—are employed, and the garden is associated with Theophrastus (ca. 372–287 B.C.), the most famous pupil of Aristotle and first systematizer of plant life. He imposed order on nature, and his systematization has inspired all subsequent botanical researchers. Of still greater cultural importance was his best-known work, *Characters*, with which he founded the long European tradition of practical wisdom and typologies, continued by Bacon, La Bruyère, Lichtenberg, Goethe, and the German romantics. As Mayer remarks in his intelligent interpretation of Huchel's poem, "Just as every garden today is a garden of Theophrastus, so all aphoristic wisdom, including this poem, has its basis in Theophrastus." [51] Tradition links the present moment with the past. "Der Garten des Theophrast" is gnomic poetry, uttering practical sagacities and introducing different "characters." There is the type of Theophrastus himself, who cultivates and nurses nature's wounds; and there are those who decree that nature be destroyed at the root. The deliberate rhyming of the lines "Mit Eichenlohe zu düngen den Boden" and "Sie gaben Befehl, die Wurzel zu roden" emphasizes this contrast.

But the traditional garden is "dead," overcome by the demand to root it out, and the poetic genre to which this poem itself belongs proves to be a thing of the past. The characters described do not coexist as ahistorical types but are separated from one another by a decisive historical gap. The wisdom of the poem appears no longer to apply as a general maxim but is addressed to one individual. The poem's aphorism,—again in Mayer's view—is really a "legacy" left by the father to his son: "The son seems to know only nature. He must also experience history, so as to learn that all nature represents at the same time a historical configuration." [52]

51. *Zur deutschen Literatur*, pp. 181–82: "Wie jeder Garten heute ein Garten des Theophrast ist, so ist alle Spruchweisheit, also auch dies Gedicht hier, bereits bei Theophrast vorgebildet."

52. *Zur deutschen Literatur*, p. 181: "Der Sohn scheint nur die Natur zu kennen. Er soll auch Geschichte erfahren, um zu lernen, dass alle Natur gleichzeitig ein geschichtliches Gebilde darstellt."

The course of history threatens to destroy and uproot nature, and with it the kind of cultural communication that had lived in it and thrived on it—"einst Gespräche wie Bäume gepflanzt," "Ein Ölbaum." All that will then be left of the tradition is a preservation of it in the memory—"Gedenke, mein Sohn," "Bewahre die Stunde" (compare, in the "Dedication" for Ernst Bloch, "Du musst es bewahren"). The lost garden, idyllic nearness to nature, remains "in the huge domain of my memory" ("im grossen Hof meines Gedächtnisses," from the motto of *Chausseen Chausseen*), and the reader is again made to think, as Mayer correctly mentions, of Hölderlin's "Andenken." The son is truly a part of his father; the poem is a monologue after all, and the poet once again takes comfort in the power of his craft to stand up against the deadening blows of history.

History is also central to the last two poems to be considered in the complex of *Chausseen Chausseen*, "An taube Ohren der Geschlechter" and "Psalm," the latter of which ends the volume. Here it becomes clear that the source of Huchel's profound resignation lies deeper, and is more far-reaching, than disappointment with East German land reform and the political pressure exerted on him in the DDR. The upset reached to his faith in the feasibility of human progress and his belief that mankind heeds the lessons provided by history.

"An taube Ohren der Geschlechter" begins with two lines which act against a normal conception of time:

> Es war ein Land mit hundert Brunnen.
> Nehmt für zwei Wochen Wasser mit. (CC, 77)

Imperfect tense is juxtaposed to an imperative: preparation is being made for an expedition now to a land that once existed, as in a fairy tale ("Es war einmal"). The speaker, who seems familiar with the route, then describes the barren wasteland that lies ahead:

> Der Weg ist leer, der Baum verbrannt.
> Die Öde saugt den Atem aus.
> Die Stimme wird zu Sand
> Und wirbelt hoch und stützt den Himmel
> Mit einer Säule, die zerstäubt.

Mayer is correct when, in paraphrasing these lines, he remarks that
the human voice does not reach the sky which it addresses but
falls back like a column of sand, "deaf ears of heaven." [53] But he
fails to observe the implications of the metaphor. The column of
sand which seems to support the sky, only to collapse to the earth
as dust, is a vision of nuclear destruction, the terrifying outcome
of the highest human aspirations. The ultimate futility of this
scientific endeavor is contained in the simultaneous use of contradictory verbs—"stützt" and "zerstäubt." The guide and speaker
then continues his description of the desert terrain, the only sign
of life being the woolly fibers torn from cattails:

> Nach Meilen noch ein toter Fluss.
> Die Tage schweifen durch das Röhricht
> Und reissen Wolle aus den schwarzen Kerzen.

The setting is now completely desolate; measured distance and
time have become indefinite and even meaningless ("Nach Meilen
noch," "Die Tage schweifen"). At the end of this section (stanzas
one and two), the speaker returns to his original advice to bring
along a substantial supply of water. The abandoned waterhole
here is covered over by green slime:

> Und eine Haut aus Grünspan schliesst
> Das Wasserloch,
> Als faule Kupfer dort im Schlamm.

Suddenly another word of advice follows, and it seems only a
historical analogy illustrating the first:

> Denkt an die Lampe
> Im golddurchwirkten Zelt des jungen Afrikanus:
> Er liess ihr Öl nicht länger brennen,
> Denn Feuer wütet genug,
> Die siebzehn Nächte zu erhellen.

In order to help you save on water, the speaker seems to say, think
how Scipio Africanus saved on oil during the Third Punic War—
how he turned off his lantern and made use of the light provided
by Carthage in flames. Such appears to be the logical connection
between the speaker's thoughts. But the real analogy is between

53. *Zur deutschen Literatur*, p. 179: "Taube Ohren des Himmels."

the wasteland, which used to have one hundred wells, and conquered Carthage, between nuclear holocaust and the flames that
ravaged the ancient Punic capital. In order to recognize the
futility of military conquest, it is said, think of how futile was the
destruction of Carthage by the Romans.

The fourth stanza is clearly separated from the rest of the poem:

> Polybius berichtet von den Tränen,
> Die Scipio verbarg im Rauch der Stadt.
> Dann schnitt der Pflug
> Durch Asche, Bein und Schutt.
> Und der es aufschrieb, gab die Klage
> An taube Ohren der Geschlechter.

The stanza is also different from the preceding ones in its symmetry: there is even a hint of a rhyme scheme in the pattern of
assonances, ä-a-u-u-a-e. It is meant as the moral of the story, telling of the Roman historian Polybius' report that the triumphant
leader, his patron and student Scipio, was brought to tears at the
sight of the total destruction wreaked on Carthage as he conquered
it, and then had salt plowed into its soil to prevent any future
harvest. Once again, Carthage is given as a warning, an example of
the futility of military conquest, and the reader is reminded of
Brecht's didactic parable in his open letter to German writers in
1951: "Great Carthage led three wars. It was still mighty after the
first, still habitable after the second. It was no longer to be found
after the third." [54]

But this last stanza is also the moral of history, and in this
respect, as Hans Mayer puts it, "a moral without a moral" ("Moral
ohne Moral"). Polybius recorded Scripio's plaint and passed it on,
but all later generations were "deaf" to it. The speaker himself is
made to recognize the futility of his own advice and to realize that
he too is recording a plaint that will not be heard. The last line
of the poem is identical with its title; the end returns to the
beginning. The static form corresponds to the content, the theme
of "historical stasis" (Mayer). The only progress discernible in
history is the magnitude of annihilation; "modern" desolation is

54. *Gesammelte Werke, 19*, 496: "Das grosse Karthago führte drei Kriege. Es
war noch mächtig nach dem ersten, noch bewohnbar nach dem zweiten. Es war
nicht mehr auffindbar nach dem dritten."

only more momentous than that of ancient times. "An taube
Ohren der Geschlechter" reads like "Bericht des Pfarrers vom
Untergang seiner Gemeinde" reflecting on itself. What can the
theme of the preacher's "report"—"Here there was no law"
("Hier war kein Gesetz")—ultimately mean if it will have to be
proclaimed endlessly to describe the full course of human history?

The last poem in the volume *Chausseen Chausseen* is entitled
"Psalm" and if what had preceded was read carefully, it requires
little commentary. The most sententious and solemn of all Huchel's
poems it begins with a paraphrase of Thomas Aquinas' idea of
generation and ends with an image of obsessively self-destructive
mankind.

Psalm

Dass aus dem Samen des Menschen
Kein Mensch
Und aus dem Samen des Ölbaums
Kein Ölbaum
Werde,
Es ist zu messen
Mit der Elle des Todes.

Die da wohnen
Unter der Erde
In einer Kugel aus Zement,
Ihre Stärke gleicht
Dem Halm
Im peitschenden Schnee.

Die Öde wird Geschichte.
Termiten schreiben sie
Mit ihren Zangen
In den Sand.

Und nicht erforscht wird werden
Ein Geschlecht,
Eifrig bemüht,
Sich zu vernichten. (CC, 84)

Again, as in "Das Zeichen," only the dead are able to "measure"
life and to recognize what is permanent. And again, as in "Winterpsalm" and especially "An taube Ohren der Geschlechter," there

is the arid desolation which is history, with the assurance here that the wasteland of the present day is also being recorded as history. Criticism of contemporary history, then, is formulated as an eschatological vision. As Walter Jens points out,[55] the question at the beginning of the volume "War es das Zeichen?" is ingeniously answered in this maxim at the end: "Die Öde wird Geschichte. / Termiten schreiben sie / Mit ihren Zangen / In den Sand." The poems in the volume move between bewildered questioning and sagacious testimony, between the cipher and the psalm.

That Huchel wrote a psalm and quoted Thomas Aquinas does not indicate a religious conversion of any kind. He never was, and has not become, a "sacred" poet. The Bible is for him, as he says in conversation, a "terrific book" ("ein tolles Buch"), as are the sources of classical mythology and the medieval scholastics, to whom he often refers. What he seeks in this allusive technique is, first of all, a mythological frame of reference, a universe of discourse to replace what he feels lost to him: the local idiom of Brandenburg. He delves backward historically into the wealth offered in the Christian and classical traditions and moves out geographically from his native terrain, setting many of his poems in Greece, the Balkan area, and northern Italy. With the coming of darkness he must leave behind the tranquil idyll of his youth. As is said, symbolically, in the poem "Le Pouldu":

> Lass alles zurück,
> Die Einfalt des Landes
>
> .   .   .   .
>
> Am Rücken der Klippe
> Stehen die Männer, sie fischen Treibholz.
> Zottige Pferde schleifen auf Kufen
> Seetang über den Strand.
> Geh fort, Gauguin. Das Dunkel flutet.
>
> .   .   .   .
>
> Lass alles zurück,
> Das Dorf, umgittert vom Garn der Netze,
> Die russumwehte Stunde nachts,
> Die Stimme der Magd. (CC, 39)

55. *Die Zeit*, December 6, 1963.

The comforting sound of the maid's voice and sight of drooping fishnets are not enough when confronting a world in which the fact of deprivation appears to run deeper than economic disadvantage. The answer will now have to be stated in a less localized idiom and within the context of a more universal mythology.

By his technique of historical and literary allusion Huchel is also seeking to express his conscious connection with the European cultural tradition, though he does not directly identify with and place faith in the teachings of Christianity, much less the Golden Age of classical antiquity. The tidy order established by Theophrastus' biological systematization and typological wisdom is felt to have broken down, and with it the harmony between poetic statement and the living nature in which it is rooted. Rather, strictly through the power of poetic evocation and reminiscence, Huchel believes himself able to preserve contact with the great humanistic cultures of the past. The tradition, then, is not a place of refuge for Huchel, as it has become for some DDR writers, but a point of reference that provides his lonely plaint with deeper significance. It helps to strengthen the sturdy "counterposition" which he has been holding over the past decade.

While he is generally indifferent to the most avant-garde poetic devices, Peter Huchel has not lost his sense of adventure, and there is nothing old-fashioned about his later poetry. He has kept pace with the times as he experienced them, gradually relinquishing one poetic tool and taking hold of another, more appropriate one. It is a far cry from his "origin" in the late 1920s, that idyll conceived out of concern over social injustice, to the dismal "winter psalm" of the 1960s, where all creation is in a condition of terrified silence; from the October light which ripened the sweet pear in harmony with the servant-girl's activity to the light which is lone witness to a frozen landscape. In between came years of National Socialism and the war, when nature itself seemed wounded, and poetic language could no longer rely for its melody on the dynamics of a rural setting. Then, at the end of the war, the poet's vision was split; he turned backward, to recapture the total destruction and chaos brought to all life by the war; and, at the same time, his hopes for a democratic reconstruction of the social and natural order were reawakened. When evoking the war, his language and imagery were fragmented and already moving away

from the local idiom, and the tone was plaintive and melancholy.
The poet was not primarily concerned with injustice specific to
society. But in the poems about agricultural reform, the style was
hymnic, more sure of itself although, like the optimistic mood,
hopelessly flat and unconvincing. The poet again turned to his
sympathy with the economically exploited and glorified the institutionalization of social justice through legislation, the historical
realization of his pastoral. His tragic disappointment with further
legislative measures formed the basis of the theme of resignation
and disillusionment which has been characteristic of his poetry
since 1955, and his late style is a continuation and refinement of
that evident in his descriptions of the war's wreckage. The idyll
of human harmony with nature is shattered once and for all, and
even the landscape itself has lost its vital dynamic. What is left
is a self-reflecting "testament" of a silenced and mortally wounded
creation, the poem turned inward and left to commune only
with the dead.

This last development, most evident in the poems published in
Huchel's "farewell issue" of *Sinn und Form*, has brought about a
situation such that the East German cultural authorities, even if
they were ready and willing to draw him back into literary life,
would be confronted with a group of texts totally at odds with
official demands. Although there is in them no straightforward
attack on specific issues, the brooding introspection and passivity
flatly deny any progress whatsoever and reflect an alienation as
deeply seated as any in the past. Further, the basically idealistic
conception of poetry, which is denied any affirmative social function, would be viewed as entirely unpresentable to East German
readers. Huchel's situation has become frozen, like the "frozen
river" in "Winterpsalm." It could be, though, as the intelligent
DDR critic Dieter Schlenstedt argues, that what he saw was
"only the brook." [56]

Since *Chausseen Chausseen* Huchel has continued writing poetry, and he may soon have the equivalent of another volume,
although very little of it has yet been published.[57] His mood re-

56. Schlenstedt, "Epimetheus—Prometheus: Positionen in der Lyrik," *alternative,* 7 (1964), 113–21. P. 120: "Er glaubt, der Fluss sei vereist—und es ist doch
nur der Bach."

57. Six of Huchel's recent poems, including the two mentioned here, were
published in an article by Ingo Seidler, "Peter Huchel und sein lyrisches Werk,"
Neue deutsche Hefte, 15 (1968), 11–32.

mains somber and pensive, and his style is still cryptic and filled
with images of desolation. For the most part he is still singing
the psalm of an unending winter. One noticeable difference from
his poetry of the beginning of the 1960s, however, is that his
negation is directed at more specific East German phenomena.
An example of this more calculated offensive is contained in his
important poem about the Berlin Wall, "Ophelia" ("Kein König-
reich, / Ophelia, / Wo ein Schrei / Das Wasser höhlt, / Ein
Zauber / Die Kugel / Am Weidenblatt zersplittern lässt"). Huchel
takes up the tradition of spectral Ophelia poems from German
expressionism (Benn, Heym, and Trakl, as well as Brecht's "Vom
ertrunkenen Mädchen"), and associates it with the gruesome situation at the Wall. Another tendency in his most recent poetry is
preoccupation with the theme of his own exiled situation. In the
poem "Exil" he tells how his "friends," the shadows and the
wind, come to visit him and talk with him. They tell him to "go
with the wind," to leave before it is too late ("Geh fort, bevor im
Ahornblatt / Das Stigma des Herbstes brennt"). But, significantly,
the "stone" (his own voice?) advises him to "remain faithful,"
since there may be some signs of renewed light and springtime:

> Sei getreu, sagt der Stein.
> Die dämmernde Frühe
> Hebt an, wo Licht und Laub
> Ineinander wohnen
> Und das Gesicht
> In einer Flamme vergeht.

There is evidently more movement and aroused energy in the
new poems. Some dialogue, no matter how dreary, seems to have
been resumed, and some human figures, although they are bitterly
treated, have begun to appear on the scene. It may be that the
words of encouragement ("Ermutigung") dedicated to him by
one of his "friends" in exile, Wolf Biermann, have had some
effect on him. Biermann writes:

> Wir wolln es nicht verschweigen
> In dieser Schweigezeit:
> Das Grün bricht aus den Zweigen
> Wir wolln das allen zeigen
> Dann wissen sie Bescheid.[58]

58. Biermann, *Mit Marx- und Engelszungen* (West Berlin, 1968), p. 61.

For Huchel the hard, frightful, silent years go on, and there is no sign that they will really brighten. "Is he the Pasternak of East Germany?" one is tempted to ask with the *Times Literary Supplement*.[59] The parallel no doubt exists, but the English reviewer has a better answer. "He is certainly one of the most courageous and humane of living contemplative poets."

59. *Times Literary Supplement*, September 28, 1967, p. 912.

4

Johannes Bobrowski: Shadow Land, Of Guilt and Community

Approaching Bobrowski

In March 1965, six months before his sudden, unexpected death at the age of forty-eight, Johannes Bobrowski was asked in an interview in East Berlin whether any living poets served as models for him in his own writing. His immediate answer was, "Peter Huchel, of course. I first read a poem of his in Soviet prison camp, in a newspaper, and it impressed me immensely. That's where I came to see people in a landscape—to such an extent that to this day I do not care for an unpeopled natural setting. I am no longer charmed by the elemental forces of a landscape, but by nature only when seen in connection with, and as a field of, the effective activity of man." Bobrowski was deeply impressed by Huchel's view of nature as a setting for human activity, his vision of "idyllic" harmony between man and nature which distinguishes his verse from the main tendency of modern German nature poetry. Indeed, Bobrowski is sometimes grouped with the "Natur-lyriker"; but because of this concern he shared with Huchel for active human presence in a natural setting, he has explicitly distanced himself from the tradition of the "pure" nature poem.[1]

1. Included in *Johannes Bobrowski: Selbstzeugnisse und Beiträge über sein Werk* (East Berlin, 1967), p. 79: "Peter Huchel natürlich! In der Gefangenschaft habe ich zum ersten Mal ein Gedicht von ihm gelesen, in einer Zeitung, und das hat mich ungeheuer beeindruckt. Da habe ich es her, Menschen in der Landschaft zu sehen, so sehr, dass ich bis heute eine unbelebte Landschaft nicht mag. Dass mich also das Elementare der Landschaft gar nicht reizt, sondern die Landschaft erst im Zusammenhang und als Wirkungsfeld des Menschen." Pp. 49–50: "Das reine Naturgedicht, das auch in diesem Jahrhundert noch gepflegt worden ist,

A few years after his return to Berlin from the Soviet Union in 1949, Bobrowski came into closer contact with Huchel. In 1952 he submitted a few poems to *Sinn und Form*, and they were published (1955) after Huchel had expressed his enthusiastic personal approval.[2] Peter Huchel "discovered" the poet Bobrowski ten years before he gained international renown and was awarded the Group 47 Prize in 1962. "He was the first person," Bobrowski recalled in the year of his death, "to tell me something about my poetry, and his words were favorable."[3]

This sympathetic contact between Huchel and Bobrowski is, I believe, of some symbolic importance. As non-Marxists writing in a Communist country, the two poets have encountered similar political circumstances in their relationship with the official currents of East German literature and cultural policy. In their poetry there is much evidence of stylistic and thematic kinship, particularly in their shared vision of human justice and of harmony between man and his natural surroundings. Bobrowski's cryptic, evocative style often closely resembles the language and rhythms of Huchel's late verse. Furthermore, both poets are profoundly concerned in their writing with the function and threatened situation of poetic language as a means of expression and communication; Bobrowski, like Huchel, viewed his art as an act of deliberate resistance against the danger of enforced linguistic sterility and subservience to ideological demands.

But, surprisingly, an intensive comparison of Huchel and Bobrowski would prove rather unrewarding because the differences between them are ultimately more telling than the similarities. Substantial differences in background account for the quite dis-

---

zum Beispiel bei Wilhelm Lehmann gelegentlich, und wie das zum Beispiel bei der 'Kolonne' in den zwanziger Jahren versucht worden ist, das halte ich nicht mehr für so erheblich. Ich glaube, dass, wenn heute ein Lyriker ein Naturgedicht schreibt, . . . er eine Beziehung sucht zu den Menschen, die in dieser Natur leben, die diese Natur auch gestalten; eine Landschaft, in der Menschen gearbeitet haben, in der Menschen leben, in der Menschen tätig sind."

2. The poems published in *Sinn und Form* were not the first written by Bobrowski. He began writing in 1943 as a German soldier on the Eastern Front. Eight of his earliest poems appeared, under the name Hannes Bobrowski, in the last issue of the periodical *Das innere Reich* (March, 1944). These poems are reprinted in the appendix, pp. 325–27.

3. *Bobrowski: Selbstzeugnisse*, p. 79: "Das war der erste, der mir etwas dazu und etwas Gutes gesagt hat."

tinct qualities of their poetry. Huchel was rooted in the province of Brandenburg and was concerned from the beginning with the fact of economic exploitation and social stratification which he saw around him in his childhood. Bobrowski, on the other hand, grew up in Tilsit (East Prussia), on the Lithuanian border, and his attention was drawn to a different kind of conflict: the disputes between the various peoples inhabiting his native area. Huchel developed his poetic means basically from Droste-Hülshoff, and to some extent from Loerke and Lehmann, and finds his own particular voice with the reflective poem; Bobrowski explicitly worked in the tradition of Klopstock and Hölderlin, his characteristic modes being the modernized ode and hymn. Of great importance, finally, is the difference between Huchel's secular humanism and Bobrowski's firm religious beliefs. As shown, Huchel could withdraw only into a state of dismal isolation once his hopes in the eradication of social injustice were shattered; whereas Bobrowski was throughout his life a believing Protestant: during the period of National Socialism he had connections with the "Confessing Church," and in the DDR he belonged to the East German Christian Democratic Union (CDU). Unlike Huchel, therefore, the Christian faith was always available to him, to support his belief in ultimate human redemption. Ironically, the same year (1962) that saw Huchel removed from his position as editor in chief of *Sinn und Form* and withdraw from East German literary life in bitter resignation brought Bobrowski full renown, and in the last three years of his life he often appeared as a spokesman for his country at international cultural conferences.

In addition, a different approach must be taken to an evaluation of Bobrowski's poetry. His career was too short, and the thematic direction of his work too removed from concrete contemporary events, to make chronological development of foremost importance, as with Huchel. To be sure, certain tendencies can be seen, such as a development from mythological to a more historical treatment of his theme, and from a hymnic to a more cryptic style. But even these trends are difficult to discern, and nothing substantial can be developed from them. Bobrowski's work is best studied by concentrating attention on the various aspects of his one major thematic concern, which his friend Klaus Wagenbach, and Bobrowski himself, called "Nachbarschaft." [4] Nearly everything he wrote derives from, or in one way or another relates to, his search for community and neighborly companionship among different peoples and among men of the same nation. [5] Even the features of his style and poetic language are best understood within this thematic context.

This chapter will concentrate on Bobrowski's three volumes of poetry, *Sarmatische Zeit* (1961), *Schattenland Ströme* (1962), and the posthumously published *Wetterzeichen* (1966), with only occasional references to the prose. [6] Although it deals with the same subjects as his poetry, Bobrowski's prose displays a different side of his character, being generally lighter in tone and more playful in temperament. The novel *Levins Mühle* (1964) has met with justified acclaim, and some of the stories included in the volumes *Mäusefest* (1965), *Boehlendorff* (1965) and *Der Mahner* (1967) are masterpieces of their kind—such as the delicate title story (1962) of *Mäusefest*, the powerful sketches "Litauische Geschichte" (1962) and "Betrachtung eines Bildes" (1965), and the amusing "De homine publico tractatus" (1964). But the second novel, *Litauische Claviere*, completed just before his death and published in 1966, is more problematic, its effectiveness severely diminishing after the promising first chapter. In my opinion Bobrowski's prose is of far less significance than his poetry, being frequently rather meager in content and annoyingly manneristic in style. Nevertheless, it can sometimes be revealing for a study of his verse.

The discussion can be arranged in three parts. The first deals with the landscape and atmosphere, unmistakably characteristic of Bobrowski's poetry, which he called "Sarmatien" and referred to time and again as the original motivation of all his writing. Involved here will be a consideration of his treatment of myth and

---

4. Cf. Klaus Wagenbach, "Nachbarschaft: Zum Tode Johannes Bobrowskis," *Die Zeit*, September 10, 1965, p. 24. Wagenbach also entitled a collection of Bobrowski's work *Nachbarschaft* (Berlin, 1967).

5. The closest English equivalent to "Nachbarschaft" is perhaps "companionship" as that word is used and explained by R. W. B. Lewis in his work on contemporary fiction, *The Picaresque Saint* (Philadelphia, 1956), pp. 29–35.

6. Bobrowski's volumes of poetry will be identified as follows. SZ: *Sarmatische Zeit* (Stuttgart, 1961; East Berlin, 1961); SS: *Schattenland Ströme* (Stuttgart, 1962; East Berlin, 1963); W: *Wetterzeichen* (East Berlin, 1966; West Berlin, 1967).

history and the tension in his poetry between vision and reality, recorded time and subjective memory. The second section discusses Bobrowski's notion of poetic language and its function, most elaborately expounded in his important poem "An Klopstock." This theoretical context can serve to define some of the characteristics of Bobrowski's unique poetic style and the typical rhythmic progression evident in many of his individual poems. Finally, the basis of the concept "Nachbarschaft" emerges from the discussion of his memorable love poems, as does the sense of obstructed community expressed in his few poems which seem to refer to society in the DDR. I will thereby attempt to determine Bobrowski's personal political viewpoint, to which he repeatedly drew attention as the "ideology" or "concern of the author" ("das Anliegen des Autors").

Although the chapter concentrates on specific texts as much as possible, no one will be subjected to exhaustive interpretation. The method of close reading of individual poems can be extremely fruitful in the case of Bobrowski, as has been demonstrated with great success by Sigfrid Hoefert, Peter Paul Schwarz, Günter Hartung, and other critics.[7] From even a casual reading it is

7. In recent years a great deal has been written about Bobrowski. Aside from the innumerable reviews and obituary notices, several longer studies have appeared, among which the following are to be especially recommended: Sigrid Hoefert, *West-Östliches in der Lyrik Johannes Bobrowskis* (Munich, 1966); Peter Paul Schwarz, " 'Freund mit der leisen Rede': Zur Lyrik Johannes Bobrowskis," *Der Deutschunterricht, 18* (1966), 48–65; Britta Titel, "Johannes Bobrowski," *Schriftsteller der Gegenwart,* ed. Klaus Nonnenmann (Olten and Freiburg, 1963), pp. 51–57; Günter Hartung, "Johannes Bobrowski," *Sinn und Form, 18* (1966), 1189–1217; Renate von Heydebrand, "Engagierte Esoterik: Die Gedichte Johannes Bobrowskis," *Wissenschaft als Dialog: Studien zur Literatur und Kunst seit der Jahrhundertwende,* ed. Renate von Heydebrand and Klaus Günther Just (Stuttgart, 1969), pp. 386–450. The last two of these articles, and the collection of essays by Hoefert, are in my opinion the best discussions thus far of Bobrowski's work. Also, the volume *Johannes Bobrowski: Selbstzeugnisse und Beiträge über sein Werk,* compiled by the publishing house where Bobrowski was active from 1959 until his death (the Union Verlag in East Berlin), is indispensable; it includes many statements by the author, some fine material on his work, and an excellent bibliography through 1966. The book by Gerhard Wolf (in the East German series "Schriftsteller der Gegenwart") *Johannes Bobrowski: Leben und Werk* (Berlin, 1967), contains some valuable biographical information but lacks original critical insight; it is further marred by the author's orthodox ideological position. There are two articles on Bobrowski in English: Jerry Glenn, "An Introduction to the Poetry of Johannes Bobrowski," *Germanic Review, 41* (1966), 45–56; and Patrick Bridgwater, "The Poetry of Johannes Bobrowski," *Forum for Modern Language*

obvious that Bobrowski is a learned poet, a *poeta doctus* in the truest sense, and his erudition is especially challenging to the reader because of the mystifying means of expression, which he himself admitted to be a "secret leaning toward hermeticism." There can be no question, therefore, that the elusive details and aesthetic subtleties of his poetry fully merit intensive critical analysis. But Bobrowski uttered a word of warning less than a year before his death which I think will remain relevant to all study of his work. "The danger exists among many friends of literature," he said, "that in recognizing literary quality they actually ignore the concern of the author, that they would rather not hear that concern and go on to busy themselves with aesthetic qualities taken out of all context. I place no value in this approach, because it is only on the basis of these problems about which I am speaking that I came to write at all, and I write for their sake." [8] Bobrowski hoped that fascination with the intriguing, inimitable art of his poetry would not exclude a recognition of the urgent moral concern which was his inspiration. Inseparable from the compelling rhythms and suggestive imagery there is a voice of profound vital humanity, which provides the substance indispensable to his verse.

Sarmatia, Myth and History

Whenever Bobrowski was asked about his own writing, he invariably gave the same reply: that he was driven to write because he wished to tell his countrymen something about which he knew more than they, their "Eastern neighbors." He repeatedly

---

Studies, 2 (1966), 320–34; both essays are informative and demonstrate a sympathetic understanding of Bobrowski's poetry, but they remain somewhat superficial in their treatment of specific texts and of the problems which ultimately most affected Bobrowski. See also the article in Dutch: Eric Standaert, "Johannes Bobrowski: Een inleiding tot zijn poëzie," *Diagram voor progressieve literatur,* 2 (1964), 35–54.

8. *Selbstzeugnisse und Beiträge.* P. 32: "eine heimliche Neigung zum Hermetismus." P. 59: "es besteht ja die Gefahr bei vielen Literaturfreunden, dass sie über einer literarischen Qualität, die sie feststellen, das Anliegen des Autors eigentlich beiseite schieben, dass sie das gar nicht hören möchten und sich dann also unverbindlich mit dem Künstlerischen befassen. Darauf lege ich keinen Wert, denn ich bin ja auf Grund dieser Probleme, die ich genannt habe, überhaupt zum Schreiben gekommen, und ich schreibe ihretwegen."

referred to the relationship of different nationalities to one another, and particularly that of the Germans to the peoples of Eastern Europe, as the "general theme" of his entire work. This historical relationship—about which he felt especially authorized to speak because of personal experiences since boyhood, profound impressions as a soldier, and his lifelong study—was seen by Bobrowski as marked from the beginning by adversity, misunderstanding, persecution, and guilt. All his writings deal with the guilt of the German people toward the indigenous people of Eastern Europe, extending from the time of the Teutonic Order to the present. He was in the widest sense a historical author, who sought to give expression to the long history of an international relationship misrepresented or totally neglected by historians until most recent times. Bobrowski saw the German East with the eyes of an exile, one who had been removed from his native terrain when new frontiers were declared. But he was an exile who, having a thorough knowledge of the long German exploitation of that area, was disturbed, not by the new frontiers themselves, but by the eventuality that recourse to war might again be urged as a means of adjusting them.[9] The very consistency of his moral position suffices to make Alfred Kurella's dogmatic contention that the "deeper interests" of Bobrowski's writing are of no use "over there" ("drüben," in West Germany) absolutely invalid.[10]

Bobrowski called the German East, Sarmatia, using the name given by ancient geographers and chroniclers (notably Herodotus, Tacitus, and Ptolemy) to a rather vaguely defined area between the Vistula River and the Caspian Sea, which corresponds roughly to central and southern Russia. Knowledge about the Sarmatian peoples is almost equally vague. They are generally considered to have been composed of various tribes of different ethnic origin, including Iranian and Slavic, and to have followed the Scythians

9. One example of what Bobrowski might have considered a successful history of this relationship may be mentioned. In the same year as the publication of his first volume, *Sarmatische Zeit* (1961), there appeared a book entitled *Land im Osten: Verheissung und Verhängnis der Deutschen* (English translation, *Slav and Teuton*) by the Austrian author Hermann Schreiber, which for the first time treated in serious, unbiased terms precisely that aspect of German history which formed Bobrowski's theme.

10. Quoted in *Selbstzeugnisse*, pp. 197–98: "Die Realia dieser Dichtung, ihr tieferes Anliegen sind drüben nicht zu gebrauchen."

from about 100 B.C. to 200 A.D. as the ruling group in Eurasia.
With the invasions of the Goths and Huns, they are thought to
have been scattered throughout central and eastern Europe. Some
chronicle traditions saw in the Sarmatians the early ancestors of
the Slavs, but these are regarded by historians as purely legendary.[11]
For Bobrowski, "the Sarmatian" or "the Eastern" ("das Östliche")
was also a very general reference, apparently including the entire
area from Finland to southern Russia, with special focus on the
Baltic states (Latvia, Lithuania, and East Prussia), Poland, and
northwestern Russia. What is important, however, is that the
epoch and landscape of Sarmatia and the Sarmatians hover between
prehistory and history, between legend and recorded actuality.
This quality of Sarmatia may explain why Bobrowski chose it as
the setting of his poetry. Bobrowski's Sarmatia is the German East
seen with the eyes of a poet, a historical landscape constituted
by mythic vision.

Characteristically, in Bobrowski's poetry neglected history is
treated in the terms and dimensions of myth, as can best be seen
in one of the first poems he wrote after the war, "Pruzzische
Elegie" (1952). As is stated in a note to this elegy, his longest
poem "calls to memory the people of Pruzze [Old Prussia], ex-
terminated by the Teutonic Order." [12] It conjures up the world
of the Old Prussians, who with the Latvians and Lithuanians com-
prised the Baltic peoples, neither Germanic nor Slavic; it celebrates
in hymnic tones their simple way of life, their primitive beliefs,
and their closeness to the natural surroundings. Its powerful
dactyls also lament the Prussians' downfall and destruction during
the thirteenth and fourteenth centuries at the hands of the Teutonic knights, acting in the name of Christianity. The Old Prussians did not share the fate of the Latvians or Lithuanians, who
managed to survive their struggles with the Teutons and established sizable territories in later centuries; rather, their resolutely
waged battles ended in their total disappearance as a people.
Through a pitiless ironic twist, their name was bestowed upon

11. See, for example, Oscar Halecki, *Borderlands of Western Civilization: A
History of East Central Europe* (New York, 1952), p. 14.

12. SZ (East Berlin edition only). P. 99: "Das Gedicht ruft die Erinnerung an
das vom Deutschen Ritterorden ausgerottete Volk der Pruzzen herauf." The
poem appears on pp. 45–47.

and borne through history by none other than their own con-
querors. Bobrowski concisely evokes their downfall in the following stanza, in which memories of Klopstock and Hölderlin
are overshadowed by the freshness of imagery and forceful rhythmic thrust:

> Volk
> der schwelenden Haine,
> der brennenden Hütten, zerstampfter
> Saaten, geröteter Ströme—
> Volk,
> geopfert dem sengenden
> Blitzschlag; dein Schreien verhängt vom
> Flammengewölke—
> Volk,
> vor des fremden Gottes
> Mutter im röchelnden Springtanz
> stürzend—
> Wie vor ihrer erzenen
> Heermacht sie schreitet, aufsteigend
> über dem Wald! wie des Sohnes
> Galgen ihr nachfolgt!—

The times when the Old Prussians still existed are recalled as
the joyous days of childhood, and the speaker sees himself among
them, partaking of their games and sacred rituals.

But even then there were evil forebodings; in the native songs
and sagas lingered a presentiment of doom:

> wie hing Gerücht im Geäst ihr! [der Linde]
> So in der Greisinnen Lieder
> tönt noch,
> kaum mehr zu deuten,
> Anruf der Vorzeit—
> wie vernahmen wir da
> modernden, trüb verfärbten
> Nachhalls Rest!

This stanza is situated between the description of the bright days
of Old Prussian life and the plaint at the Prussians' brutal extinction. Forming a kind of transition, it is thematically crucial because

it suggests this ancient people's tragic awareness of its own destiny, as expressed in its vanished songs and culture. The "Pruzzische Elegie" is itself an "Anruf der Vorzeit" and therefore contains as an essential element a reflection on its own nature. The vanished nationality is the poem's subject, which attains mythic grandeur through being invoked at the beginning like the epic muse or an entire pantheon: "Dir / ein Lied zu singen." But the description of Old Prussian life and its downfall is framed by a characterization of the "song" itself. After the initial address ("Dir"), the entire first stanza tells of the "Lied": "hell von zorniger Liebe— / dunkel aber, von Klage / bitter." The two closing stanzas explain how the spirit of Old Prussian life is preserved: the landscape itself seems to speak of it—mountain ridges and rivers—as well as sagas, and also the present song. The poem ends,

> heute ein Gesang, vor Klage
> arm—
>
> arm wie des Fischers Netzzug,
> jenes weisshaarigen, ew'gen
> am Haff, wenn die Sonne
> herabkommt.

The elegy is filled with love for the Old Prussians and anger over their cruel fate. But it is above all a plaint (*elegos*), made dismal and lean from lamenting ("vor Klage arm"). The closing simile probably refers to an ancient legend about Perkun, the Baltic sun deity. Foreseeing a massive Swedish invasion, Perkun descended among his worshipers ("wenn die Sonne herabkommt") and succeeded in preserving the sea's fish by withdrawing them from near the shoreline. Bobrowski alludes to this same legend in two other poems.[13] The comparison in "Pruzzische Elegie" is between the scantiness, in those times, of a fisherman's net and the "thin" quality of the song itself.

The description of the song as sparse appears to refer not only to the result of the speaker's lament, or to the virtual lack of any significant remnants of Old Prussian culture. It is also a characterization of the elegiac genre as Bobrowski used it. Since he could

13. "Die Frauen der Nehrungsfischer" (SZ, 17) and "Absage" (SZ, 85). See with regard to this mythological allusion Hoefert, *West-Östliches*, pp. 4–5.

rely on neither a consistent mythological frame of reference nor
the convention of the elegiac distich, Bobrowski attempted to
develop his own form and technique of the historical elegy. The
following lines illustrate his unique elegiac style:

> Namen reden von dir,
> zertretenes Volk, Berghänge,
> Flüsse, glanzlos noch oft,
> Steine und Wege—
> Lieder abends und Sagen,
> das Rascheln der Eidechsen nennt dich.

Clearly these lines contain none of the full, assured resonance
characteristic of earlier elegies, such as those of Goethe or Hölderlin or even Rilke. Bobrowski seems to have recourse only to
random flashes of imagery, disparate associations which must of
themselves evoke a sense of broad historic totality.

Bobrowski wrote several other poems in which reference is
made to the lost culture of Old Prussia. In "Der Wachtelschlag"
(SS, 5–7) the fate goddess Laima is mentioned, and in the intriguing poem "Gestorbene Sprache" (SZ, 30) Bobrowski even
uses words from the nearly extinct language. As Sigfrid Hoefert
has shown in his detailed analysis of "Gestorbene Sprache," that
poem contains the same sense of foreboding as does "Pruzzische
Elegie." [14] Again it is as though these ancient peoples expressed
in their vocabulary and spiritual beliefs a prophetic awareness of
their oncoming doom. Finally, words from Old Prussian are of
central thematic interest in the poem "Namen für den Verfolgten"
(W, 54).

Sarmatia, however, also includes the cultural landscapes of
ancient Lithuania, Latvia, ancient Russia, and Finland. These areas
are evoked in poems about their songs ("Litauische Lieder," "Let-
tische Lieder," and "Russische Lieder"), their cities ("Wilna,"
"Nowgorod," "Die Ostseestädte," "Humlegard," and "Die Wol-
gastädte"), and most frequently their rivers. Most of these works
do no more than suggest mythological settings—often personal,
dreamlike landscapes in the manner of Chagall, whose paintings
Bobrowski greatly admired (see the poem "Die Heimat des
Malers Chagall," SZ, 64). But as is evident from temporal specifica-

14. *West-Östliches*, pp. 6–11.

tions in some of the titles ("Der Ilmensee 1941," "Kaunas 1941," "Kathedrale 1941," "Dorfkirche 1942"), a great many of them are to be read with a view to recent history. Often poems which seem purely mythological may be seen to suggest historical references when they are juxtaposed to similar texts whose titles include particular dates.

The poem "Der Don," for instance, one of Bobrowski's best, contains in its third and final stanza an allusion to the *Song of Igor's Campaign*:

> Dort
> singt der Diw,
> im Turm,
> er schreit an die Wolke, der Vogel
> ganz aus Unglück, er ruft
> über die Felsenufer,
> befiehlt zu hören den Ebenen.
> Hügel, öffnet euch, sagt er,
> tretet hervor gerüstet,
> Tote, legt an den Helm. (SS, 67)

In the Old Russian epic (lines 115–20) Prince Igor and his army are warned by the song of the prophetic daeva that their campaign against the Kumans will end in disaster. Such an allusion helps to evoke the atmosphere of the area around the Don River, providing it with a familiar cultural dimension. But the daeva's call clearly performs a different function here than it does in the source. More than an evil omen, it becomes a command, the bird imploring the dead victims (thus the tragic confrontation has already occurred) to rise up armed from their graves.

The implications of the enigmatic, mythical setting of "Der Don" may be clarified by a comparison with an explicitly historical landscape in a poem written in the same month (August 1960), "Dorfkirche 1942" (SS, 72). The scenes at the beginning of the two poems are nearly identical. In both, buildings on an elevation are surrounded by fire or smoke, indicating human life or flaming destruction or both; and at the bottom of the steeply inclined shoreline is a frozen river.

Der Don

Hoch, aus Feuern
die Dörfer. Über den Fels
fallen die Ufer. Aber
der Strom gefangen, Eishauch
wehte er, Stille finster
folgte ihm nach.

Dorfkirche 1942

Rauch
um Schneedach und Balkenwand.
Über den Hang hinab
Krähenspuren. Aber der Fluss
im Eis.

In both poems there follows the sight of high walls, set off against the sky. This scene is presented as a kind of miraculous vision in "Der Don" ("Einmal, / die Ufer drüben / flogen davon, wir sahn / hinter den Feldern, weit, / unter dem Frühmond, Mauern / gegen den Himmel.") and as a quick flurry of images in "Dorfkirche 1942" ("Dort / Aufschein, zerstürzt / Stein, Gemäuer, der Bogen, / geborsten die Wand"). Finally, "Dorfkirche 1942" also ends with the call of a bird: "der [Wind] auf den Höhen umher / geht, finster, der eigene / Schatten, er ruft, rauhstimmig / die Krähe / schreit ihm zurück." The crow here does not explicitly address the dead, as does the daeva in "Der Don," but the wind is referred to as "der eigene Schatten" and is said to blow up on the heights, the site of the destruction of the village church. In several ways, then, the wind seems associated with death.

Both poems progress from a direct juxtaposition of village life and frozen death (the icy river) through the sight of destruction to a final, desperate scream of communication between the living and the dead. In the closing stanza of each poem there is a shift to the present tense. The similarity between the two poems, one of them explicitly describing a landscape during the war, indicates that it is incorrect to disassociate a seemingly mythical, ahistorical setting such as that in "Der Don" from the poet's personal experience of Russia at a concrete historical moment. Bobrowski's

adaptation of the situation from the *Song of Igor's Campaign* is
made in accordance with his intensely felt recollection of the
atrocious destruction brought to the area of the Don by his own
people. In general, his entire vision of the eastern landscape, no
matter how unspecified temporally, is unmistakably conditioned
by what he witnessed during the war. He at one time even referred
to his choice of theme and subject matter as "a kind of war
wound." [15]

Nevertheless, Sigfrid Hoefert is perfectly correct in asserting
that there is no specific reference in "Der Don" and that the end
of the poem is left open. Rather than settling on a particular
interpretation, he assumes the dead to stand as a warning and reminder of the absurdity and irreparable destructiveness of war—
a reading, however, as he himself admits, also only a plausible
speculation.[16] The problem of historical specificity, I think, largely
derives from the fact that Bobrowski characteristically treats history as myth or as inextricably bound up with the mythic dimension. As was clear from Bobrowski's epic vision of ancient Prussia
in "Pruzzische Elegie," history tends toward myth, and the range
and generality of reference is thereby magnified; and, as shown
by comparing the poems "Der Don" and "Dorfkirche 1942," the
sense of historical relevance is present even in an apparently
mythical setting and makes possible a concreteness and intensifica-
tion of mythical allusion.

A different, though equally illuminating, quality of Bobrowski's
verse derives from the poet's personal idea of historical development, which might be termed his myth of history. According to
the (somewhat too schematic) analysis by Jerry Glenn, this
"myth" is basically triadic in conception, composed of an initial
stage of unity and tranquility, a second period extending through
the present of chaos and anxiety, and an occasionally envisioned
age of peace in the future.[17] The distant past, frequently introduced
by the word "einst" or "damals," is generally associated with a
childhood state of happiness and oneness with nature and is personified by such figures as gypsies, wandering Jews, and the un-

15. *Selbstzeugnisse*, p. 51: "so etwas wie eine Kriegsverletzung."
16. *West-Östliches*, pp. 35, 36.
17. Cf. Glenn, "Introduction," p. 48.

specified "ancestor" ("Ahn"). The second phase corresponds roughly to the more recent past, in which the unity with nature is split and the primitive personages are replaced by agents of persecution, usually represented by the hawk, the wolf, the hunter, or murderers ("die Würger"). The nature of future redemption is most difficult of all to determine, although it is invariably mentioned only in relation to the past.

For the most part Bobrowski's poetry about development through history describes the transition from the first temporal stage to the second, from original harmony to ensuing destruction. The "Pruzzische Elegie" is an obvious example of this movement in history, and in many other poems—such as "An Nelly Sachs" (SS, 57–58) and "Kathedrale 1941" (SS, 70–71)—the age of destruction is connected with the reign of National Socialist brutality.

Most often, however, this passage of time is not directly associated with historical events. The poem "Gedenkblatt" (SS, 32) clearly illustrates Bobrowski's mythic conception of temporal development. It begins with a formulaic introduction ("Jahre, / Spinnenfäden, / die grossen Spinnen, Jahre—") and goes on to tell of the activities and gestures of simple gypsies in a rural setting: "es sind die Zigeuner gezogen / mit Pferden den Lehmpfad. Der alte Zigahn / kam mit der Peitsche, die Frauen / standen im Hoftor, redend, / in aufgehobenen Armen / die Handvoll Glück." Suddenly, however, they are no longer there, and ominous murderers dominate the landscape ("Später blieben sie aus. / Da kamen die Würger mit bleiernen / Augen."). An old woman then directly witnesses the gypsies' disappearance, which may be associated with their extermination in the Third Reich, and expresses her sympathetic concern: "Einmal, die Alte / oben im Dach / hat den Entschwundenen nachgefragt." In the third, final stanza there is a marked change to the present tense. Here the speaker literally "makes present" a sense of the past by seeing what nobody sees any more: gypsies making their way along a dusty path. The last stanza reads:

> Hör den Regen strömen
> über den Hang, sie gehn,
> die keiner mehr sieht,

> auf dem alten Lehmpfad,
> eingehüllt in die stäubenden
> Wasser, Windkronen der Fremde
> über dem Schwarzhaar,
> leicht.

The fact of physical extinction, therefore, is transcended by a feat of active remembrance, as is the otherwise unbridgeable lapse in time. The word "Fremde" is surely to be understood at least in part temporally. There is the suggestion that the "foreignness" or distance which hovers above the gypsies' heads helps salvage them from oblivion, preserving their happy state above time. The image corresponds in its position in the stanza to the "Handvoll Glück" (in stanza one) which the gypsy women held in their outstretched arms before the age of destruction set in.

"Gedenkblatt" is best read together with the brilliant poem at the beginning of *Sarmatische Zeit*, "Anruf" (SZ, 5–6). It opens with an invocation to the days of childhood:

> Wilna, Eiche
> du—
> meine Birke,
> Nowgorod—
> einst in Wäldern aufflog
> meiner Frühlinge Schrei, meiner Tage
> Schritt erscholl überm Fluss.

In those sunny days there was an old story-teller by the fire, who spoke on into the night. But now his youthful audience has departed, leaving him to sing all alone, surrounded only by wolves. Here again, in the last strophe, there is a change to the present tense. But this time the speaker specifically states that the old, ancestral world perseveres through time, and that what remains is of sacred significance. Here is the last stanza:

> Heiliges schwimmt,
> ein Fisch,
> durch die alten Täler, die waldigen
> Täler noch, der Väter
> Rede tönt noch herauf:
> Heiss willkommen die Fremden.
> Du wirst ein Fremder sein. Bald.

The holy fish which still swims about in the age-old landscape is really a spoken legacy, uttered by past generations. Again the word "foreign" ("Fremd") is to be taken temporally. The speaker's forebears call upon him (the second sense of "Anruf") to recall them, even identify with them, for he will himself be a forebear in the near future. The sense of the age of destruction is to force subsequent generations to reject the notion that they are unique and that it is possible to have a sharp, conclusive break in history. The future, near and distant, can not be entirely alien to the past or the present but is intimately related to them, as though by ties of blood.

The novel *Levins Mühle* (subtitled, "34 Statements About My Grandfather") is about sin and guilt. The fifteenth sentence, which in a way holds the argument of the entire book, also speaks of the identity of generations and is therefore directly relevant to the poem "Anruf."

> The fifteenth sentence does not belong to the plot, though it is part of us. It states, not quite exactly: fathers' sins afflict the children down to the third and fourth member.
>
> There we are, speaking of fathers and grandfathers, and ought to know that these fathers or grandfathers are for their part also children, in the third or fourth or twenty-seventh generation. There is no end to it once we start searching around. There we come across guilty people and more guilty people and find fault with them and would like to silently think of ourselves as exceptions.
>
> Although of course this whole story, for instance, is being told for our sake.[18]

Perhaps the greatest crime is for present generations to exclude themselves from the guilt of the past, and to shut the door on

18. Bobrowski, Johannes, *Levins Mühle: 34 Sätze über meinen Grossvater* (Frankfurt, 1964), p. 165.

> Der fünfzehnte Satz gehört nicht zur Handlung. Wenn auch zu uns, er heisst, nicht ganz genau: Die Sünden der Väter werden heimgesucht an den Kindern bis ins dritte und vierte Glied.
> Da reden wir also über die Väter oder Grossväter und müssten doch wissen, dass diese Väter oder Grossväter ihrerseits ebenfalls Kinder sind, im dritten oder vierten oder siebenundzwanzigsten Glied. Da gibt es kein Ende, wenn wir erst anfangen herumzusuchen. Da finden wir Schuldige über Schuldige und halten uns über sie auf und nehmen uns unterdessen vielleicht stillschweigend aus. Obwohl doch zum Beispiel die ganze Geschichte hier unsertwegen erzählt wird.

their ancestors. The third reference of "invocation" ("Anruf")
may be the words of welcome spoken to the "strangers" of an
earlier time, which exhibit the speaker's awareness that he himself
will be a stranger before long. The poem, then, refers back to the
beginning, where just such a welcome is uttered: "Wilna, Eiche /
du—meine Birke, / Nowgorod—."

Also revealing as to Bobrowski's myth of history, and particularly his vision of the future, is the last poem in *Sarmatische Zeit,*
"Absage."

> Feuer,
> aus Blut die Lockung:
> der schöne Mensch. Und wie Schlaf
> das Vergangene, Träume
> an Flüssen hinab,
> auf den Wassern,
> segellos, in der Strömung.
>
> Ebenen—die verlornen
> Dörfer, der Wälder Rand.
> Und ein dunner Rauch
> in den Lüften,
> steil.
>
> Einst,
> wulstigen Munds, Perkun
> kam, eine Feder im Bart,
> kam in der Hufspur des Elchs,
> der Stotterer kam,
> fuhr auf den Strömen, Finsternis
> zog er, ein Fischernetz, nach.
>
> Dort
> war ich. In alter Zeit.
> Neues hat nie begonnen. Ich bin ein Mann,
> mit seinem Weibe ein Leib,
> der seine Kinder aufzieht
> für eine Zeit ohne Angst. (SZ, 85)

The past is stated to be like deep slumber, dreams drifting about
in the landscape. First there is an elegiac vision, expressing the
sense of historical loss by a reversion to myth and prehistory:

the god of sun and thunder, Perkun, brought darkness to the entire land. The allusion—the "darkness" is called a fishnet ("Finsternis / zog er, ein Fischnetz, nach")—is probably again to the legend already used at the end of "Pruzzische Elegie." The cryptic final stanza, the meaning of which has given rise to some debate among critics (Jerry Glenn and Dieter Hasselblatt), consists of three parts and states three temporal relationships. For an understanding it is best to bear in mind the poem "Anruf," which "Absage" was meant to complement. First the speaker acknowledges that he was present in those ancient settings, and identifies with all the past: "Dort / war ich. In alter Zeit." This is followed by a gnomic statement, in the present-perfect tense, linking the past with the present: "Neues hat nie begonnen." Despite Jerry Glenn's objection, there is no evading the reminiscence of the words of Solomon, "there is nothing new under the sun." The sentence does not mean, as Glenn contends,[19] "during ancient times nothing new began," but "nothing new has begun from the beginning until today." My interpretation is confirmed grammatically by the following sentence, which closes the poem. In the present tense, it ends with a reaching out to the future: "Ich bin ein Mann, / mit seinem Weibe ein Leib, / der seine Kinder aufzieht / für eine Zeit ohne Angst."

In his interpretation Jerry Glenn disagrees with the comments of Dieter Hasselblatt, who attributes to this last stanza a disturbing inconsistency between changelessness and change.[20] But neither critic succeeds, in my opinion, in explaining the deliberate paradox in Bobrowski's conception. Because of the rigidity of the "temporal system" that he would impose, Glenn is forced to characterize the "alte Zeit" as a "self-contained, unchanging period of harmony between man and nature, comparable, perhaps, to the Garden of Eden before the Fall." [21] But in this poem, as often in Bobrowski's work, the ancient times are not at all paradisal; Perkun comes with ominous darkness rather than blessings. In the past, rather, blissful harmony alternates with destruction, and in this sense there is nothing new even in the present. By rejecting Glenn's reading, however, one is still confronted with the dilemma of two seem-

19. "Introduction," p. 49.
20. Hasselblatt, *Lyrik Heute* (Gütersloh, 1963), pp. 222–23.
21. "Introduction," p. 49.

ingly contradictory conceptions of history: static uniformity and progressive development into a future free of anxiety.

The solution is suggested in the initial phrase of the poem: "Feuer, / aus Blut die Lockung: / der schöne Mensch." In a speech on the theme, "Guilt named, guilt banished," Bobrowski made the statement, "A writer has to do with man, who in the ten thousandth year of his history is still a man." Earlier in the same speech he mentioned the origin of this notion and discussed precisely that discrepancy, expressed in the poem "Absage," between history as uniformity and as progress. "In Johann Gottfried Herder," he noted, "in 'Ideas,' I read: Man in the ten thousandth year of his history is born with the same passions as in the second. . . . In the same 'Ideas,' however, there is the conception of a progressive humanization." Bobrowski went on to speak on the function of literature—or rather, of his own literary endeavor: "Literature—that is, the kind of literature with which we are dealing—works through the past, past in the widest sense, and therefore also its superannuated manifestations. This is what literature does, and always with a view toward the present, maybe even toward the future." [22]

Humanity, then, is the persistent, uniform factor throughout all history, and in this sense "nothing new has begun" since the dark days of Perkun. There can be progress in history, but only by an increase in humanity, a development which Bobrowski frequently called, quoting Wilhelm von Humboldt, "the humanization of conditions" ("die Vermenschlichung der Verhältnisse"). The transition from "alte Zeit" to "eine Zeit ohne Angst" comes only with a complete identification with the past. But it also depends upon intimate human love and devotion in the present: "Ich bin ein Mann, mit seinem Weibe ein Leib."

In order to fully understand Bobrowski's Sarmatia it is necessary to make one further assertion about it. As is suggested by

22. *Selbstzeugnisse*. Pp. 32–33: "Der Schreiber hat es mit dem Menschen zu tun, der im 10 ooosten Jahr seiner Geschichte noch ein Mensch ist." Pp. 26–27: "Bei Johann Gottfried Herder, in den Ideen, lese ich: Der Mensch im 10 ooosten Jahr seiner Geschichte mit den gleichen Leidenschaften geboren wie im zweiten. . . . In den gleichen Ideen aber findet sich die Konzeption einer fortschreitenden Humanisierung." "Literatur, d.h. die Literatur, von der wir hier handeln—, arbeitet Vergangenheit auf, Vergangenheit im weitesten Sinne, also auch ihre überständigen Erscheinungsformen. Das tut sie also, und sie tut es im Blick auf Gegenwart, meinetwegen auf Zukunft."

the title, "Sarmatische Zeit," Sarmatia is a spatial landscape conceived of temporally. This concept becomes clear in Bobrowski's second novel, *Litauische Claviere*. The plot deals with two men from Tilsit, Professor Voigt and Concertmaster Gawehn, who in 1936 wish to collaborate on an opera about the Lithuanian national poet, Christian Donelaitis. They cross the Memel River to Wilkischken in the Lithuanian district to visit a schoolteacher, Potschka, who is an expert on Donelaitis' life and work. During their day in the border region they witness countless scenes of conflict between the native Lithuanian population and the German or Germanized defenders of the Reich. They finally return to Tilsit, filled with doubt that such an opera can be written at that particular time in history. At this point, two-thirds through the book (p. 140), the actual plot breaks off, and there appears a startling description of a huge surveyor's tower ("Trigonometrischer Punkt"). Potschka, on whom the idea of the Donelaitis opera has made a deep impression, stands on top of the symbolic wooden edifice and looks out into the surroundings: "Into a landscape. Into a darkness. In which there is this luminousness." ("In eine Landschaft. In eine Dunkelheit. In der es diese Helle gibt.") What he actually surveys, however, is not a landscape, but time.[23] The passage continues, "Into a time. If one knows: what that is, time." ("In eine Zeit. Wenn man das weiss: was das ist, Zeit.")

There follows a reflection on the nature of time, in which my earlier suggestion about the convergence of past, present, and future is corroborated.[24] Bobrowski begins here, as so often in his work, with the past; in fact, the "Trigonometrischer Punkt" may be considered a device for "working through" the past in the author's own meaning. From it Potschka surveys the landscape, seeing first "lifeless objects" ("houses, a village, windows"), and then people. What Potschka really sees, though, is the past: a Lithuanian wedding in Donelaitis' time and the last day of the

23. For a symbolic use of the surveyor's tower similar to that in Bobrowski's novel, see Hans Magnus Enzenberger's poem "Trigonometrischer Punkt" in the volume *blindenschrift* (Frankfurt, 1964), pp. 80–81.

24. *Litauische Claviere*, p. 140: "Das Gegenwärtige? Das schon immer, indem es bemerkt wurde, abgeschlossen ist, vergangen, Vergangenheit geworden. Das Zukünftige? Das immer herankommt, ganz nah heran, und nie eingetreten ist, immer draussen geblieben. Die Vergangenheit? Abgeschlossen, abgetan, nicht mehr zu rufen, weil ohne Gehör. Erkennbar vielleicht in leblosen Gegenständen, Gestorbenes, in einem Augenblick unkenntlich geworden."

poet's and preacher's life in 1780. The landscape seen from the
tower is, in fact, time, which Potschka had been enabled to survey
as though through a precision lens. Potschka identifies with what
he sees to such an extent that he seems to die with his hero and
mistakes his own sweetheart, Tuta, for Donelaitis' wife, Anna
Regina.

Finally, however, at the very end of the book, the present breaks
in: the tower disappears, the traces of Potschka's vision fade, and
he recognizes the voice calling his name to be Tuta's. She says,
about the possibility of returning to the past: "To go there, that
is no good any more. We can not go there." Potschka's answer,
which closes the novel, is a call to realize the relevance of the
past in the present and the future. "Now he speaks, slowly, with a
mouth that will learn to speak, with a voice that will still find its
sounds, today or tomorrow—call it over here, where we are." [25]
In its conventional usage, "Wo wir sind" has spatial reference,
but here it means "Where we are in time"; it means our present
which, for Bobrowski, is "continually approached" by the future,
and is continually becoming the past. The last three chapters of
Litauische Claviere constitute a kind of coda which may detract
from the quality of the novel because of its artificial effect: it
seems to have been tacked on to the plot as an afterthought. But
as a unit it is revealing with regard to Bobrowski's conception
of space as time: the "Trigonometrischer Punkt" is an instrument
which converts the view of a spatial landscape into an awareness
of temporal relationships.

Two of Bobrowski's most important poems, "Die Sarmatische
Ebene" (SZ, 35–36) and "Gegenlicht" (SZ, 37–38), illustrate this
same transformation of spatial into temporal vision. Both poems
begin with a kind of formulaic incantation, in which the senses of
dimension (time and space) and perception (sight and sound) are
made to blend. In the especially brilliant first stanza of "Die
Sarmatische Ebene" internality and externality are juxtaposed and
then seem to merge in the image of the "singing" plain:

Seele,
voll Dunkel, spät—

25. P. 171: "Hingehen, das geht nicht mehr. Hingehen nicht. . . . Jetzt spricht
er, langsam, mit einem Mund, der das Sprechen erlernen, mit einer Stimme, die
ihre Laute noch finden wird, heute oder morgen: Herrufen, hierher. Wo wir
sind."

der Tag mit geöffneten
Pulsen, Bläue—
die Ebene singt.

In both texts there follows a basically geographic, spatial landscape. The plains and forests are evoked, as are the people who
inhabit that terrain. The second stanza of "Gegenlicht" reads:

Auf den Ufern der Ströme,
weit,
als sie der weite
Himmel umarmt hielt,
hörten wir Singen
im Wälderschatten. Der Ahn
ging verwachsenen Gräben nach.

The Sarmatian plain creates a feeling of a broad, all-embracing
terrain, and its "song" penetrates to the cities and towns. Traces of
organic life begin to appear, cattle is seen trudging along ash-
strewn paths, and finally people are introduced, signaling to one
another ("Und ein Kind / folgt ihm / pfeifend, es ruft / von den
Zäunen / die Greisin ihm nach").

At this point in "Die Sarmatische Ebene" there is a break, and
the plain becomes fully animated and personalized. It is addressed
as "riesiger Schlaf, / riesig von Träumen"; streams are seen rushing along its "hips." It is here, I believe, that the nature of the
speaker's vision shifts. The plain now serves not so much as a
huge, geographic landscape, extending to the end of a distant
horizon; it has, rather, become the preserver of time. By the end
of the poem the beauty praised is no longer of spatial, but of
temporal, significance.

da die Völker geschritten
auf Strassen der Vögel
im frühen
Jahr ihre endlose Zeit,

die du bewahrst
aus Dunkel. Ich seh dich:
die schwere Schönheit
des ungesichtigen Tonhaupts
—Ischtar oder anderen Namens—,
gefunden im Schlamm.

These are the last two stanzas of "Die Sarmatische Ebene." With
the line, "da die Völker geschritten," the suggestion of past time
suddenly enters a poem which was until then entirely in the
present tense. In the earlier description of the plain the dimension
of time was of no significance, since attention was directed toward
evoking the landscape's spatial components (cities, villages, trodden
paths, and the like). With the mention of the human inhabitants
of the terrain, however, the vision must take on the temporal
dimension, and awareness develops of a "depth" from present into
past time. The paths have become "routes of birds" ("Strassen der
Vögel"), those eternal markers of time, and in the lines, "im
frühen / Jahr ihre endlose Zeit," nearly every word expresses
the temporal factor. At the end of the poem the plain is addressed
again; this time, however, it attracts the speaker not as a vast,
spatial stretch of land, but as a monument of former primitive
times. The ultimate beauty of the ancient plain, like that of an
old statue, is that it preserves early, otherwise unrecoverable time
and holds it up to the present. In this sense the single poem "Die
Sarmatische Ebene" is representative of the volume in which it
appears, and could itself have been entitled "Sarmatische Zeit."

Also a miniature *ars poetica*, though much more personal than
"Die Sarmatische Ebene," is the poem "Gegenlicht."

Gegenlicht

Dämmerung.
Wie das Grasland
hertreibt, die breite Strömung,
Ebenen. Kalt, unzeitig
der Mond. Ein Flügelschlag nun.

Auf den Ufern der Ströme,
weit,
als sie der weite
Himmel umarmt hielt,
hörten wir Singen
im Wälderschatten. Der Ahn
ging verwachsenen Gräben nach.

Vogelherz, leicht, befiederter
Stein auf dem Wind.

In die Nebel
fallend. Gras und die Erde
nehmen dich an, eine Spur
Tod, einen Schneckenpfad lang.

Aber
wer erträgt mich,
den Mann mit geschlossenen Augen,
bösen Mundes, mit Händen,
die halten nichts, der dem Strom
folgt, verdurstend,
der in den Regen
atmet die andere Zeit,
die nicht mehr kommt, die andre,
ungesagte, wie Wolken,
ein Vogel mit offenen Schwingen,
zornig, gegen den Himmel,
ein Gegenlicht, wild. (SZ, 37–38)

After the landscape has become increasingly humanized, there
is the unusual image of a bird's heart drifting about in the air
("Vogelherz, leicht, befiederter / Stein auf dem Wind"). Not
until the end of the poem does it become apparent what this sign
might refer to. First there follows another change of direction: the
speaker describes himself. The characterization is not at all ap-
proving, and he even begins by asking who will tolerate him
("Aber / wer erträgt mich). These lines constitute the first half
of the final stanza, the speaker listing various features of his own
appearance. In the last lines he describes his own activity. It becomes clear that the bird's heart, or "feathered stone," also refers
to the speaker ("der in den Regen / atmet"). The speaker characteristically, and as though by nature, places against one time
"the other time," by which is meant that he forces the past ("Zeit,
die nicht mehr kommt") into juxtaposition with the present.

Beginning with the image of the bird's heart, a gradual transformation takes place from a basically spatial vision to one dominated by temporal contrasts and relations. This change is most
evident in the difference in the quality of light at the beginning
and at the end. The poem opens with the one-word line, "Dämmerung." Although it generally connotes a certain time of day,

this word here functions strictly within a spatial setting, being followed by the lines, "Wie das Grasland / hertreibt, die breite Strömung, / Ebenen." Light is understood in the usual physical sense, having no connection with historical or temporal relationships. At the end of the poem the word "Gegenlicht" appears, and judging only from the two final lines it would seem that there has been no change, that here too light is perceived only spatially ("zornig, gegen den Himmel, / ein Gegenlicht, wild"). The structural device of this pair of lines is a chiasmus, and the "Gegenlicht" appears to be a radiance emitted to counter the light of heaven. But from the preceding lines the reader is already aware that the opposition is really between two "times": the speaker "breathes" into the present "the other time" ("die andere Zeit, die nicht mehr kommt"). Thus what would seem an opposition in space is in fact a juxtaposition of periods of time. Similarly, the words "zornig" and "wild" might be taken to be adjectives, modifying "Gegenlicht"; but when read in the context of the entire stanza they must be interpreted as adverbs describing the activity of the speaker. "Angrily" and "wildly" he forces the recovery of time unrecoverably lost, refusing to leave unsaid what he himself calls "unsaid," "die andere [Zeit], ungesagte."

There is something desperate and challenging about the speaker's gesture here, as though he were performing a duty that it would be much easier to neglect. "Gegenlicht," I believe, is a poem about the responsibility of temporal consciousness. Not only is there a change from a spatially envisaged landscape to impressions of temporal interrelations, but this poem also evokes the urgency and personal necessity of such a transformation. Once the speaker is aware of human activity in the landscape, and his view turns inward into himself, he can no longer merely conjure up an intriguing setting in and for itself. Rather, he now feels compelled to see the landscape which seemed geographically distant as actually removed in time and to forcefully place it in relation to the present. He not only discovers lost time but "breathes" it back into the present. The speaker's act is recollection, given special vitality and immediacy because it is presented as though it were a physical act ("ein Vogel mit offenen Schwingen"). "Gegenlicht" analyzes the faculty of remembrance—that is, time consciousness as opposed to, or as an extension of, space consciousness—and is therefore typical of many of Bobrowski's poems about Sarmatia as myth and history.

But regardless of the approach taken to Bobrowski's myth of Sarmatia, the factor of recollection is of decisive importance, remaining constant as an ultimate function of poetic vision and even as a moral imperative. The discussion of the intermingling of history and myth showed that the treatment of history and the association of myth with recorded history both serve to intensify the speaker's remembrance of earlier times. "Pruzzische Elegie" laments the historical downfall of the Old Prussians, but the recollection receives its actual force from the epic proportions and high tone generally accorded to a realm of mythic stature. The poem "Der Don" centers around a mythological allusion to the Old Russian epic, but, as can be demonstrated by its similarity in structure and imagery to "Dorfkirche 1942," the memory of ancient Russia is inevitably connected with the same area during World War II.

What I have called Bobrowski's myth of history, his mythic conception of temporal development, is also dominated by the power of recollection. In the poem "Gedenkblatt" the speaker "makes present," as is reflected even grammatically, the old gypsies, now extinct; he sees them there—"sie gehn, die keiner mehr sieht"—and the fact of physical absence is thereby overcome by a determined act of remembrance. The same relation of past and present is expressed in "Anruf," except that in this poem the urgency of recollection is emphasized by a projection into the future. Those in the present, it is stated, must remember the past for the sake of historical continuity, because they will themselves soon be looked upon as belonging to the past.

Finally, in discussing Bobrowski's characteristically temporal conception of a spatial landscape, recollection appeared as the awareness of depth in time. In "Die Sarmatische Ebene" the plain was first felt to be a broad, geographic surface but then was seen to assume temporal significance, as a beautiful monument to primitive times. A full act of memory, however, not only involves a plunge into the past, but earlier time must be "called back" into the present. Potschka becomes aware of this need at the end of *Litauische Claviere*, after the "Trigonometrischer Punkt" has enabled him to survey the "landscape" of Lithuania in Christian Donelaitis' time. And, according to my interpretation, the speaker's act in the poem "Gegenlicht" appears to be a determined juxtaposition of the present and the distant past—a forceful, almost physical act of recollection.

The history of Bobrowski's Sarmatia is the history of a relation between peoples, the Germans and their "eastern neighbors"; it must be recalled because the guilt and persecution which pervade it must not be forgotten. Past forces of destruction still lurk in nature and will continue to haunt the present until they are seized and made to confront forceful acts of resistance. Such confrontations often occur in Bobrowski's poetry, such as in "Tod des Wolfs" (SS, 25–26), "Der Adler" (SS, 11: "Den Adler hab ich genagelt / meinem Haus an den First"), and "Hechtzeit" (W, 8: "Den erbitterten Hecht / riss ich vom Grund los, / schlug ich gegen den Stein"). In the poem "Namen für den Verfolgten" (W, 54) the fact of persecution is counteracted, or at least recognized, in the process of poetic utterance itself. The speaker "gives names" to a persecuted victim; significantly, the names are words from Old Prussian. At the end he names the elder tree—the same image that appears in one of Bobrowski's best-known and most beautiful poems, "Holunderblüte" (SS, 29). Here a specific victim of persecution is mentioned, the Russian writer Isaak Babel; and persecution is directly related to the faculty of memory and the crime of forgetfulness:

> Es kommt
> Babel, Isaak.
> Er sagt: Bei dem Pogrom,
> als ich Kind war,
> meiner Taube
> riss man den Kopf ab.
>
> Häuser in hölzerner Strasse,
> mit Zäunen, darüber Holunder.
> Weiss gescheuert die Schwelle,
> die kleine Treppe hinab—
> Damals, weisst du,
> die Blutspur.

Leute, ihr redet: Vergessen—
Es kommen die jungen Menschen,
ihr Lachen wie Büsche Holunders.
Leute, es möcht der Holunder
sterben
an eurer Vergesslichkeit.

"Holunderblüte" is a warning against forgetfulness, and it is clear that the need to combat forgetfulness to a great extent explains Bobrowski's entire idea of Sarmatia and his deep concern for time and history. Understandably, therefore, it is also basic to his conception of poetic language.

Language: Recollection and Communication

Bobrowski's main theme was Sarmatia, the history of the relationship between the Germans and their neighbors to the east. It is "a long history," he wrote, "of calamity and guilt, since the days of the Teutonic Order, which stand on my people's account. Not that it can ever be erased or atoned for, but it is worth hope and an honest attempt in German poetry. I have one taskmaster to help me: Klopstock." [26] This statement of poetic intention was written for Hans Bender's anthology of postwar German poetry, *Widerspiel* (1962), and it must have aroused the curiosity of many readers that a "new" poet should pledge his indebtedness to Friedrich Gottlieb Klopstock (1724–1803). Amid scores of "modernist" manifestos proclaiming as the ultimate value the magical forces of nature, political engagement, surrealist trauma, or linguistic experimentation, and containing not even one casual mention of an earlier tradition or author, there appears a word of grateful allegiance to one individual poet. Even more surprising, the model is not one of the "fathers" of modernism, such as Rimbaud, Valéry, or Trakl, or even Rilke or Hölderlin, but Klopstock, who is often felt to have been completely overshadowed by developments in German lyric poetry that he himself only initiated.

26. *Selbstzeugnisse*, p. 23: "Eine lange Geschichte aus Unglück und Verschuldung, seit den Tagen des deutschen Ordens, die meinem Volk zu Buch steht. Wohl nicht zu tilgen und su sühnen, aber eine Hoffnung wert und einen redlichen Versuch in deutschen Gedichten. Zu Hilfe habe ich einen Zuchtmeister: Klopstock."

Yet, despite this apparent anachronism, Bobrowski's reference
to Klopstock should not be brushed aside as a mere cleverness,
intended to shock worshipers of avant-garde feats of daring into
an awareness of continuity and tradition. Though such an intention was unquestionably present, Klopstock was Bobrowski's
"taskmaster" in a true and more profound sense. An explanation
of this peculiar and complex indebtedness is therefore crucial to
an understanding of Bobrowski's poetry, and particularly of his
conception of poetic language and its function. It also helps in an
analysis of his characteristic style and technique.

The primary reason for Bobrowski's allegiance is that he regarded his own poetry as belonging to the tradition of the German
ode and hymn begun by Klopstock. Like Klopstock's, his poems
are typically invocational and elevated in tone, and his attitude
toward nature and the entire cosmos is one of deep and pious
reverence. In a phrase of Klopstock's time, Bobrowski's verse
represents a modernized "sublime style" ("erhabene Schreibart").
Anni Carlsson and Manfred Seidler have described this point of
contact in their essays on Bobrowski and Klopstock. They illustrate the often striking similarities in imagery and vocabulary and
in techniques of syntax and rhythm, though they do not, I think,
sufficiently emphasize the great importance of Klopstock's pioneering use of free rhythms. Indeed, Klopstock's development from a
strict adherence to classical ode patterns to the more dynamic free
rhythm, in which traces of the ode and elegy forms remained, was
identical to the course of Bobrowski's own career. But Anni
Carlsson and Manfred Seidler do cite some passages in which there
is a very definite contact, such as the closing stanzas of Klopstock's "Frühlingsfeier" and of Bobrowski's poem "Nänie." [27]

Most revealing is Anni Carlsson's comparison of two passages
evoking a stream. Klopstock's stanza reads,

27. Carlsson, "Johannes Bobrowski und Klopstock," *Neue Zürcher Zeitung*,
January 16, 1966; Seidler, "Bobrowski, Klopstock und der antike Vers," *Lebende
Antike*, ed. Horst Meller and Hans-Joachim Zimmermann (Berlin, 1967), pp.
542–54. Klopstock's "Frühlingsfeier" ends with a line about Jehova, "Und unter
ihm neigt sich der Bogen des Friedens"; Bobrowski's "Nänie," dedicated to
Dietrich Buxtehude, ends,

über dem Regen
farbenstrahlend aus Nebeln
der Bogen—Frieden
ist uns versprochen. (SS, 38)

Ferner Gestade, die Woge schnell,
Dem Blick gehellt bis zum Kiesel ist—
Das Gebüsch blinket er durch oder wallt
In die Luft, hohes Gewölk duftend—der Strom.

Bobrowski's poem ("Landstrasse," SS, 19–16) contains the same
sense of anticipation created by the syntactic structure (with the
fully characterized subject finally appearing at the end) and the
same rhythmic accumulation:

             an den Berg
legt sich, er atmet von Lüften,
mit Flössen und abends dem Segel
der Blinde, der Strom.

In each case the sentence begins slowly with a halting, paratactic
rhythm, then speeds up and seems to swell as the periods are longer
and the syntax unbroken ("Das Gebüsch blinket er durch oder
wallt / In die Luft," "mit Flössen und abends dem Segel / der
Blinde"). This dynamic rushing movement culminates at the
final stop, and the source of the entire atmosphere is named—"der
Strom."

There are, of course, marked differences, such as Bobrowski's
greater reliance on the noun as opposed to Klopstock's verbal
style, and the sparsity and conciseness of Bobrowski's evocation
when compared with the hieratic fullness of Klopstock's lines.
But the characteristics of Bobrowski's technique are better studied
in the context of his theme of the obstacles confronting poetic expression. Most significant in Bobrowski's poem is the clear recurrence of the linguistic and rhythmic energy first introduced into
modern German poetry by Klopstock. It is precisely this achievement of Klopstock that Bobrowski praises in his only brief elabora-
tion on his esteem for the "master." He wrote, "I would have to
give an entire lecture on what I see in Klopstock: vitalization of
the language, full utilization of linguistic possibilities, new conception of metrics. . . . For me he is a master who, I am certain, will
surpass in his effect in Germany everything that came after." [28]

28. *Selbstzeugnisse*, p. 78: "Darüber müsste ich einen ganzen Vortrag halten, was
ich an Klopstock sehe: Verlebendigung der Sprache, ein Ausnutzen der sprachli-
chen Möglichkeiten, Neufassung der Metrik. . . . Das ist für mich ein Meister,

Yet despite the great importance of this formal indebtedness, Bobrowski's acquaintance with Klopstock's work was more profound than could be reflected in stylistic influence or in a spoken tribute to his immense contribution to the history of German poetry. The kinship, as Bobrowski felt it, extended to his most basic thematic concerns and became especially relevant to the relationship between his idea of history and his conception of language. This more penetrating allegiance to his "taskmaster" forms the theme of one of his greatest poems:

An Klopstock

Wenn ich das Wirkliche nicht
wollte, dieses: ich sag
Strom und Wald,
ich hab in die Sinne aber
gebunden die Finsternis,   5
Stimme des eilenden Vogels, den Pfeilstoss
Licht um den Abhang

und die tönenden Wasser—
wie wollt ich
sagen deinen Namen,   10
wenn mich ein kleiner Ruhm
fände—ich hab
aufgehoben, dran ich vorüberging,
Schattenfabel von den Verschuldungen
und der Sühnung: 15
so als den Taten
trau ich—du führtest sie—trau ich
der Vergesslichen Sprache,
sag ich hinab in die Winter
ungeflügelt, aus Röhricht   20
ihr Wort. (W, 20)

Grammatically the poem is an enigma: it appears to comprise a full sentence, but there is no conditional clause to complete the thought introduced by the initial subjunctive. From a first reading it seems that lines nine and ten provide the continuation and that the

---

der, ich bin sicher, in seiner Wirkung in Deutschland alles überholen wird, was nachher gekommen ist."

entire sentence reads, "Wenn ich das Wirkliche nicht wollte, wie wollt ich sagen deinen Namen." But the condition of the words "wie wollt ich sagen deinen Namen" immediately follows in lines eleven and twelve ("wenn mich ein kleiner Ruhm / fände"), and the whole passage, lines nine through twelve, is a unit set off from the main thought by hyphens. Besides, I do not think that an opposition between the speaker's longing for "das Wirkliche" and the naming of Klopstock is intended. Aside from this section, however, there is not a single other subjunctive usage and therefore no other possible main clause.

I believe the poem to be a conditional clause which is not completed grammatically. The only conclusion that may be drawn from the initial condition is that the opposite is true—that is, that the speaker "wants" "das Wirkliche" and that what follows will specify what "das Wirkliche" means. In order to understand the poem's direction as a whole, and the ultimate resolution which I find present, it is best to consider the various individual parts in their sequence. It is also important to mention any possible connections to the work of Klopstock, which unquestionably forms a background of reference here. Bobrowski may not have consciously alluded to specific passages of Klopstock, but general parallels and thematic associations are nevertheless of crucial interest and can hardly be considered merely accidental. Of particular relevance are Klopstock's poems "Die Erinnerung" (154),[29] "Die Sprache" (131–33), "Unsere Sprache" (113–15) and "Der Zürchersee" (53–55), and his writings on the nature of poetic language, especially "Gedanken über die Natur der Poesie" (992–97) and "Von der heiligen Poesie" (997–1009). Some of these connections are made by Manfred Seidler in his essay, but not in specific reference to the poem "An Klopstock."

The word "dieses" is a pronoun standing for "das Wirkliche," and what follows, after the colon in line two, is an illustration of what is meant by "wanting the real" ("das Wirkliche wollen"). Two activities characterize the speaker and stand in contrast to one another. He names things ("ich sag Strom und Wald"), *but* he has "bound" phenomena "into the senses." The contrast is between two different kinds of perception, one being a passive,

---

29. References are to Klopstock, *Ausgewählte Werke*, ed. Karl August Schleiden (Munich, 1962).

intuitive receiving and naming, the other an active, deliberate capturing. In one case the objects perceived are static and isolated ("Strom und Wald"), in the other case the phenomena are apprehended in motion ("Stimme des eilenden Vogels"). The objects of the process of naming seem to be no more than lifeless labels when compared with the vitality and reality of the passage beginning "die Finsternis." To interpret one step farther, "to want the real" may be the same as this act of "binding into the senses" nature's movement and action. In this respect "das Wirkliche" would be defined as "the actual" and as "the active."

But, assuming at this point that the poem is concerned with poetic perception and expression, as becomes evident in the second stanza, it may be shown that "das Wirkliche" has still another meaning. Klopstock's reflections on poetry are of help. In "Gedanken über die Natur der Poesie" he states that "the deepest secrets of poetry lie in the *action* to which it moves our soul. In general, action is *essential* to our enjoyment. Common poets would have us lead a plant life with them." "Action" here is the effect of poetry on the soul of the reader. The notion of poetry's effect is basic to Klopstock's aesthetic theory; it is, in a word, a "Wirkungsästhetik." [30] In another passage in the same treatise he defines the "essence of poetry" as its capacity to "preoccupy the most *refined* forces of our soul to such a high degree that each of them affects the others and thereby sets the *entire* soul in motion." Similarly, in "Von der heiligen Poesie" (1756), it is stated that "the ultimate and highest effects of works of genius are that they move the entire soul." [31]

According to these statements, in the poem "An Klopstock" the

30. *Werke*, p. 993: "Die tiefsten Geheimnisse der Poesie liegen in der *Aktion*, in welche sie unsre Seele setzt. Überhaupt ist uns Aktion zu unserm Vergnügen *wesentlich*. Gemeine Dichter wollen, dass wir mit ihnen ein Pflanzenleben führen sollen" (emphasis Klopstock's). Cf. Karl August Schleiden, *Klopstocks Dichtungstheorie als Beitrag zur Geschichte der deutschen Poetik* (Saarbrücken, 1954), esp. pp. 25 ff.

31. *Werke*. P. 992: "Das Wesen der Poesie besteht darin, dass sie, durch die Hülfe der Sprache, eine *gewisse Anzahl* von Gegenständen, die wir *kennen*, oder deren Dasein wir *vermuten*, von einer *Seite* zeigt, welche die *vornehmsten* Kräfte unsrer Seele in einem so hohen Grade *beschäftigt*, dass eine auf die andre wirkt, und dadurch die *ganze* Seele in Bewegung setzt" (emphasis Klopstock's). P. 1000: "Die letzten und höchsten Wirkungen der Werke des Genie sind, dass sie die ganze Seele bewegen."

term "das Wirkliche" is used in its original denotation, meaning
the same as "das Wirksame." The speaker wants a poetic perception which is not only "actual" and "active," but also "effective"
in that it transfers inward the motion of the perceived objects.
He does not want to simply record the names of things but to "set
the entire soul in motion," which he can do by "binding" nature's
motion "into the senses." Another passage from Klopstock, the
beginning of his poem "Die Sprache," may be relevant to Bobrowski's use of the word "gebunden": "Des Gedankens Zwilling, das
Wort, scheint Hall nur, / Der in die Luft hinfliesst; heiliges Band /
Des Sterblichen ist es, erhebt / die Vernunft ihm, und das Herz
ihm!" (131). Language "binds" mortals to one another, thus forming the basis of human society, and also to the divine powers, by
elevating their thoughts and feelings to highest dignity.[32] In both
cases the real effect of the word is contrasted with what it seems to
be, a mere transitory resonance ("scheint Hall nur"). The contrast in Bobrowski's poem is similar to Klopstock's, at least insofar
as the reality and effectiveness of poetic perception is associated
with the element of binding. The notion of language as a "bond"
between mortals, and therefore as the basis of community, is suggested at the end of "An Klopstock," and particularly in Bobrowski's own poem "Sprache" (W, 37), which will be discussed sub-
sequently.

The next section of the poem "An Klopstock" (lines nine
through twelve)—after the description of "real," "effective"
perception—is the parenthetical sentence "wie wollt ich sagen
deinen Namen, / wenn mich ein kleiner Ruhm / fände." The verbs
"wollt" and "sagen" remind the reader of the second line of the
poem ("wollte, dieses: ich sag"); but this passage, and in particular
the word "Ruhm," can only be understood in the context of what
follows in the remainder of the second stanza. To look ahead
briefly, the end of the poem deals with the relation of the poet
and of language to history. The poet recalls the past, and with
language he enters into earlier times. Such an act, and the power
of language, draw the poet's immediate thoughts from the passage
of his own life to figures permanently fixed in the past; the puzzling phrase, "ich hab aufgehoben, dran ich vorüberging," may be
explained by this result of the act of recollection. The poet's at-

32. Cf. Schleiden, p. 29.

tention turns to the thought of immortality. It is in this sense, I
believe, that the word "Ruhm" is meant, and seems to refer directly
to the famous stanzas toward the end of Klopstock's ode "Der
Zürchersee":

> Reizvoll klinget des Ruhms lockender Silberton
> In das schlagende Herz, und die Unsterblichkeit
> Ist ein grosser Gedanke,
> Ist des Schweisses der Edeln wert!
>
> Durch der Lieder Gewalt bei der Urenkelin
> Sohn und Tochter noch sein, mit der Entzückung Ton
> Oft beim Namen genennet,
> Oft gerufen vom Grabe her (54)

The word "Ruhm" in Bobrowski's poem may mean the sense of
immortality derived from the capacity of the poetic word to recall,
and enter into, the past.

In Klopstock's poem, as very often in the work of Bobrowski,
the past represents the lifetime of distant ancestors. But the poem
"An Klopstock" names the past in a more general way. It is called
"Schattenfabel von den Verschuldungen / und der Sühnung,"
which describes in a concise formula all his writing; as mentioned,
Bobrowski defined the main theme of his work as "a long history
of calamity and guilt," and it is worth noting that Klopstock's
magnum opus, *Der Messias*, has a similar theme: "Sing, unsterbliche
Seele, der sündigen Menschen Erlösung." In his prose statement of
theme Bobrowski explicitly mentions that the misfortune and guilt
of the past cannot be erased or atoned for; in his poem, however,
he speaks of "Verschuldungen / *und der Sühnung*." The difference may be that "An Klopstock" is a practical "attempt," in poetry, at atonement. There is not only an awareness of the misdeeds
and tragic events in history, but also a confidence in the power of
language to penetrate into the past in all its darkness. The speaker
arrives at this confidence only gradually through the course of the
poem. The development is most evident in the use of the word
"sagen."

At first, in lines two and three, "to say" is merely to record
the objects of passive perception ("ich sag Strom und Wald"),
and then gives way to an active capturing of phenomena in motion
(lines four through eight). Next, at the beginning of stanza two,

"to say" means to recall ("sagen deinen Namen"), which the speaker would do if he were inspired by the thought of immortality ("ein kleiner Ruhm"). At the end, the speaker "says" by actively leading language "down into" the past: "sag ich hinab in die Winter." "Finsternis" in line five, "Schattenfabel" in line fourteen, and "Winter" in line nineteen, all refer, I believe, to Bobrowski's dark "shadow land" of the past. (See the poem "Schattenland," W, 19.) They are all, perhaps, concretizations of the concept "das Wirkliche." But each is understood differently. "Finsternis" is nature apprehended as action, and not merely as a static set of phenomena. "Schattenfabel" is the landscape of the past as it is recalled; once again, a landscape conceived of historically. "Winter," finally, is the same nature, but descended into by the speaker in an act made possible only by the force of language. The speaker's longing for "das Wirkliche" may ultimately be a hope for atonement, and the poem expresses the awareness that atonement comes only with a penetration into the past; and penetration into the past, in turn, can happen only by active faith in the power of poetic language.

Clarification of one more phrase, "der Vergesslichen Sprache," may explain why it is Klopstock who is chosen as a kind of partner for these basic reflections on the role of the poet. Who are "the forgetful ones" in whose language the speaker places his faith, and what is it of which they are forgetful? The most obvious connection might be with the closing of "Holunderblüte": "Leute, es möcht der Holunder sterben an eurer Vergesslichkeit." People tend to forget earlier persecution and thereby perpetuate the same guilt in the present. The speaker in "An Klopstock," therefore, would lead the language of "the forgetful" down into the past and, in so doing, force them to remember earlier misdeeds which still linger in the present. But the speaker emphasizes that he has faith in ("trau ich") the language of the forgetful, and that Klopstock himself used it ("du führtest sie"). This positive attitude toward talk of forgetfulness would seem to contradict Bobrowski's entire endeavor to combat estrangement and discontinuity between periods in history. The poem "Holunderblüte" is a warning directed against people who say to "forget it" ("Leute, ihr redet: Vergessen—").

The answer, rather, is that Bobrowski thought of "forgetful-

ness" in a slightly different way in "An Klopstock" than elsewhere, and in a sense closer to Klopstock's own conception. The
"forgetful ones" are mortal human beings, who characteristically
forget that they are immortal. Bobrowski, like Klopstock before
him, uses the language of mortals; in his poetry, like Klopstock in
his, he reminds men of their immortality. It is precisely this idea of
poetry and its function which is pronounced in Klopstock's most
famous theoretical statement. "The ultimate purpose of higher
poetry," he states in "Von der heiligen Poesie" (1756), "and at the
same time the true mark of its value, is moral beauty. And this
alone also has the merit of setting our entire soul in motion. The
poet whom we mean must elevate us above our short-sighted way
of thinking and tear us away from the stream by which we are
pulled along. It must powerfully remind us that we are immortal
and could be much more ecstatic already in this life." [33] In terms
of this statement, all the various strands in the poem "An Klopstock" may be seen to converge: the notion of "das Wirkliche" as
the actual, the active and the effective; the sense of "Ruhm" as the
feeling of immortality inspired by poetic recollection of the past;
and the idea of "die Vergesslichen" as mortals whom poetry, in
their language, must remind of their immortality. Ultimately the
poet-speaker's confidence in the language of the forgetful is the
same as his longing for "das Wirkliche," as is evident even in a
casual remark. In a letter to his friend Peter Jokostra, Bobrowski
wrote, "I have an unbroken faith in the effectiveness of the
poem." [34]

Bobrowski shared many thematic concerns with his "Zuchtmeister," Klopstock. They all involve moral categories, and all
pertain to Klopstock's conception of "moral beauty." Significantly, they refer to the relationship of poetic perception and
time, and particularly to the capacity of poetic language to recapture past time and thereby to elevate the thoughts of men in the

33. *Werke*, p. 1001: "Der letzte Endzweck der höhern Poesie, und zugleich das
wahre Kennzeichen ihres Werts, ist die moralische Schönheit. Und auch diese
allein verdient es, dass sie unsre ganze Seele in Bewegung setze. Der Poet, den
wir meinen, muss uns über unsre kurzsichtige Art zu denken erheben, und uns
dem Strome entreissen, mit dem wir fortgezogen werden. Es muss uns mächtig
daran erinnern, dass wir unsterblich sind, und auch schon in diesem Leben, viel
glückseliger sein könnten."

34. Quoted in Jokostra, *Die Zeit hat keine Ufer* (Munich, 1963), p. 55: "Ich
habe ein ungebrochenes Vertrauen zur Wirksamkeit des Gedichts."

present. In Klopstock's poetry this recollection is characteristically expressed as a greeting of beloved friends of the past, as in the stanzas of "Der Zürchersee." Even better examples are the three similar odes "Die frühen Gräber," "Die Erinnerung," and "Die Sommernacht." The last stanza of "Die Erinnerung" reads:

> Ach mich reisst die Erinnerung fort, ich kann nicht widerstehn!
> Muss hinschaun nach Grabstätten, muss bluten lassen
> Die tiefe Wund', aussprechen der Wehmut Wort:
> Tote Freunde, seid gegrüsst! (154)

In Bobrowski's poem "An Klopstock" the lines "ich hab aufgehoben dran ich vorüberging" express an act of remembrance, as does the final use of the verb "sagen": "sag ich hinab in die Winter." Two terms sometimes used by Bobrowski for recollection through language are to "call over" ("herrufen") and to "retrieve" ("einholen").[35] To capture lost time does not mean to return to the past but to call it back, to retrieve it through a poem back into the present.

Yet "moral beauty" as the end purpose of poetry not only entails thought of the past; its effect is ultimately manifest in the present. The reason for elevating human thoughts is "to make men more moral" ("die Menschen moralischer zu machen"), as Klopstock noted, and to show them that they "can be much more ecstatic already in this life." The stanza which marks the climax and culmination of "Der Zürchersee" is not that which speaks of "Ruhm" and the thought of immortality, but one which is a praise

---

35. The word "herrufen" appears repeatedly at the end of the novel *Litauische Claviere;* the verb "einholen" is used in two significant places: in a comment on his poem "Der Ilmensee 1941" Bobrowski said, "Ich habe mit ihm [dem Gedicht] einen Eindruck von 1941, der örtlich und zeitlich auf Zentimeter und Minute festliegt, eingeholt" (quoted in Seidler, p. 550); and the story "In eine Hauptstadt verschlagen" (1964) ends with the words:

> Aber gesprochene Worte doch, lebendige Sprache. Atem. Gehör, Blicke. Alles mit Organen getan, die von Blut tönen. Möglichkeiten der Wiederkehr? Zu dem, was war? Und vorausgegangen ist für ein paar Schritte?
> einholen
> einholen
> jetzt
> gleich.

(*Mäusefest*, p. 79)

of intimate friendship. It is explicitly stated that the joy of human community in this life is superior to the abstract virtues addressed earlier in the poem:

> Aber süsser ist noch: schöner und reizender,
> In dem Arme des Freunds wissen ein Freund zu sein,
> So das Leben geniessen,
> Nicht unwürdig der Ewigkeit!

The highest dignity of man is expressed in his immediate personal contact with others, and the highest value of language is as the basis of human community—what Klopstock called "heiliges Band des Sterblichen." The idea of communication and community is not directly present in the poem "An Klopstock," but it is expressed in many others, and is of basic importance to a consideration of Bobrowski's humanism. One fundamental bond between the two poets is evident in Bobrowski's poem to Klopstock: both are obsessed by the yearning for a sense of intimate community between men, for a "friendship" transcending the barriers of time and space. Bobrowski's longing for "das Wirkliche" in his poem to Klopstock is identical, when all his work is taken together, to Klopstock's "devout wish" ("frommer Wunsch") at the end of "Der Zürchersee": "Wäret ihr auch bei uns, die ihr mich ferne liebt, . . . / O so bauten wir Hütten der Freundschaft uns!" Perhaps Bobrowski's poem is to be understood as one of these "huts of friendship," built of ideas and values uppermost in the minds of both poets.

The poem "An Klopstock" begins with a contrast—or rather, a personal conflict—within the speaker, expressed in the lines, "ich sag Strom und Wald, ich hab an die Sinne aber gebunden die Finsternis." Two kinds of poetic perception are presented, the second of which is felt to be appropriate to "das Wirkliche," the desired actuality and effectiveness. The first is passive perception, and expression by simple naming of things, whereas the second is poetry as action, both in the capturing of impressions and in the active "speaking into" past time ("sag ich hinab in die Winter"). Poetic activity in this sense involves the speaker's consciousness of temporal relationships. Poetry is effective reminiscence because it recalls the past and in its effect reminds the present.

The second half of "An Klopstock" is concerned primarily with

coming to terms with past guilt ("Schattenfabel") and suggesting
a hope of atonement. But the initial conflict of naming, as against
capturing, what would be forgotten is contained in the condition
which extends through the whole poem ("Wenn ich das Wirkliche
nicht wollte"); it was of crucial importance for Bobrowski in all
his work. It is the central theme, I believe, of his often quoted
"Immer zu benennen." Although this poem is frequently mentioned as the key to Bobrowski's poetry, it has still not been satisfactorily interpreted, nor has it been shown in precisely what way
it is relevant to the rest of his writings.[36] A brief consideration of
"Immer zu benennen" will lead me to some observations on the
style characteristic of Bobrowski's poetry in general.

> Immer zu benennen
>
> Immer zu benennen:
> den Baum, den Vogel im Flug,
> den rötlichen Fels, wo der Strom
> zieht, grün, und den Fisch
> im weissen Rauch, wenn es dunkelt   5
> über die Wälder herab.
>
> Zeichen, Farben, es ist
> ein Spiel, ich bin bedenklich,
> es möchte nicht enden
> gerecht.   10
>
> Und wer lehrt mich,
> was ich vergass: der Steine
> Schlaf, den Schlaf
> der Vögel im Flug, der Bäume
> Schlaf, im Dunkel   15
> geht ihre Rede—?
>
> Wär da ein Gott
> und im Fleisch,
> und könnte mich rufen, ich würd
> umhergehn, ich würd   20
> warten ein wenig. (SS, 86)

36. The best discussion thus far is by Bernhard Böschenstein in *Doppelinterpre-*
tation, pp. 103–105. The poem is also analyzed by Jerry Glenn and Günter Hartung in their articles.

The four stanzas are clearly demarcated, each constituting a separate unit of thought. The first is an explicit allegiance to the technique of naming; Bobrowski lists some of the "things" he names in all his poems: the tree, the bird, the stream and its jagged shoreline. It is noteworthy that these elements are here all present in the singular; they are perceived individually, without any interconnection except that they are all objects of the speaker's naming. The phrase "Immer zu benennen" implies that the speaker identifies with this kind of poetic utterance and recognizes its necessity. But in the second stanza the validity of this technique is placed in question. First the method is characterized ("Zeichen, Farben, es ist / ein Spiel"); there follows an expression of personal inadequacy: "ich bin bedenklich, / es möchte nicht enden / gerecht." To name things and their external, physical properties comes naturally to the speaker; it seems his instinctive mode of expression. But it is no more than a game and must appear a questionable enterprise, inadequate to anyone who would "do justice" to things. The word "gerecht" occupies a line by itself, forming the center, as it were, of the poem. Once again, the categories of physical beauty versus "moral beauty" from Klopstock's aesthetics seem to apply to Bobrowski's theme.

The moral perception of phenomena is not natural to the speaker but is acquired; stanza three begins, "Und wer lehrt mich, / was ich vergass." Moral perception involves the faculty of memory and an awareness of temporal dimensions. What the speaker has forgotten and must be taught is then enumerated, and the list seems only a repetition of the first stanza. One difference, however, is that the phenomena are here given in the plural and are therefore perceived not individually but as classes. More important, the object of perception is not the "things" themselves but their "sleep" ("Schlaf"); they are connected with one another not only in their grammatical function but also by an attribute common to all. Now "sleep," I believe, stands for death or the former existence of things. Time and again in Bobrowski's poetry the word "Schlaf" has this connotation; the words in "Absage" (SZ, 85), "und wie Schlaf das Vergangene," are typical. Sleep is the deep, dark past, the time of the "Schattenfabel." By merely naming things in their individual, physical presence the speaker does not do them justice. He must struggle to capture them in their "sleep"

—that is, in their absence from present time. He must, again, "bind darkness into the senses" because, as the lines read here, "im Dunkel geht ihre Rede." A poetic expression which is to be "just" ("gerecht") must include a dialogue with things through time, in their full temporal interconnection.

To acquire such expression is truly a challenge. The final stanza seems to imply a disbelief in God but means only that God and Christ cannot be relied on to teach the speaker what he has forgotten.

Wär da ein Gott
und im Fleisch,
und könnte mich rufen, ich würd
umhergehn, ich würd
warten ein wenig.

Most noticeable here is the impatient, restless tone, brought about especially by the repetition of the phrase "ich würd" at the end of the line. A mood of dire urgency has increasingly taken hold of the speaker, leaving him no longer content with the "game" of signs and colors which he normally plays. He cannot wait any more because God cannot be expected to call him to the task of "poetic justice" in the moral sense in which Bobrowski means it. It is he himself who tends to forget, and it is therefore his own responsibility to take up communication with what is forgotten.

The poem "Immer zu benennen" is clearly Bobrowski's *ars poetica* as concerns its theme. But the poem, in its entire structure and not only the first stanza, also provides an excellent guide to the poetic style so unmistakably his own. Attempts thus far to describe Bobrowski's style have generally been based on the technique endorsed in the first lines, "Immer zu benennen. . . ." The faith in the mystic identity between things and their names offers an explanation for his paratactic, enumerative style "in which the word alone is capital, often, rather than the period or the phrase." This observation—in which by "word" is meant "noun"—is offered in the *Times Literary Supplement* of September 21, 1962. The reviewer (probably Michael Hamburger) continues: "A double counterpoint is established: the word alone connotes the cosmos of its ideal relations; meanwhile the rhythm proceeding

dwells, over and over, on one word or on a small verbless whirl of
words which is then resolved back into the rhythmic procession
as a fresh finite verb carries the thrust of speech further. Each
poem is a crosswork of halt and thrust, of singularity and complicity." There can be no doubt about the excellence and accuracy
of this description. The irregular, erratic alternation between a
slow deliberating and lingering over individual nouns and a rapid,
rushing rhythmic thrust is apparent in nearly every poem.

But it is important to recognize that this naming technique is
characteristic primarily of the beginnings of the poems. Bobrowski's friend Manfred Bieler speaks of "the audacious vigor of
the beginning, the clinging to the sometimes still colorless discovery, the seizing of the word." [37] As though to break the silence,
the poetic speaker latches on to one individual word and then to
another, often unrelated, one. He probes and falters, struggling to
set up associations and some scheme by which to orient himself.
He is determined, but at this stage only because of his conviction
that things always have to be named. The first lines of the poems
are usually almost static rhythmically and threadbare in syntax,
whatever verbs there are appearing in participial form. The rhythm
seems to flicker, like dim candlelight which a mighty wind
threatens to extinguish; or, in a different simile, it is like a tiny
rivulet trickling from one low point on the earth to the next. The
opening stanza of "Wintergeschrei" is an example: "Krähen,
Krähen, / grünes Eis, Krähen / über dem Strom. Erstarrt / Ges-
träuch, seine Flucht / uferhinauf." (SS, 24)

Gradually, however, as the speaker begins to find his way about
among the things he names, and to perceive dimensions and directions, momentum gathers, and syntactical patterns are completed.
The second phase in the structure of Bobrowski's poetry (there
are three according to the model I propose) is characterized by
an apprehension of contacts, particularly between the poetic ego
and the setting it has conjured. Frequently full sentences appear,
often with a first-person subject. Sometimes the difference between
the first lines and the middle of the poem is only that the speaker
seems to have become aware of his own presence in the landscape
and of his activity in it, as in the poem "Erzählung":

37. In a review of *Sarmatische Zeit* in *Neue Deutsche Literatur, 10* (1962),
142: "die verwegene Kraft des Beginns, das Festhalten an der mitunter noch farb-
losen Entdeckung, der Griff nach dem Wort."

Heller Sand, Spuren,
grün, und der fliegende Wald
Finsternis, hoch der stählerne Fisch
fährt durch die Bäume,
über die Wipfel auf, ich
setz nur den Schritt,
weiter den Schritt. (SS, 21)

But, as is clear from the second stanza of "Immer zu benennen,"
the transition from the first stage to the second actually involves
a feeling of the inadequacy of mere naming and conjuring and of
personal responsibility with respect to the connectedness of things
in time.

After the initial sense of spatial connections, therefore, an awareness of time develops, as does a wish to do justice to nature in its
historical continuity. Characteristic of this stage in the poem is
the use of the words "einst," "einmal," and "damals" at the beginning of the second stanza, and the frequent shift from present
to past tense between the first stanza and the second.[38] The quality
of the lyrical voice is less the probing, incantatory one of the
beginning than a straightforward, though still tense, narrative. The
rhythm has become more evenly measured in its smooth cadences,
the periods generally extending over longer syntactical stretches
than mere flashes and flurries of individual nouns and verbless
clusters. The middle of the poem is usually spoken in full, declarative sentences. It is here, in the middle of the poem, that the
"message" of the phenomena seems to be apprehended. In "Immer
zu benennen," for example, the speaker comes into contact again
with the "sleep" of things and follows the course of their "speech"
("im Dunkel geht ihre Rede").

Further, in the middle of Bobrowski's poems the speaker very
often reflects on the meaning of the poetic subject—be it a river,
a church, or a biographical figure—or on his own situation and
impressions. These first two stages—the staccato beginning and the
more fluent middle section—as well as the third are clearly

38. Some examples of the first technique are the poems "Schattenland" (W,
19), "Auf der Taurischen Strasse" (SZ, 57), and "Die Memel" (SZ, 78); and the
shift in tenses can be seen in "Nowgorod" (W, 17), "Gestorbene Sprache" (SZ,
30), "Heimweg" (SS, 85), "Wagenfahrt" (SZ, 22), "Abend der Fischerdörfer"
(SS, 69), "Spur im Sand" (SZ, 32), "Auf einen Brunnen" (W, 9), and "Winterlicht" (SZ, 82). The "Pruzzische Elegie" has the same basic structure.

exemplified in the poem "Ebene," a structurally typical poem and
one of Bobrowski's best.

> See.
> Der See.
> Versunken
> die Ufer. Unter der Wolke
> der Kranich. Weiss, aufleuchtend
> der Hirtenvölker
> Jahrtausende. Mit dem Wind
>
> kam ich herauf den Berg.
> Hier werd ich leben. Ein Jäger
> war ich, einfing mich
> aber das Gras.
>
> Lehr mich reden, Gras,
> lehr mich tot sein und hören,
> lange, und reden, Stein,
> lehr du mich bleiben, Wasser,
> frag mir, und Wind, nicht nach. (SS, 12)

There is the "static," almost stuttering beginning, the slow gathering of momentum and rhythmic thrust as awareness of dimensions
and spatial relationships increases, and then the awakened sense of
temporality ("der Hirtenvölker Jahrtausende"). The speaker finds
contact and companionship with the wind and with his own place
in the setting as the poetic style opens up to full syntax and
longer rhythmic periods.

The third stanza, and third stage, of the poem is entirely in the
imperative, dominated by verb forms. The speaker addresses
directly three of the four noun objects ("Gras," "Stein," "Wasser"), and these nouns are set off by commas for emphasis; but
they seem overwhelmed by the torrent of nine verbs: four imperatives, all at the start of lines, and five infinitives. Accordingly,
the tone is one of pressing urgency and impatience, corresponding
in poetic practice to the negative theoretical condition at the end
of "Immer zu benennen," where the speaker indicates that he
would wait a while ("ich würd umhergehn, ich würd warten ein
wenig") if there were a God who could help him communicate
with what he has forgotten. The implication (in "Immer zu benen-

nen") is that there is no such God and that he therefore cannot wait.

The end of "Ebene," and of a great many of Bobrowski's poems, is like a desperate, obsessive, impatient scream of communication, an intensely urgent wish to hear and to be heard by the surrounding phenomena. I say like a "scream" intentionally, because the verbs "schreien" and "rufen" are of crucial importance in the poet's vocabulary. The "scream" ("Geschrei") sometimes has negative associations, characterizing the forces of destruction in nature, as opposed to the gentle speech ("reden") of innocent, victimized things.[39] But for the most part it is the victims—very often tortured birds—who scream, and because he identifies with their suffering, so does the poetic speaker. This howl of agony and warning is heard at the end of the poems "Der Don" and "Dorfkirche 1942" and many others. The speaker's voice always joins in the cry, as is most evident in poems about persecuted individuals —"Vogelstrassen 1957" (SS, 52–53) and "An Nelly Sachs" (SS, 57–58). In these two poems there is also a clear identification of the scream and the poetic song itself; the same is true of "Mit Liedern Sapphos" (W, 18) and the magnificent poem "Petr Bezruč" (SS, 48). At other times—as in "Der Wachtelschlag" (SS, 5–7) and "Nowgorod" (W, 17–18)—the scream is an impassioned expression of ardent religious faith. The words "Schrei," "Geschrei," and "Ruf," and their verb forms, appear almost invariably toward the ends of the poems, and by physical analogy they seem to epitomize the poem's diction and the speaker's mood at that final moment.

The scream is one version of the sense of urgency and the intensity of expression which characterize the last lines of a great many of Bobrowski's poems and also much of his prose (for example, Potschka's demand to "call the past over to where we are" at the end of Litauische Claviere, or the artist Philippi's determined "no" which forms the thirty-fourth and last statement in Levins Mühle). When it is not an imperative or a screaming cry, the final intensity is expressed by an exclamatory utterance, intent listening, restless activity, or not infrequently by a prophetic intimation of the future. Some typical poem endings are: "so ruft, /

39. As in the poems "Nachtweg" (SZ, 68), "Winterlicht" (SZ, 83), and "Der Judenberg" (SS, 46).

Augen, ruft, Wange, ruf, Mund / ruf Hosianna" ("Ostern");
"lauschen, legen / das Ohr an die Erd" ("Nordrussische Stadt");
"ich gehe / über den Strom" ("Heimweg"); "Schöpferin, lehn
dich ins Licht. / Sing dir den Mund blass" ("Der litauische Brunnen"); "fahrt hinaus / wartet nicht auf die Nacht" ("Am Tage");
"aus dem höchsten / Fenster schrei mich ins Licht!" ("Franzö-
sisches Dorf"). All of these examples, and many others, illustrate
the same intensity of experience and desperate impatience as was
expressed in the speaker's yearning for "das Wirkliche" in "An
Klopstock," and his unwillingness to "wait a while" in "Immer
zu benennen." The poetic speaker seems to sense that he is running
out of breath and must do or say something at once, before it is
too late. After conjuring up a landscape and finding his place in
it, he must now make his presence known by a fervent vocal, or
physical, gesture.

  Bobrowski's characteristic poem is triadic in structure, each of
the three stages marked by a particular subjective mood and a
particular mode of diction. The three-stanza poem is the form
most frequently used (a total of 65 out of 168 poems have three
stanzas), and the three-stage development is also apparent in innumerable other poems of two, four, five, or six stanzas. At the
beginning the mood is one of uncertainty and disorientation, and
the style is incantatory, nominal, and sharply paratactic, characterized by a probing grasp after individual nouns and noun
clusters and an erratic, staccato rhythm. The speaker "names"
objects, without yet possessing any sense of their spatial and
temporal interconnections or of his own position toward them.
As this sense develops, the rhythmic momentum builds and the
second stage emerges. The speaker seems to have gained a point of
focus and reference, though he is never fully at ease, and can
reflect on and take up contact with his surroundings. The style is
narrative, with a more even rhythm and with full, declarative
sentences. A kind of balance is reached between nominal and
verbal usage. Toward the end, however, the verb reigns supreme.
In the third phase the style is again paratactic, but this time verb
forms prevail, and the rhythmic staccato has the effect, not of
faltering fits and starts, but of an onward rush, again and again
defying all obstructions. The speaker seems to stutter here not
out of a scarcity of words and images, which he must wrench, one

by one, out of his imagination, as was true in the first lines; rather, he stammers because of an overwhelming abundance of thoughts and wishes to be expressed. Suddenly he discovers that he really has too much to say, and he bursts forth with a torrent of emphatic, demanding statements. The poem ends on an imperative, often an optative, note.

The style and linguistic techniques of Bobrowski's poetry may be directly related to his conception of poetic language and its function. Two tasks are assigned to the language of poetry: recollection and communication. Poetry has a responsibility with regard to things in time; it must not only "always name" them ("Immer zu benennen"); it must also develop an awareness of their coherence and connectedness in a temporal dimension. It must "call" them into contact with one another through time. This act of poetic recollection forms the basis of the transition between the first and the second phases in the poem. But poetic language is also obligated to communicate; it must insist on a dialogue with all objects, organic and inorganic, present and past, near and far. The lyrical voice has to make itself heard through the darkness, and the speaker must hear the sounds emitted in the unreachable distance. Communication is the axis on which the poem turns from its middle section to the end.

Both functions, recollection and communication, involve a bitter struggle, because they constitute attempts to break through and transcend impregnable barriers. For this reason the style is uneasy and tense throughout the poem, which usually leaves the overall impression of one extended, vocal outburst, alternating retarded motion and violent lunges forward, "a crosswork of halt and thrust, singularity and complicity" (*Times Literary Supplement*). But there is within this general and unmistakable aura of Bobrowski's poems a definite pattern of development, in which differing personal attitudes and stylistic modes can be discerned and in which the linguistic medium itself seems to serve radically differing purposes. In addition, this movement from incantation to narration to exclamation may be satisfactorily explained in the framework of Bobrowski's theory of language as it is expressed in the poems "An Klopstock" and "Immer zu benennen." Crucial in the general sequence are the factors of recollection and communication, the dual raison d'être of poetic language.

Recollection is an imperative quality of poetry for Bobrowski because of his sense of the profound guilt and persecution pervading past history, particularly of the people who speak his native German language, and his responsibility to make an attempt at atonement. Communication, because it is conceived of as a penetration into the dark past and a "recalling it" to the present, is obviously to some extent the same act as poetic recollection. But there is another reason for the primacy of this function in Bobrowski's mind, which I have already mentioned in connection with "An Klopstock." Communication is for him the basis of human society; language is the medium which links man to man ("heiliges Band des Sterblichen"), making them "neighbors" and providing them with the only true sense of community. Bobrowski in his poetry seeks to reach a listener, a human addressee, because, as he noted, "A writer has to do with man, who in the ten thousandth year of his history is still a man" and who, in spite of everything, still "remains within reach for the direct address, for urgent questioning." [40]

The same attitude is expressed in one more poem about the nature of language which, unlike "An Klopstock" and "Immer zu benennen," requires no explanation at all. I quote the last stanza of "Sprache":

> Sprache
> abgehetzt
> mit dem müden Mund
> auf dem endlosen Weg
> zum Hause des Nachbarn (W, 37)

The speaker in Bobrowski's poems is on his way next door, no matter how far that may be. His society is a "neighborhood," based on the communication between one man and another, ardently searching out the possibility of realizing, or restoring, an intimate I-thou relationship. When this possibility is fulfilled, a condition of inseparable love may be reached; when it is frustrated, there is only anxiety and alienation.

---

40. *Selbstzeugnisse*, pp. 32–33: "Der Schreiber hat es mit dem Menschen zu tun, der im 10 ooosten Jahr seiner Geschichte noch ein Mensch ist, was stolz klingen soll, wie es heisst, aber nicht so stolz ist,—der aber doch wohl erreichbar bleibt für die direkte Anrede, für die dringliche Befragung."

"Nachbarschaft," Love and Anxiety

In an interview for East Berlin radio Bobrowski was once asked his opinion of the theory current among "leading late bourgeois poets" ("führende spätbürgerliche Lyriker") that "the love poem is no longer possible today." Bobrowski answered by expressing his firm belief that the love poem was "always possible and also always legitimate." After one sentence, however, he immediately turned his defense of love poetry not against the dangers of dehumanization in modern "bourgeois" poetry, as the interviewer had obviously expected, but rather against tendencies and attitudes in the lyric in his own country. "But there is even among us," he said, "for instance among a whole group of lyric poets, an aversion against love poems, based more or less on the general idea that the love poem places too great an emphasis on the I-thou relationship, an affair between two people, and forces concerns proper to society too far into the background. I do not think that that is a valid argument. This I-thou relationship must remain in the love poem. It will not do, I believe, perpetually to look over the beloved's shoulder at the entire world. That is not love, that is something else. I believe that society must by all means place great value on the retention of this intensive I-thou relationship in poetry. I consider it a precondition for society." [41]

Bobrowski wrote only a few love poems, but they form an essential core of his work, and some of them are true masterpieces of German poetry. Invariably they express that intimate I-thou relationship which he felt to be indispensable to all society; and

41. *Selbstzeugnisse*, pp. 50–51: "Ich glaube, dass das Liebesgedicht immer möglich ist und auch immer legitim. Es gibt aber selbst bei uns, zum Beispiel bei einer ganzen Reihe von Lyrikern, eine Aversion gegen Liebesgedichte, die ungefähr darauf ausgeht, dass das Liebesgedicht von sich aus die Ich-Du-Beziehung, eine Angelegenheit zwischen zwei Leuten, zu stark betont und Belange, die der Gesellschaft angehören, zu weit zurückdrückt. Ich bin nicht der Ansicht, dass das ein Argument ist. Diese Ich-Du-Beziehung muss dem Liebesgedicht erhalten bleiben. Es geht nicht an, glaube ich, über die Schulter der Geliebten hinweg dauernd auf die ganze Welt zu sehen. Das ist keine Liebe, das ist etwas anderes. Ich glaube, dass die Gesellschaft durchaus darauf Wert legen muss, dass diese intensive Ich-Du-Beziehung im Gedicht gerettet bleibt. Ich halte es für eine Vorbedingung für Gesellschaft."

without exception the relationship is so intense that all attention must be directed toward its realization; it is never sidetracked
by anxious glances at the great world outside. The faith implicit
throughout is that the larger forces of social and historical change
can be favorable only when time and energy are devoted to culti-
vating such private love. Good neighbors in history and among
peoples can emerge only when men know well who lives next
door and are joined in inseparable unity with those in their immediate presence. In all of Bobrowski's love poems the binding force
is the factor of communication, even though at times the lovers
seem to communicate in a most unusual way.

In some cases the dialogue is explicit and open, the lover asking
questions and the beloved finally answering. The poem "Am
Strom" (SZ, 27), for instance, for which Bobrowski was awarded
the Viennese Alma-Johanna-Koenig Prize in 1962, ends:

> Lauscht ich über den Strom?
> Dem Vogel nach oder drunten
> dem Grundfisch?—"Lieber, immer
> Sprunglaut hör ich und droben
> Flügelschlag. Geh mir nicht fort."

In "Liebesgedicht" (SZ, 16), a curious poem in which the speaker
identifies with the rising and setting moon, the beloved does not
answer directly, but her voice nevertheless seems to hover in the
atmosphere:

> Und ich frag dich,
> die neben mir lag,
> nach einem Mond
> gestern, wann er verging—du
> antwortest nicht, an die Wolke
> streift der Lichtstein, der tönt
> von deiner Stimme.

At the end of the poem the lover lives on, even though the moon
has already passed, because he has heard her voice:

> Gestern—
> ich bin vergangen—
> heute—

ich hab dich gehört—
und ich atme noch immer.

Equally remarkable, and similar because the speaker ends by
"hearing" the beloved speak, is "Vogelnest" (W, 41). In this
poem, with its unusually short lines, the lovers appear as two birds
building a nest together. But because of the strange, bewildering
sentences which are blurted out (the poem begins, "Mein Himmel
/ wechselt mit deinem"), it becomes clear that what is being built
is not really a bird's nest. The second stanza, in which a site for
the nest is found, is an act of exchange and harmonious utterance:

Wir vertauschen
unsere Augen,
wir finden
ein Lager:
Regen,
wir sagen
wie eine Geschichte
die halben Sätze
Grün,
ich hör:

The green foliage consists, in fact, of the "half sentences" spoken
in the lines of the poem. The odd poetic structure may therefore
be explained as an attempt to assimilate the poem's visual, and
aural, effect to the process of constructing a nest piece by piece.
Once again the speaker "hears" ("ich hör") at the end of the
poem, and in the last stanza the metaphoric identification of the
act of nest-building and love as communication is complete: "Zu
meiner Braue / hinauf / mit Vogelreden / dein Mund / trägt
Federn und Zweige." Throughout the poem there is an alternation
between the first and the second person ("ich" and "du"), followed by their unity: in the first stanza, "Mein Himmel" and
"deinem," "meine Taube" and "deine," and then "zwei Schatten";
in the second, the sequence at the beginning of the first four lines,
"Wir"-"unsere"-"wir"-"ein"; and in the third stanza, "Zu meiner
Braue," "dein Mund," and then unity in "Federn und Zweige"—
the nest itself. The bird's nest, to paraphrase the metaphor, is the
result of an act of mutual exchange and harmonious activity, and

above all of intensive dialogue, hearing and speaking, between the lovers.

Most typically in Bobrowski's love poetry this act of communication is not an outspoken and outwardly audible dialogue, but an interplay of inner senses. Such a turn inward characterizes the love scene in the poem "Mitternachtsdorf" (W, 14), where all the lovers hear is the flow of blood through each other's veins: "Lass uns schlafen einer / des andern Schlaf und hören / nicht die Sterne und alle / Stimmen im Finstren, das Blut / nur wie es fällt und zurücksinkt." The lovers have penetrated into each other so deeply that they no longer need to externalize their utterances; they can understand each other from the beat of the pulse in their veins.

The same internal, speechless communication occurs in the two exquisite love poems "Seeufer" (SZ, 76) and "Einmal haben" (SZ, 77). "Seeufer" contains three stanzas and has basically the three-part structure characteristic of Bobrowski's poetry. (Another love poem in which this form is even more clearly evident is "Erzählung," SS, 21.) The first stanza is a long dependent clause which merely "names" the living objects remaining on a tide-swept shoreline: "Was noch lebt / im Treibsand / unter der grossen Fische / Flossenflügel, schwindendes / Grün, Algen, ein Seemoos." In the second stanza, containing the predicate part of the sentence ("ist"), the speaker finds himself with his beloved. The two lovers seem to be what was washed onto the shore, and love itself is what is left after the sand is dry. Once again the "word of love"— I believe that this is the sense of the stanza—is unspoken, yet heard within, in the beating of the pulse: "ist wie ein Wort, ungesagt, / gehört in der Höhlung des Mundes, / im Beben der Schläfe, / im Haar. Wir treiben ans Ufer, / mit bläulichen Händen Liebe, / weiss." The third stanza begins with an imperative, as occurs so frequently in Bobrowski's poems. Here, however, the last lines show no sign of impatience and urgency; the words serve as gentle assurance to the beloved that the warmth and intimacy of their love will find refuge from the cold outdoors: "Komm / es ist kalt, hören / wird uns das Stroh, die Decke / über dem Seufzer / die knisternde Holzwand." Their love itself is this tiny, tranquil enclosure in which communication is possible, and they are finally whispered into slumber: "Der Schlaf, ein Geflüster, / legt sich zu uns." It is in such delicate little poems as "Seeufer" that the poet Bobrowski is at his best, the speaker's timid, reticent voice standing up to, and overpowering, the huge and perilous forces of nature around him. There is courage in the simple words, "Komm, es ist kalt"—courage gained from the faith that a word spoken, or even unspoken, is heard at least within the narrow confines of intimate love.

The situation is similar in "Einmal haben." Here the lovers appear with the light of love in their hands at the beginning ("Einmal haben / wir beide Hände voll Licht—"); their bold confrontation with the icy, inimical landscape occupies the middle of the poem: "—dann / stehen wir gegen den Hang / draussen, gegen den weissen / Himmel, der kalt / über den Berg / kommt, die Kaskade Glanz, / und erstarrt ist, Eis, / wie von Sternen herab." The effect created by the succession of enjambments and then the erratic rhythm ("die Kaskade Glanz, und erstarrt ist, Eis") corresponds perfectly to the striking image of the entire frozen sky tumbling over the precipice like a mammoth waterfall of ice. The second stanza, with which the poem ends, is short and expresses a different mood; it contains only five gentle lines, as compared with the fourteen restless, violent lines which preceded. Once again, as at the end of "Seeufer," refuge is found in intense, close love. Once again the act of communication involves not words or sounds, but is entirely internal, the lovers' pulses made to beat in time. The stanza reads, "Auf deiner Schläfe / will ich die kleine Zeit / leben, vergesslich, lautlos / wandern lassen / mein Blut durch dein Herz."

"Schläfe," "Blut" and "Herz" are key words in Bobrowski's love lyrics. The temple and blood are the media of this internalized communication, the pulse and the heartbeat, and it is they which triumph over the inimical, wintry surroundings. This confrontation between the force of love's voice and an icy landscape is crucial in the poem "Wintergeschrei" (SS, 24). In the first half of the poem (the first stanza and the beginning of the second), the setting is entirely frozen, and the syntax nearly static: "Krähen, Krähen, / grünes Eis, Krähen." But then, in the middle of the second stanza, there is the sight of blood ("aber / ein wenig Blut / dein Herz / mitten im Eis"), which then becomes a "call" that seems to finally melt the ice. The poem ends,

dein Ruf
eine Rauchspur über
der Sandbank,

wo unermüdend waren
Umarmungen, immer
lebte der Strom.

The "scream of winter" is the expression of the pulsating heart of love, the unspoken voice given off by tireless embraces in a climate which offers no other warmth than that of immediate, physical contact. It is the most desperate, and most desperately yearned for, version of that same act of communication which is present in Bobrowski's other love poems, "Am Strom," "Liebesgedicht," "Vogelnest," "Seeufer," and "Einmal haben."

The turning point of "Wintergeschrei" is the sight of a spot of red in the middle of a massive icy terrain. In the poem "Am Fluss" (SS, 18) the speaker also perceives a trace of red: "Da ist ein Streifen Rot, / eine Spur / Rot, wir sind es allein"; again, the poem ends with an internal dialogue of the throbbing pulse: "es liegt deine Schläfe (ein Klopfen / langsam, nicht mehr zu hören, / nie mehr) auf meinem Mund." But here the patch of red does not appear on one solid surface of green ice but is a strip between two other colors: "Rot, wir sind es allein / zwischen Grün und Blau, / Himmel und Erde." The poem begins with this same contrast of colors and between sky and earth. First there is the blue sky, a huge arch above the lovers, and then the green of the tree-lined riverbank on which they lie. This polarity is not followed through in this poem (which I consider a less impressive text anyway), but it is of central importance in much of his other verse, including some of his love poems. Basically the tension is between lightness and heaviness, dryness and dampness, the ethereal and the earthy. In "Am Strom," for example, the contrast is between the bird flying above the stream and the fish down in its depths. Earlier in the poem, the beloved seems to possess a sacred, ethereal quality ("Du kamst / den Mondweg, von Ostra Brama / kamst du herab"), and the speaker-lover longs for the heavy, moist earth: "Füll mir die Hände mit Sand, / die Feuchte will ich, die Schwere."

This tension is characteristic of Bobrowski's poetry in general, not only of his love-poems, and it has been discussed by some critics.[42] Most interesting in this regard is the remarkable two-stanza "Dryade" (SS, 17). Overtly it is not a love lyric, but the Dryad's effect on the speaker clearly suggests an intimate relationship. He is a tree, his roots deep into the earth and soaking in all the dampness of the cool soil. As he feels the liquids gushing upward within him, the second stanza begins:

> Lass,
> in den Nacken hinab,
> lass fallen dein Haar, ich hör
> in meinen Händen, ich hör
> durch die Kühle, ich hör ein Wehen,
> hör anheben die Strömung,
> steigende Flut,
> den Taumel
> singen im Ohr.

The speaker seems possessed by a spirit within him which he feels rushing upward from the earth. He speaks as though in a trance, the dynamic rhythm building up greater and greater momentum with the repetition of the words "ich hör." What the speaker "hears" is not a voice of any kind but his own pulse, the sap flowing through his veins—or rather, a throbbing, mounting pulsation which has entered into him. The poem "Dryade" may be viewed as a variation of Bobrowski's love theme, with the characteristic act of internal communication taking place this time within an individual state of mind. The trance of the speaker corresponds to a condition of ecstatic love without an object, the tension between earthiness and ethereal lightness having completely penetrated into the being of an individual lover. He is firmly rooted into the earth, and yet he seems borne upward by the rushing flood of sap within him.

The interpretation of "Dryade" in the context of Bobrowski's love poetry makes greater sense when the poem is juxtaposed with one final love poem, entitled "Ungesagt" (SS, 20). It consists of a single stanza:

42. See, for example, Schwarz, "'Freund mit der leisen Rede,'" pp. 62–65. However, Schwarz does not specify that "Am Strom" and "Ungesagt" are love poems.

Schwer,
ich wachse hinab,
Wurzeln
breite ich in den Grund,
die Wasser der Erde
finden mich, steigen,
Bitternis schmeck ich—du
bist ohne Erde,
ein Vogel den Lüften, leichter
immer im Licht,
nur meine Angst noch
hält dich
im irdischen Wind.

The polarity here is between the lover as a tree rooted to the ground ("Schwer") and the beloved as a bird ("ohne Erde," "leichter"). As the "waters of the earth" rise in his trunk he thinks of her flying in the sky above, appearing free of all contact with the earth. The axis of the poem is the middle line, "Bitternis schmeck ich—du." It is, therefore, in this poem that the I-thou relation is most obviously present and "retained." It is imperiled by the great distance between the lovers and by the fact that the beloved may at any time fly off into the higher reaches of the atmosphere and leave him alone, planted in the cold earth. But they are bound by the taste of "bitterness" on his lips: his "Angst" keeps her within his reach ("nur meine Angst noch hält dich im irdischen Wind"). The lovers seem to have an "unspoken" agreement (the title "Ungesagt" is a key word for all of Bobrowski's love poetry) that as long as his condition on earth is unbearable alone, they will cling to each other and remain within intimate range.

Bobrowski's love poems are set in an inimical winter landscape; they are unvoiced, yet fulfilled, acts of internal communication which defy a climate in which any dialogue whatsoever is threatened by the very existence of a world outside. Intimate love is refuge from the world, yet it stands up to the world, and as realized communication, it is the only basis on which a human community free of anxiety can be construed. Poetic language aims at "Nachbarschaft"—the notion that inspired all of Bobrowski's literary productivity—which is ultimately grounded in an intensive I-thou relationship and defiantly challenges all "alienated" and all "collectivized" societies.

The poem "Absage" (SZ, 85), discussed earlier, ends with the stanza,

> Dort
> war ich. In alter Zeit.
> Neues hat nie begonnen. Ich bin ein Mann,
> mit seinem Weibe ein Leib,
> der seine Kinder aufzieht
> für eine Zeit ohne Angst.

The first two lines refer to the distant past, and the third sentence to the sense that nothing has changed since the days of the ancient Prussian deity Perkun. The final words prophesy a future in which there will be an end to guilt and persecution. The transition from the present "age of anxiety" (to use Auden's phrase [43]) to that blissful future is contained in the fourth line. A "time without anxiety" will only come as the result of the "humanization of conditions," intimate devotion and personal unity here and now, and not because of the eventual intervention of some transcendent divinity. The model of Bobrowski's faith was commendable social behavior, rather than ascetic seclusion; as he himself put it, "our idea of a Christian way of life is based precisely on the fact that we are not a secret sect but must take our place in society." [44]

For the most part Bobrowski's sense of human suffering and injustice in history was formed by his experience of National Socialism and the war. An "age of anxiety" was for him one in which entire peoples could be persecuted and exploited by brutality like that of National Socialism. All his many works devoted to humble and tortured Jews, Poles, and Lithuanians were written out of profound sympathy for their irreparable agony and out of a profound consciousness of the guilt of his own, the German people. The poems to Gertrud Kolmar, Else Lasker-Schüler, and Nelly Sachs in the middle of *Schattenland Ströme*, for example,

43. The connection is suggested by Glenn, "Introduction," p. 49.
44. *Selbstzeugnisse*, p. 44: "Unsere Vorstellung von christlicher Lebensführung basiert ja gerade darauf, dass wir nicht eine verborgene Sekte sind, sondern in der Gesellschaft zu stehen haben."

are all attempts to identify with the suffering brought to those three persecuted Jewish poetesses. Love in this context is the force of redemption from the horrors present in the age of the Nazis; the poem "Else-Lasker-Schüler" (SS, 55–56) ends with the stanza, "Liebe / (du sprichst aus dem Grab) / Liebe tritt, eine weisse / Gestalt, / aus der Mitte des Grauens."

There was another reason for Bobrowski's continual reminder of the horrors of the recent past: his concern over, and his hope that he could help to combat, nationalistic and revanchist tendencies in postwar German society. The revival of such sympathies, particularly in West Germany, deeply troubled him, since they could only lead to a revival of massive destruction. In this regard he was in basic agreement with the policies of the DDR toward Germany's eastern boundaries and the illegality of nationalist organizations.[45] Another attitude Bobrowski felt to be conducive to anxiety and injustice in the postwar period is anti-Communism. His brilliant autobiographical essay entitled "Fortgeführte Überlegungen" and his powerful story "Der Mahner," [46] both written in the last year of his life, were intended as warnings against anti-Communist "hysteria," and both are of course extolled by East German and sympathetic West German commentators. Indeed, they are basic to Bobrowski's attitude toward the DDR, which was explicitly that of a non-Marxist who affirmed "the structure and future of socialist society." [47]

Despite his fundamental allegiance to the country, however, Bobrowski saw little resemblance between the DDR and his ideal of a congenial human community. In order to fully understand his concept of anxiety and alienation as obstacles to love and com-

45. In an autobiographical sketch Bobrowski once wrote about his own literary intentions: "Hauptthema: Der Versuch, das unglückliche und schuldhafte Verhältnis des deutschen Volkes zu seinen östlichen Nachbarvölkern bis in die jüngste Vergangenheit zum Ausdruck zu bringen und damit zur Überwindung revanchistischer Tendenzen beizutragen." (Selbstzeugnisse, pp. 24–25) In another interview (pp. 72–73) Bobrowski expressed his approval of the East German law intended to curtail the emergence of nationalist and chauvinist feelings in Germany.

46. "Fortgeführte Überlegungen" was written for the collection of essays Antikommunismus und Proexistenz, ed. Günter Wirth (East Berlin, 1965), pp. 37–39; "Der Mahner" first appeared in Sinn und Form, 17 (1965), 805–809. Both pieces are included in Der Mahner.

47. Selbstzeugnisse, p. 44: "Ich habe oft erlebt, das es gerade eindrucksvoll für den Gesprächspartner ist, wenn ein Nichtmarxist sich zu Gestalt und Zukunft der sozialistischen Gesellschaft bekennt."

munication, it is necessary to recognize Bobrowski's skepticism and reservation toward the East German society in which he lived. It is, of course, never easy to ascertain when he was referring specifically to the situation in the DDR, and indeed there is virtually nothing in the works published during his lifetime which alludes to contemporary events even indirectly (except one story, "Dunkel und ein wenig Licht," which is set in West Berlin). Bobrowski has become known as a writer immersed in the past, and for the bulk of his work this description is an entirely apt one. But as one reviewer for the *Times Literary Supplement* (February 22, 1968) mentioned when discussing his posthumously published collections (the stories in *Der Mahner* and the poems in *Wetterzeichen*), "the direction of his work was changing fast in 1965: 'Sarmatia' was giving way to the world of today."

Der Mahner contains the playful anecdote entitled "Das Stück," in which fun is poked at the way in which only "constructive criticism" is permitted. Albert Erich Knolle wants to write a play, which he will call "The Mishap" ("Die Panne," an allusion to Friedrich Dürrenmatt), and it is to be "critical." But when he submits the first three acts to the chief dramaturge, Dr. Obcrüber, "objections arose, like blisters." Knolle is then set on the right track and finishes writing the play. "Now the play is finished and is called 'Mishap Avoided.' Knolle has gone through a development and has imparted a constructive turn to his criticism. The criticized event or object proved to be only apparently worthy of criticism. The main character had been subject to an error which was finally resolved, and insight emerged triumphant." [48] There can be no question that beneath this light humor lay a contempt for the whole socialist-realist enterprise and its trivial demands for "the positive," which Bobrowski and his countrymen encountered for more than a decade.

But "Das Stück" is not localized, and its tone is too jocular to be regarded as serious opposition. The real basis of Bobrowski's skepticism is suggested in the following poem written in 1965:

48. In *Der Mahner*, pp. 61–62: "Jetzt ist das Stück fertig und heisst Die verhinderte Panne. Knolle hat eine Entwicklung durchgemacht und seiner Kritik eine aufbauende Wendung beigebracht. Der kritisierte Vorgang oder Gegenstand erwies sich nur als scheinbar kritikwürdig. Die Hauptperson war einem Irrtum unterlegen. Der löste sich auf, die Einsicht triumphierte breit."

Entfremdung

Zeit
geht umher
in Kleidern
aus Glück
und Unglück.

Der im Unglück
spricht mit der Klapperstimme
der Störche, die Störche
meiden ihn: sein Gefieder
schwarz, seine Bäume Schatten,
da ist Nacht, seine Wege
gehn in der Luft. (W, 80)

"Alienation" according to this text has nothing in common with
the Marxist concept, since it is not a factor of the labor process in
capitalist society nor is it rooted in a particular historical period.
Rather, time itself appears to be only a kind of masquerade, alter-
nately donning the garbs of "fortune and adversity." "Entfremdung"—"estrangement"—is taken literally: a time "dressed in"
misfortune, or "Entfremdung," is one in which people are "strange"
to one another, in which any attempt at communication meets with
failure. The unfortunate one speaks the language of others, but
they "avoid him," and he becomes a stranger in what seemed his
natural habitat. "Entfremdung," in short, is the opposite of "Nachbarschaft," since the wish to engage in congenial dialogue is frustrated and ignored.

The same fundamental problem is present in the two related
poems, "Antwort" (W, 46) and "Nachtfischer" (W, 47), which
I would like to suggest refer to the situation and late poetry of
Peter Huchel. (Certainly it is remarkable that among his many
poems and stories about poets and artistic personalities not one
is dedicated to Huchel, whom of all living poets Bobrowski held
in the highest esteem.) Both are dated 1963, the year in which
Huchel vanished from literary life in the DDR. Indeed, "Nachtfischer," which begins with the lines, "Im schönen Laub / die
Stille / unverschmerzt. / Licht   mit   den   Händen / über   einer
Mauer," is strikingly similar in theme and imagery to Huchel's
poem about the Berlin Wall, "Ophelia." Even more relevant, be-

cause Bobrowski's speaker begins by addressing an individual person, is the poem "Antwort"; it opens: "Über dem Zaun / deine Rede." The second and third stanzas strike the reader familiar with Huchel's late poetry as direct allusions to the poems published in the last issue of *Sinn und Form* under Huchel's editorship. Stanza two strongly resembles the poem "Traum im Tellereisen" (especially the lines, "ein Testament gestürzter Tannen, / geschrieben / in regengrauer Geduld"). Bobrowski's passage reads,

Auch im gestürzten Holunder
das Schwirrlied der Amseln, der Grille
Gräserstimme
kerbt Risse ins Mauerwerk, Schwalbenflug
steil
gegen den Regen, Sternbilder
gehn auf dem Himmel,
im Reif.

The third, final stanza of "Antwort" may have reference to Huchel's poems "Psalm" and "Der Garten des Theophrast" (1962), and here the theme of anxiety and impeded communication is most clearly evident. The final three lines exhibit the urgency characteristic of the conclusions of Bobrowski's poems; otherwise, however, the stanza could be a direct quote from Huchel. Bobrowski's lines read:

Die mich einscharren
unter die Wurzeln,
hören:
er redet,
zum Sand,
der ihm den Mund füllt—so wird
reden der Sand, und wird
schreien der Stein, und wird
fliegen das Wasser.

Once again, as in "Entfremdung," vocal utterance is threatened, and the poetic subject seems to have lost his orientation in the world to which he belonged. But because of the insistent tone in the last lines the poem ends on a note of defiant determination and even triumph, as though by an act of will the person addressed

will break through the alienated situation to which he is condemned. "Antwort," then, may be just that—an answer to Peter
Huchel's "Winter Psalm" of melancholy isolation.

Related to the thematic complex of "Antwort" and "Nachtfischer" is the poem "Strandgänger" (W, 50–51), also written in
1963. In the middle of the poem are the lines, "die Wälder aus
Grillenstimmen / heraufgehn / über die Öde," and this time the
subject, a beachcomber, is desperately asked for advice in the last
lines: "Dich werd ich fragen: / Wie heiss ich? / Wo bin ich? /
Wie lang noch / bleibe ich hier?" The word "hier" occurs often,
and in crucial positions, in Bobrowski's late poetry, and I believe
it must be taken literally as a reference to his immediate locality.
The poem "Stadt" (W, 62), for instance, is an expression of the
speaker's (and poet's) reaction to the situation in the city of East
Berlin. The second stanza speaks of violent persecution, with the
same image of the slain pigeon that appeared in the poem about
persecution in general, "Holunderblüte." This time, however, the
word "hier" is used to specify geographically the site of the injustice:

> Hier
> sprengen die Steine, gemalte
> Wände, die Treppe
> bricht, um die Taubenkadaver
> —ihre Standarten—
> stellen sich Rattenheere auf.

Stanza three of the poem also begins "Hier," as if to remind the
reader of the location: "Hier wird, / sagt man, / grünen ein Baum
/ und den Himmel halten, / sagt man, / auf Zweigen und Blättern." By repeating the phrase "sagt man," the speaker expresses
his skepticism; he doubts what is said about the bright, blossoming
future "here," in this city. He cannot believe the words of optimism plastered on the terrifying banners of bands of rats.

The poem "Stadt" is best read in conjunction with the anecdote,
included in Der Mahner, entitled "Im Verfolg städtebaulicher
Erwägungen" (1965). The narrator notices from the window of
his house that changes are being made in one of the sidestreets in
his neighborhood. Old houses are being torn down, one by one,
and the inhabitants continually move next door, until they are

finally on the corner. The narrative ends with the following reflection:

> Yes, new houses can be built in the place of old ones; every-
> thing new, a new name for the street, new inhabitants, they
> have precise, fully detailed ideas when it comes to the future.
> But how that was with the old, with what came before, the
> past, there they are left with guess-work. That has been, and
> is past, time, and lost time. Like idle gossip.[49]

Bobrowski was profoundly skeptical toward the spirit of optimism
proclaimed in his country. Prediction and planning for the future
were for him empty and false as long as they involved neglect of
the past and the present, which also have their needs and require
consideration. He was all in favor of social progress, but not when
it is achieved through mechanical rationalization and by doing
violence to circumstances as they exist and have existed. The true
prophet, for Bobrowski, looks for guidance in past time because
he knows that a blueprint for the future is accurate and just only
when it is sketched in accordance with the entire continuum of
history. It was not possible, for him, to at once build a better
future, a "new Germany," and persecute humanity in the present.

All of Bobrowski's objections to the situation "here" in the
DDR, as he saw it, and his entire moral credo, are pronounced
in his last poem:

Das Wort Mensch

Das Wort Mensch, als Vokabel
eingeordnet, wohin sie gehört,
im Duden:
zwischen Mensa und Menschengedenken.

Die Stadt
alt und neu,
schön bleibt, mit Bäumen

---

49. In *Der Mahner*, p. 66:

Es können ja neue Häuser an die Stelle der alten gesetzt werden; alles neu,
ein neuer Name für die Strasse, neue Bewohner, man hat präzise, ausreichend
detaillierte Vorstellungen, wenn es um die Zukunft geht. Aber wie das mit
dem Alten, Früheren, dem Vergangenen gewesen ist, da bleibt man auf Ver-
mutungen angewiesen. Das ist gewesen, und ist vergangen, Zeit, und verlorene
Zeit. Wie Geschwätz.

auch
und Fahrzeugen, hier

hör ich das Wort, die Vokabel
hör ich hier häufig, ich kann
aufzählen von wem, ich kann
anfangen damit.

Wo Liebe nicht ist,
sprich das Wort nicht aus. (W, 83)

It severely offended the humanist Bobrowski to read and hear
such jargon as "In our republic man stands in the foreground,"
so typical of the inevitable rhetoric of East German newspapers
and officialdom. He was keenly aware that jargon is not language,
"die Vokabel" is not "das Wort," because it is used not to communicate but to deceive. Any claim to "humanism" was for him
a lie—empty, mechanical terminology existing only on paper—
when love and neighborliness are absent. His moral legacy is the
same as the warning issued by his friend Erwin Strittmatter, that
there can be "no socialism without human hearts" ("kein Sozialismus ohne Menschenherzen!"). The irony of ironies, and a sign
either of blindness or progress, is that the poem "Das Wort
Mensch" was first published in *Neues Deutschland* (June 8, 1966).

It would be a mistake to consider this change in the direction of
Bobrowski's poetry just before his death—his final shift of attention to present-day society—in isolation, outside of the context of
his general theme, that "long history of calamity and guilt" of
which he had been writing since the early 1950s. As is stated in
that same perceptive review from the *Times Literary Supplement*,
of February 22, 1968: "This was an entirely consequential development, for it was precisely Bobrowski's year-long absorption
in the eastern European past that qualified him to turn to the
present (in which the past is re-enacted), while his moral commitment made it inevitable that he would do so." Sarmatia was the
landscape in which Bobrowski developed his moral responsibility
toward historical development; society in postwar Germany, East
and West, provided him with contemporary conditions to which
it could finally be applied.

The reviewer for the *Times Literary Supplement* closes with the prediction: "His work will live on because his theme and the sheer quality of his work are timeless." Bobrowski himself was sensitive to the fact that the real "effect" of literature, including its political effect, depends to a very great extent on its aesthetic quality.[50] One such indirect effect is that quality can be emulated, and artistically valuable works may help create an atmosphere in which other work of quality can be produced. In a study of the development of lyric poetry in the DDR, the verse of Johannes Bobrowski is of key importance for precisely such an impact on the prevailing literary climate.

In 1962, just after the publication of his first volume, Bobrowski stated that he "would like above all to help raise the level of our poetry." A year later, in 1963, when asked what he regarded as the year's most impressive cultural event, he answered, "that our poetry has been set in motion somewhat." [51] The years 1963–1965 are generally acknowledged to represent the blossomtime of East German poetry—a brief but highly significant "lyrical inter-mezzo," after which it would never be the same again. The role of the example set by Bobrowski's work cannot, I think, be over-emphasized. In 1961, for the first time after more than a decade of predominant versified clichés and the banalities of socialist realism, there appeared poetry of genuine originality and genius; for the first time the whole question of the "German past" was explored with the inspiration and subtlety indispensable to great art. Finally, public tribute was paid not only to commendable poetic inten-tions, of which there was an overabundance, but to the irresistible, timeless merit of "sheer quality." (A coincidence worth noting is that only three months after Bobrowski's death, as a result of the Eleventh Plenum of the Party's Central Committee in December, 1965, the promising interlude of brilliant poetry was brought to an abrupt halt.)

At the same time, however, as Bobrowski was also aware, he

50. See, for example, his statement quoted in *Selbstzeugnisse*, p. 81: "Ich habe zum Beispiel oft betont, dass ich auf restaurative Erscheinungen, auf Faschismus, Chauvinismus usw., zu ihrer Bekämpfung Macht angewendet wünsche. Allerdings erwarten Zweckoptimisten, die der Literatur diese Macht einfach zuschreiben, all-zuviel. Inwieweit Literatur hier etwas leistet, wird nicht so sehr vom guten Willen, als von ihrer Qualität abhängen."

51. *Selbstzeugnisse*. P. 25: "Ich möchte vor allem an der Hebung des Niveaus der Lyrik bei uns mitarbeiten." P. 34: "Das für mich bedeutungsvollste Ereignis: dass in unserer Lyrik einiges in Bewegung gekommen ist."

did not serve as a direct model for the young poets who began to emerge in the 1960s. He recognized that they belong to a different "generation," as it were, and that the flowering of East German poetry derived from a source from which he himself had always been distant: Bertolt Brecht. "The generation of poets that I have in mind here," he noted in 1965, "they are all more or less pronounced Brechtians. And my own relation to Brecht is not very strong. Of course I like him a great deal, especially as a poet. Otherwise, though, I am not a particularly avid admirer." [52] The Brechtians—that is the best name to apply to all younger poets of any importance writing in the DDR in the 1960s. Günter Kunert, Volker Braun, Sarah and Rainer Kirsch, Karl Mickel, Bernd Jentzsch, Wolf Biermann—they are all different, having learned slightly different lessons, but they all learned most from Brecht, and they constitute his "posterity" ("die Nachgeborenen") in the country where he spent the last years of his life. They are, unlike Huchel and Bobrowski, explicitly public poets; their poetry is shaped not so much by inward, personal visions of potential justice as by their stances and attitudes toward the society in which they grew up. They are epigones, still standing too much in the shadow of their master to have created poems of the stature of Huchel's or Bobrowski's best. But they are the new generation, the Enzensbergers and Rühmkorfs of East Germany, and it is they who will decide the future course of poetry in the DDR.

52. *Selbstzeugnisse*, p. 78: "Die Generation, die ich hier im Auge hatte, die sind alle mehr oder weniger ausgesprochene Brechtianer. Und ich habe kein so starkes Verhältnis zu Brecht. Ich mag ihn natürlich sehr, vor allem als Lyriker. Sonst bin ich kein so überschwenglicher Bewunderer."

Part Three: Revisions

5

Premonitions and Provocations: Günter Kunert, Volker Braun, Karl Mickel, and Wolf Biermann

Contradictions and the Critical Stance

In the late 1930s, while in exile from Hitler's Germany, Bertolt Brecht wrote a few paragraphs on "the critical stance" ("die kritische Haltung") in poetry. "It is all wrong," he said, "to think of *criticism* as something dead, unproductive and, so to speak, long-bearded. Herr Hitler wishes very much to propagate this conception of criticism. In reality, the critical stance is the only productive one, the only stance worthy of mankind." A poem was for Brecht worthless if it did not give evidence, however subtly, of the rich diversity, the ambiguity, the compelling dialectic of things and social circumstances. In his essay of the same years, on "The Dialectic," he wrote: "Poems grow flat, empty and stale when their subject matter is robbed of its contradictions." The ideas of "the critical stance" and the contradictory nature of reality were integrally connected in Brecht's mind, and they were both basic to his theory of realism in art. Even later, in the 1950s, he defended socialist realism only if it was "at the same time a critical realism." The realist's "critical stance," accordingly, must address itself not only to the antagonisms inherent in capitalist society, but also to the contradictions still present in socialism. "Realist artists," he said in 1954, "depict the *contradictions* in men and their relations to one another, and show the conditions under which they develop." Significantly, the work that most impressed Brecht in his reading of that same year, 1954, was the treatise "On Contradiction" by Mao Tse-tung.[1]

1. Brecht, *Gesammelte Werke, 19.* P. 393: "Es ist völlig verkehrt, *Kritik* als etwas Totes, Unproduktives, sozusagen Langbärtiges zu betrachten. Diese Auf-

The great majority of recent East German poetry is "realistic"
precisely in Brecht's sense: it is characterized by a "critical stance"
toward the society in which it was conceived and expresses the
poet's sensitivity to "contradictions" in the reality with which he
is most familiar. The young poets do not at any point reject East
German society or voice a preference for the other half of Germany. For them, West Germany does not even represent a real
alternative—partially, of course, as they themselves admit, because
they know so little about it. Their attention is drawn to the situation in their country, which they feel to be their own and the
"better country" ("dieses bessere Land"). But they sense that it
is better, not "the best"; its superiority is only relative, and contradictions, human misery, and alienation have not disappeared.
The young poets know that they are addressed in Brecht's poems
"An die Nachgeborenen" (1938) and "An die Studenten im wie-
deraufgebauten Hörsaal der Universität" (1954), and they appreciate the battles waged for the sake of the new society. But they
do not feel that they have escaped those "gloomy times" ("die
finsteren Zeiten") fought through by the past generation, or that
it has yet come to pass that "man is a helper to his fellowman," as
Brecht had hoped in "An die Nachgeborenen." Brecht's posterity,
therefore, cannot make too many allowances in judging the old
comrades ("An die Nachgeborenen" ends, "Gedenkt unsrer / Mit
Nachsicht") because in the country they have constructed, "happiness" ("Glück") is still hard to come by.

"In diesem besseren Land," "Glück ist schwer in diesem Land"
—these two lines, from two recent East German poems, suggest
the full ambiguity of sentiment among younger poets in the DDR.
The first is from a long poem by Heinz Czechowski (b. 1935),
which also contains the lines "Widerspruch seh ich. / Zweifel
spür ich"; it was taken as the title of the most recent, and by
far the best, anthology of East German poetry, edited by the poets
Adolf Endler (b. 1930) and Karl Mickel (b. 1935). The line

---

fassung von Kritik wünscht Herr Hitler zu verbreiten. In Wirklichkeit ist die
kritische Haltung die einzig produktive, menschenwürdige." P. 394: "Flach, leer,
platt werden Gedichte, wenn sie ihrem Stoff seine Widersprüche nehmen." P.
543: "Unser sozialistischer Realismus muss zugleich ein kritischer Realismus sein."
P. 547: "Realistische Künstler stellen die *Widersprüche* in den Menschen und
ihren Verhältnissen zueinander dar und zeigen die Bedingungen, unter denen sie
sich entwickeln." On Mao Tse-tung, see *Werke, 20,* 343.

"Glück ist schwer in diesem Land" was used by Peter Hamm as the title for his fine article on East German poetry of the 1960s.[2] It is from a sonnet by Rainer Kirsch (b. 1934), which expresses the attitude symptomatic of the newest development in poetry of the DDR and was clearly intended as a response to Brecht's poem to his posterity:

> Meinen Freunden, den alten Genossen
>
> Wenn ihr unsre Ungeduld bedauert
> Und uns sagt, dass wir's heut leichter hätten,
> Denn wir lägen in gemachten Betten,
> Denn ihr hättet uns das Haus gemauert—
>
> Schwerer ist es heut, genau zu hassen
> Und im Freund die Fronten klar zu scheiden
> Und die Unbequemen nicht zu meiden
> Und die Kälte nicht ins Herz zu lassen.
>
> Denn es träumt sich leicht von Glückssemestern;
> Aber Glück ist schwer in diesem Land.
> Anders lieben müssen wir als gestern
> Und mit schärferem Verstand.
>
> Und die Träume ganz beim Namen nennen,
> Und die ganze Last der Wahrheit kennen.[3]

Friends and enemies are not so clearly distinguishable any more, and feelings of love and hatred must now be more cautiously differentiated than before. Optimistic hope and dreams of a blissful future must also be closely examined in order to determine whether they are not really easy dreams or opportunism. The speaker addressing his "friends," the "old comrades," is impatient to carry on their struggle—or rather, to convince them that their struggle is not yet complete. His indulgence in judging them, his "Nachsicht," is tempered by a stance critical of their complacency and their dogmatic, oversimplified view of reality.

The theme of conflicting generations, which inevitably involves

2. "'Glück ist schwer in diesem Land': Zur Situation der jüngsten DDR-Lyrik," *Merkur, 19* (1965), 365–79.

3. Sarah and Rainer Kirsch, *Gespräch mit dem Saurier* (East Berlin, 1965), p. 67; also in Peter Hamm, ed., *Aussichten* (Munich, 1966), pp. 88–89. For an example of a poetic "response" to "An die Nachgeborenen" by a writer in the West, see Enzenberger's poem "Weiterung," *blindenschrift* (Frankfurt, 1964), p. 50.

criticism of the existing order, is central to all recent poetry in the
DDR and has received far more forceful poetic expression in the
poems of Volker Braun and the songs of Wolf Biermann than in
this sonnet by Rainer Kirsch. It is worth reiterating the obvious:
dissent does not, of itself, make for good poetry; a poem does
not increase in value the more harshly it is treated by the censor.
The "critical stance," too, can become an empty mode; conversely,
some of the most impressive texts by these young poets do no
more than declare a basic affirmation, despite all grievances, of the
possibility of East German society. Rainer Kirsch's poem is worthy
of notice, not because of any outstanding literary quality, but
because it voices in clear terms the mood typical of his generation
of poets in his country. It is a mood of dissatisfaction and impatience, a sense of premonition that all is not well in this land
where the old warriors have settled down to rest, and a will to
provoke them and their whole society into facing up to new and
equally challenging tasks. The old answers, it is felt, do not apply
to many of the new questions, and the teachers can once again
learn from their pupils. The brilliant little poem by Brecht,
written in the last years of his life, is most relevant to the new
generation:

> Lehrer, lerne!
>
> Sag nicht zu oft, du hast recht, Lehrer!
> Lass es den Schüler erkennen!
> Strenge die Wahrheit nicht allzusehr an:
> Sie verträgt es nicht.
> Höre beim Reden! [4]

The "old comrades," of course, have not failed to respond, nor
have they responded in the spirit of Bertolt Brecht. The critical
attitudes evident in much of the new poetry is claimed to constitute a revival of outdated "bourgeois" sentiments and a rejection
of socialist values. Rainer Kirsch's sonnet "Meinen Freunden, den
alten Genossen," for example, was condemned in 1963 by dele-
gates of the Writers' Union for presenting too subjective a view
of the question of generations and for ignoring the "worldwide

4. *Werke, 10,* 1017.

historical process within which the conditions of the struggle have changed."[5] Kurt Hager of the Central Committee is disturbed by "moods of pessimism and skepticism" in some of the more recent poetry, which are for him "incompatible with the revolutionary traditions of our socialist-realist literature."[6] Subjectivism, nihilism, anarchistic resignation, "unhistorical" confusion of issues and generalization of social critique, concentration on the minute details of everyday reality at the expense of the larger ideological context, lack of clarity and elusiveness of poetic expression and reference, the corruptive influence of Western attitudes and literary fashions—all of these charges have been lodged against the prevailing tendencies in recent East German poetry by old-guard dogmatists, who are deeply troubled by the obvious dissolution of literary uniformity in the DDR.[7] The decisive crackdown was finally implemented in December 1965, with the decisions of the Central Committee's Eleventh Plenum. But such decisions are only stop-gap measures, which may serve to tentatively counteract a critical stance but cannot eliminate the real contradictions that inspired it. "Art is not capable of converting bureaucratic theories of art into works of art. *Only boots can be made to measure.*" The "old comrades" have ignored these words, written by Brecht in 1954.[8]

5. "Entwicklungsprobleme der Lyrik seit dem V. Deutschen Schriftstellerkongress," *Neue Deutsche Literatur*, *11* (September 1963), 70: "Die wichtigen Fragen nach dem Unterschied zwischen dem Charakter des Kampfes früher und heute, nach dem Verhältnis zwischen den Generationen werden einseitig beantwortet: Der weltgeschichtliche Prozess, unter dem sich die Bedingungen des Kampfes geändert haben, wird nicht gefasst."

6. Quoted by Hamm, "'Glück ist schwer'," p. 366: "Bei einem Teil unserer Dichter gibt es Stimmungen des Pessimismus und der Skepsis, die mit den revolutionären Traditionen unserer sozialistischen realistischen Dichtkunst unvereinbar sind."

7. One example of this anxiety on the part of the older generation is the painfully long essay by Professor Hans Koch, "Haltungen, Richtungen, Formen," *Forum*, *20* (August 1966). Professor Koch is one of the original FDJ (Freie Deutsche Jugend) "pioneers" and author of some of the most dogmatic works on Marxist-Leninist literary theory.

8. *Werke*, *19*, 545: "Die Kunst ist nicht dazu befähigt, die Kunstvorstellungen von Büros in Kunstwerke umzusetzen. *Nur Stiefel kann man nach Mass anfertigen*" (emphasis Brecht's).

Günter Kunert's Parabolic Premonitions

Günter Kunert (b. 1929), the oldest and most prolific of the
new generation, has stood directly at the center of the ideological
crossfire of the 1960s. Defended in his theoretical position and to
some extent emulated in literary practice by the younger poets,
Kunert was bitterly attacked by spokesmen for the official policy.
An editorial about him was headlined, "Why do we need this
poet?" ("Wozu brauchen wir diesen Dichter?"), and accused him
of ahistorical resignation, social and political "disengagement," and
contributing to the "destruction of reason." Rudolf Bahro in
Forum charged that Kunert has "grown tired of socialism," and
Kurt Hager believes to have detected in some of his poems a
"direct affront, hardly even concealed, against our republic." [9]
All of Kunert's "accusers" in the 1960s, however, are careful
to emphasize that their objections refer to specific, recent texts and
not to his entire work; it is his poetic development which is viewed
as the "genuine tragedy." [10] The reason for such selective caution
is quite illuminating. When Kunert began writing in the late
1940s, his exceptional talent was immediately recognized by none
other than the "poet of the nation," Johannes R. Becher. On
January 19, 1950, Becher noted in his diary: "Günter Kunert need
not attend any literary boarding school, he goes to the school
which is life itself, and he is an attentive and gifted pupil. . . .
A poet has emerged out of our new reality, his poems consecrate

9. Editorial, *Forum*, 20 (May and June 1966). Bahro, *Forum*, 20 (June 1966):
"Kunert ist sozialismusmüde geworden". Hager, quoted in Hamm, " 'Glück ist
schwer'," p. 366: "Günter Kunert z.B. schrieb eine Reihe von Gedichten, die
kaum noch versteckte Angriffe gegen unsere Republik enthalten." A similar
criticism of Kunert occurs in the useful essay by Klaus Werner, "Zur Brecht-
Rezeption bei Günter Kunert und Hans Magnus Enzensberger," *Weimarer Beiträge* (Brecht-Sonderheft, 1968), pp. 61–73.
10. Bahro, *Forum*, 20 (May and June, 1966): "Die Entwicklung Kunerts ist
eine echte Tragödie." See also Kurt Hager, "Freude an jedem gelungenen
Werk," *Neue Deutsche Literatur*, 11 (August 1963), 61–72. Hager is compelled to
defend Kunert from attacks even against his early work: "Jetzt graben einige die
Gedichte von Kunert von vor zehn Jahren aus, obwohl an diesen Gedichten gar
nichts auszusetzen ist und die Kritik sich mit sehr konkreten Werken Günter
Kunerts beschäftigte und nicht etwa mit seinem gesamten Schaffen, . . . keines-
wegs mit allen Gedichten, sondern mit einigen seiner letzten Gedichte und Werke
und der in diesen konkreten einzelnen Werken zum Ausdruck kommenden nihi-
listischen Anschauung."

our activities and aspirations; this is genuine youth." [11] There was
no limit to Becher's praise for young Kunert, who became the
"pet" of the old, prestigious poet—his "grasshopper" as Becher
chose to nickname him.

Kunert's earliest poems, published in the volumes *Wegschilder
und Mauerinschriften* (1950) and *Unter diesem Himmel* (1955),
have very little in common, stylistically or in temperament, with
Becher's own poetry. In fact, they seem to have been written in
direct opposition to the elevated, rhetorical sentiments of Becher's
hymns to his recovered homeland and to the artificial "classicism"
of his late sonnet cycles. Kunert's mood is from the beginning
cool and distanced, sheared of any high-pitched emotionality, and
his poetic manner is laconic, conversational, even colloquial. His
origins are not to be found in any German tradition—not even in
Brecht, at first—but derive in their straightforward simplicity and
chatty style from popular American poetry—Carl Sandburg and
Edgar Lee Masters (to whom Kunert dedicated a poem [12]). The
bulk of this verse is of a highly perishable quality, being severely
hampered by a willful use of the line (Kunert is still uncomfortable with both long and short periods) and by the bald, uninspiring vocabulary. Yet the poems do achieve striking vitality because
of the sensitively captured dramatic situation. Examples are "Traf
jemand"—where the speaker comes face to face with Life in a
subway station—and particularly very short poems such as the
following:

DIE SONNE SCHEINT. AUS DEN FENSTERN
Des neuen Hauses sehen die Frauen
Auf spielende Kinder. Über den
Himmel fliegt ein Flugzeug, über
Die Gesichter zieht ein Schatten.
Sie erinnern sich. [13]

11. Becher, *Auf andere Art so grosse Hoffnung: Tagebuch 1950* (East Berlin,
1951), pp. 48-9, quoted by Bahro in *Forum*, 20 (May 1966): "Günter Kunert muss
kein Literaten-Internat besuchen, er geht in die Schule, die das Leben ist, und er
ist ein aufmerksamer und talentierter Schüler. . . . Aus unserer neuen Wirklichkeit ist ein Dichter entstanden, seine Gedichte segnen unser Tun und Trachten:
das ist Nachwuchs, echt, und kein künstlich gezüchteter, kein künstlich hinaufbe-
lobigter. . . ."

12. "Edgar Lee Masters," *Unter diesem Himmel* (East Berlin, 1955), p. 22; also
in *Erinnerung an einen Planeten* (Munich, 1963), p. 23.

13. *Himmel*, p. 36; also in *Erinnerung*, p. 22.

With delicate control and lapidary simplicity of style, Kunert evokes in its everyday concreteness a moment tense with suggestive significance for Germany of the postwar years. One is reminded somewhat of Günter Eich's poems from the later 1940s, published in his volumes *Abgelegene Gehöfte* (1948) and *Untergrundbahn* (1949).

Kunert's early poetry is didactic "Trümmerlyrik," written in the confidence that the survivors crawling from under the rubble have learned from their experience. The metaphor embracing both his first volumes is that of social change as a journey. Man and his community are on the way to transformation, and the poems were conceived of as "signposts" ("Wegweiser"), messages posted to remind men of their rationality. As Kunert put it, they were to "steer the thoughts of the reader in a direction: in the direction of truth." What most impressed Johannes R. Becher was not the explicit distrust of "feeling," the deliberately dampened emotionality which most clearly distinguishes these poems from most other verse written in the DDR at the time. Rather, Becher approved of the young poet's honest faith in social progress and collective human regeneration, his conviction that the world is "too valuable to be left unchanged." [14] The assumption throughout, as is clear in many of the poems, is that the basis of such transformation, and the journey's ultimate destination, can only be Communism, under the direction of the Party. (See "Ich und du," "Partei" and Becher's favorite, "Erst dann.") Kunert's youthful socialist didacticism (always neatly expressed but often verging on a placative moralism) is what impressed the "old comrades" in his early poetry; and therefore its absence—or actually its refinement and greater subtlety in later years, tempered by the author's growing skepticism—was for them a severe disappointment and indicated the "tragic perversion" of a promising career.

Kunert learned from the new reality, and not at a "literary boarding school." After *Unter diesem Himmel* six years passed before any new volumes of his poetry were published (*Das kreuzbrave Liederbuch* and *Tagwerke*, both 1961). In the meantime Bertolt Brecht had praised his talent highly, and this time the

14. *Himmel*, p. 7: "Die Gedichte sind allenfalls Wegweiser, welche die Gedanken des Lesers in eine Richtung lenken: in die der Wahrheit. . . . die Welt ist veränderungswert. . . . Das heisst: zu wertvoll, sie unverändert zu lassen."

encounter was to mean a crucial "discovery" for Kunert as well. Brecht introduced Kunert to dramatic writing. His amusing anti-American play, *Der Kaiser von Hondu* (1960), and a radio opera, *Fetzers Flucht* (1959), on the touchy subject of the border between East and West Germany, which brought him under serious official attack for the first time, exhibit the obvious influence of Brechtian techniques. Equally obvious, however, is the fact that Kunert is not a dramatist; all his plays and scenarios—as well as his recent novel, *Im Namen der Hüte* (1967)—confirm the fact that his real talent lies in the short forms—poems and prose sketches. The great importance of Brecht in Kunert's career is revealed by his perfection of the narrative parable poem, the genre in which he commands most respect. By studying Brecht's poetry Kunert came to master his handling of the line and rhythmic units, and his cool, witty sensitivity received the ironic bite for which it had seemed to be groping in the early poems. In the prefatory note to *Unter diesem Himmel* Kunert called himself a "satirist"; only later in the 1950s, however, after experience had sobered his initial moral enthusiasm and the poet Brecht had supplied the proper instruments and gesture, did this description become a fully apt one.

Das kreuzbrave Liederbuch (1961) contains little of interest, mainly because Kunert is generally unimpressive as a writer of songs and ballads. *Tagwerke* (1961), subtitled "Gedichte, Lieder, Balladen," suffers from the same deficiencies, but some of the included poems are indicative of the development of Kunert's attitude and poetic technique since his earlier verse. He is still anxious for social change, as is clear in the forceful, sweeping poem which opens the volume, "Gesang vom Durst"; but he has grown significantly more sensitive to the dialectical nature of historical progress. The emphasis is on the "contradictions" involved in day-to-day life (the "Schlusswort an den Leser" begins, "Gewöhn dich dran: Der Widerspruch stirbt nie"). Poems affirming the difference made by socialism alternate with others in which the lofty claims and outworn ideals extolled by the "new society" are satirized, and some in which there is even a mood of desperation over the guilt and inhumanity persisting despite social transformation. In "Von der Schuld," for instance, the speaker again finds himself in a subway station (the frequent locus of

Kunert's poems). Rather than encountering Life, he this time finds
himself surrounded by the faces of the guilty new rulers on posters
and billboards. After his wild flight through a labyrinth of tunnels,
the speaker reports:

> Schaudernd sehe ich in
> Plakatfratzen,
> Papiernen Reklamelarven
> Die Gesichter derer, die
> Hier hinunterzögen, wenn
> Von der Stadt oben nichts bliebe
> Als sie. . . . (*Tagwerke*, 53)

In other cases the specific target of Kunert's irony is somewhat
more evident, as in "Farbe," where workers on the Palace of
Justice in Paris accidentally spill a can of red paint:

> Die
> Vorbeikamen und sahen
> Gingen mit rascheren Schritten davon:
> Sie
> Wussten auf einmal
> Wer sie regierte. (*Tagwerke*, 81)

The most obvious method of parabolic presentation is the establishment of a hypothetical distance in geographical setting and
historical circumstances, as in "Farbe" or the poem "Kansas City,"
where the governor does not demand too much of his subjects:
"Nur / Das Denken sollen sie ihm überlassen." Kunert's best-
known, and most notorious, parable of this kind is the following:

> ALS UNNÖTIGEN LUXUS
> Herzustellen verbot was die Leute
> Lampen nennen
> König Tharsos von Xantos der
> Von Geburt
> Blinde.[15]

Long ago and far away an ancient monarch, blind from birth,
forbade the making of lamps as an unnecessary luxury; anyone at

---

15. *Verkündigung des Wetters* (Munich, 1966), p. 21; also in *Der ungebetene
Gast* (East Berlin and Weimar, 1965), p. 75.

any time deprived of what he feels to be a necessity—including Kunert's own countrymen at the time he wrote the poem—will understand the relevance of this parable. The brilliant structure of the poem, with its clause in the present tense ("was die Leute Lampen nennen") interspersed between references to the past ("verbot" and "König Tharsos"), allows for such a transfer of allusion. Producers of "light," restricted in their work by overseers who know nothing about it, might recognize particularly cogent associations in this poem. (Is there a pun on the words "Luxus" = *lux?* Maybe King Tharsos really can see, but only the kind of lamps he deems necessary.)

Another, more complex, possibility of the satiric parable is to equate abstractions (historical processes or social conditions) with concrete objects. Kunert employs this technique, still crudely, in the poem "Zwei Arten," in which two different types of progress are compared with a handsome horse-drawn coach and with an automobile. The car is greasy and unattractive, and its driver can be seen yelling at the chugging engine. The poem ends:

> Aber er fährt.
>
> Dies ist ein Gleichnis und trifft zu
> Auf jedwede neue Weise fortzuschreiten:
> Heisse sie Auto oder heisse sie
> Kommunismus. (*Tagwerke,* 58)

Kunert masters this technique of the "Gleichnis," the parable as a concretization of an abstract concept, in the later poem "Wie ich ein Fisch wurde."[16] Here the full depth of the poet's skepticism and sense of premonition by the early 1960s is unmistakably evident. One fine day ("Am 27. Mai um drei Uhr") the rivers of the earth swell up and chase the frightened citizens from their homes up to the mountaintops. But then the oceans, too, surge, leaving no survivors: "Und sie schluckten alles das, was noch vorhanden, / Ohne Unterschied, und das war allerhand." Just as he himself is to be towed under, at his dying breath, the speaker recalls what he had once been taught:

> Nur wer sich verändert, den wird nicht verdriessen
> Die Veränderung, die seine Welt erfährt.

16. *Erinnerung,* pp. 41–42; *Gast,* pp. 12–13.

Leben heisst: Sich ohne Ende wandeln.
Wer am Alten hängt, der wird nicht alt.

He decides, therefore, to follow this teaching and adapt himself
to "the new element" ("dem neuen Element") by transforming
himself into a fish. He feels relieved now, and rescued from the
deluge, but then a new fear arises. The poem ends:

Aber [ich] fürchte jetzt die Trockenheiten,
Und dass einst das Wasser wiederum verrinnt.

Denn aufs neue wieder Mensch zu werden,
Wenn man's lange Zeit nicht mehr gewesen ist,
Das ist schwer für unsereins auf Erden,
Weil das Menschsein sich zu leicht vergisst.

Adjustment to new conditions seemed the right solution in the
moment of crisis; change, one was advised, in accordance with the
revolutionary historical process. The question arises, however,
whether in the course of such a transformation humanity itself
might not be manipulated out of existence. The inhuman sacrifices
which become the rule during an intensive revolutionary campaign
may result in the complete sacrifice of all traces of human dignity;
will it not then be frightfully difficult to rehumanize an entire
society? This sardonic parable, a fine example of Kunert's precise
poetic calculation, reflects the still unsuccessful process of de-
Stalinization in the DDR. This local, historical phenomenon is no
doubt at the center of Kunert's concern. But a parable by definition contains various levels of reference, and emphasis may
properly be placed on the poet's presentiments about the treachery
of human transformation in general.[17]

In any case, "Wie ich ein Fisch wurde" does illustrate the severe
change in Kunert's attitude, since his earlier writings, toward
historical development and the possibility of progressive social
change. In the 1960s some of his very best poems still voice the
ironic yet steadfast commitment characteristic of Brecht; among
these are "Ich bringe eine Botschaft," "Film—verkehrt einge-

17. Cf. Hamm, " 'Glück ist schwer'," p. 368; see also the prefatory note (on
the dust jacket) to *Gast:* "Gezielt . . . ist auf die Gefahr der Entmenschli-
chung, auf den möglichen, unwiederbringlichen Verlust der Conditio humana."

spannt," and "Von den Genüssen: der dritte"; these are by no means to be omitted from a consideration of Kunert's political stance.

> In den Träumen
> Der noch Niedergedrückten und in den
> Gedanken der bereits Aufrührerischen, wie
> In den Taten
> Der sich schon Erhebenden
> Findet ihr, was
> Von uns bleibt. ("Vom Vergehen," *Gast*, 9)

The difference from his verse of the previous decade is the bleak, skeptical temperament; Kunert has incorporated into his dialectic the eventual futility of human aspirations. His mood is cynical, sarcastic, melancholy, at times almost fatalistic; his style, still conversational, has become tensely cryptic and deliberately disjointed. The poem "Geschichte" (*Verkündigung*, pp. 27–28), fiercely attacked in official circles in the DDR, is an example of the latest development. It begins, "Leichter mal mal schwerer mal unerträglich: / Die während Bürde. / Das allzeit fällige Urteil"; the fourth stanza is a bold retraction of one of the treasures of revolutionary, antifascist literature. In Brecht's poem "Die unbesiegliche Inschrift" (ca. 1937), a captured resistance fighter carves the words "Hoch Lenin!" on the wall of his prison cell; and after several unsuccessful attempts to cover over the inscription with paint, the military guard finally sees that the only remedy is the removal of the entire wall.[18] The indelible image which occurs to Kunert's speaker when he thinks of revolutionary change is a hero quite different from Lenin:

> Die Revolution wo finden wir sie und wieder.
> Unterm tückischen Marmor liegt siebenmal siebenfach
> Sisyphos verdammt und unaufweckbar.
> Lang lebe die unbesiegliche Inschrift.

History, especially in Germany (stanza six), is a record of the futility of human action and, ultimately, may be no more than the individual's struggle for survival. The closing lines of "Geschichte" read:

18. *Werke*, 9, 668–69.

Geschichte sage ich und weiter noch: Wenig bleibt.
Glücklich wer am Ende mit leeren Händen dasteht.
Denn aufrecht und unverstümmelt dasein ist alles.
Mehr ist nicht zu gewinnen.
Was dauert ist grau und unauffällig
Unter allen Tritten.

This bleak aspect of Kunert's attitude in recent years is, in my opinion, a pessimism often annoyingly moralistic and overbearing, and the expression of feeling strikes me as too strained to achieve full impact. The language, different from that in the earlier poetry, is used with very uneven success; it frequently seems too derivative from Enzensberger and other West German writers. Kunert is sometimes stronger when he responds to other contemporary poems in his own idiom, as in "Ikarus 1964," which appears to be an answer to Peter Rühmkorf's "Anti-Ikarus." [19] But Kunert is obviously experimenting with new stylistic possibilities. The beginning of "Notizen in Kreide," for example,—a poem that is also considered objectionable in the DDR—shows that the writings of Gottfried Benn, more than those of Brecht, have provided Kunert with the tone and poetic gesture suitable to his recent attitude:

Eingerichtet auf dem Gestirn
Unseres Schmerzes
Als Baracke. Aber fester denn jede Festung
Und dauernder. Ausgesetzt
Den bittersten Wettern. Ewiges Provisorium:
Ich. (*Verkündigung*, 1)

In addition to the influence of Benn, echoes from Rilke can be heard ("Ausgesetzt auf den Bergen des Herzens"), just as Rilke's famous line, "Dasein ist alles," is taken over by Kunert at the end of the poem "Geschichte." Most important as an alternative, or supplement, to Brecht is another modern master of the parable technique, Franz Kafka. The impact of Kafka on Kunert's work is clearly evident in some of his fine prose sketches, collected under the titles *Tagträume* (Munich, 1964) and *Die Beerdigung findet in aller Stille statt* (Munich, 1968), and in the atmosphere of some of his short poetic aphorisms ("Sprüche"), such as, "In den

19. Cf. Paul Konrad Kurz, "Vom Erhaben zum Anti-Ikarus," *Stimmen der Zeit* (Freiburg), December 1967, pp. 375–92.

Herzkammern der Echos / Sitzen Beamte. Jeder / Hilferuf hallt /
Gestempelt zurück." [20] The controversial poem entitled "Unter-
schiede" must also be considered in this context:

> Betrübt höre ich einen Namen aufrufen:
> Nicht den meinigen.
>
> Aufatmend
> Höre ich einen Namen aufrufen:
> Nicht den meinigen.[21]

These little Kafkaesque scenes reflect a state of dire anxiety,
anonymity, and alienation in a bureaucratized and (as is clear in
"Notizen in Kreide") mechanized world. One of Kunert's gravest
concerns is his explicit skepticism with regard to technological
advance, his conviction that "only the height of naiveté can still
equate technology and social, humanitarian progress." [22] The
work of Franz Kafka supplied Kunert with the general setting for
his poetic evocation of a world dehumanized by technological
overdevelopment. In the poem "Interfragmentarium (Zum Werk
Franz K.s)" Kunert attempts to re-create the atmosphere of
Kafka's "Metamorphosis" ("Die Verwandlung"). Though this
poem is of importance within the context of the East German
cultural situation because of official rejection of Kafka, it is, for
my taste, rather unimpressive artistically. By the mid-1960s the

20. *Gast*, p. 75; *Verkündigung*, p. 39.

21. *Gast*, p. 29; *Erinnerung*, p. 59. Hans Mayer regards these lines as a typical
text in "slave language" ("Sklavensprache"), incomprehensible to anyone not
directly familiar with the situation of cultural politics in the DDR (*Zur deutschen Literatur der Zeit*, pp. 386–87). The first stanza, according to Mayer, refers
to the reaction of the East German intellectual when he is denied recognition or
an award because of his objectionable performance of one kind or another; and
the second to his relief that, this time, he is not being accused by the political
authorities. This interpretation may have its validity, particularly since the poem
was received in just this way by some East German readers. (See Rostock *Ost-
see-Zeitung*, January 12–13, 1963.) But, as Kunert rightly insists in private conversation, the matter is not as simple as Mayer suggests, and if the text has any
value, it will manage to transcend such a narrow frame of reference. Mayer's
generalization of the term "Sklavensprache" to account for all literature in the
DDR is, in my opinion, a gross oversimplification.

22. *Forum, 20* (May, 1966), p. 23: 'Ich glaube, nur noch grosse Naivität setzt
Technik mit gesellschaftlich-humanitärem Fortschritt gleich. Auch wenn sie mich
mit dem gerade gängigen Terminus 'Skeptiker' abstempeln: Wir können unsere Erfahrungen nicht ignorieren, erst recht nicht die Welt, in der zwischen technischem
Können und menschlichem Dasein die Kluft wächst."

Kafkean strain in Kunert's work, the mood of despair and of the compellingly logical absurdity of existence, had to a great extent overshadowed the impact of Brecht. In the career of Günter Kunert contemporary German literature has a fascinating kind of counterpart in reverse to Peter Weiss, whose development, as is well known, passed through an initial phase of prose writings in the manner of Kafka to a heavy reliance, in his plays, on the work of Brecht.[23] The difference, in my estimation, is that whereas Weiss came into his own with his discovery of Brecht, Kunert's turn to Kafka has, thus far, been to the detriment of his literary productivity.

Kunert's detractors in the DDR label him disillusioned with Marxism and charge him with "mystifying history" because he has not sufficiently distinguished between technology in socialist society and under capitalism. These accusations are no doubt valid at the vulgar Marxist level at which they are made. Kunert's Marxism, however, is operating at a level once removed from the orthodox. Marx is dead ("Marx ist tot") if he is deified as the bringer of one all-embracing answer to mankind, of a final order to the world. Kunert presents this image of the tentative death of Marx in the title poem of his most recent volume published in West Germany, *Verkündigung des Wetters* (1966). In this work Marxism means more than the empty slogans and pipe dreams of "Marxist" propaganda:

> Was mehr bedeutet
> Als eingeschneites Gebein als eingeschreinter Regen
> Als zwischen Buchdeckel gepresster Sonnenschein
> Als
> Die feierliche Verkündigung des Wetters. (P. 86)

Marx is a hero without an apotheosis, and he should be acknowledged without ceremonious proclamation because his effects remain of immanent and immediate concern ("Denn Marx / Ist nicht aufgefahren am dritten Tag sondern / An gar keinem. Sondern ist da / Und dort / Im furchtbaren fruchtbaren Chaos irdischer / Ordnung"). Kunert has one hope to counteract all his premonition: "arrival"—"Anzukommen," not in any final sense,

23. Cf. John Millful, "From Kafka to Brecht: Peter Weiss' Development towards Marxism," *German Life and Letters*, 20 (1966), 61–71.

with a specific destination in sight, but as a continual rebirth and reinitiation. He concludes the poem:

Wohl aber
Wie der so verletzliche Fleischbalg
Aus dem Leib einer Frau ankommt
Im aufdämmernden Irgendwo: Immer wieder
Am Anfang. Immer wieder am Start. Immer
Wieder zu neuem Beginn.
Wie der Regentropfen, wie die Schneeflocke.

In his visions of chaos and "mystification" of history, Kunert has not at all grown tired of the socialist possibility; rather, his commitment has increased with his awareness that chaos is a component of order and that history is not understood unless its mysteries are taken into account. Kafka may not wholly supplant Brecht, but he is a necessary complement to the Brechtian ethic of political engagement. Kunert is no longer a simple believer; he is no longer Johannes R. Becher's "grasshopper." (Kunert's new and still un-published poem, "Exegese J. R. Bechers," is directly relevant here.) His conviction has been refined and revised so as to resemble closely that of Ernst Bloch: the image of an eventual "arrival" at the point of origin and such a phrase as "Im aufdämmernden Irgendwo" indicate the decisive impact of Bloch's unorthodox anticipatory perspective in *Das Prinzip Hoffnung*.

Kunert's main difficulty is that he has not yet developed a poetic idiom appropriate to his revised position. His major achievements still remain the narrative parable poems and miniature aphoristic settings in the manner of Brecht, and much of his more recent verse is spoiled by its overbearing, strained feeling and cramped mode of expression. His art has until now been most cogent as the art of ambiguous simplicity—the disturbing, sarcastic understatement. Nevertheless, his very latest poems, which focus on concrete situations and day-to-day circumstances (such as "Nachlasslager, Kleine Alexanderstrasse, Berlin"), are promising,[24] and his current work at adaptation from the Polish of Zbigniev Herbert may help him settle on some fruitful techniques.

24. A number of these recent poems have appeared in a pamphlet entitled *Album 8* (East Berlin, 1968).

Günter Kunert more than anyone else is to be regarded as *the* representative poet of East Germany, his career encompassing the entire development of his country from the beginning and demonstrating all the weaknesses, and the strengths, of poetry in the DDR. He may never have proclaimed allegiance to his country as forthrightly and loudly as others, and his reaction to its brutality has been unusually radical. But as a poet he has grown with it, and the hopes and disappointments expressed in his poetry were inspired by the accomplishments and the failures of East German society. He was the first to recognize the need to adjust poetic techniques and critical stance to the new conditions and to confront the new contradictions, emerging in the later 1950s. His poem "Anpassung" (ca. 1958) ends with advice to those still reaching for the old poetic tools:

> Die Steinaxt gilt noch als Waffe, aber
> Sie ist nicht mehr gefährlich. (*Tagwerke*, 49)

Volker Braun and Karl Mickel: Provocations and Antimyths

The two most highly regarded young poets now writing in the DDR, aside from Wolf Biermann, are Volker Braun (b. 1939) and Karl Mickel (b. 1935). Both grew up in Dresden, rather than Berlin, and both are now active in East Berlin cultural life: Braun with the Berliner Ensemble and Mickel as an editor of literary periodicals and of the anthology *In diesem besseren Land* (1966). The poetry of Braun and Mickel has been favorably, but critically, received in the DDR, and each poet has had one book of verse published in the West as well as in the East.[25]

As is apparent from the titles of these two volumes—Braun's *Provokation für mich* (1965) and Mickel's *Vita nova mea* (1966) —both are poets of the "new life," the "new spirit" in the DDR; both, like Kunert, are concerned with confronting contemporary conditions in their country and with "provoking" change, further development, and alternatives to the status quo. The poems are meant to confront reality and stimulate it, they are "provocations"

25. Braun, *Provokation für mich* (Halle, 1965), *Vorläufiges* (Frankfurt, 1966); Mickel, *Vita nova mea. Mein neues Leben* (East Berlin, 1966), *Vita nova mea* (Reinbek, 1967).

of the *vita nova*. But in these titles the first-person references, "mich" and "mea," are also of greatest importance. The two young provocateurs speak for themselves; they have distinct, individual poetic temperaments and illustrate the remarkable, though not unlimited, range and differentiation which has been reached in East German poetry of recent years.

Volker Braun's poetry is boisterous and rings with youthful vitality:

> Kommt uns nicht mit Fertigem! Wir brauchen Halbfabrikate!
> Weg mit dem faden Braten—her mit dem Wald und dem Messer!
> Hier herrscht das Experiment und keine steife Routine.
> Hier schreit eure Wünsche aus: Empfang beim Leben. (*Provokation*, 10; *Vorläufiges*, 7)

This pioneer world disdains convenient instruction booklets and armchair optimism. Any job done is finished only for the time being, tentatively: the key word in Braun's vocabulary, and the title of a poem, is "Vorläufiges." The speaker in these "provocations" often seems an ambitious Boy Scout leader, rolling up his sleeves and shouting to his troop to use their heads for a change: "Nix zum Herunterdudeln! Hier wird ab sofort Denken verlangt. / Raus aus den Sesseln, Jungs!" The official East German youth organization, the FDJ, has been trying for years to awaken this kind of spirit. The difference, however, between Braun's poems and the usual versified pep talk is that Braun really means what he is saying and knows how to say it.

Brecht, of course, has helped him, especially the early Brecht, as well as Mayakovsky and Whitman. The young poet has also learned from reading Pablo Neruda, and there are even faint echoes of Hölderlin's odes, although they are transferred to a very concrete, realistic context. Braun's most impressive technique is the controlled shift of poetic gestures, the startling modulation in the speaker's tone of voice. Long-winded rhetorical passages alternate with sharp exclamations and urgent questioning; expressionist flurries of images and genitive metaphors mingle with colloquial turns of phrase from Braun's own Saxon idiom—what he calls his "Kälberdeutsch." He provokes by enthusiasm and irony, by an

elevated tone and by flippant asides, and very often by the abrupt
variation of these gestures. The overall poetic effect, though not
the political standpoint, is sometimes remarkably similar to that
of Hans Magnus Enzensberger, whom Braun feels to be his
counterpart in the West.

In my opinion, the poem "Jugendobjekt" illustrates Volker
Braun at his best:

> Blassrot ziehn sie die Sonnenscheibe hoch über dem Rhinluch,
> Blassrot und rund schwimmt sie in der Himmelssuppe,
> Blassrot und rund und spät, wenn wir schon wackeln
>
> Wenn wir schon wackeln in der unnachgiebigen Erdsuppe,
> Wenn wir schon wackeln und schwitzen an diesen lumpigen
>   Handbaggern
> Unter der blauen Sonnenfahne, wenn wir schon schwitzen
>
> Ehe sie die Sonne hochziehn und für die paar Piepen,
> Für den versengten Rücken und Dreck im Ohr und billige
>   Blutwurst
> Und für getrocknete Felder und Butter, Leute, Butter!
>
> Ja, für Butter, mit diesen erbärmlichen Handbaggern, schau-
>   feln wir
> Uns die Brust voll Ruhm und Hoffnung, schaufeln ein Vater-
>   land her,
> Eh sie noch richtig hochkommt, die Sonne, über den Gräben
>   im Rhinluch
>
> Eh sie noch richtig gelb und bunt durch den blauen Himmel
>   schwingt,
> Schwingen wir unsere lumpigen Suppenschaufeln unter der
>   Sonnenfahne,
> Eh sie noch gelb und bunt wie blanke Butter hochschwingt,
>   die Gute! (*Provokation*, 17; *Vorläufiges*, 13)

Early in the morning, in the Havel region of Brandenburg, a
group of teenagers is busy dredging a marsh so that the land may
be used for pasture. The staggering cumulative syntax evokes well
the efforts of the toiling youngsters; Braun uses the technique of
the poetic fugue, similar to that in Paul Celan's famous poem
"Todesfuge." Very brilliantly a sharp dialectic is set up in the
first two stanzas between the glaring sun, swimming about in the

"soupy" blue sky, and the young dredgers tottering over their shovels in the swamp. In the third stanza the element of challenge is finally apparent, first suggested by the word "späte" in line three of the poem: they must race to get the job done before the sun rises to its full height and the oppressive heat makes working impossible. At the same time, however, they become aware of the purpose of their labor; the word "Butter!" at the end of stanza three marks the climax of the poem.

What then follows is the resolution; in stanza four the youthful workers recognize that they are sweating for their own welfare and for the sake of their country. But the real synthesis does not come until the very end. By the last stanza the sun itself has been activated ("schwingt" instead of "schwimmt"), and its movement in the sky is identified with the activity of the workers in the common verb "schwingen." Finally, in the delicately controlled color imagery, the challenge of their labor becomes identified with its purpose: the yellow, noontime sun seems like churned butter. Nature—at first a threatening, inimical force, impeding their efforts—is by the end a helping hand, and even the highest source of inspiration: "die Gute!"

"Jugendobjekt" is a fuguelike ode to the purposefulness and ultimate moral value of productive physical activity, the "naturalization of man and humanization of nature" which Marx envisioned as the essence of unalienated human labor. Volker Braun has in this poem achieved the rare feat of giving forceful expression to such an ideal in its full dialectic richness, without ending in abstract platitudes and empty sentimentalism. The contradictions and their eventual synthesis lie entirely in the object confronted ("Objekt") and in the vital interplay between man and his surroundings. Labor is affirmed not in a vague song of praise, or through the mouth of some hypothetical lifeless farmhand—as was so often the case in typical socialist-realist verse; rather, the affirmation develops in the experience of the labor process itself.

Theme and setting are similar in Braun's other powerful poem, "Flüche in Krummensee." Insight into the real challenge of getting a job done, the ultimate sense of the sweat and swearwords accompanying hard labor—this spirit, so vulgarized in the commonplaces of typical agitational work poetry, lends forceful motivation to all of his best verses. The sense of self-fulfilling productivity forms Braun's personal metaphor for the significance of his country in history:

> Vielstimmig brichts los, gewaltiger
> Eindruck für zeitfremde Leute, Chor aus Spott und Empörung über
> Gelüstlose Gestalten, die nicht das Ende des Ackers
> Kennenzulernen wünschen und auf die Uhr schaun, als wäre nicht
> Ihre Stunde gekommen in diesem
> Lärmgewohnten Jahrhundert. (*Provokation*, 15; *Vorläufiges*, 10–11)

Braun protests not against reality but *for* it, by demonstrating the changeability embodied in concrete, active experience.[26] In the representative poem "Provokation für mich (als im dritten Viertel des 20. Jahrhunderts die Gedichte entbehrlich wurden)" the same theme is expressed in relation to Braun's notion of the function of poetry: literature "praises the positive" only when it is truly operative, when it enters into the process of life itself. Also impressive is the three-part "Liebesgedichte für Susanne M. in Flensburg," in which the mood of impatience and ambitious activity is associated with the problem of the two Germanies, the "divided heaven." The third part, following a deliberately idealized avowal of love and renunciation by an East German boy to a girl in West Germany, is entitled "Anmerkung für Bürger der Deutschen Demokratischen Republik." It is Braun's "provocation" to his own society, beginning with the stanza:

> Lasst keins der Häuser mehr träg
> Herumstehn, grabt sie nicht zum Wegfauln ein
> Lasst die Strassen nicht länger lustlos
> Sielen im Regenbett, verbaumelt nicht in Gerüsten
> Unsere Zeit, kleistert Stuck nicht, seid
> Nie mehr verlegen vor euren Fäusten!
> Lasst kein Stück Himmel blass und nackt westwärts treiben. . . .
>   (*Provokation*, 44; *Vorläufiges*, 23)

26. On the basis of this attitude, in the poem "Rezension in der Landessprache," Braun eloquently attacked the noncommittal stance of Hans Magnus Enzensberger. (*Provokation für mich*, pp. 47–48.)

Braun's poems are of course not all as strong as the cited ones. The attempts at "jazz lyric" ("Jazz" and "Tramp-Blues") are rather artificial, and many of the love poems are ruined by sentimental moralizing. Long poems, such as "Der schiefe Schornstein" and "Landgang," become tediously complex, and political texts about the German question, such as "Die Mauer" and "Wir und nicht sie," [27] are in my estimation trite and exhibit a somewhat contrived revolutionary posture. But they are all only the experiments of a young and lively writer; as is evident in "Jugendobjekt," Braun has more than time and extraordinary talent on his side. He genuinely understands the meaning of Brecht's "Aufbaulied":

> Besser als gerührt sein, ist: sich rühren
> Denn kein Führer führt aus dem Salat! [28]

If Volker Braun's "new life" is the "vita activa," Karl Mickel's is the "vita contemplativa." Braun's poetic situation abounds with vital experience; Mickel's is delicately filtered through strange, elusive personae. Mickel is the learned poet: he experiments with traditional forms (sonnet, elegy, epistle, song) and adapts from classical and metaphysical writers, such as Catullus and John Donne. At the end of his volume *Vita nova mea* (1966) he includes two literary essays, one on a hymn of Klopstock, the other on Schiller's "Die Bürgschaft." His own poems are reflective monologues, most impressive within the context of myths radically reworked and reinterpreted. More than Braun, he has turned provocation and irony inward, and it is often manifest in the speaker's moods and whims rather than in the outward gesture. Whereas Braun is clearly a physical poet, Mickel's verse is in the widest sense metaphysical.

In many of his poems Mickel does no more than toy with old forms, and his success is very uneven. His little "Elegie" has its tender charm,

> Nicht schlafen nicht wachen das Herz
> Durchs Schlüsselloch aufsteigt Orion Schnee

27. "Fünf Gedichte auf Deutschland," published in *Kursbuch* 4 (1966), ed. Hans Magnus Enzensberger, pp. 64–72.
28. Brecht, *Werke, 10*, 956.

Inmitten des Zimmers am Boden
Das letzte Grün ein Laubblatt rasselnd [29]

but most often he accomplishes very little of consistent value.
His use of rhyme, which is very frequent, strikes me as generally
quite uninspired. A group of his poems is entitled "Fragmen-
tarisch," and many of the texts seem to be just that: unfinished,
meager work except for occasional flashes of brilliance. In general
Mickel appears still in a formative stage, his style often hampered
by a kind of manneristic chattiness and his poetic posture sometimes painfully affected and self-centered.

Yet there is some extremely fine poetry in the volume *Vita nova
mea*. The long, meditative poem "Dresdner Häuser" gathers momentum and ends with gripping force. In "Petzower Sommer"
Mickel has created some remarkably powerful dactyllic lines:
"Latten, zu Zunder gedörrt, Zaun unter zögernden Schritten: /
Lautlos zerfällt er, er knirscht zwischen Sohle und Holz." At
times the speaker's stubborn individualism, which in many poems
has an irritating effect, lends a dramatic cogency to the biting
irony. In the following poem, harshly criticized by official commentators (Prof. Hans Koch) in the DDR, Mickel apparently
applies the myth of Tantalus to the condition of a "dismembered"
Germany. The speaker here, at any rate, will not let himself be
"torn apart" by other people's tales of woe but will go about his
own business, collectedly and expecting no grace from above. The
poem is, I think, quite intriguing, its bathos technique strikingly
similar to the style of Peter Hacks, especially in his play *Moritz
Tassow* (1965):

Nicht meine Schulter ists, die Demeter
Abnagte aus Versehn, nicht auf mein Fleisch
Bevor sie's kaute, tropften ihre Tränen.
Mein Vater heisst nicht Tantalos, ich heisse
Nicht Pelops folglich, unverkürzt
An Arm, Bein, Kopf und Hoden bau ich
Kartoffeln an und Lorbeer hier in Preussen.
Ich warte nicht auf Götter zur Montage
Normal wie üblich ist mein EKG
Wenn ich ein Messer, scharf und schneidend, seh. (*Vita*, 67)

29. *Vita nova mea*, p. 50; references are to the West German edition.

In another mythological poem, "Odysseus in Ithaka," Mickel's persona is the great hero returning from battle. His homeland, however, is not the majestic paradise of which he has long been dreaming, but a stuffy, decaying heap of rubble. Nor was his queen Penelope, whose three hundred suitors he is now expected to slay, worth the long, trying journey home: "Die Sau. Für Kirkes Schatten soll ich / Dreihundert abtun? Keinen. Troia reicht. / Ich will kein Gott sein, hinter mir zerfällt / Die sich selber fallen lässt, die Welt" (*Vita*, 52). Professor Hans Koch sees in this version of the myth a "destructive retraction of useful classical ideals" and clear evidence of the "sickness which threatens to eat away at this poetic talent." [30]

Mickel's supreme achievement, and the single most impressive mark of his talent, is the poem "Der See":

See, schartige Schüssel, gefüllt mit Fischleibern
Du Anti-Himmel unterm Kiel, abgesplitterte Hirnschal
Von Herrn Herr Hydrocephalos, vor unsern Zeitläuften
Eingedrückt ins Erdreich, Denkmal des Aufpralls
Nach rasendem Absturz: du stösst mich im Gegensinn
Aufwärts, ab, wenn ich atemlos nieder zum Grund tauch
Wo alte Schuhe zuhaus sind zwischen den Weissbäuchen.

Totes gedeiht noch! An Ufern, grindigen Wundrändern
Verlängert sichs, wächsts, der Hirnschale Haarstoppel
Borstiges Baumwerk, trägfauler als der Verblichene
(Ein Jahr: ein Schritt, zehn Jahr: ein Wasserabschlagen
Ein Jahrhundert: ein Satz). Das soll ich ausforschen?
Und die Amphibien. Was sie reinlich einst abschleckten
Koten sie tropfenweis voll, unersättlicher Kreislauf
Leichen und Laich.

                    Also bleibt einzig das Leersaufen
Übrig, in Tamerlans Spur, der soff sich aus Feindschädel-
Pokalen eins an ("Nicht länger denkt der Erschlagene"
Sagt das Gefäss, "nicht denke an ihn!" sagt der Inhalt).

So fass ich die Bäume ("hoffentlich halten die Wurzeln!")
Und reisse die Mulde empor, schräg in die Wolkenwand

---

30. *Forum*, 20 (August, 1966): "eine leere, zerstörische 'Zurücknahme' auch der 'nutzbaren' klassischen Ideale"; "die Krankheit, die dieses Talent auszuzehren droht."

Zerr ich den See, ich saufe, die Lippen zerspringen
Ich saufe, ich saufe, ich sauf—wohin mit den Abwässern!
See, schartige Schüssel, gefüllt mit Fischleibern:
Durch mich durch jetzt Fluss inmitten eurer Behausungen
Ich lieg und verdaue den Fisch   (*Vita*, 43–44)

The most striking vision in the poem is of a world without transcendence, a demythologized nature.[31] The lake is the monument
of a fallen heaven, the fractured skull of a dethroned, cosmic
Hydrocephalos. Earthly nature is a vast "antiheaven." But as early
as the first stanza there is a hint of another, countervailing tendency
in the poem: the sudden descent of the transcendent deity seems
to force the poetic ego upward, as he submerges to the bottom
of the lake: "du stösst mich im Gegensinn / Aufwärts, ab, wenn
ich atemlos nieder zum Grund tauch." (The phrase "zum Grund"
and the verb "zerren" in stanza four, as well as the entire tone of
the poem, seem to suggest an allusion to Franz Fühmann's poem
"Die Richtung der Märchen.") The first two stanzas of "Der
See" consist of associative observations of the relative, sheerly
physical, and senselessly circular nature of existence, revolving
about the question, "Das soll ich ausforschen?" The second part,
beginning with a historical reminiscence, resorts to the fantasies of
the speaker's active imagination: he is like the great conqueror
Tamburlaine when he gulps, swallows, and digests the whole lake
and all the refuse clinging to its bottom. The poem seems to relate
the tale of Jonah in reverse. Professor Koch is correct in recognizing the temperament of the poem as similar to that of Brecht's
first play *Baal*; he is wrong when he contends that the poem ends,
conclusively, in the intestinal tract of this overinflated ego.[32]

It is revealing to compare "Der See" with Volker Braun's poem
"Jugendobjekt." Both begin with the sight of nature as an inimical
force. In both, physical, culinary metaphors prevail ("Himmels-
suppe," "Butter," "See, schartige Schüssel," "Ich saufe, ich saufe,
ich sauf"); the world and human activity are understood in terms
of the digestive system. Even the actions in the two poems are

31. For a detailed interpretation of this highly intricate text I refer to the brilliant analysis by Dieter Schlenstedt in *Forum*, 20 (June 1966), 18–19. Schlenstedt's
essay is the lengthiest, and by far the most penetrating, critical discussion of a
single poem published in the DDR to date.

32. *Forum*, 20 (August, 1966): "Saufen, saufen, dass die Lippen zerspringen,
liegen, verdauen—Schluss."

similar: the speaker in "Der See" is also involved in a task of
dredging. The main difference, clearly, is in the purpose of these
acts and in their results. In Braun's poem the young workers confront the challenge of nature by recognizing the productive value
of collective labor; at the conclusion they sense the ultimate harmony of their effort and the processes of nature, the identity between their distant goal and the immediate surroundings. The
speaker in "Der See," on the other hand, undertakes his task entirely as an individual; more important, his act seems to occur not
externally, in concrete, physical reality, but on another plane altogether, in the realm of fantasy (another connection with Fühmann, about whom Mickel has written an excellent essay [33]).
Neither the poet Mickel nor the poetic speaker takes the effort in
full earnest; it is really only a suggestion of how the "insatiable,
circular course" of life and death ("unersättlicher Kreislauf
Leichen und Laich") might be escaped. Unlike Braun's "Jugendobjekt," with its sharp, clear resolution ("die Gute!"), "Der See"
is explicitly open-ended, containing no punctuation at all after the
final word. (In an earlier version the poem ended with a colon.)
    "The play lacks wisdom" ("dem Stück fehlt Weisheit"), was
Brecht's comment on his own early drama *Baal* when he looked
back on it in 1954. The protagonist, he remarked, "is asocial, but
in a asocial society." [34] Karl Mickel's "Baalian spirit" ("baalsches
Weltgefühl"), as expressed in "Der See," is also lacking in
"wisdom" if Brecht intended that word to mean certainty as to
the ultimate unity of man and nature in more than a physical sense.
The ego in Mickel's sarcastic "antimyths" is asocial because he is
without an intuitive assurance of the feasibility of reaching a
higher value by collective human effort. The poet Mickel is
continually seeking, whereas Volker Braun, in all his youthful
restlessness, is forever finding.

Wolf Biermann, East Germany's Enfant Terrible

    Wolf Biermann (b. 1936), the best-known and most contro-
versial of all young poets in the DDR, stands apart from his

33. "Von der Richtung der Märchen," *Neue Deutsche Literatur*, 10 (1962),
116–20.
34. Brecht, *Baal. Der böse Baal der asoziale: Texte, Varianten und Materialien*,
ed. Dieter Schmidt (Frankfurt, 1968), pp. 110–11.

contemporaries in several important respects. His stance, the most radically provocative of all, has a unique element.

To begin with, his biography is different. When Biermann moved to East Berlin in 1953, full of enthusiasm for the Communist cause to which his parents had been devoted (his father was killed in Auschwitz in 1943), he came not from the provinces of East Germany, but from West German Hamburg. His commitment to the DDR resulted from a conscious decision which he has never regretted. Throughout the 1950s he worked very actively, first as a student of political economy at Humboldt University, then from 1957 to 1959 as a dramatic assistant with the Berliner Ensemble. All the while he willingly did his stints at rural collectives, encouraging the downtrodden workers not to lose heart. Even today, after all he has been through, he has no desire to live in the West, "not if the streets were paved with gold."

Another factor which distinguishes Bierman from his colleagues is the potential popularity of his work. He learned his techniques from the traditions of the political song of François Villon, Heine, Béranger, and Brecht; the satirical chanson of Frank Wedekind and Kurt Tucholsky; and, above all, from the music of Hanns Eisler, whose friendship and support he cherished highly. The result was an assortment of texts in clear, straightforward language about problems immediately affecting the widest contemporary audience and written to catchy tunes with guitar accompaniment. In short, Biermann is a model of literary "Volkstümlichkeit," and he has no need for an esoteric "slave language." Both "partisan" and "popular," he meets precisely the qualifications of "people's poet of the nation" set forth by East German cultural authorities. Yet Biermann, their most faithful pupil, has brought them little comfort because his realism is not only socialist, and readily accessible to the masses, but also truthful. In fact, it is precisely because his poetry is so obviously that of a true believer, and so highly contagious, that its "realism" represents such a threat to the establishment.

Despite symptomatic similarities, Biermann's confrontation with the cultural policy makers, his "political case," differs qualitatively from all others in intensity, logical consistency, and conclusiveness. His story has been related in detail by Marcel Reich-Ranicki and

Dieter E. Zimmer and in English by Margaret Vallance.[35] There were two crucial occasions of repressive proceedings against him: first in 1961, during the rehearsals of his play *Berliner Brauttag*, on the theme of the divided Germany, when he lost his temporary candidacy for Party membership and was forbidden to perform anywhere in the DDR until June 1963; and again in 1965, after a run of enormously successful appearances in both East and West Germany and the publication of his first volume, *Die Drahtharfe*, in West Berlin, when his public career was brought to an abrupt and final halt as a result of the Central Committee's notorious Eleventh Plenum. The charges against him are all contained in the article in *Neues Deutschland* (December 1965) which began the final campaign, an example of polemics of the basest sort: "skepticism," "anarchistic philosophy," "self-complacent egocentricity," "bourgeois individualism," giving solace to the forces of imperialism, betrayal of his own father's antifascist legacy, and sexual perversity.[36] In February 1966 the decisive "lex Biermann" was passed.

These political facts cannot be omitted from a discussion of Biermann's work; they influence directly and decisively nearly everything that he writes, particularly because he is such an overtly public poet. But clearly, a literary study must treat these facts more as an incidental background and must focus on the poetry itself. Biermann has continued to write since the Eleventh Plenum, and a statement that he made in mid-December 1965, just when the pressure was strongest, is worth remembering. "I intend," he said then, "to spend a good while writing in peace and quiet, because in ten years not a soul will be interested in the scandals put out about my person, but only in what useful texts I can lay on the table."[37] Three years later, in 1968, his second volume

---

35. Reich-Ranicki, "Wolf Biermann und die SED," *Wer schreibt, provoziert* (Munich, 1966), pp. 184–88; Zimmer, "Wolf Biermann wird nicht vergessen," *Die Zeit*, June 9, 1967, pp. 17–18; Vallance, "Wolf Biermann: The Enfant Terrible as Scapegoat," *Survey*, no. 61 (October, 1966), pp. 177–86.

36. *Neues Deutschland*, December 5, 1965: "Skeptizismus," "anarchistische Philosophie," "selbstgefällige Ich-Sucht," and so on. For an informative account of the situation in the DDR at the time of the Eleventh Plenum, see *Der Spiegel*, December 22, 1965.

37. *Der Spiegel*, December 22, 1965: "ich [habe] die Absicht. . . , für längere Zeit in Ruhe zu arbeiten, da sich in zehn Jahren kein Mensch mehr für die

of songs, *Mit Marx- und Engelszungen,* was published in West Berlin.

Not all of Biermann's songs have met with objections from the authorities. Some of his love songs were even published in East German anthologies, and his ballads about the Spanish Communist Julian Grimau and about the mailman William L. Moore from Baltimore—who was killed in 1963 when marching in Alabama for civil rights—were widely acclaimed in the DDR, as were his songs about Vietnam. More memorable is the beautiful song, "Warte nicht auf bessre Zeiten," which is similar in mood to Volker Braun's "provocations" against laziness and resignation and which was often printed in East German newspapers. The gentle refrain reads, "Wartet nicht auf bessre Zeiten / Wartet nicht mit eurem Mut / Gleich dem Tor, der Tag für Tag / An des Flusses Ufer wartet / Bis die Wasser abgeflossen / Die doch ewig fliessen." (66) [38]

The Buckow ballads ("Buckower Balladen," the title an allusion to Brecht's late poems, the "Buckower Elegien"), which recapture life in the small towns and on the collective farms, best illustrate Biermann's mastery of the ballad style. In one of them the women in a small village spend all of a rainy morning waiting on line for fish, only to find out that they were wrong to be cursing state ownership of the fish industry:

> Die alten Weiber von Buckow
> die schimpfen auf den Staat,
> weil en nur am Sonna'mt
> frische Fische hat.
> Der Staat heisst Fiete Kohn
> ein Fischer jung und stark.
> Ein junges Weib von Buckow
> verschläft mit ihm bis acht.
> Das hat die Weiber von Buckow
> so bös und nass gemacht. (19)

The irony, of course, is that blame ultimately does fall to the centralized bureaucracy, which allows a perfectly excusable hu-

---

Skandale, die um meine Person inszeniert wurden, interessieren wird, sondern einzig dafür, welche brauchbaren Texte ich auf den Tisch legen kann."
38. Page references are to *Die Drahtharfe.*

man foible to inconvenience other citizens to an irritating degree. In another of these satiric songs of country life, the marvellous "Ballade von der Buckower Süsskirschenzeit," all activity and springtime youthfulness on the collective are hampered by the same note posted everywhere, on the cherrytrees and on the girls: "DAS VOLKSEIGENTUM WIRD STRENG BEWACHT!" (15–16).

Biermann's best ballad of this kind is the one about Buckow's pipelayer, Fredi Rohsmeisl (11–13). One night Fredi is caught doing the twist ("das war verboten") with his fiancée and, after a scramble with the police, is given a three-months' sentence for counterrevolutionary activities. Fredi is deeply embittered by the affair, having lost all faith in justice:

> Er ist für den Sozialismus
> Und für den neuen Staat
> Aber den Staat in Buckow
> Den hat er gründlich satt.

These lines have, I think correctly, been taken as a statement of Biermann's own attitude toward the DDR, as well as that of many of his countrymen: they do believe in socialism and what the East German state stands for, but they often find the concrete day-to-day situation ("Buckow") intensely depressing. But Fredi's story does not end there. With the years, and the flight of the tenth Sputnik, conditions began to change somewhat. At the same café in which he was arrested, some years later, Fredi notices his own prosecuting attorney twisting on the dancefloor. The final refrain also contains an element of Biermann's own belief: "Junge, ich hab Leute sich ändern sehn / Junge, das war manchmal schon einfach schön. / Aber nützt uns das? (Ja.)." Things do change, even in Buckow, and sometimes it helps to keep one's eyes open.

Biermann's Buckow ballads are precise and ingeniously controlled, and they compare favorably with some of the best poems by Brecht himself. But Biermann is also a poet of Berlin, the divided city, and of "poor," dismembered Germany of which it is the symbolic core: "Mein Vaterland hat eine Hand aus Feuer, hat eine Hand aus Schnee / und wenn wir uns umarmen, dann tut das Herz mir weh." Here it is his "cousin" Heinrich Heine, that other "sufferer for Germany," from whom Biermann has learned, and again he does justice to his master:

> Berlin, du deutsche deutsche Frau
> Ich bin dein Hochzeitsfreier . . .
> Ich kann nicht weg mehr von dir gehn
> Im Westen steht die Mauer
> Im Osten meine Freunde stehn
> der Nordwind ist ein rauher (50).

Heine's ironic sentimentalism, his half-jocular weeping over the misery that is Germany, has found a faithful continuation in Biermann's little songs:

> Es senkt das deutsche Dunkel
> Sich über mein Gemüt
> Es dunkelt übermächtig
> In meinem Lied.
> Das kommt, weil ich mein Deutschland
> So tief zerrissen seh
> Ich lieg in der bessren Hälfte
> Und leide doppelt weh. (*Mit Marx*, 77)

Significantly, in the last few years Biermann has been busy with a long poem entitled "Deutschland—Ein Wintermärchen."

Finally, Biermann is the author of poetic "appeasements and revisions" ("Beschwichtigungen und Revisionen"). The tenor of these poems, most bitterly resented in the East—and therefore most frequently quoted in the West—is clearly illustrated in "Antrittsrede des Sängers":

> Die einst vor Maschinengewehren mutig bestanden
> fürchten sich vor meiner Guitarre. Panik
> breitet sich aus, wenn ich den Rachen öffne und
> Angstschweiss tritt den Büroelephanten auf den Rüssel
> wenn ich mit Liedern den Saal heimsuche, wahrlich
> Ein Ungeheuer, eine Pest, das muss ich sein, wahrlich
> Ein Dinosaurier tanzt auf dem Marx-Engels-Platz
> Ein Rohrkrepierer, fester Kloss im feisten Hals
> der Verantwortlichen, die nichts so fürchten wie
> Verantwortung. (53)

Biermann speaks from his own position as a young poet impatient for change, and he hurls words of "reckless abuse" ("Rücksichtslose Schimpferei," another poem) at the old-timers, now totally corrupted, who are content to do nothing but gloat over the change which they themselves accomplished years ago. These poems are all addressed to the old socialist warriors by a spokesman for their true posterity, a youthful activist possessed by his awareness of new battles. In "An die alten Genossen" Biermann gives his answer to Brecht's poem "An die Nachgeborenen"; one stanza serves to show the force of Biermann's voice, especially when compared with that of his contemporary Rainer Kirsch in the sonnet "Meinen Freunden, den alten Genossen":

> Ihr sprecht mit alten Worten
> Von den blutigen Siegen unsrer Klasse
> Ihr zeigt mit allen Händen auf das Arsenal
> Der blutigen Schlachten. Voll Eifersucht
> Hör ich Berichte eurer Leiden
> Vom Glück des Kampfes hinter Stacheldraht
> Und bin doch selbst *nicht* glücklich:
> Bin unzufrieden mit der neuen Ordnung. (67)

Biermann is stubbornly individualistic in his hatred for what is called socialism and the harmony of collective society and in his skepticism about what is considered rational. He feels that as an individual, in person, he can best speak for what he knows to be the true need of socialism and genuine rationality. Another of these self-portraits, which he is confident portrays more general sentiments than merely his own, contains the lines, "Ausgerüstet mit den Messern der Vernunft bin ich / . . . Käuflich bin ich für die Währung barer Wahrheit / In den Bunkern meiner Skepsis sitz ich sicher" (75). Biermann resists the old comrades' rigidity with an uncompromising insistence of his own: "Ich will beharren auf der Wahrheit / ich Lügner" ("Rücksichtslose Schimpferei").

I would say that Biermann's "appeasements and revisions" are not as satisfactory aesthetically as his Brechtian Buckow ballads, or his Berlin songs in the manner of Heine. Despite the striking poignancy of his political rhetoric, the emotions are perhaps too personally felt; with the lack of distance the speaker's sarcasm and bitterness are often too high-strung to remain under control. But it is in these poems that his ideological intentions and the nature of his critical attitude are most evident. Not only does Biermann demand change and criticize concrete reality in his society; he also reflects on the significance of such demands and such criticism. Not only does he refuse to glorify existing conditions and broad-

cast his optimistic hope in a brighter future, as East German poets
of a decade earlier had done and as the "old comrades" would
have him continue to do; an even more basic factor in his dialogue
with the older generation is his concern with the meaning of this
refusal, the implication of his own insistence upon honesty at all
costs. Wolf Biermann's most fundamental poetic confession is
contained in a stanza of the poem entitled "Tischrede des Dichters":

> Ich soll vom Glück Euch singen
> einer neuen Zeit
> doch Eure Ohren sind vom Reden taub.
> Schafft in der Wirklichkeit mehr Glück!
> Dann braucht Ihr nicht so viel Ersatz
> in meinen Worten.
> Schafft Euch ein süsses Leben, Bürger!
> Dann wird mein saurer Wein Euch munden.
> Der Dichter ist kein Zuckersack! (63)

Biermann's concern is with the contradiction between realism
and the obligatory affirmative "perspective" in poetry. His attention is drawn to a situation in which the poetic celebration of an
unrealized future has lost all provocative effect and serves only
as a substitute for the deficiencies of reality. The "critical stance"
characteristic of recent poetry of the DDR is in Biermann's work
itself of thematic importance; his songs express the idea that when
realistic poetry is not critical it ceases to be realistic. For this
reason Biermann's practice of placing himself, as a person, in the
center of his poems (as in "Antrittsrede des Sängers," "Tischrede
des Dichters," and "Selbstporträt an einem Regensonntag") is not
to be interpreted as a kind of selfish poetic narcissism. It is, rather,
a technique directly appropriate to his theoretical interest in himself—a young critical poet—and his work—poetic provocations—
as a social phenomenon:

> Wenn ich euch nun hin und wieder
> bittere Balladen brülle
> Lieder voller Traurigkeiten
> redet euch dann ja nicht ein:
> *Mir* gings schlecht, und

ich sei traurig
ich sei voller Bitterkeiten

Ihr erinnert euch: es sind doch
nur so traurig bitter finster
unsere ansonsten grossen
und so schön bewegten Zeiten
("Kwischenlied," *Mit Marx*, 64)

He recognizes his own personal dilemma and the challenge he
represents as a decisive function of the historical reality reflected
in his art.

Biermann has reached the peak of his achievement thus far in
his "Ballade auf den Dichter François Villon" (31–36). Here all
three elements of his poetry are perfectly integrated: the simple
ballad style of the Buckow poems with their concentration on the
details of everyday life; the Heine-like ironic sentimentality of
the poems about Berlin and the condition of Germany; and, very
brilliantly, the attitude of the "appeasements and revisions," with
that crucial thematic concern for the meaning of the poet's
critical stance.

François Villon, the fifteenth-century French poet whom Biermann calls his "big brother," is reincarnated in East Berlin and
takes up lodging at the poet-speaker's apartment. Disconcerted
by the oppressive air, and in order to evade the inevitable snoopers,
"Villon retreats into Biermann's wardrobe and drinks solidly, ven-
turing out only when reliable kindred spirits come to visit his
host. When Marie comes to Biermann, however, Villon has to
leave the wardrobe; he chooses to spend these nights walking
along the Wall playing tunes on the barbed wire [*Die Drahtharfe*].
The frontier guards shoot at him, but he bleeds only red wine and
spits out the bullets. The People's Police find this behaviour dis-
orderly and wake Biermann at 3 A.M. to relieve him of his lecher-
ous, rebellious guest." [39] Throwing open the doors of the closet,
they encounter not Villon, but a pool of vomit flowing gradually
to the floor. The poem contains several allusions to Villon's work,
such as his fictitious lover "la grosse Margot," his "requestes"
("Bittgesänge") or verse appeals for mercy from the authorities,

39. "Who is Afraid?" *Times Literary Supplement*, December 2, 1965, p. 1095.

and the lines "Er wollt nicht, dass sein Hinterteil / Ihm schwer am Halse hinge," which are a paraphrase of the image in "Le Quatrain (que feit Villon quand il fut jugé à mourir)." Each of the six sections in Biermann's poem ends with a four-line "Pointe," which has a similar function to the "envoy" in Villon's ballads.

But Biermann's relation to Villon is not so much in poetic technique or even in an identification with his "big brother's" scurrilous, mischievous vitality. He is primarily interested in the poet's behavior under the threat of political authority. At first the speaker only notices how Villon manages to hide at the right moment ("Wenn Leute bei mir schnüffeln gehn / Versteckt Villon sich immer"). Then he recalls Villon's troubles ("War oftmals in den Fängen / Der Kirche und der Polizei / Die wollten ihn aufhängen") and how his poetry always came to the rescue: "Mit seinen Bittgesängen hat / Villon sich oft verdrückt / Aus Schuldturm und aus Kerkerhaft / Das ist ihm gut geglückt." In the third section, which leads up to Villon's midnight stroll on the Wall, some hint is given of the oppressive atmosphere native to East Berlin: "Der Wodkaschnaps aus Adlershof / Der drückt ihm aufs Gehirn / Mühselig liest er das 'ND' [*Neues Deutschland*] / (Das Deutsch tut ihn verwirrn)." Then, in the second half of the poem, time and place of the episode become unmistakable: Villon provokes the border guards by strumming, "aus Jux," the barbed wire to the rhythm of their bullets, and Biermann is brought face to face with the country's infallible "order" ("Es lässt sich nichts verbergen / In unserm Land ist Ordnung gross").

But Villon's host has learned a lesson from the visit. Biermann does not deny that he knows "a certain Franz Fillonk" but, "a faithful son of the DDR," he points out the culprit's hideout, thanking the keepers of law and order for finally ridding him of that unruly intruder. The poem is by the end a "requeste en forme de ballade" of the kind composed by Villon to save his skin time and again:

> "Jawohl, er hat mich fast verhetzt
> Mit seinen frechen Liedern
> Doch sag ich Ihnen im Vertraun:
> Der Schuft tut mich anwidern!
> Hätt ich in diesen Tagen nicht

Kurellas Schrift gelesen
Von Kafka und der Fledermaus
Ich wär verlorn gewesen
Er sitzt im Schrank, der Hund
Ein Glück, dass Sie ihn endlich holn
Ich lief mir seine Frechheit längst
ab von den Kindersohln
Ich bin ein frommer Kirchensohn
Ein Lämmerschwänzchen bin ich
Ein stiller Bürger. Blumen nur
In Liedern sanft besing ich."

In this answer to the police officers, poet-speaker Biermann makes
certain to emphasize the difference between his own songs, the
height of sweet innocence, and the nasty tunes of his uninvited
guest. He tells them that the truly saving grace during this terrifying visit was his reading of Alfred Kurella's essay (1963) on Franz
Kafka, in which the relevance of Kafka's work to the socialist
world is categorically rejected.[40]

The ultimate theme of this magnificent "Ballade auf den Dichter
François Villon" is the question of the acceptable literary canon,
the relationship between literary expression and cultural authority.
Villon's social pranks, both in the Paris of his time and on the
Wall of contemporary Berlin, are to be understood as metaphors
for the impertinence and subversive playfulness of Biermann's own
poems; and the sacred and secular authority forever on the medieval poet's heels are the official watchdogs of East German culture.
After all, it is precisely Biermann's poetry to which the phrase
"freche Lieder" is most commonly applied, and with regard to
"Kurellas Schrift," it is precisely such Communists as Biermann
(and Kunert) who recognize the obvious relevance of Kafka to
phenomena in the socialist countries.[41] With Villonlike cunning
he turns these uncomfortable associations into arguments in his
own defense.

40. Kurella's essay, entitled "Der Frühling, die Schwalben und Franz Kafka,"
was published in the East Berlin weekly *Sonntag*, August 4, 1963, pp. 10–12.

41. Very interestingly, a delegate from another East European country—
probably Czechoslovakia—is reported to have made the following comment on
Party measures against Biermann in 1965: "The SED has never been fond of
Kafka, but it now seems intent on converting Kafka's terrifying visions into
reality." (Quoted in *nachtdepesche*, December 21, 1965.)

François Villon appears in the poem as the speaker's legendary roommate and, at the critical moment, as his convenient scapegoat. By the closing lines he has become the very expression of his disgust:

> Die Herren von der Polizei
> Erbrachen dann den Schrank
> Sie fanden nur Erbrochenes
> Das mählich niedersank.

These lines end the ballad, a masterful parable which comments on its own social function. It provokes society by ridiculing its prudish intolerance and stands as proof of its own thesis because of the intolerance with which it was received. This paradox inherent in the self-reflective irony of the Villon poem, and of Biermann's work as a whole, was well described in the *Times Literary Supplement* of December 2, 1965: "the east German reader . . . would welcome the outspokenness of the text, but his simultaneous laughter at the grotesque humour of the story can only serve to achieve a reconciliation between him and the system which governs his life; the reconciliation would however be based on mutual compromise, since the system itself would change the moment it permitted such laughter." Biermann calls his verse provocations "appeasements and revisions" because these two words express the contradiction involved in critical provocation as such: to demand "appeasement"—that is, toleration of criticism —is to demand a "revision" of the existing order, and a "revision" of the system will call for "appeasement" in just this sense.

The poet Wolf Biermann, like his friend Professor Robert Havemann, is a living defiance of society in the DDR. An outgrowth of its values and all it represents, he is the glaring antagonism born of its own dialectic, its own child who lives to haunt it and terrify it into a realization of its promises. He is a symbol of the division of Germany, but also of its ultimate unity, because if there is ever to be a future for that country, it will only come when one half recognizes a challenge to the other as a challenge to itself. The last and most cogent word on the phenomenon Wolf Biermann, and the phenomenon Germany, in these dismal years of its dismal history, was written by Dieter E. Zimmer for *Die*

Zeit (June 9, 1967): "The case of Wolf Biermann—one day it will have to be described in full, for it is a German case like few others. It could only occur in this country, which brought forth National Socialism and Auschwitz, whose two separate halves cling to each other 'like two cripples,' and like two senile old men take turns screaming about their sicknesses into each other's ears —each one deriving its self-esteem from the ailments of the other." [42]

A Final Prospect

Of the other young poets in the DDR, the husband-and-wife team of Rainer and Sarah Kirsch (b. 1934, 1935) is probably most worth mentioning. Their volume *Gespräch mit dem Saurier* (1965), contains a selection of poems by each of them. Harmless and often uninspiring songs and fairy-tale poems alternate with occasional traces of very real talent. Sarah Kirsch is best in her gentle love poems ("Ich bringe dir einen feuchten Fisch / einen schöngebauchten Flaschenfisch komm"), and in her imaginary poetic voyages, such as "Bootfahrt" and "Kleine Adresse." In "Trauriger Tag" (published in Peter Hamm's anthology *Aussichten*) she is a tiger, roaming aimlessly through the rainy streets of East Berlin: "Ich brülle am Alex den Regen scharf: / das Hochhaus wird nass, verliert seinen Gürtel / (Ich knurre: Man tut was man kann)." Rainer Kirsch is of a more philosophical temperament and is stronger at the ironic, didactic poem, such as "Beobachtung von deinem Hals aus" and "Auszog das Fürchten zu lernen." [43] They complement each other well, but of the two I would say that Sarah Kirsch has shown a more natural and spontaneous poetic gift.

Two very young poets, both born in 1940, have published some fascinating works in anthologies: Friedemann Berger and Bernd

42. "Wolf Biermann wird nicht vergessen," *Die Zeit*, June 9, 1967, p. 18: "Der Fall Biermann—eines Tages wird er vollständig beschrieben werden müssen, denn er ist ein deutscher Fall wie kaum ein anderer. Nur in diesem Land konnte er sich abspielen, das den Nationalsozialismus und Auschwitz hervorbrachte, dessen beide geschiedene Hälften 'wie zwei Krüppel' aneinandergeklammert sind und sich greisenhaft gegenseitig ihre Krankheiten in die Ohren schreien—und jeder bezieht sein Selbstbewusstsein aus den Gebrechen des anderen."

43. Included in Hildegard Brenner, ed., *Nachrichten aus Deutschland* (Reinbek, 1967), pp. 318–19.

Jentzsch. Berger, more than anyone else in the DDR, has been experimenting with radically new linguistic and formal possibilities; I quote from the beginning of his poem "Bäume nicht":

nicht zwischen den Stein
ins
Land
grabt
wo ich zusprach dem Sieben-
schwanz
(—heisst's—)
wo ich blies die Siebenloch-
flöte (*Nachrichten*, 378)

Even more exciting is Bernd Jentzsch, who has already proven himself a truly original nature poet. Poems such as "Die grünen Bäume starben in uns ab" and such lines as the following, from "In stärkerem Masse," are indications of unmistakable talent:

Zapfentrommler Wald grüner Landsknecht
mehrfach getarnt: dich erkenn ich am Tritt
deiner Bäume. Ruhelos stampfen sie auf
auf mich zu, in stärkerem Masse, verdoppeln
das ist mir bekannt, ihre Besuche, nachts
oder dienstags, zu Ostern, zu jeglicher Stunde
erscheinen, wer weiss das nicht, die kürzlich
im Waldgrab verblichen: Erschlagne, Gehenkte.[44]

All in all, the poetry written in the DDR in the last ten years represents an undeniable contribution to the history of German literature. It may not quite stand up to some of the best political lyrics of Hans Magnus Enzensberger, Günter Grass, or Peter Rühmkorf; but Kunert's parables, Braun's provocations, Karl Mickel's antimyths, and Biermann's satirical ballads more than merit consideration together with the works of the most outstanding West German poets of their own age, such as Rolf Haufs (b. 1935), Volker von Törne (b. 1834) and Christoph Meckel (b. 1935). Most important, their poetry is fruitfully studied in relationship to their own society; it was written in explicit or implicit response to a given literary past and a given ideological

44. *Nachrichten*, p. 377; also in *Aussichten*, p. 240.

situation. With techniques and a critical spirit inherited from
Brecht, these poets express an attitude of vital dissent, sensing and
announcing the contradictions around them and impatiently provoking anyone who seeks comfort in the existing order of things.
The dialectic, they know, deals unkindly with those relaxing in
its path. With Brecht they know that "real progress is not to be
progressive, but to progress." [45]

Brecht, whose spirit never ceases to haunt the country which
he chose as his home, was by no means their "discovery": his style
obviously had its influence throughout the 1950s in the poetry
of such uninteresting writers as Werner Lindemann (b. 1926),
Paul Wiens (b. 1922), Heinz Kahlau (b. 1931) and Günther
Deicke (b. 1922). What they did discover and absorb for the first
time, though, was Brecht's irony and dialectical sharpness, his
awareness of the contradictions and antagonism in social reality.
The real significance of the new critical development can only be
fully appreciated when it is played off against the usual apologetic,
"partisan" poetry witten at the same time. The Party still has its
"court poets," whom it can use to demonstrate the unbroken continuity of the East German literary tradition from the beginning.
  Uwe Berger (b. 1928) and Helmut Preissler (b. 1925), for example, along with scores of others, are writers of the "literary
order." Their verse, rhymed pipedreams, is of no artistic value
whatever but is written to soothe and placate readers into the
illusion that all is well and getting better. [46] Theirs is a poetry
which does not seek to probe the intricacies of human situations,
but only to manipulate public taste and opinion and to be manipulated by institutionalized social functions. Their real forebear is

45. Quoted by Hamm, "'Glück ist schwer,'" p. 368: "Wirklicher Fortschritt
ist nicht Fortgeschrittensein, sondern Fortschreiten."
46. See, for example, the lines of Helmut Preissler:

  Ein Land, drin Frieden Heimat find',
  sei unser deutsches Land,
  ein Land, dem gute Zeit beginnt:
  ein rotes Zukunftsland.
(Zwischen Gräsern und Sternen [East
                          Berlin, 1963], 67)

For a valuable discussion in which a contrast is drawn between Biermann and
Helmut Preissler, see Hans Mayer, "Die DDR-Literatur und ihre Widersprüche,"
Zur deutschen Literatur der Zeit, pp. 374-93.

not Bertolt Brecht, who never believed in allowing rulers their peaceful slumber, but Kurt Barthel, Max Zimmering, and other nonpoets of earlier times. But with the years it has become clear to all poets worthy of the name that more room is needed than the "order" can offer and that, to be true socialists and true realists they will necessarily work directly counter to the dictates of prescribed socialist realism. Their art, they feel, is most genuinely socialist when it is without a vow of allegiance to socialism as an established, codified system; and it is realistic only when it will not refrain from examining present reality because of a faith in the promises of a more glorious future. Prophecy in poetry is not mere prediction; it requires vision and not merely eyesight.

"Adjustments" by East German writers to political demands were usually unfortunate in the 1950s, but they were understandable because their society was undergoing significant changes at all levels of life. Today, however, such an adjustment is inexcusable—the sign either of intellectual naïveté or outright opportunism, or both. Poetry, by virtue of its own differentiation and quality, has gained the upper hand, forcing adjustments and loopholes in the literary order itself. In the future there are bound to be many stringent crackdowns and blasts of cold air, and the monotonous pattern of recent years will have no abrupt end. But the poetry of Johannes Bobrowski and Peter Huchel, and the example set by Brecht, have initiated a trend which is irreversible in its implications, a climate marked not by empty affirmations but by shadings of critical negation. Interaction and resistance will prevail, rather than authority and helpless submission.

Appendix

Wartime Poems of Franz Fühmann.

Poems 1–5 appeared in the series *Das Gedicht: Lyrik junger Menschen*, published by Heinrich Ellermann, Hamburg, eighth year, fifth series (February, 1942); 6–9 were given to me by the author; 10–12 appeared in *Das Reich*, June 25, 1944, and poem 13 in *Das Reich*, January 28, 1945.

1. *Griechischer Auszug*

Unser Schiff ist mit dreihundert Kriegern gegen Süden gefahren.
Die Helme glänzten in der Sonne mit schimmernden Funken.
Fern am Land haben tausend Bürger uns jubelnd Abschied gewunken,
und alles lag schwer trunken an Deck, wir lachten zukünftiger Gefahren.
Die Wellen haben flüsternd des Schiffes Planken gekost.
Wir haben getrunken und schneeig glänzende Fische gefangen,
vom salzigen Windhauch brannten uns Stirnen und Wangen.
Da haben wir zum Spass um den kommenden Tod gelost.
Wir hatten die Insel schon von ferne aufleuchten gesehn.
Die furchtbaren Speere hielten wir fest in der Faust gedrückt.
Die Gottheit hat uns ein leuchtendes Siegeszeichen geschickt.
Wir haben uns noch einmal umarmt und alles schien unsagbar schön.
Dann stiess unser Schiff mit dreihundert Kriegern ans Land.
Wir haben die Lanzen hoch in die Lüfte geschwungen,
dann haben wir mit dem furchtbaren Gegner gerungen
und unser Gott hat sich zürnend von uns abgewandt.

317

Die Berge widerhallten vom gellen Kriegsgeschrei.
Schon viele sanken hin, und das Blut schoss heiss aus dem Herzen.
Mein Kamerad neben mir wand sich in zuckenden Schmerzen.
Wir schritten den ganzen Tag, dann kam die Nacht schwarz wie
  Blei.
Von dreihundert Kriegern kehrten noch zwanzig zum Schiffe
  zurück.
Wir lösten die Anker und fuhren hinaus in die Nacht.
Und unser Steuermann hat wild aufgelacht.
Wir liefen auf ein Riff—uns verliess das Glück.
Die Götter wollten unser Weihopfer nicht mehr.
Der Morgen kam und das Schiff barst in Trümmer.
Der heulende Sturm erstickte das bange Gewimmer.
Die Wellen schäumten. Der Strudel schwoll. Wir versanken im
  Meer.
Die Sonne ist hoch in den stahlblauen Himmel gestiegen.
Unser Schiff lag tot mit zerborstenem Kiel und Planken.
Dreihundert brave Krieger haben gekämpft und versanken.
Still lag die Flut. Die Götter haben geschwiegen.

2. *Stunde in April*

Über kühle Wasser steigt der Mond.
Reglos steht ein Baum.
Aus den Tälern tönt ein weiches Singen.
Sehnsucht hat die Erde übermannt.
Alle Steine fangen an zu klingen.
Alle Menschen warten auf den tiefsten Traum.

3. *Kalter Schnee im Dezember*

Der Schnee rieselt leise aus geöffnetem Himmel—
Die Götter reissen die alten Gestirne aus ihren Bahnen.
Flocken fallen zu Boden in überstürzendem Gewimmel,
überdecken das Leben—das letzte verwelkende Ahnen.
Die lebendigen Wässer haben Eispanzer bedeckt,
das Atmen der Blumen ist in der lastenden Hülle erstickt,
Schneebäume haben die heiligen Bäume niedergedrückt . . .
Nur meine Sehnsucht hat sich hoch in die Nacht gereckt.
Die Götter haben die Sterne aus den alten Bahnen gerissen,
und aus den Löchern im Firmament fällt schneeweiss der Tod.
Meine Sehnsucht bäumt sich noch einmal auf und loht,
dann umfängt auch sie der Tod mit kalten und weissen Küssen.

4. *Nacht am Peipussee*

Aus der ungeheuren Weite
wächst der unendliche See
schwer und stumpf wie Blei.
Dröhnend schlagen die Wellen.

Dunkelnde Bäume wachsen
gespenstisch aus schillerndem Sumpf.
Tiefschwarzer Himmel gespannt—
Stille ward über dem Wasser.

Langgedehnter Flug von Vögeln.
Müd und schwer die Stunden lasten.
Irgendwo ein Lagerfeuer.
Hie und da ein harter Schritt.

Nächtlicher nie noch die Nacht.
Banger noch keine Stunde.
Eine blutende Wunde
wird unser kleines Herz.

5. *Jede Nacht erglühen neue Sterne*

Jede Nacht erglühen neue Sterne.
Immer wieder werden Sonnen neu geboren.
Neue Welten brechen aus der Ferne.
Neue Götter sprechen zu den tauben Ohren.

Neue Götter haben sich den Welten neu vermählt.
Und der Tag bricht an mit Tubaklang.
Harte Herzen werden in der Sonne neu gestählt.
Neue Menschen wachsen schön und rank.

Jede Nacht erstrahlt ein neues Licht.
Ewig wechselt Leben mit dem Tod.
Und die ewigstarke Liebe spricht—
Eine neue Weltensonne loht.

6. *Dämmrung*

Sieh den Mond sich erheben, Geliebte
Die Nebel, sie steigen gschwind.
Dass doch die Zeichen der Götter
Immer tödlich uns sind.

Die Augen sie weinen sich blind
und die Nacht ist weit wie ein Meer

Fährt auf feurigem Wagen ein Engel daher
Bestimmt unsres Lebens schütteres Los.

Die Nacht naht tief wie ein Meer
Die Liebenden stehn wie ein Kind
und es steigen die Monde so schwer
Die Nebel fallen geschwind

Und hüllen die strahlenden Sterne ein
Voll Grauen erhebt sich ein Wind:
Dass doch die Zeichen des Lebens
Immer voll Schrecknissen sind . . . !

7. Russland

Über die Weite weg
Ein Licht.
Geht das Korn auf aus dumpfen Samen
Geht die Sonne auf aus tiefen Tälern
Geht ein Bauer schliesslich hin zu seiner Saat.

Lebensverbrannt
Da ein Misston erstand
Da der Hass gross auferstand
Da die Sintflut sich ausgebreitet

Trommelgetön
Noch ehe es Tag ward
Irres Gestöhn
Noch ehe es Form ward—

Da—
und ferne reitet der Tod.
Schrecklich ist er anzusehn
Kupferrot
Ein Mal auf der Stirn
Schlägt einen Reif um das berstende Hirn—

Russland du hast uns Pfähle ins Herz gerammt!
Russland—du hast uns Sünder zur Acht verdammt
Russland—du hast uns zum letzten Bekenntnis entlammt
Russland—du Land der verzehrenden Ewigkeiten
Russland—du Land der vernichtenden Todesweiten
Russland—du dunkle Mutter der irdischen Leiden
Russland!

8. *Cäsar*

Aufruhr, der ihm überm Kopf zusammen
schlug und der die besten seiner Schar
mordete, ganz Gallien in Flammen
und in Rom das grosse Unheilsjahr
da die Ohnmacht seiner Senatoren
und das Brüllen feiler Massen sich
fürchterlich verband vor seinen Ohren
und wie Schatten um sein Denken strich

und er hören musste: Not um Not
und Verzweiflung, da und: allerorten!
Frieden säte er, doch aus den Worten
seines Mundes war ein Schwert geworden—
er schlug zu und erntete nun Tod

aber dieser Tod war ihm so schwer
dass es ihm ganz schwarz war von Gesichtern
dieser Fallenden und vor den Lichtern
einer Hölle stand der Julier

zwischen Staat und zwischen Anarchie
taumelnd und im Fall nach Höhe ringend
bis er fiel. Und fiebernd sah er die
Völker seines Staates, zukunftszwingend
seine Fundamente untergraben
und es graute ihm: Es kommt der Tod
und er sah. Und er liess nun den Schlag
ohne sich noch in der Hand zu haben
auf sich niederdröhnen dass er drunter
eisern würde und ein Zukunftsstern
seiner Stadt. Er aber sahs nur bunter
sein um Rom und aller Glanz war fern.

9. *Kupferner Spiegel / Wien*

Nicht jene viel zu vielen vollen Formen
des Angedrängten schildern, das, was klar
und offensichtlich, ohne Kommentar
geschrieben steht, in Falten, in enormen

Bildern der Haut—nicht dies. Metall sieht tief
mit seiner Purheit in das Echtgeborne

das Auserkorne, meidet das Verlorne
der Offenheit, die in den Strassen rief

wie eine Dirne, laut, es zu bestaunen
hier aber siehst du Zug um Zug entfallen
bis nur aus ursprünglichem Licht und Blut
sich wesenhaft die wahren Züge ballen
zu einem Bildnis deiner, tief im braunen
Metall, ein Bild, das fertig ist und gut.

10. *Nach der Schlacht*

Noch beten können!
Noch ein Stück Seele nehmen
aus zerfallenen Himmeln!
Erde lag in welken Händen gebettet,
eine Blüte hatten wir angestarrt
verwundert,
dass sie noch keimte aus diesem Blut—

In den Kellern nahte uns diese Nacht
ohne Bett,
ohne Obdach der Seele.
Gewölbe hingen schwarz in den Raum.
Pforten waren gesprengt, doch keiner
trat ein als der Tod.

Hinweggenommen die Liebe des Traums.
Milde Weise nicht mehr um uns,
was zum Sternkreis aufwärts drang
schrie aus geöffneten Adern, schrie
aus dem Wetzstein,
den der Schnitter trug,
und dann sanken die Garben.

Starben ohne Bett, ohne Wort
auf den Strassen sanken sie hin
über unsren Häuptern.
Leise fiel
Regen vom Himmel auf die ragenden Toten
Leise
rauschend wie ein Lied.

Weiter klang es in uns,
wir wussten es nicht.

Hatten die Hände geschlossen
zum Kreise, wilde Gesichter darüber
staubbedeckt, schwerevoll—
Leise—
schwang sich eine lichte Weise
hin ins ewige Leuchten der Sterne,
nicht mehr achtend
der Schlacht . . .

11. *Finnische Grenze*

Nichts war die Trauer mehr
Riesengross hob sich der Brand.
Schweigend und leidend leer
lag Land.

Wälder mit schwarzem Geäst,
wurzellos wild,
trieben als schrecklichen Rest
ihrer Vernichtung ein einziges Bild:

Skelette, ragend und kahl,
hatten das Grünen verlorn.
Überall war ein Mal
blutiger Herrschaft geborn.

Zorn stieg und Hass in die Welt.
Blume im Dorn verdarb.
Rauschendes Ährenfeld
sank hin und starb.

12. *Bauerngebet*

Lass uns ins Morgenrot bauen
Gott mit dem goldenen Haar!
Zeig uns als Zeichen im blauen
Himmel ein fruchtbares Jahr,

zeig uns den Tod und dahinter
stell uns das knospende Reis.
Führ uns durch glitzernden Winter
hin zu dem kreissenden Eis,

ziehe die Kreise nun dichter
ewig um reifende Saat!

Schenk uns zur Nacht neue Lichter,
weis uns am Tage den Pfad,

rette uns vor der Maschinen
tödlichem treibenden Schwarm.
Gib uns die Gnade zu dienen,
halt uns im segnenden Arm!

13. *Das Mass*

Nicht mehr in schönem
Bogenbau der kunstvollen Verse,
nicht mehr im Flug mit den eilenden Vögeln
und nicht mehr
im vertrauten
Du auf Du mit der schwärmenden Gottheit der Jugend
wird uns Gedicht und Wort—

uns ist gesetzt mit Mass:
in kargen Worten zu sagen,
dass über dem Tod
Menschen wandeln,
Menschen leben,
ihre heiligsten Pflichten erfüllen.

Mehr bedarf's nicht,
und es ziemt nicht
tönender Wunder der Worte zu Nacht.
Werk, Rausch und Schönheit misslang uns. Kein
Klang mehr war dem Grauen gerecht und kein
Schweigen mehr
dem Adel der Sterbenden.

Karg und klar ist die Zeit.
Ehern waltet die Not.
Zucht und Demut vollenden das Leid.
Dies sei die Sprache unser:
Zucht und Mass. In der Stille weilend,
treibend im Pulsschlag des Ungeheuren
und versöhnend dem Tag die Nacht.

EARLY POEMS OF JOHANNES BOBROWSKI.

Published under the name Hannes Bobrowski in *Das Innere Reich*, *10* (1943–1944), 351–354.

1. *Welebitzy*

Es sinkt der Tag. Da löst aus der Mauer sich
des Walds ein Stück von Röte, gezackt, sich dort,
ein wildes Leuchten wie von Feuern
noch und daneben versinkt's schon nächtlich.

Blick lang die leeren Felder hinab zum Fluss,
bis Schlaf dir stumm das Auge betäubt und dich
ein Frieren ankommt, so als wäre
Winter schon und alles Rot geträumt nur.

Dann aber reisst der Himmel den Blick empor.
Da lodern Feuer auf und da steigt ein Wald
so mächtig, dass die Erde drunten
trüb nur mehr scheint und ein blinder Spiegel.

2. *Pleskau*

Den Berg hinunterblicken und lang noch stehn
am Morgen auf verfallener Mauer. Da
liegt weit das Land, ins Leichentuch der
Nebel verhüllt, unter feuchtem Himmel.

Der Fluss führt stumm das Herz dir und traurig fort.
Halt's fest! es käm' dich anders ein Schauer an—
so kalt wie jene Strassen Trümmer
bleichender Kirchen mit Drohwort säumen.

Der Berg trägt widerwillig und müde nur
Die mächt'ge Krone, die sich zur Höhe zwingt,
dass endlich sich die Kuppel rmünde
über der Türme verlor'ner Mühe.

3. *Der Friedhof*

Dort, wo gemach die Eb'ne in Wellen sich
zum Hügel aufschwingt, steht noch in gelbem Laub
ein Bäumepaar allein, ertrinkend
Kreuze noch dort in dem Herbstgesträuche.

Und still hinab verliert in die Weite sich
ein Weg. Den halten Bäume dir rot im Blick
lang noch, wenn schon ins Grenzenlose
alles verwehte—, vom Wind getrieben.

Da wandle die verwachsenen Pfade noch
zum Hügel auf und steh bei den Kreuzen lang,
und blick nach Westen, wo das letzte
Feuer versinkt in ein armes Glühen.

4. *Wind*

Wer treibt dich, wilder Bruder, die Strassen hin,
die Acker ab und über die Seen noch?
Führt dich (wie uns) Gesetz und Auftrag?
Oder verwirft dich ein Schicksal stündlich?

Dein Reich, unendlich weit, über Wolken weit—
zu ahnen manchmal, morgens, auf Bergen, wenn
das Haar uns fliegt vor deinem Atem
und sich das Herz wie im Feuer härtet.

Da möcht' der Mut dir glauben, du führest frei,
und deinen Willen ehren mit rascher Tat.
Doch wer darf frei sein, den die Gottheit
nicht in die Freiheit befahl, sehr strenge!

5. *Steinkreuz*

Dem, den du trägst, ist Erd' und Himmel klein.
Er reisst sie sterbend in sein Herz hinein.
Und ich erfahr' im Anblick eines Steines,
wie tiefste Lieb und tiefstes Leid sind Eines.

6. *Anruf*

Hoch überm See die schweigende Nowgorod.
Noch sinne ich das wohl, und es zieht das Herz
sich mir zusammen,—und doch ist ein
Frieden bereitet in der Zerstörung.

Den aber nennen! In das zerstörte Haus
gehn nur im Traum Gedanken noch ein vom Einst—
wie Möwen überm müden Flusse,
und auch ihr Schreien zerbricht im Winde.

Noch stehen Türme, die ihrer Kuppeln Last,
zerbrochnen Kronen gleich, aus der Trümmer Leid
aufheben, doch es fügt der Himmel
nur das zertretene Bild zusammen.

7. *Klosterkirche*

Dreieinigkeit! Es öffnen zu Dreien sich
die Bögen der Apsiden. Und vierfach schart
der Kuppeln Zahl, gleich den Aposteln,
sich um die Mitte, die kreuzbekrönte.

Vier Säulen ragen mächtig, als trügen sie
die schwere Last der Erd, und kein Bogen wölbt,
zu helfen, sich herüber: in ein
Kreuz sind gebunden die hohen Räume.

Leer sehn die Fensterhöhlen, leer bleibt die Tür,
geborsten ist das Dach, und es neigt der Turm
sich schon herüber, und es wächst der
Regen zerbrochnes Gerät des Frommseins.

8. *Abend*

Zerstörten Treppen gleichend das Ufer geht,
ein Trümmerfeld von Häusern, aufleuchtend weiss
und rötlich, stumm hinab. Ein Turm. Dort
grünlich ein Stück noch von Kirchendächern.

Und Strauchwerk, wuchernd, das die Vernichtung bald
verschweigen wird. Da führt schon der graue Fluss
den weiten Bogen, bis der See sich
meergleich dem wandernden Blick eröffnet.

Und erst wo ohne Grenzen das Auge ist
und Nacht im Tag schon aufwächst und Schweigen wohnt,
findt sich das Herz zurück. Da steht das
frierende Segel des Monds im Dämmern.

Bibliography

Note: An asterisk (*) indicates that the item was first published in the DDR.

I. Primary Sources

1. Poetry and Prose

Biermann, Wolf. *Die Drahtharfe*. Berlin, 1965. *The Wire Harp*, trans. Eric Bentley. New York, 1968.

———. *Mit Marx- und Engelszungen*. Berlin, 1968.

Bobrowski, Johannes. *Boehlendorff und andere Erzählungen*. Stuttgart, 1965.

*———. *Boehlendorff und Mäusefest: Erzählungen*, 2nd ed. Berlin, 1966.

———. *Das Land Sarmatien: Gedichte*, ed. Horst Bienek. Munich, 1966.

*———. *Der Mahner*. East Berlin, 1967; West Berlin, 1967.

*———. "Fortgeführte Überlegungen," *Antikommunismus und Proexistenz*, ed. Günter Wirth. Berlin, 1965, pp. 37–39.

*———. *Im Windgesträuch*. Berlin, 1970.

———. *Levins Mühle: 34 Sätze über meinen Grossvater*. Frankfurt, 1964.

*———. *Litauische Claviere*. East Berlin, 1966; West Berlin, 1968.

———. *Mäusefest und andere Erzählungen*. Berlin, 1965.

———. *Nachbarschaft: 9 Gedichte, 3 Erzählungen, 2 Interviews, 2 Grabreden, 2 Schallplatten, Lebensdaten*, ed. Klaus Wagenbach. Berlin, 1967.

———. *Sarmatische Zeit*. Stuttgart, 1961; East Berlin, 1961.

———. *Schattenland Ströme*. Stuttgart, 1962; Easter Berlin, 1963.

———. *Shadow Land*, selected poems trans. Ruth and Mathew Mead. London, 1966.

*———. *Wetterzeichen*. East Berlin, 1966; West Berlin, 1967.

Braun, Volker. "Fünf Gedichte auf Deutschland," *Krusbuch 4* (1966), 64–72.

*———. *Provokation für mich*. Halle, 1965.

———. *Vorläufiges*. Frankfurt, 1966.

————. *Wir und nicht sie.* Frankfurt, 1969.

*Fühmann, Franz. *Aber die Schöpfung soll dauern.* Berlin, 1957.

*————. *Das Judenauto: 14 Tage aus zwei Jahrzehnten.* Berlin, 1962.

*————. *Die Nelke Nikos.* Berlin, 1953.

*————. *Die Richtung der Märchen.* Berlin, 1962.

*————. *Kabelkran und blauer Peter*, 2nd ed. Rostock, 1962.

*————. *König Ödipus: Gesammelte Erzählungen.* Berlin and Weimar, 1966.

*Hermlin, Stephan. *Balladen*, ed. Sina Witt. Leipzig, 1965.

*————. *Der Flug der Taube.* Berlin, 1952.

*————. *Dichtungen.* Berlin, 1956.

————. *Die Städte: Gedichte,* ed. Alfred Karnein. Munich and Esslingen, 1966.

————. *Die Zeit der Gemeinsamkeit; In einer dunklen Welt: Zwei Erzählungen.* Berlin, 1966.

*————. *Erzählungen.* Berlin and Weimar, 1966.

*————. *Gedichte.* Leipzig, 1963.

————. *Gedichte und Prosa*, ed. Klaus Wagenbach. Berlin, 1965.

*————. *Mansfelder Oratorium.* Berlin, 1950.

*————. *Nachdichtungen.* Berlin, 1957.

————. *Strassen der Furcht.* Singen, 1944.

*————. *Zweiundzwanzig Balladen.* Berlin, 1947.

————. *Zwölf Balladen von den Grossen Städten.* Zürich, 1944.

Hermlin, Stephan (with Jo Mihaly and Lajser Ajschenrand). *Wir verstummen nicht: Gedichte in der Fremde.* Zürich, 1944.

*Huchel, Peter. "Bericht aus Malaya," *Neue Deutsche Literatur, 4* (1956), 65–74.

————. *Chausseen Chausseen.* Frankfurt, 1963.

*————. "Das Gesetz," *Sinn und Form, 2* (1950), 127–36.

————. *Die Sternenreuse: Gedichte 1925–1947.* Munich, 1967.

*————. *Gedichte.* Berlin, 1948; Karlsruhe, 1948.

*Kirsch, Sarah, and Rainer Kirsch. *Gespräch mit dem Saurier.* Berlin, 1965.

*Kunert, Günter. *Album 8.* Berlin, 1968.

*————. *Das kreuzbrave Liederbuch.* Berlin, 1961.

*————. *Der ungebetene Gast.* Berlin and Weimar, 1965.

————. *Die Beerdigung findet in aller Stille statt.* Munich, 1968.

————. *Erinnerung an einen Planeten.* Munich, 1963.

————. *Im Namen der Hüte.* Munich, 1967.

*————. *Kramen in Fächern.* Berlin, 1969.

*————. *Notizen in Kreide.* Leipzig, 1969.

————. *Tagträume.* Munich, 1964.

*————. *Tagwerke.* Halle, 1961.

————. "Twofold Monologue—Short-Circuited and Other Poems," trans. Christopher Middleton, *Dimension: Contemporary German Arts and Letters* (Austin, Texas), *1* (1968), 504–15.

*————.*Unschuld der Natur.* Berlin and Weimar, 1966.

*Kunert, Günter. *Unter diesem Himmel.* Berlin, 1955.
———. *Verkündigung des Wetters.* Munich, 1966.
*———. *Wegschilder und Mauerinschriften.* Berlin, 1950.
Mickel, Karl. *Vita nova mea.* Reinbek, 1967.
*———. *Vita nova mea. Mein neues Leben.* Berlin and Weimar, 1966.

2. Theoretical Statements

*Abusch, Alexander. *Kulturelle Probleme des sozialistischen Humanismus: Beiträge zur deutschen Kulturpolitik 1946–1961.* Berlin, 1962.
*———. *Literatur im Zeitalter des Sozialismus: Beiträge zur Literaturgeschichte 1921 bis 1966.* Berlin and Weimar, 1967.
*Ackerman, Anton. *Gibt es einen besonderen deutschen Weg zum Sozialismus.* Berlin, 1946.
*Ammer, Karl. *Sprache, Mensch und Gesellschaft.* Halle, 1961.
Balluseck, Lothar von. *Literatur und Ideologie 1963: Zu den literatur-politischen Auseinandersetzungen seit dem VI. Parteitag der SED.* Bad Godesberg, 1963.
*Becher, Johannes R. *Die sozialistische Kultur und ihre nationale Bedeutung.* Berlin, 1958.
*———. *Über Literatur und Kunst,* ed. Marianne Lange. Berlin, 1962.
Bender, Hans, ed. *Mein Gedicht ist mein Messer: Lyriker zu ihren Gedichten.* Munich, 1961.
*Beyer, Ingrid. *Der Künstler und der Sozialismus.* Berlin, 1963.
Bloch, Ernst. *Auswahl aus seinen Schriften,* ed. Hans Heinz Holz. Frankfurt, 1967.
———. *Das Prinzip Hoffnung.* 3 vols. Frankfurt, 1959.
*Braemer, Edith. "Volksverbundenheit und Parteilichkeit," *Forum,* 20 (August 1966), 16–19.
Brecht, Bertolt. *Gesammelte Werke in 20 Bänden,* ed. Suhrkamp Verlag and Elizabeth Hauptmann. Frankfurt, 1967.
———. *Über Lyrik,* 2nd ed. Frankfurt, 1968.
"Das Jahr '45": Dichtung, Bericht, Protokoll deutscher Autoren, ed. Hans Rauschning. Gütersloh, 1970.
*"Der Kampf gegen den Formalismus, Für eine fortschrittliche deutsche Kultur," *Einheit,* 6 (1951), 579–92.
"Ein Briefwechsel zwischen Anna Seghers und Georg Lukács," *Internationale Literatur,* 9 (1939), 97–121.
*"Entwicklungsprobleme der Lyrik seit dem V. Deutschen Schriftstellerkongress," *Neue Deutsche Literatur,* 11 (September 1963), 55–71.
*Fühmann, Franz. "Louis Fürnberg," *Sinn und Form,* 19 (1967), 779–87.
"Greif zur Feder, Kumpel!" Protokoll der Autorenkonferenz des Mitteldeutschen Verlages Halle (Saale) am 24. April 1959 im Kulturpalast des elektrochemischen Kombinats Bitterfeld. Halle, 1959.
Grundlagen der marxistisch-leninistischen Ästhetik. Berlin, 1962.
*Haase, Horst. "Lyrik und Klassenkampf," *Forum,* 20 (August 1966), 14–15.

*————. "Was kann Lyrik leisten? Aktuelle Probleme der Lyrik in der DDR," *Neue Deutsche Literatur*, *15* (May 1967), 25–39.

*Hager, Kurt. "Freude an jedem gelungenen Werk," *Neue Deutsche Literatur*, *11* (August 1963), pp. 61–72.

*————. *Zur geistigen Situation der Gegenwart*. Berlin, 1961.

Havemann, Robert. *Dialektik ohne Dogma? Naturwissenschaft und Weltanschauung*. Reinbek, 1964.

*Hermlin, Stephan. *Begegnungen 1954–1959*. Berlin, 1960.

*————. *Der Kampf um eine deutsche Nationalliteratur*. Berlin, 1952.

*————. "Nachwort," Georg Heym, *Gedichte*, pp. 119–22. Leipzig, 1967; Frankfurt, 1967.

*————. "Über Tradition und Moderne: Ein Beitrag zur Budapester PEN-Diskussion," *Sinn und Form*, *17* (1965), 786–88. Reprinted in *Du/Atlantis*, *7* (1966), 895, and *Die Zeit*, November 27, 1964.

Hermlin, Stephan, and Hans Mayer. *Ansichten über einige Bücher und Schriftsteller*. Weisbaden, 1947; East Berlin, 1947.

*Herting, Helga. *Das sozialistische Menschenbild in der Gegenwartsliteratur*. Berlin, 1966.

Hinweise für schreibende Arbeiter. Leipzig, 1961.

*"In diesem besseren Land: Lyrik-Debatte," *Forum*, *20* (April 1966), 19–23. Continued in subsequent issues through the year 1966.

*Iwanow, Wassili. *Der sozialistische Realismus*. Berlin, 1965.

*John, Erhard. *Einführung in die Ästhetik*. Leipzig, 1964.

*————. *Probleme der Kultur und der Kulturarbeit*. Berlin, 1965.

Joho, Wolfgang. "Wir begannen nicht im Jahr Null," *Neue Deutsche Literatur*, *13* (May 1965), 5–11.

*Kantorowicz, Alfred. *Deutsche Schicksale: Intellektuelle unter Hitler und Stalin*, 2nd ed. Vienna, 1964; expanded from *Deutsche Schicksale; neue Portrats*. Berlin, 1949.

————. *Deutsches Tagebuch*. 2 vols. Munich, 1959, 1961.

*Koch, Hans. "Haltungen, Richtungen, Formen," *Forum*, *20* (August 1966), pp. 5–12, 22–23.

*————. *Marxismus und Ästhetik: Zur ästhetischen Theorie von Karl Marx, Friedrich Engels und Wladimir Iljitsch Lenin*. Berlin, 1961.

*————. *Unsere Literaturgesellschaft: Kritik und Polemik*. Berlin, 1965.

*Koelwel, Eduard. *Von der Art zu Schreiben: Essays über philosophische und dichterische Ausdrucksmittel*. Halle, 1962.

Kultur in unserer Zeit: Zur Theorie und Praxis der sozialistischen Kulturrevolution in der DDR, ed. Institut für Gesellschaftswissenschaften beim ZK der SED. Berlin, 1965.

Kulturkonferenz der KPD, Protokoll. Berlin, 1945.

*Kunze, Reiner, Gerhard Wolf, and Klaus Pfützner. *Fragen des lyrischen Schaffens*. Halle, 1960.

*Kurella, Alfred. "Der Frühling, die Schwalben und Franz Kafka," *Sonntag*, August 4, 1963, pp. 10–12.

*————. *Der Mensch als Schöpfer seiner selbst: Beiträge zum sozialistischen Humanismus*. Berlin, 1958.

*Lange, Marianne. *Kulturrevolution und Nation,* Berlin, 1966.
*———. ed. *Zur sozialistischen Kulturrevolution 1957–1959: Dokumente.*
    2 vols. Berlin, 1960.
Literatur und Repression: Sowjetische Kulturpolitik seit 1965, ed. Helen
    von Ssachno and Manfred Grunert. Munich, 1970.
Loose, Gerhard. "Grundbegriffe des sozialistischen Realismus," *Monats-*
    hefte, 57 (1965), 162–70.
*Lukács, Georg. "Das Problem der Perspektive. Referat, gehalten am 11.
    Januar 1956 auf dem 4. Deutschen Schriftstellerkongress," *Beiträge zur*
    Gegenwartsliteratur, 2 (1956), 75–82. Reprinted in: Lukács, *Schriften*
    zur Literatursoziologie, pp. 254–60.
———. *Schriften zur Literatursoziologie,* ed. Peter Ludz. Neuwied, 1961.
*Lunatscharsky Anatoli. *Die Revolution und die Kunst: Essays, Reden,*
    Notizen, ed. and trans. Franz Leschnitzer. Dresden, 1962.
"Lyrik im Gespräch" (comments by Volker von Törne, Bernd Jentzsch
    Friedemann Berger, Heinz Kahlau, and Helmut Heissenbüttel), *alterna-*
    tive, 7 (1964), 1–10.
*Marx, Karl, and Friedrich Engels. *Über Kunst und Literatur: Eine Sammlung*
    aus ihren Schriften, ed. Michail Lifschitz. Berlin, 1948.
*Mayer, Hans. "Zur Gegenwartslage unserer Literatur," *Sonntag,* Decem-
    ber 2, 1956. Reprinted in: Mayer, *Zur deutschen Literatur der Zeit,* pp.
    365–73.
Mjasnikow, Alexander. "Sozialistischer Realismus und Literaturtheorie,"
    Sinn und Form, 19 (1967), 669–716.
Raddatz, Fritz J., ed. *Marxismus und Literatur.* 3 vols. Reinbek, 1969.
Riklin, Alois, and Klaus Westen, eds. *Selbstzeugnisse des SED Regimes.*
    Cologne, 1963.
*Schiller, Dieter. "Über Verständlichkeit von Gedichten," *Forum,* 20
    (June 1966), 20–23.
Schubbe, Elimar, ed. *Dokumente zur Kunst-, Literatur- und Kulturpolitik*
    der SED. Stuttgart, 1969.
*Seghers, Anna. *Die grosse Veränderung und unsere Literatur.* Berlin, 1956.
"Sie sprechen verschiedene Sprachen?: Schriftsteller aus beiden Teilen
    Deutschlands im Gespräch (Hans Werner Richter, Heinz von Cramer,
    Günter Grass, Uwe Johnson; Paul Wiens, Hermann Kant, Max Walter
    Schulz)," *alternative,* 7 (1964), 97–100.
*Ulbricht, Walter. *Dem Dichter des neuen Deutschland Johannes R.*
    Becher. Berlin, 1959.
*———. *Whither Germany? Speeches and Essays on the National Ques-*
    tion. Dresden, 1966.
*Ulbricht, Walter, and Kurt Hager. *Parteilichkeit und Volksverbundenheit*
    unserer Literatur und Kunst: Reden auf der Beratung des Politbüros des
    ZK der SED und des Präsidiums des Ministerrates mit Schriftstellern
    und Künstlern am 25. und 26. März 1963. Berlin, 1963.
"Wie sie uns sehen": Schriftsteller der DDR über die Bundesrepublik, ed.
    Karl Heinz Brokerhoff. Bonn and Bad Godesberg, 1970.

Zhdanov, A. A., Maxim Gorky, Nikolai Bukharin, Karl Radek, and A. Stet-
sky. *Problems of Soviet Literature: Reports and Speeches at the First
Soviet Writers' Congress.* New York, 1935.
Zhdanov, A. A. "Speech at the First All-Union Congress of Soviet Writers, 1934," *On Literature, Music and Philosophy* (London, 1950), pp.
9–18.
Zwerenz, Gerhard. *Ärgernisse: Von der Maas bis an die Memel.* Cologne,
1961.

3. Anthologies

Anderle, Hans Peter, ed. *Mitteldeutsche Erzähler: Eine Studie mit Proben
und Porträts.* Cologne, 1965.
Balluseck, Lothar von, ed. *Gedichte von drüben: Lyrik und Propaganda-
verse aus Mitteldeutschland.* Bad Godesberg, 1963.
Bender, Hans, ed. *Widerspiel: Deutsche Lyrik seit 1945.* Munich, 1962.
Besten, Ad den, ed. *Deutsche Lyrik auf der anderen Seite: Gedichte aus
Ost- und Mitteldeutschland.* Munich, 1960.
Böhme, Herbert, ed. *Rufe in das Reich: Die heldische Dichtung von Lange-
marck bis zur Gegenwart.* Berlin, 1934.
Brenner, Hildegard, ed. *Nachrichten aus Deutschland: Lyrik, Prosa, Dra-
matik. Eine Anthologie der neueren DDR-Literatur.* Reinbek, 1967.
*Deicke, Günter, ed. *Im werdenden Tag: Gedichte unserer Zeit.* Leipzig,
1958.
*Deicke, Günther and Uwe Berger, eds. *Deutsches Gedichtbuch.* Berlin,
1959.
"Die roten Strassen: Politische Lyrik aus den 20er Jahren," *alternative, 9*
(1966), 81–115.
*Drews, Richard, and Alfred Kantorowicz, eds. *Verboten und Verbrannt:
Deutsche Literatur 12 Jahre unterdrückt.* Berlin, 1947.
*Endler, Adolf, and Karl Mickel, eds. *In diesem besseren Land: Gedichte
der Deutschen Demokratischen Republik seit 1945.* Halle, 1966.
Fuchs, Walter R., ed. *Lyrik unserer Jahrhundertmitte.* Munich, 1965.
Hamm, Peter, ed. *Aussichten: Junge Lyriker des deutschen Sprachraums.*
Munich, 1966.
*Jentzsch, Bernd, and Klaus-Dieter Sommer, eds. *Auswahl 66: Neue Lyrik
—Neue Namen.* Berlin, 1966.
Jokostra, Peter, ed. *Ohne Visum: Lyrik-Prosa—Essays aus dem Osten
geflohener Autoren.* Gütersloh, 1964.
*Lammel, Inge, and Günter Hofmeyer, eds. *Lieder der Partei.* Leipzig,
1961.
"Lyrik, Prosa und Dramatik: Schriftsteller in der DDR," *alternative, 6*
(1963), 105–49.
*Menschen und Werke: Vom Wachsen und Werden des neuen Lebens in
der Deutschen Demokratischen Republik,* ed. Deutscher Schriftsteller-
Verband. Berlin, 1952.

Morawietz, Kurt, ed. *Deutsche Teilung: Ein Lyrik-Lesebuch aus Ost und West*. Wiesbaden, 1966.

Nilsen, Jan Andrew and Sebastian Lybeck, eds. *En di diktare är ingen sockersäck: nio obekväma poeter i DDR*. Stockholm, 1968.

Pfeffer, Ernst, ed. *Deutsche Lyrik unter dem Sowjetstern*. Frankfurt, 1961.

Schlösser, Manfred, ed. *An den Wind geschrieben: Lyrik der Freiheit 1933–1945*. Darmstadt, 1960.

*Sommer, Klaus-Dieter, and Gerhard Wolf, eds. *79 Songs und Chansons*. Berlin, 1966.

Stroh, Franz and Gören Löfdahl, eds. *Zweimal Deutschland?* Stockholm, 1966.

Vesper, Will, ed. *Die Ernte der Gegenwart: Deutsche Lyrik von heute*. Munich, 1940.

Wolf, Christa, and Gerhard Wolf, eds. *Wir, unsere Zeit: Gedichte aus zehn Jahren*. Berlin, 1959.

*Wolf, Gerhard, ed. *Sonnenpferde und Astronauten: Gedichte junger Menschen*, Halle, 1964.

*————, ed. *Sputnik contra Bombe: Lyrik, Prosa, Berichte*. Berlin, 1959.

II. Secondary Literature

1. Reference and General Works

*Albrecht, Friedrich. *Schriftsteller und Arbeiterklasse*. Berlin, 1969.

*Albrecht, Günter, Kurt Böttcher, and others. *Deutsches Schriftstellerlexikon: Von den Anfängen bis zur Gegenwart*. Wiemar, 1962.

Baring, Arnulf. *Der 17. Juni 1953*. Cologne, 1965.

Bartholemes, Herbert. *Das Wort "Volk" im Sprachgebrauch der SED: Wortgeschichtliche Beiträge zur Verwendung des Wortes "Volk" als Bestimmungswort und als Genitivattribut*. Düsseldorf, 1964.

Bender, Peter. *Offensive Entspannung: Möglichkeit für Deutschland*. Cologne and Berlin, 1964.

"Bestseller drüben," *alternative*, 7 (1964), 11–17.

Betz, Werner. "Der zweigeteilte Duden," *Der Deutschunterricht, 12* (1960), 82–98.

————. "Vom geeinten zum geteilten Wörterbuch?" *Merkur, 16* (1962), 89–94.

————. "Zwei Sprachen im Deutschland?" *Merkur, 16* (1962), 873–79.

Bilke, Jörg Bernhard. "DDR-Literatur: Tradition und Rezeption in Westdeutschland (Ein Literaturbericht)," *Der Deutschunterricht, 21* (October, 1969), Beilage (zu Heft 5), 1–12.

Blumenfeld, Yorick. *Seesaw: Cultural Life in Eastern Europe*. New York, 1968.

Brandt, Heinz. *Ein Traum, der nicht entführbar ist: Mein Weg zwischen Ost und West*. Munich, 1967.

Brant, Stefan. *Der Aufstand: Vorgeschichte, Geschichte und Deutung des 17. Juni 1953*. Stuttgart, 1954.

———. *The East German Rising*. London, 1955.

Brenner, Hildegard. "Das DDR-Lesebuch," *alternative*, 8 (1965), 237–40.

Bütow, Hellmuth G. *Die Entwicklung des dialektischen und historischen Materialismus in der Sowjetzone*. 3 vols. Berlin, 1960–63.

Childs, D. *East Germany*. London, 1970.

Croan, Melvin. "East German Revisionism: The Spectre and the Reality," *Revisionism: Essays on the History of Marxist Idea*, ed. Leopold Labetz, pp. 239–56. New York, 1962.

———. "Intellectuals under Ulbricht," *Survey*, 55 (1960), pp. 35–45.

Demetz, Peter. *Marx, Engels, and the Poets: Origins of Marxist Literary Criticism*. Chicago, 1967.

Deuerlin, Ernst, ed. *DDR: Geschichte und Bestandsaufnahme*. Munich, 1966.

———. ed. *Potsdam 1945: Quellen zur Konferenz der "Grossen Drei."* Munich, 1963.

Dönhoff, Marion Gräfin; Rudolf Walter Leonhardt; and Theo Sommer. *Reise in ein fernes Land: Bericht über Kultur, Wirtschaft und Politik in der DDR*. Hamburg, 1964.

Dörnberg, John. *The Other Germany*. Garden City, New York, 1968.

*Doernberg, Stefan. *A Short History of the GDR*. Berlin, 1964.

*———. *Kurze Geschichte der DDR*. Berlin, 1964.

Duhnke, Horst. *Stalinismus in Deutschland: Die Geschichte der sowjetischen Besatzungszone*. Cologne, 1955.

Eschenburg, Theodor. *Die deutsche Frage: Die Verfassungsprobleme der Wiedervereinigung*. Munich, 1959.

Fischer, Ernst. *Kunst und Koexistenz: Beitrag zu einer modernen marxistischen Ästhetik*. Reinbek, 1966.

Freund, Gerald. *Germany Between Two Worlds*. New York, 1961.

Friedrich, Carl J., and Henry A. Kissinger, eds. *The Soviet Zone of Germany*. New Haven, Conn., 1956.

Friedrich, Gerd. *Der Kulturbund zur demokratischen Erneuerung Deutschlands: Geschichte und Funktion*. Cologne, 1952.

———. *Die freie deutsche Jugend: Auftrag und Entwicklung*. Cologne, 1953.

*Geerdts, Hans-Jürgen, ed. *Deutsche Literaturgeschichte in einem Band*. Berlin, 1965. See esp. the last section, "Die deutsche Nationalliteratur nach 1945," pp. 641–720.

Gente, Hans-Peter. "Versuch über 'Bitterfeld'," *alternative*, 7 (1964), 126–31.

Glenn, Jerry H. "Approaching the Contemporary German Lyric: A Selected, Annotated Bibliography," *Modern Language Journal*, 51 (1967), pp. 480–92.

Görlich, J. Wolfgang. *Geist und Macht in der DDR*. Freiburg, 1968.

Grunert-Bronnen, Barbara, ed. *Ich bin Bürger der DDR und lebe in der Bundesrepublik: 12 Interviews*. Afterword by Uwe Johnson. Munich, 1970.

Handbuch der Deutschen Demokratischen Republik, ed. Deutsches Institut für Zeitgeschichte in Verbindung mit dem Staatsverlag der Deutschen Republik. Leipzig, 1964.

Hangen, Welles. *The Muted Revolution: East Germany's Challenge to Russia and the West*. New York, 1966.

Hartmann, Frederick H. *Germany Between East and West*. Englewood Cliffs, N.J., 1965.

Höllerer, Walter, ed. *Ein Gedicht und sein Autor, Lyrik und Essay*. Berlin, 1968.

———. *Theorie der modernen Lyrik: Dokumente zur Poetik I*. Reinbek, 1965.

*Höppner, Joachim. "Über die deutsche Sprache und die beiden deutschen Staaten," *Weimarer Beiträge*, 8 (1963), 576–85.

Hornsby, Lex, ed. *Profile of East Germany*. New York, 1967.

Jänicke, Martin. *Der dritte Weg: Die antistalinistische Opposition gegen Ulbricht seit 1953*. Cologne, 1964.

Jokostra, Peter J. *Die Zeit hat keine Ufer: Südfranzösisches Tagebuch*. Munich, 1963.

Just, Klaus Günter. "Zwischen Verlorenem Paradies und Utopie: Politische Dichtung in Deutschland," in *Übergänge: Probleme und Gestalten der Literatur* (Bern, 1966), pp. 42–57.

Keith-Smith, Brian, ed. *Essays on Contemporary German Literature*. London, 1966.

*Klein, Alfred. *Bürgerliche und sozialistische Arbeiterdichtung*. Berlin, 1969.

Korlén, Gustav. "Führt die Teilung Deutschlands zur Sprachspaltung," *Der Deutschunterricht*, 21 (October 1969), 5–23.

Kersten, Heinz. *Aufstand der Intellektuellen*. Stuttgart, 1955.

*Klemperer, Victor. "Verantwortung für die Sprache," *Neue Deutsche Literatur*, 3 (March 1955), 122–26.

Krippendorf, Ekkehart. "Eine Lektion in deutscher Geschichte und geteilter deutscher Gegenwart," *Offene Welt: Zeitschrift für Wirtschaft, Politik, und Gesellschaft*, September, 1967, pp. 80–89.

Kunisch, Hermann, ed. *Handbuch der deutschen Gegenwartsliteratur*. Munich, 1965.

Langenbucher, Hellmuth. *Nationalsozialistische Dichtung: Einführung und Übersicht*. Berlin, 1935.

Lennartz, Franz. *Deutsche Dichter und Schriftsteller unserer Zeit*, 10th ed. Stuttgart, 1969.

Lilge, Herbert. *Deutschland von 1955–1963: Von den Pariser Verträgen bis zum Ende der Ära Adenauer*. Hannover, 1965.

Ludz, Peter Christian. "East Germany: The Old and the New," *East Europe, 15* (April 1966), 23–37.

———. *Parteielite im Wandel*. Cologne, 1968.

———. ed. *Studien und Materialien zur Soziologie der DDR*. Cologne, 1964.

Lust, Peter. *Two Germanies: Mirror of an Age*. Montreal, 1966.

Marcuse, Herbert. *Soviet Marxism: A Critical Analysis*. New York, 1958; 2nd ed., 1961.

Merritt, Richard L. "Politics, Theater, and the East-West Struggle: The Theater as a Cultural Bridge in West Berlin," *Political Science Quarterly, 80* (1965), 186–215.

Moser, Hugo. "Die Sprache im geteilten Deutschland," *Wirkendes Wort, 11* (1961), 1–21; extended as *Sprachliche Folgen der politischen Teilung Deutschlands*. Düsseldorf, 1962.

Münch, Ingo von, ed. *Dokumente des geteilten Deutschland*. Stuttgart, 1968.

Nawrocki, Joachim. *Das geplante Wunder: Leben und Wirtschaften im anderen Deutschland*. Hamburg, 1967.

Nette, Wolfgang. *DDR Report*. Düsseldorf and Cologne, 1968.

Neurig, Karl. "Bitterfelder Seitenwege," *alternative, 7* (1964), 131–34.

Noack, Paul. *Die deutsche Nachkriegszeit*. Munich, 1966.

Nonnenmann, Klaus, ed. *Schriftsteller der Gegenwart: 53 Porträts*. Olten and Freiburg, 1963.

Otto U. *Die literarische Zensur als Problem der Soziologie der Politik*. Stuttgart, 1968.

*Paulick, Wolfgang, ed. *Junge Schriftsteller der Deutschen Demokratischen Republik in Selbstdarstellungen*. Leipzig, 1965.

Plat, Wolfgang. *Begegnung mit den anderen Deutschen: Gespräche in der Deutschen Demokratischen Republik*. Reinbek, 1969.

Price, Arnold H. *East Germany, a Selected Bibliography*. Washington, D.C., 1967.

"Professor Havemann's Views," *East Europe, 13* (April 1964), pp. 21–22.

Proletarisch-revolutionäre Literatur 1918 bis 1933: Ein Abriss. Berlin, 1965.

Reich, Hans. *Sprache und Politik: Untersuchungen zu Wortschatz und Wortwahl des offiziellen Sprachgebrauchs in der DDR*. Munich, 1968.

Richert, Ernst. *Das zweite Deutschland: Ein Staat, der nicht sein darf*. Frankfurt and Hamburg, 1966.

———. *Die DDR-Elite oder Unsere Partner von Morgen?* Reinbek, 1968.

———Die neue Gesellschaft in Ost und West: Analyse einer lautlosen Revolution*. Gütersloh, 1969.

———. "Ulbricht and After," *Survey*, No. 61 (1966), 153–65.

Richter, Hans Werner, ed. *Bestandsaufnahme: Eine deutsche Bilanz 1962*. Munich, 1962.

———. *Die Mauer oder Der 13. August*. Reinbek, 1961.

Riemschneider, Ernst. *Some Changes in the German Language in Soviet Occupied Germany Since 1945*. University of Kentucky, 1960. Master thesis, extended as *Veränderungen der deutschen Sprache in der sowjetisch besetzten Zone Deutschlands seit 1945*. Supplement 4 to *Wirkendes Wort*, 1963.

*Rilla, Paul. *Vom bürgerlichen zum sozialistischen Realismus: Essays*. Leipzig, 1967.

Rühle, Jürgen. *Das gefesselte Theater*. Cologne, 1957.

Rühle, Jürgen. *Literatur und Revolution: Die Schriftsteller und der Kommunismus*. 2nd ed., Munich and Zurich, 1963.

——. *Literature and Revolution: A Critical Study of the Writer and Communism in the Twentieth Century*. New York (Praeger), 1969.

SBZ von A bis Z: Ein Taschen- und Nachschlagebuch über die Sowjetische Besatzungszone Deutschlands, 9th ed., ed. Bundesministerium für gesamtdeutsche Fragen. Bonn, 1965.

Schenk, Fritz. *Im Vorzimmer der Diktatur: 12 Jahre Pankow*. Cologne and Berlin, 1962.

*Schriftsteller der DDR und ihre Werke: Biographisch-Bibliographischer Nachweis. Leipzig, 1955.

Smith, Jean Edward. *Germany Beyond the Wall: People, Politics . . . and Prosperity*. Boston, 1967.

*Statistisches Jahrbuch der DDR. Berlin, annually since 1955.

Stern, Carola. "East Germany," *Communism in Europe*, ed. William E. Griffith (Cambridge, Mass., 1966), *2*, 43–154.

Sturz, Jürgen. "Auf dem Weg nach Bitterfeld: Schriftsteller 'aus den eigenen Reihen'," *alternative*, 7 (1964), 122–24.

——. "Innerdeutsche Sprachentfremdung," *alternative*, 7 (1964), 135–41.

Tertz, Abram. *The Trial Begins and On Socialist Realism*. New York, 1960.

Tudyka, Kurt P., ed. *Das geteilte Deutschland: Eine Dokumentation der Meinungen*. Stuttgart, 1965.

Von Bitterfeld bis Oobliadooh: Die andere deutsche Literatur. Berlin, 1967. Bibliography of recent East German literature compiled by the "Amerika Gedenkbibliothek" in West Berlin)

Wagner, Helmut. "The Cultural Sovietization of East Germany," *Social Research, 24* (1957), 395–426.

Weber, Dietrich, ed. *Deutsche Literatur seit 1945 in Einzeldarstellungen*. Stuttgart, 1968.

Weber, Hermann, ed. *Der deutsche Kommunismus: Dokumente*. Cologne, 1963.

——. ed. *Völker hört die Signale: Der deutsche Kommunismus 1916–1966*. Munich, 1967.

*Weiskopf, F. C. "'Ostdeutsch' und 'Westdeutsch' oder Über die Gefahr der Sprachentfremdung," *Über Literatur und Sprache* (Berlin, 1960), pp. 416–33.

Zimmer, Dieter E., ed. *Die Grenzen literarischer Freiheit: 22 Beiträge über Zensur im In- und Ausland*. Hamburg, 1966. Includes Hans Peter Anderle, "DDR," pp. 150–58.

Zwerenz, Gerhard. "Das gespaltene Wort," *Der Monat, 12* (1960), 76–88.

——. "Junge Intelligenz unter Ulbricht," *Neue Gesellschaft*, July–August, 1958, pp. 311–14.

2. *Works of Criticism*

Adorno, Theodor. "Rede über Lyrik und Gesellschaft," *Noten zur Literatur I*, pp. 73–104. Frankfurt, 1958.

Balluseck, Lothar von. *Dichter im Dienst: Der sozialistische Realismus in der deutschen Literatur*. Wiesbaden, 1956; 2nd ed., 1963.

———. *Kultura: Kunst und Literatur in der Sowjetischen Besatzungszone*. Cologne, 1952.

Bilke, Jörg Bernhard. "Auf den Spuren der Wirklichkeit. DDR-Literatur: Traditionen, Tendenzen, Möglichkeiten," *Der Deutschunterricht, 21* (1969), 24–60.

———. "DDR-Literatur: Tradition und Rezeption in Westdeutschland," *Der Deutschunterricht, 21* (1969), 1–12.

———. "Die zweite deutsche Literatur," *Die Welt der Bücher, 3* (March 1967), 370–80.

Behrmann, Alfred. "Metapher im Kontext: Zu einigen Gedichten von Ingeborg Bachmann und Johannes Bobrowski," *Der Deutschunterricht, 20* (1968), 28–48.

Berger, Kurt. "Schleichwege zum Chaos: Kleine Studie über nationalsozialistische Lyrik," *Die Sammlung, 2* (1946), 68–81.

Besten, Ad den. "Deutsche Lyrik auf der anderen Seite," *Eckart, 28* (1959), 224–63.

Brant, Sabine. "The Production of Literature," *Survey*, no. 55 (1960), 58–65.

Brenner, Hildegard. "Von verschiedenen Möglichkeiten in dieser Anthologie zu lesen," *Nachrichten aus Deutschland*, pp. 6–14. Reinbek, 1967.

Bridgwater, Patrick. "The Poetry of Johannes Bobrowski," *Forum for Modern Language Studies* (University of St. Andrews), *2* (1966), 320–34.

Carlsson, Anni. "Johannes Bobrowski und Klopstock," *Neue Zürcher Zeitung*, January 16, 1966.

Castorp, Claus. " 'Das Blut ist getrocknet, die Tragödie ist gelaufen . . .': Ostdramatik auf dem Hintergrund des Status quo: Hacks, Lange, Müller," *Europäische Begegnung, 6* (1966), 110–15.

Conrady, Karl Otto. "Zur Lage der deutschen Literatur in der DDR," *Geschichte in Wissenschaft und Unterricht, 17* (1966), 737–48.

Demetz, Peter. "*Galileo* in East Berlin: Notes on the Drama in the DDR," *The German Quarterly, 37* (1964), 239–45.

———. "Literature in Ulbricht's Germany," *Problems of Communism, 11* (1962), 15–21.

Domin, Hilde, ed. *Doppelinterpretation: Das zeitgenössische deutsche Gedicht zwischen Autor und Leser*. Frankfurt and Bonn, 1966.

Drewitz, Ingeborg. "Metamorphosen der DDR-Literatur," *Deutsche Studien, 7* (1969), 147–58.

———. "Wege der Literatur in BRD und DDR: Zur Realität der Hoffnung," *Neue Deutsche Hefte, 16* (1969), 90–110.

Eder, Horst. "Ostdeutsche Theaterlandschaft: Ein Beitrag zur Realität des europäischen Intellektuellen," *Wort in der Zeit, 12* (1966), 69–73.

Empson, William. *Some Versions of Pastoral.* New York, 1950.

Enzensberger, Hans Magnus. "Poesie und Politik," *Einzelheiten II: Poesie und Politik,* pp. 113–37. Frankfurt, 1963.

Forster, Leonard. *German Poetry 1944–1948.* Cambridge, 1949.

*Franz, Michael. "Zur Geschichte der DDR-Lyrik," *Weimarer Beiträge, 15* (1969), 561–619.

Friedrich, Hugo. *Die Struktur der modernen Lyrik: Von Baudelaire bis zur Gegenwart.* Hamburg, 1956.

*Geerdts, Hans-Jürgen. *Literatur unserer Zeit.* Rudolstadt, 1961.

*———. "Zur Beurteilung der nationalen und internationalen Stellung und Bedeutung der Literatur der Deutschen Demokratischen Republik," *Wissenschaftliche Zeitschrift der Ernst Moritz Arndt-Universität Griefswald, 16* (1967), 151–58.

"German Writing Today," *Times Literary Supplement,* September 23, 1960. See esp. "East Germany," pp. xvi–xviii.

Glenn, Jerry. "An Introduction to the Poetry of Johannes Bobrowski," *Germanic Review, 41* (1966), 45–56.

Gross, Walter. " 'Zeit ohne Angst': Zu den Gedichten von Johannes Bobrowski' " *Reformatio, 14* (1965), 603–16.

Hamburger, Käte. *Die Logik der Dichtung.* Stuttgart, 1957; 2nd. ed., 1968.

Hamm, Peter. "Die Wiederentdeckung der Wirklichkeit," *Aussichten,* pp. 321–27. Munich, 1966.

———. " 'Glück ist schwer in diesem Land': Zur Situation der jüngsten DDR-Lyrik," *Merkur, 19* (1965), 365–79.

———. "Vermächtnis des Schweigens: Der Lyriker Peter Huchel," *Merkur, 18* (1964), 480–88.

*Hartung, Günter. "Johannes Bobrowski," *Sinn und Form, 18* (1966), 1189–1217.

Hasselblatt, Dieter. *Lyrik heute: Kritische Abenteuer mit Gedichten.* Gütersloh, 1963.

Heise, Hans-Jürgen. "Peter Huchels neue Wege," *Neue Deutsche Hefte, 11* (1964), 104–11.

Heydebrand, Renate von. "Engagierte Esoterik: Die Gedichte Johannes Bobrowskis," *Wissenschaft als Dialog: Studien zur Literatur und Kunst seit der Jahrhundertwende,* ed. Renate von Heydebrand and Klaus Günther Just (Stuttgart, 1969), pp. 386–450.

———. "Überlegungen zur Schreibweise Johannes Bobrowskis: Am Beispiel des Prosastücks 'Junger Herr am Fenster'," *Der Deutschunterricht, 21* (October 1969), 100–25.

*Hochmuth, Arno, ed. *Literatur im Blickpunkt: Zum Menschenbild in der Literatur der beiden deutschen Staaten,* 2nd ed. Berlin, 1967.

Hoefert, Sigfrid. "Der Nachhall finnischer Dichtung in der Lyrik Johannes Bobrowskis," *The German Quarterly, 41* (1968), 222–30.

————. *West-Östliches in der Lyrik Johannes Bobrowskis.* Munich, 1966.
Hoffmann, Charles W. *Opposition Poetry in Nazi Germany.* Berkeley, Calif., 1962.
Hohoff, Curt. "Moden und Masstäbe zeitgenössischer deutscher Lyrik," *Welt und Wort, 14* (1959), 135–36.
Holthusen, Hans Egon. "Natur und Geschichte in Huchels Gedicht," *Hommage für Peter Huchel,* pp. 72–77. Munich, 1968.
Hommage für Peter Huchel: Zum 3. April 1968, ed. Otto F. Best. Munich, 1968.
Horst, Eberhard. "Günter Kunert: Verkündigung des Wetters, Im Namen der Hüte," *Neue Rundschau, 78* (1967), 678–84.
"In Memoriam Johannes Bobrowski," *Merkur, 20* (1966), 128–37.
Jens, Walter. *Deutsche Literatur der Gegenwart.* Munich, 1962.
**Johannes Bobrowski: Selbstzeugnisse und Beiträge über sein Werk.* Berlin, 1967.
Jokostra, Peter. "Zur Situation der Dichtung in Mitteldeutschland," *Merkur, 14* (1960), 680–87.
*Kähler, Hermann. *Gegenwart auf der Bühne: Die sozialistische Wirklichkeit in den Bühnenstücken der DDR von 1956–1963/64.* Berlin, 1966.
Kloehn, Ekkehard. "Die Lyrik Wolf Biermanns," *Der Deutschunterricht, 21* (October 1969), 126–33.
Kobligk, Helmut. "Zeit und Geschichte im dichterischen Werk Johannes Bobrowskis," *Wirkendes Wort, 19* (1969), 193–205.
Kopelew, Lew. "Gibt es zwei deutsche Literaturen?" *Neue Zeit: Wochenschrift für Weltpolitik* (Moscow), December 22, 1965, pp. 22–24.
Krolow, Karl. *Aspekte zeitgenössischer deutscher Lyrik.* Munich, 1963.
————. *Schattengefecht.* Frankfurt, 1964.
Kunisch, Hermann. *Die deutsche Gegenwartsdichtung: Kräfte und Formen.* Munich, 1968.
Kurz, Paul Konrad, S.J. "Vom Erhabenen zum Anti-Ikarus: Selbst- und Weltbewusstsein des Menschen in der deutschen Lyrik seit 1945," *Stimmen der Zeit* (Freiburg), no. 180 (December 1967), 326–37, 375–92.
Lange, Victor. "Ausdruck und Erkenntnis: Zur politischen Problematik der deutschen Literatur seit dem Expressionismus," *Neue Rundschau, 74* (1963), 93–108.
Lehmann, Wilhelm. "Mass des Lobes: Zur Kritik der Gedichte von Peter Huchel," *Deutsche Zeitung und Wirtschaftszeitung,* February 8, 1964, p. 17.
*Leschnitzer, Franz. *Von Börne zu Leonhard oder Erbübel—Erbgut?* Rudolstadt, 1966.
Lüdtke, Reinhold. "Über neuere mitteldeutsche Lyrik im Deutschunterricht der Oberstufe," *Der Deutschunterricht, 20* (October, 1968), 38–51.
*Lukács, Georg. *Skizze einer Geschichte der neueren deutschen Literatur.* Berlin, 1953; Neuwied, 1963.

Lynen, John F. *The Pastoral Art of Robert Frost.* New Haven, Conn., 1960.

*Maurer, Georg. *Der Dichter und seine Zeit: Essays und Kritiken.* Berlin, 1956.

*————. "Näher der Wurzel der Dinge: Das Märchenmotiv bei Franz Fühmann," *Neue Deutsche Literatur, 12* (1964), 111–27.

————. "Was vermag Lyrik?" *Kürbiskern, 2* (1966), 78–85.

*————. "Zur deutschen Lyrik der Gegenwart," *Der Dichter und seine Zeit,* pp. 32–67. Berlin, 1956.

Mayer, Hans. "Die Literatur der DDR und ihre Widersprüche," *Zur deutschen Literatur der Zeit,* pp. 374–93. Reinbek, 1967.

*————. "Stephan Hermlins 'Zwölf Balladen von den Grossen Städten'," *Deutsche Literatur und Weltliteratur* (Berlin, 1957), pp. 649–54.

————. "Über die Einheit der deutschen Literatur," *Zur deutschen Literatur der Zeit,* pp. 344–57. Reinbek, 1967.

————. "Zu Gedichten von Peter Huchel," *Zur deutschen Literatur der Zeit,* pp. 178–88. Reinbek, 1967.

————. *Zur deutschen Literatur der Zeit: Zusammenhänge, Schriftsteller, Bücher.* Reinbek, 1967.

*Mickel, Karl. "Von der Richtung der Märchen," *Neue Deutsche Literatur, 10* (1962), 116–20.

Müller, Joachim. "Der Lyriker Johannes Bobrowski–Dichtung unserer Zeit," *Universitas, 23* (1968), 1301–11.

Peddersen, Jan. "Die literarische Situation in der DDR," *Handbuch der deutschen Gegenwartsliteratur,* ed. Hermann Kunisch, pp. 746–58. Munich, 1965.

Piontek, Heinz. *Männer die Gedichte machen: Zur Lyrik heute.* Hamburg, 1970.

Pongs, Hermann. *Dichtung im gespaltenen Deutschland.* Stuttgart, 1966.

Raddatz, Fritz J. "DDR-Literatur und marxistische Ästhetik," *Germanic Review, 43* (1968), 40–60.

————. "Tradition und Traditionsbruch in der Literatur der DDR," *Merkur, 19* (1965), 666–81.

Ranicki, Marceli [Marcel Reich-Ranicki], "Stephan Hermlin," *Z dziejów literatury niemieckiej 1871–1954,* pp. 345–51. Warsaw, 1955.

Reblitz, Irma. "Das Porträt: Johannes Bobrowski—Konfession eines universalen Humanisten," *Europäische Begegnung, 6* (1966), 661–66.

Reich-Ranicki, Marcel. "Der exemplarische Weg des ostberliner Erzählers Franz Fühmann," *Die Zeit,* March 31, 1967, pp. 25–26.

————. *Deutsche Literatur in West und Ost: Prosa seit 1945.* Munich, 1963.

————. "Kamerad Fühmann," *Deutsche Literatur in West und Ost,* pp. 422–33. Munich, 1963.

————. *Literarisches Leben in Deutschland: Kommentare und Pamphlete.* Munich, 1967.

————. *Literatur der kleinen Schritte: Deutsche Schriftsteller heute.* Munich, 1967.

————. "Stephan Hermlin, der Poet," *Deutsche Literatur in West und Ost,* pp. 386–410. Munich, 1963.

————. "The Writer in East Germany," *Survey,* no. 61 (October, 1966), 188–95.

————. *Wer schreibt, provoziert: Kommentare und Pamphlete.* Munich, 1966.

————. "Wolf Biermann und die SED," *Wer schreibt, provoziert,* pp. 184–88. Munich, 1966.

Rischbieter, Henning, and Ernst Wendt. *Deutsche Dramatik in West und Ost.* Velber, 1965.

Sanders, Rino. "Peter Huchel: Chausseen Chausseen," *Neue Rundschau,* 75 (1964), 324–29.

*Schiller, Dieter. "Die Entwicklung der Lyrik in der Deutschen Demokratischen Republik," *Weimarer Beiträge, 8* (1962), 357–80.

Schiwelbusch, Wolfgang. "Neuere Dramatik in der DDR," *Frankfurter Hefte, 23* (1968), 783–90.

Schleiden, Karl August. *Klopstocks Dichtungstheorie als Beitrag zur Geschichte der deutschen Poetik.* Saarbrücken, 1954.

*Schlenstedt, Dieter. "Analyse [Karl Mickel, 'Der See']," *Forum, 20* (June 1966), 18–19.

————. "Epimetheus—Prometheus: Positionen in der Lyrik," *alternative, 7* (October 1964), 113–21.

Schonauer, Franz. "DDR auf dem Bitterfelder Weg," *Neue Deutsche Hefte, 13* (1966), 91–117.

————. *Deutsche Literatur im Dritten Reich: Versuch einer Darstellung in polemisch-didaktischer Absicht.* Olten and Freiburg, 1961.

————. "Peter Huchels Gegenposition," *Akzente, 12* (1965), 404–14.

Schöne, Albrecht. *Über politische Lyrik im 20. Jahrhundert.* Göttingen, 1965.

"Schriftstellerporträt: Christa Reinig," *alternative, 7* (1964), 18–22.

*Schulz, Max Walter. *Stegreif und Sattel: Anmerkungen zur Literatur und zum Tage.* Halle, 1967.

Schwarz, Peter Paul. " 'Freund mit der leisen Rede': Zur Lyrik Johannes Bobrowskis," *Der Deutschunterricht, 18* (1966), 48–65.

Schweilert, Uwe. "Gedichte aus dem anderen Deutschland: Zwei neue Lyrik-Anthologien aus der DDR," *Die Zeit,* September 19, 1967, p. 12.

Seidler, Ingo. "Peter Huchel und sein lyrisches Werk," *Neue Deutsche Hefte, 15* (1968), 11–32.

Seidler, Manfred. "Bobrowski, Klopstock und der antike Vers," *Lebende Antike: Symposium für Rudolf Sühnel,* ed. Horst Meller and Hans-Joachim Zimmermann, pp. 542–54. Berlin, 1967.

Seidlin, Oskar. "Eichendorffs 'Zwei Gesellen'," *Versuche über Eichendorff* (Göttingen, 1965), pp. 169–92. Reprinted in *Interpretationen I: Deutsche Lyrik von Weckherlin bis Benn,* ed. Jost Schillemeit (Frankfurt, 1965), pp. 173–97.

Sitte, Eberhard. "Deutsche Lyrik auf der anderen Seite in unserem Deutsch-unterricht," *Der Deutschunterricht, 14* (1962), 88–105.

Standaert, Eric. "Johannes Bobrowski: Een inleiding tot zijn poëzie," *Diagram voor progressieve literatur, 2* (1964), 35–54.

*Stein, Ernst. *Wege zum Gedicht.* Halle, 1963.

*"Stephan Hermlin," *Erich Weinert, Stephan Hermlin, Kuba,* pp. 53–66. Berlin, 1955.

Titel, Britta. "Johannes Bobrowski," *Schriftsteller der Gegenwart: 53 Porträts,* ed. Klaus Nonnenmann, pp. 51–57. Olten and Freiburg, 1963.

Vallance, Margaret. "Wolf Biermann: The Enfant Terrible as Scapegoat," *Survey,* no. 61 (October 1966), 177–86.

Vormweg, Heinrich. *Die Wörter und die Welt: Über neue Literatur.* Neuwied, 1968.

———. "Varianten, realistisch und grotesk," *Merkur, 21* (1967), 1196–1200.

Wallmann, Jürgen P. "Stimmen aus der DDR," *Argumente: Informationen und Meinungen zur deutschen Literatur der Gegenwart,* pp. 196–225. Mühlacker, 1968.

Walwei-Wiegelmann, Hedwig. "Zur Lyrik und Prosa Günter Kunerts," *Der Deutschunterricht, 21* (October 1969), 134–44.

Weber, Werner. *Zeit ohne Zeit: Aufsätze zur Literatur.* Zurich, 1960.

Wellershoff, Deiter. *Literatur und Veränderung: Versuche zu einer Meta-kritik.* Cologne, 1970.

*Werner, Klaus. "Zur Brecht-Rezeption bei Günter Kunert und Hans Magnus Enzensberger," *Weimarer Beiträge* (Brecht-Sonderheft, 1968), pp. 61–73.

Wiegenstein, Roland H. "Zur Situation der Schriftsteller in der DDR," *Neue Rundschau, 77* (1966), 330–34.

Wiese, Benno von. "Die deutsche Lyrik der Gegenwart," *Deutsche Literatur in unserer Zeit,* ed. Wolfgang Kayser, pp. 32–57. Göttingen, 1959.

Wilk, Werner. "Peter Huchel," *Neue Deutsche Hefte, 10* (1963), 81–96.

Winter, Helmut. "East German Literature," *Essays on Contemporary German Literature,* ed. Brian Keith-Smith, pp. 261–80. London, 1966.

*Wolf, Gerhard. *Deutsche Lyrik nach 1945.* Berlin, 1965.

*———. *Johannes Bobrowski: Leben und Werk.* Berlin, 1967.

*———. "Kontur eines Dichters," afterword to Stephan Hermlin, *Gedichte,* pp. 121–32. Leipzig, 1963.

*———. "Motive des Lyrikers Bobrowski," *Johannes Bobrowski: Selbstzeugnisse und Beiträge über sein Werk,* pp. 134–49. Berlin, 1967.

*Zak, Eduard. "Der Dichter Peter Huchel," *Neue Deutsche Literatur, 1* (1953), 164–83.

*———. *Der Dichter Peter Huchel: Versuch einer Darstellung seines lyrischen Werkes.* Berlin, 1953.

Zimmer, Dieter E. "Wolf Biermann wird nicht vergessen," *Die Zeit,* June 9, 1967, pp. 17–18.

Index